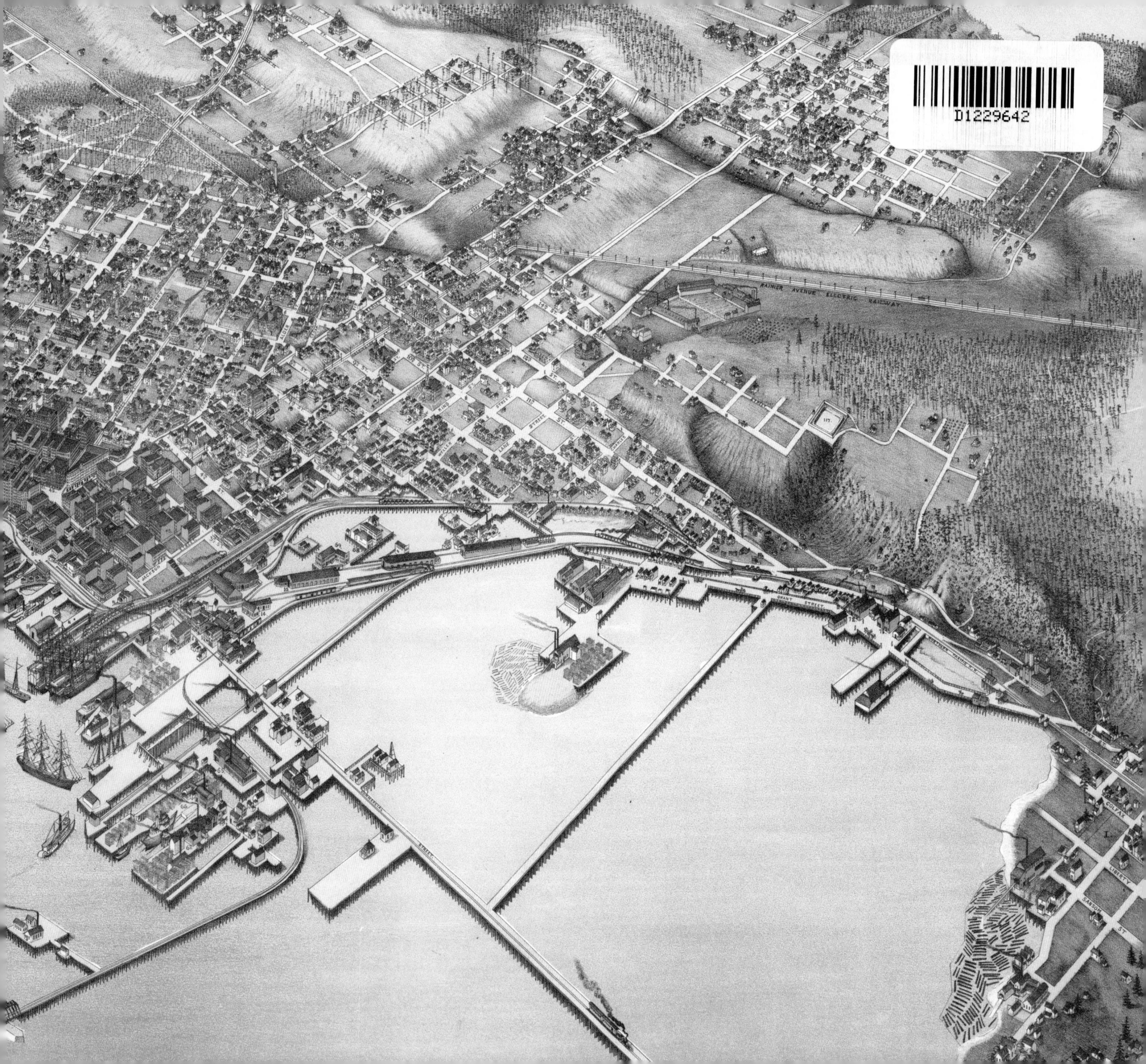

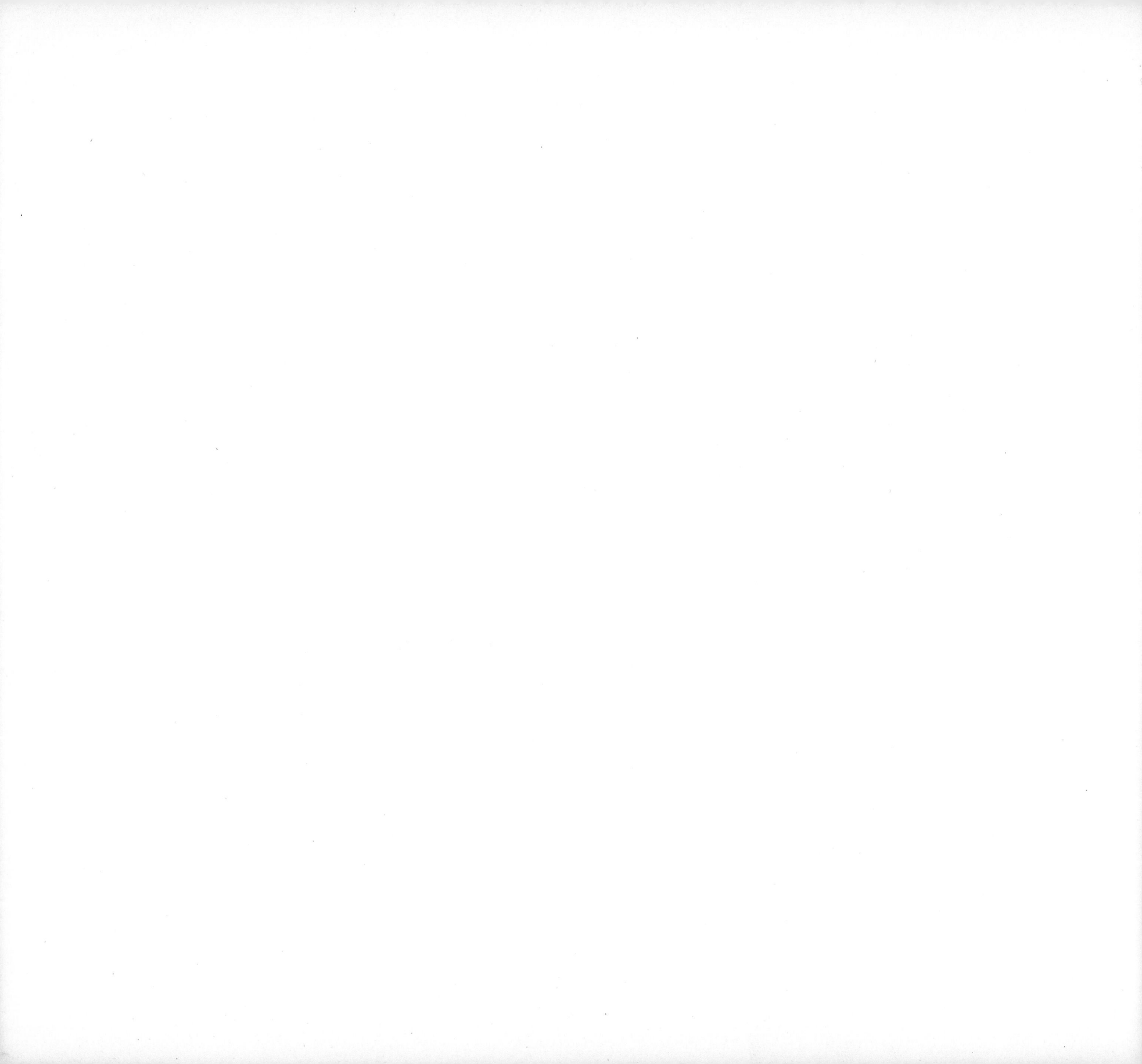

LOST SEATTLE

Acknowledgments

With love to Mai and Ansel, who endured months of insanity while I wrote. Thanks to Paul Middents and Ben Lukoff. The Seattle Public Library was essential to this work, from stacks to the Seattle Room to images to the digital *Seattle Times*. Paul Dorpat's deep website and Historylink's encyclopedia were referenced too often to list in the bibliography below. Thank you to everyone contributing to Wikipedia as well as archive.org, loc.gov and books.google.com.

Selected bibliography

Bagley, Clarence. *History of Seattle*. S. J. Clarke, 1916.
Ballard News-Tribune. *Passport to Ballard: the Centennial Story*. Ballard News-Tribune, 1988.
Becker, Paula and Alan Stein. *Alaska-Yukon-Pacific Exposition*. History Ink, 2009.
Becker, Paula and Alan Stein. *The Future Remembered*. Seattle Center Foundation, 2011.
Best, David Grant. *Portrait of a Racetrack*. Best Editions, 1992.
Blanchard, Leslie. *The Street Railway Era in Seattle*. H. E. Cox, 1968.
Burke, Edward. *Seattle's Nippon Kan*. E. Burke, 2011.
De Barros, Paul. *Jackson Street After Hours*. Sasquatch Books, 1993.
Grant, Frederic James. *History of Seattle, Washington*. American Publishing and Engraving, 1891.
Grind, Kirsten. *The Lost Bank*. Simon & Schuster, 2012.
Hines, Neal O. *Denny's Knoll*. University of Washington Press, 1980.
Ho, Chuimei, Bennet Bronson et al. Various articles. CINARC.org. 2009–2013. Web.
Hunt, Herbert and Floyd C. Kaylor. *Washington, West of the Cascades*. S. J. Clarke, 1917.
Marshall, John Douglas. *Place of Learning, Place of Dreams*. UW Press, 2004.
Miyamoto, S. Frank. *Social Solidarity Among the Japanese in Seattle*. University of Washington Press, 1981.
Ochsner, Jeffrey Karl and Dennis Anderson. *Distant Corner*. University of Washington Press, 2003.
Prosser, William. *A History of the Puget Sound Country*. Lewis Publishing, 1903.
Rayner, Alice D. *Path We Came By*. Plymouth Congregational Church, 1937.
Robinson, Julius. *The Georgetown Story*. Georgetown Designs, 1979.
"Sonicsgate [Online Director's Cut]," YouTube video, 1:59:37. Posted by "Sonicsgate" on Jan 22, 2010.
Thompson, Nile. *Building for Learning*. Seattle Public Schools, 2002.
Watts, Slick. *Tales from the Seattle SuperSonics*. Sports Publishing, 2005.

Picture credits

Seattle Public Library: 8, 10–12, 15–18, 19 bottom, 22–24, 26–27, 28 left, 31, 39 left, 43, 46, 51 left, 55, 56 right, 59 bottom, 63 right, 71–76, 81, 83, 86 left and top, 88 left, 90, 96, 104 right, 110, 112, 116–117, 120 right. **Seattle Municipal Archives:** 36, 42, 44 right, 51 right, 53, 56 left, 58, 60–62, 63 left, 67 top, 68–69, 78–79, 80 bottom, 82, 86 bottom, 88 right, 92, 98, 99 left, 101, 103 left, 106–107, 109, 119 bottom, 120 left, 123 right, 139 right. **University of Washington Libraries:** 9, 14, 20 left, 21, 25, 28 right, 29, 33, 39 middle, 54, 57, 64 right, 66, 70, 89, 93, 129. **Washington State Archives:** 7, 13, 30, 37, 47, 50, 80 top, 94, 97, 108 bottom, 134. **Rob Ketcherside:** 48 bottom, 59 top, 64 left, 91, 103 sidebar, 128 left, 132 right, 135, 140 left (David C. Cook). **Paul Dorpat:** 19 sidebar, 32 (courtesy of Lawton Gowey), 39 sidebar, 40, 48 top (courtesy of Waterfront Awareness), 52 (courtesy of Lawton Gowey), 87. **Anova Image Library:** 48 sidebar, 67 bottom, 67 sidebar, 95 top right, 104 left, 128 middle, 139 left. **Library of Congress:** 20 right, 100 sidebar, 111, 114–115, 124 bottom, 126–127, 136–137. **Museum of History & Industry:** 34–35, 38, 41, 45, 49, 77, 95 left, 102, 113, 142. **Corbis:** 85, 105, 121, 125. **Getty Images:** 118, 119 top, 130. **Joe Mabel:** 100 left, 128 right, 132 left. **Collection of Don Bugh:** 44 left. **Koji D. Kanemoto:** 65. **National Archives and Records Administration:** 84. **Choking Sun:** 95 bottom right. **Dennis Bratland:** 99 right. **Scott Durham:** 108 top. **King County Archives:** 122. **PH1 Harold J. Gerwien:** 123 left. **The Boeing Company:** 124 top. **Achim Hepp:** 131 bottom. **Jeramey Jannene:** 131 top. **K.lee:** 133. **Clark Humphrey:** 138. **Chihuly Garden and Glass:** 140 right.

Endpapers

Front: Bird's-Eye View of Seattle, 1891 (Library of Congress).
Back: Bird's-Eye View of Seattle, 1878 (Library of Congress).

First published in the United Kingdom in 2013 by
PAVILION BOOKS
10 Southcombe Street, London W14 0RA
An imprint of Anova Books Company Ltd

ISBN: 978-1-90910-863-9

A CIP catalogue record for this book is available from the British Library.

10 9 8 7 6 5 4 3 2

Repro by Rival Colour Ltd, UK
Printed by 1010 Printing International Ltd, China

www.anovabooks.com

LOST SEATTLE

Rob Ketcherside

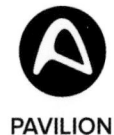

PAVILION

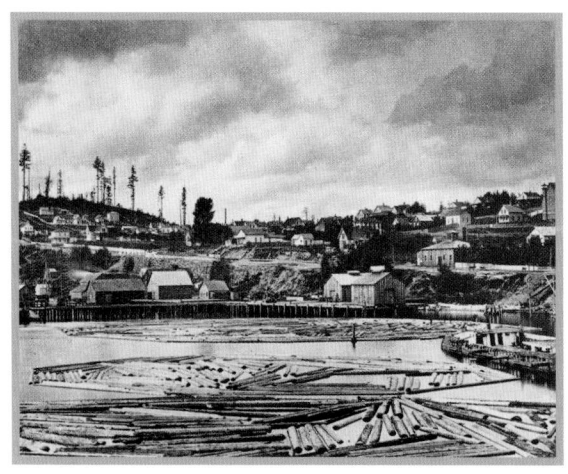
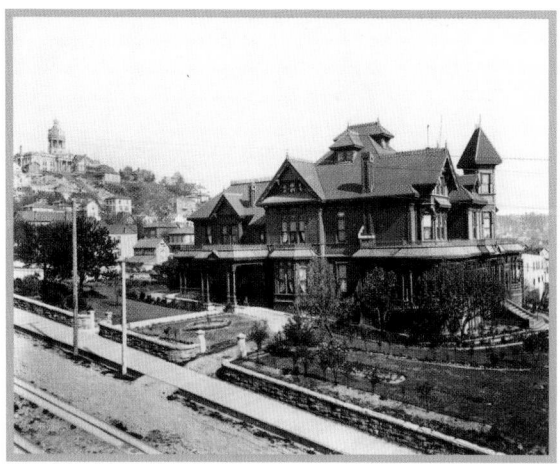
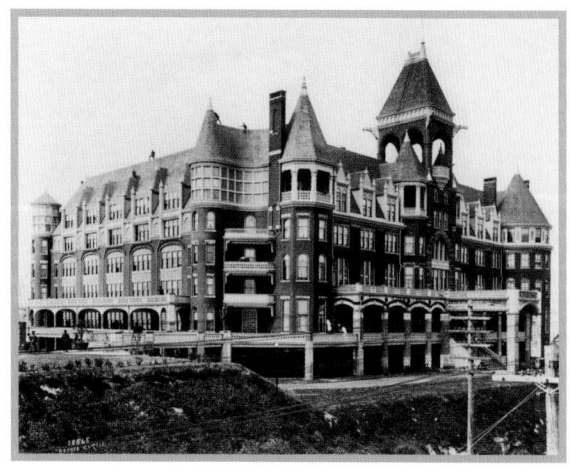
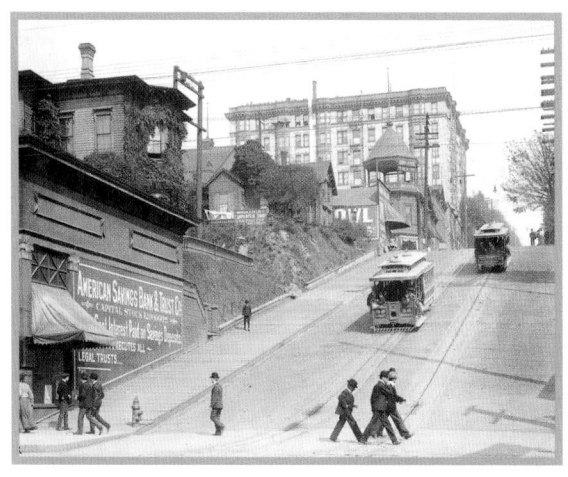
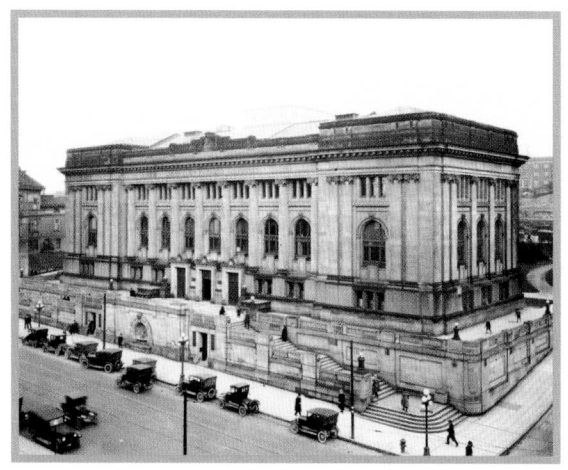
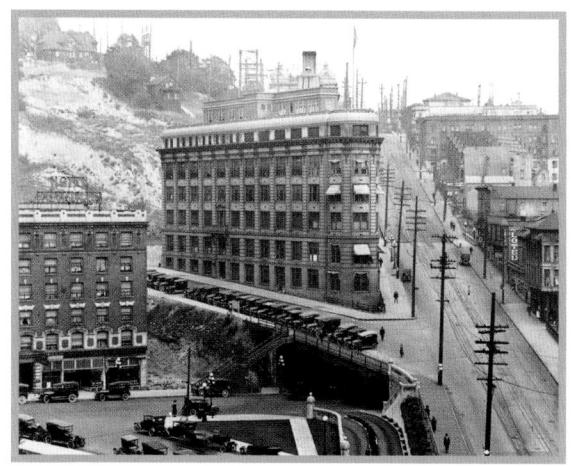
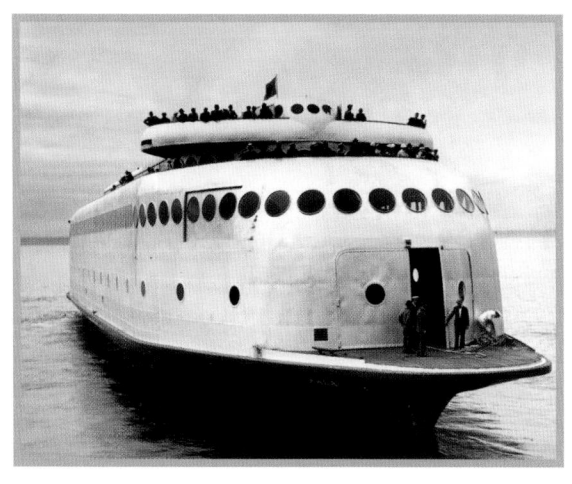
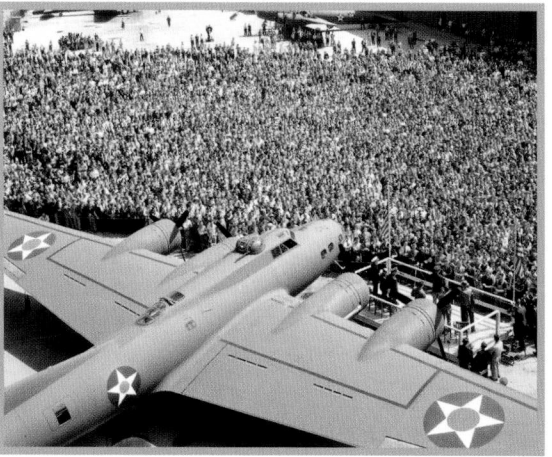
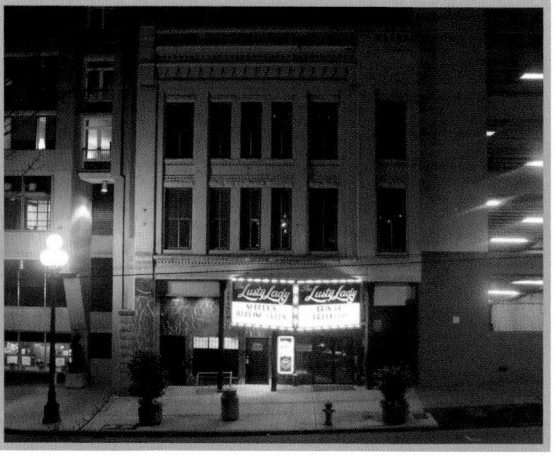

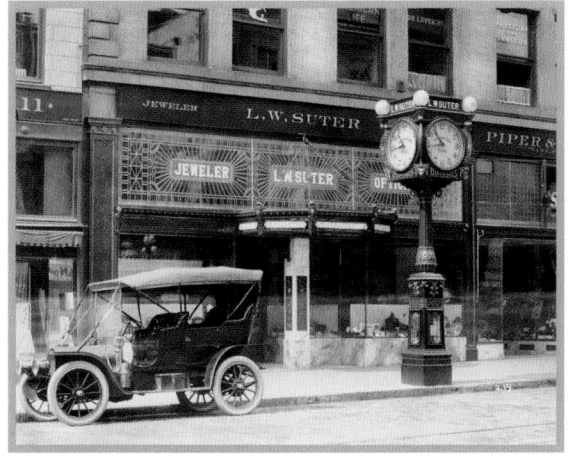

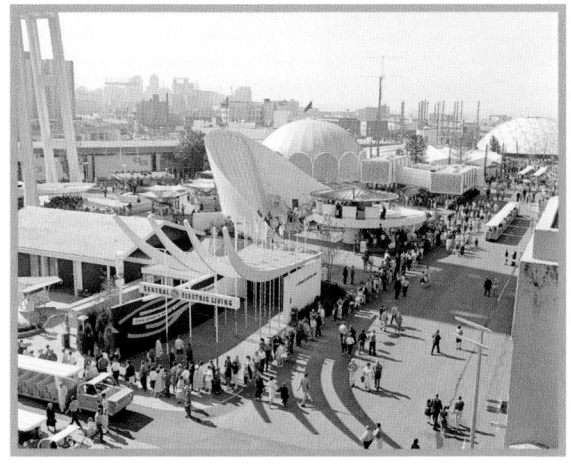

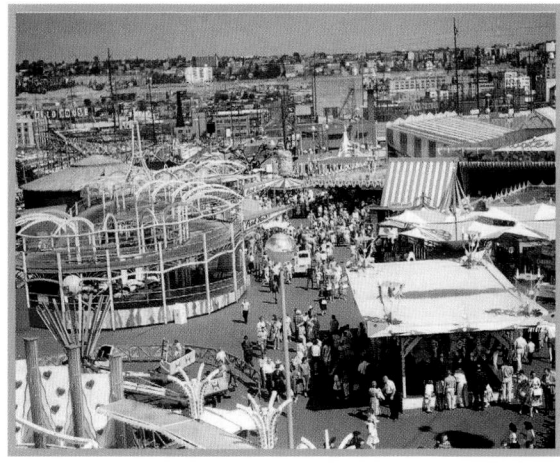

LOST IN THE...

INTRODUCTION

Since the mid-1920s the most regularly lamented loss in the Emerald City has been the Seattle Spirit. Every city has an element of boosterism and an effort driven by the chamber of commerce to draw new business. The Seattle Spirit represented that and so much more, from the time of first settlement and on through every early challenge to this upstart city.

To put Seattle in perspective, consider what was happening in New York and Chicago as the pioneers settled Elliott Bay in the 1850s. New York carved out Central Park, displacing half as many people as lived in all of Washington Territory. Chicago raised the city six feet and secured dominance in the national grain trade. These were real cities solving problems of growth while Henry Yesler, Doc Maynard, and the Denny family were in Seattle swimming a steam engine ashore for the mill, building docks, and starting to fill the tide flats. Seattle's pioneers were a stubborn community working together to build something new.

In the decade after the Civil War, the second wave of pioneers came with even more determination. James Colman, Thomas Burke, Frank Osgood, Jacob Furth and others proved willing to make personal sacrifices for the common good. The Seattle Spirit was an aggressive optimism based on the belief that when the city succeeds, the individual succeeds. The clearest early example came in 1883 after the Northern Pacific opted to grab land on Commencement Bay and end the transcontinental railroad in Tacoma instead of Seattle. What did Seattle's leading citizens do? With their own hands they began building the Seattle & Walla Walla Railroad. It never made it to Walla Walla, or even Tacoma for that matter. But it got to Renton and scared the Northern Pacific into building a connection to Seattle.

When Seattle burned in 1889 that rail line proved its worth. Tacoma firefighters raced to the scene and trains hauled loads of emergency supplies. Despite the setback, Seattle Mayor Robert Moran declared that Seattle would rebuild better than before. He led by example by turning his own burned-down boiler repair shop into an entire shipyard. Seattle began its legendary phoenix rise from 64 acres of ashes.

In 1897 Seattle convinced miners to stop in and buy all of their provisions on the way to the Klondike Gold Rush. Then Seattle lobbied for a federal Assay Office branch to take in the gold that was found. The commission of the battleship *Nebraska*, the Carnegie Library, the Federal Building, the World's Fair in 1909, and the endless series of earthmoving regrades were all tangible effects of the Seattle Spirit's "going and getting" philosophy. Touring the regrades while visiting for the fair, the leader of the Chicago Association of Commerce said, "The ancestor of the Seattle Spirit was a Chicago hustler." He recognized Seattle's civic dynamic as an echo of Chicago's city building.

The Seattle Spirit's most egregious flaw was the exploitation of nature. The regrades displaced homes and businesses. Worse, they caused landslides that wiped out buildings without warning. The removal of creeks, rechanneling of the Duwamish River and filling of the waterfront and tideflats devastated local fisheries. The impacts were all battled out in the courts, and the need to build and rebuild the city prevailed.

The Seattle Spirit died out in the mid-1920s with the death of Thomas Burke and withdrawal of John Chilberg, the last of the second-generation pioneers. Growth was no longer personality-driven: business decisions were more likely to be selfish, and bureaucracy became a tool for exploiting the city itself. The introduction of federal housing and renewal money in the 1930s and the interstate highway system in the 1960s were particularly damaging. Entire neighborhoods were upturned. Flight to the suburbs made parking garages more valuable than historic buildings. As architect B. Marcus Priteca watched another of his theaters get demolished for a parking garage he said "I wish Seattle would just stop growing." He expected them all to be torn town, but luckily Seattle has held on to a few.

There are many easily accessible histories of Seattle, from popular books to extensive websites. While those were certainly leveraged, this book was created through extensive combing of old newspapers and long out-of-print tomes. Many standards of Seattle history are given quite new treatment. In the article Interurban Railways, the early years of the intercity rails are untangled and Columbia City's origins given much-deserved attention. While discussing the beginnings of the Green Lake Aqua Theatre, Seafair's forgotten connection to Minneapolis festivals is unveiled. Naval Air Station Seattle provides the opportunity to mention Seattle's first air defenses.

A few topics are quite unique to this book. Joseph Mayer's production of street clocks is hardly understood outside of a small circle of enthusiasts. Discussion of Seattle's regrades usually ends at Denny Hill, but here space is also devoted to the almost-forgotten Yesler Hill and Jackson Ridge. Although the remaining Ramps to Nowhere on SR-520 are receiving attention recently, newcomers have never heard of the much more iconic Interstate 5 ramps.

Seattle history fans should have fun spotting the forgotten trivia sprinkled through other stories. Every account of John Collins's original Occidental Hotel says that he tore it down, but it actually burned. No story of Luna Park mentions the family's return to Seattle and one grandson's rise to vice-president of WaMu. Firland Sanatorium had other facilities alongside the tuberculosis hospital, including an entire building devoted to "delousing" prostitutes.

In order to lose, you must first gain. Each of the following stories describes the genesis of a place, event or institution and its role in the cultural or economic heritage of Seattle. The vignettes describe connections to people important to Seattle's history or the designs of talented architects. All of the subjects were important landmarks of Seattle that we have lost forever.

RIGHT *Golden Potlatch celebrations at Pioneer Square and First Avenue in 1912. (See page 63.)*

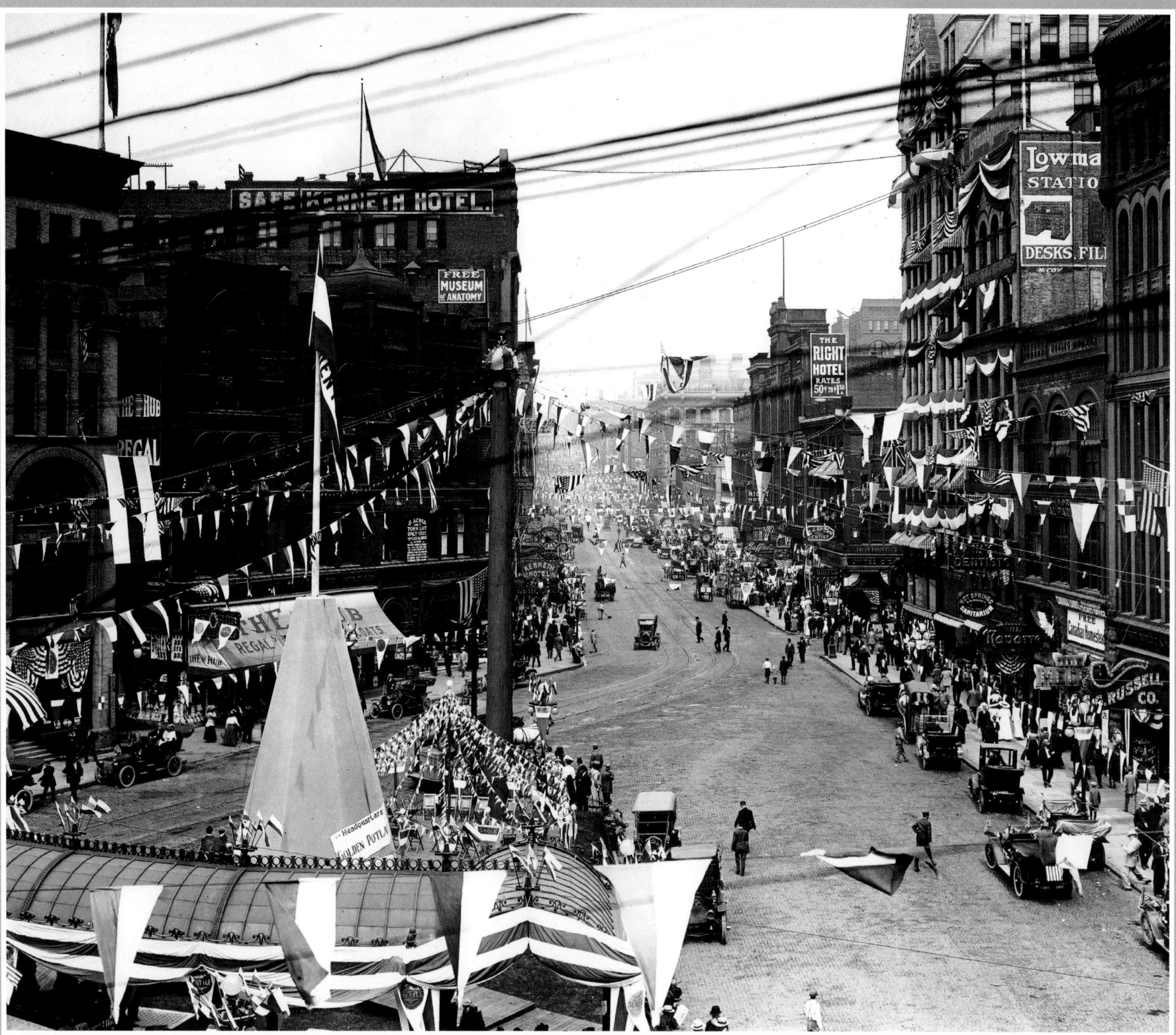

Yesler's Mill CLOSED 1889

Seattle was founded in 1851 at Alki Point out on Puget Sound. A year later the settlement moved into Elliott Bay to what is now Pioneer Square. On the end of a narrow spit of land Henry Yesler built the town's first industry, and Yesler's sawmill started cutting logs in 1853. Its steam engine was the only one at a mill among the townsites on Puget Sound and the first in Washington Territory. Today the mill would be at just about the intersection of Yesler Way and Post Avenue.

The mill planed boards to ship south to San Francisco, still booming after the 1849 gold rush. The lumber was freighted to Pacific Isles, Asia, and Australia. It allowed Seattle's houses and shops and hotels to take a more refined look than the rough log cabins of the surrounding country. And the sawdust from all of that cut timber was used to fill the swampland and bogs separating the new town and the bottom of First Hill.

As the streets were platted out, the mill became the endpoint of a road running right up the hill. It replaced a trail to Lake Washington, and was straightforwardly named Mill Street. Because of its steepness it came to carry the myth of being the original Skid Road, a road to skid logs down. Sure, it wasn't really the first, but it was the only urban timber route with a real skid and where gravity could do the job alone.

In Seattle's early years the importance of Yesler's Mill cannot be overstated. Settlers cleared their land and made cash from their timber. And it gave work to the men who built Seattle: founder Arthur Denny, banker Dexter Horton, builder Hillary Butler, and businessman George Frye were among the near unanimous list of pioneers to work the mill. Names that now are only found on streets like those of Hanford and Holgate filled the pay ledger.

The demand for 8,000 board feet per day required more labor than the American imperialists could provide themselves. So the local and seasonal native population joined them. Their names are left out of most histories except in nicknames like Curley, Yesler's foreman. His real name, Suquardle, is barely mentioned in scholarly works. We've forgotten the names of the native peoples in his camp.

Curley was a key figure in early Seattle history. The popular story is that he arrived in advance of a rebellious uprising of native peoples in 1856, turning the Battle of Seattle into a siege instead of the massacre that happened in the White River Valley.

Henry Yesler began investing his time and money in other ventures, and eventually he decided to lease out the mill. He served as mayor twice, as County auditor, and developed land holdings in the region.

In 1869 the little mill was rebuilt, modernized and enlarged. It was rebuilt again in 1875 when James Colman took over Yesler's Mill on lease. It suffered a major fire in 1879 but was reconstructed.

The city prophetically renamed Mill Street to Yesler Avenue in 1888. The mill went idle in early 1889 as competing mills took away business. And then Seattle's Great Fire burned it down for good in June.

Yesler rebuilt his mill as a shipping wharf, and built a new mill out on Lake Washington. Other mills relocated to Ballard, which became the industrial center for Seattle.

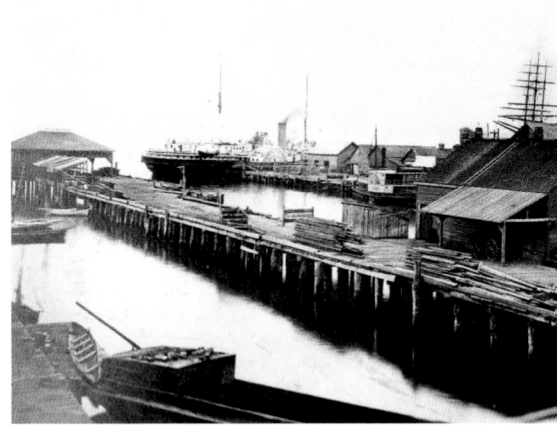

ABOVE *Yesler's wharf in 1880 with the sidewheeler* Dakota *in the distance.*

RIGHT *Yesler's wharf with logs for the mill and cut lumber in about 1888.*

OPPOSITE PAGE *Log booms of Yesler's Mill with Denny Hill in the background in 1878.*

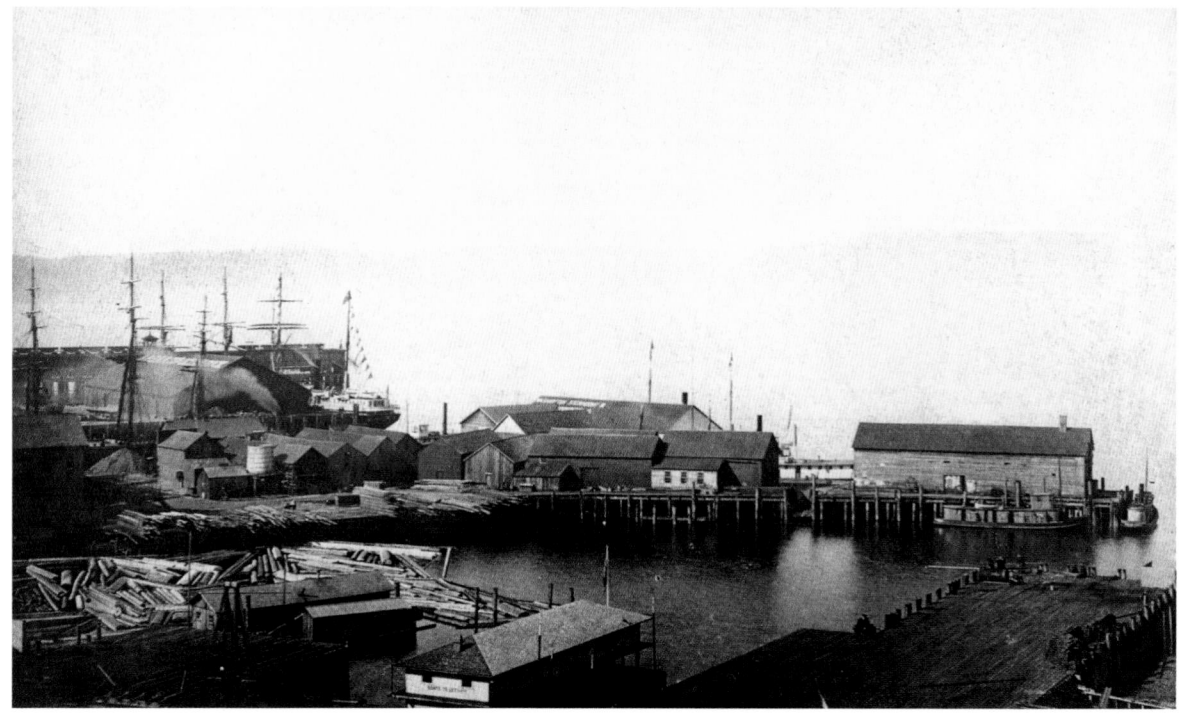

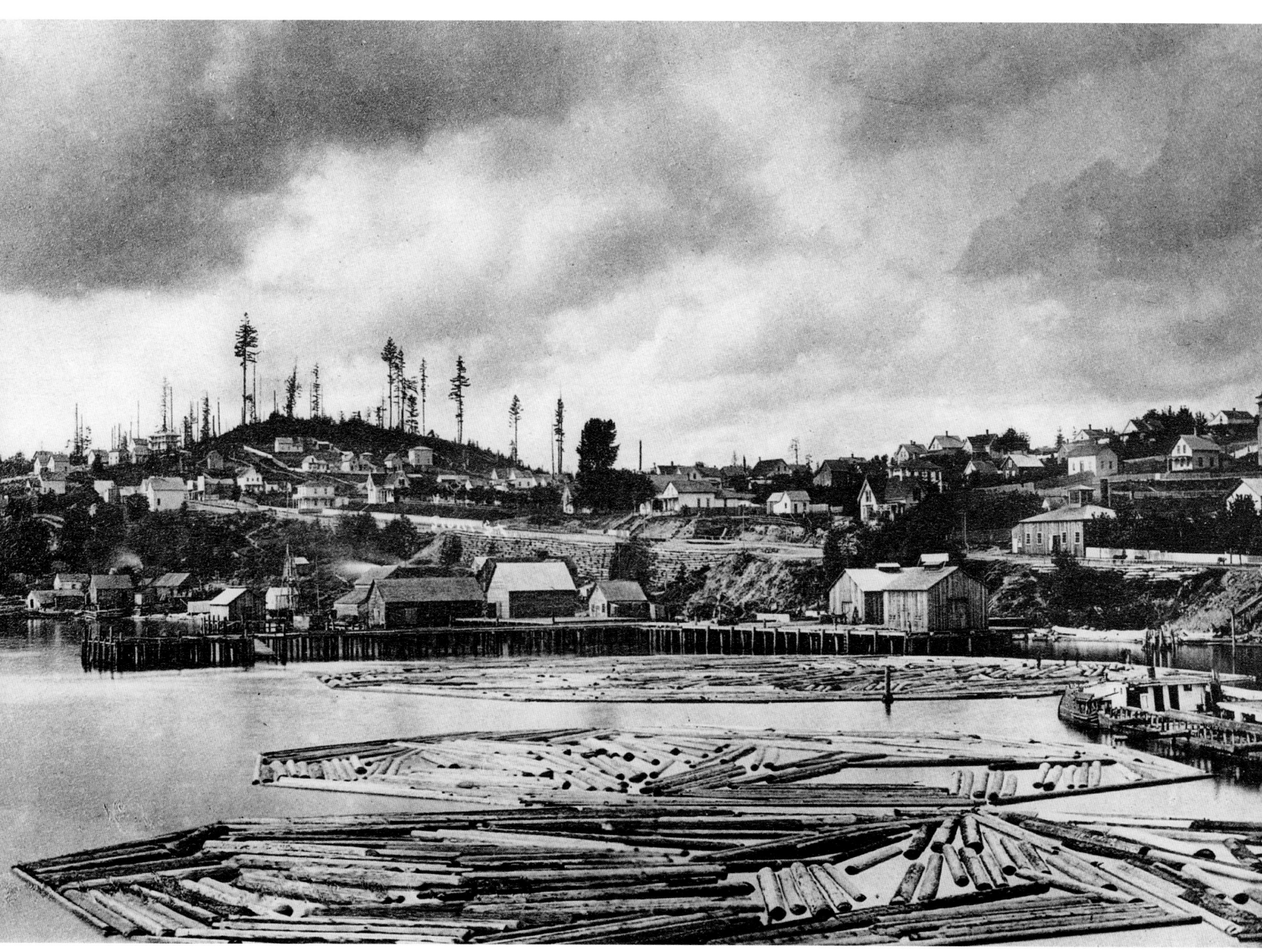

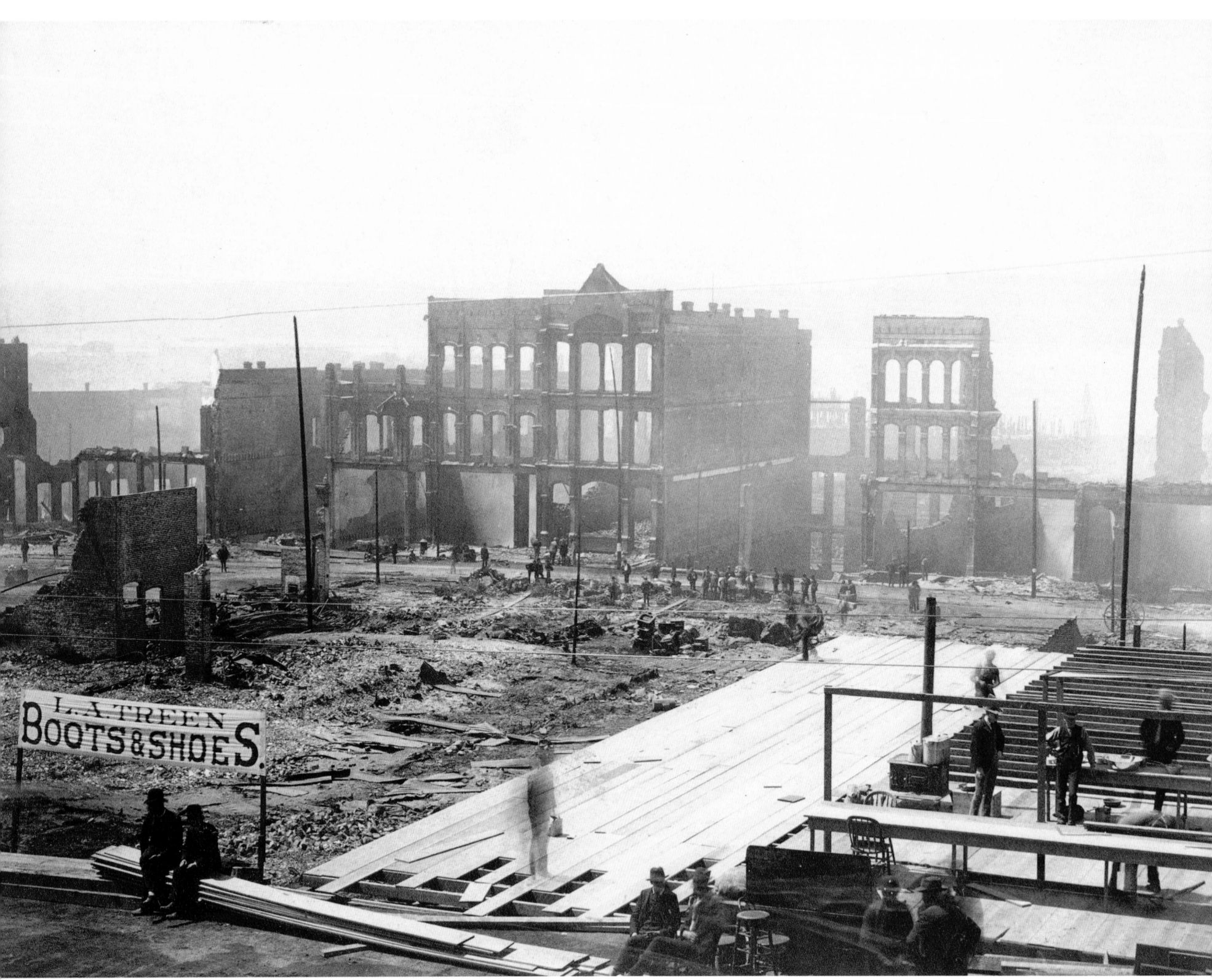

Great Fire BUBBLED OVER 1889

On June 6 1889, 64 acres of the core of Seattle were reduced to smouldering rubble. It started in a pot of glue at a cabinetmaker's shop at Front Street (First Avenue) and Madison Street. Worker John Berg panicked when he saw the pot. He threw a bucket of water on it which spread the fire to the whole store. The building was quickly engulfed and the northerly breezes of Seattle summer afternoons pushed the fire downhill into the city center.

Major conflagrations were common in dense, wood cities of the late 1800s, where the buildings stood shoulder to shoulder and even the sidewalks were wood. Spokane and Ellensburg, Washington also burned in 1889. Cities across the country including Jacksonville, Chicago, San Francisco, and Galveston suffered major fires within a few years. Indeed, there is some irony that Seattle's original business was to feed lumber for San Francisco's insatiable need after a seemingly endless series of fires.

In October 1884 an insurance inspector mistakenly certified Seattle as safe from fire. The two steam fire engines were rolled out and connected to fire plugs. Two hoses each simultaneously sprayed water over the top of Seattle's tallest buildings, the Occidental Hotel and Yesler-Leary Building. He saw enough to lower insurance premiums.

Seattle was primed for a spectacular fire, though. The uphill springs, which were inspected during the wet fall, had low pressure in the summer. The backup system, emergency lines out into Elliott Bay, only worked at high tide. And Seattle grew each year, adding buildings and drawing down water. It took little to light the city on fire in 1889.

As the fire spread, business owners and residents responded by moving all of their valuables out into the street. Thomas Carroll, a young employee at jeweler L. P. Smith's shop, piled jewelry, silver and valuables, and found a horse to pull it up onto First Hill. *Seattle Post-Intelligencer* board secretary Samuel Crawford raced from Bainbridge Island in time to save the paper's records from the office at Mill Street and Post Avenue. Militia composed of pastors, businessmen, and other leading citizens patrolled the streets to make sure nothing was stolen.

Before abandoning their offices the telegraph companies wired for help. A hose team from Tacoma made it by train in time to help check the flames. Port Townsend, Olympia, Portland and even Victoria, B.C. sent fire engines, hoses and men. But it was too late when they arrived. A mile of waterfront and a quarter-mile inland was smouldering wreckage, accented with pieces of brick walls or chimneys.

Devastation was not limited to the commercial and office buildings along Front or around Mill Street (Yesler Way). Every wharf south of University Street, every warehouse, mill, factory and lumber yard along the waterfront was destroyed. The glow could be seen from Tacoma, and the sky looked blood red from the top of Seattle's hills.

Under the advice of experts from San Francisco, Seattle's first building code was enacted less than a month after the Great Fire. It ensured that stone and brick construction would slow the spread of fire.

From the very day of the fire, farflung newspapers reported on the determination of Seattle to rebuild a better city than before. With the law in place, reconstruction was immediate. Dozens of buildings were underway in July. By the end of the year, the number topped 250.

Another fire in 1892 at First and Yesler consumed most of Schwabacher Hardware, but the new fire laws kept it contained.

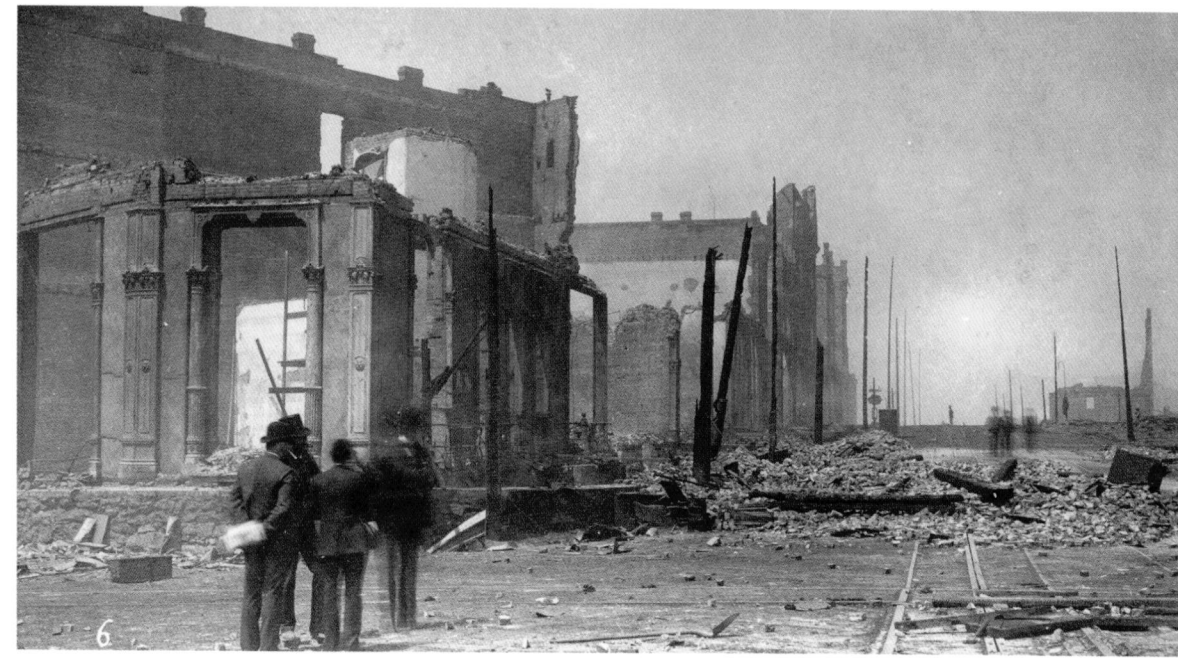

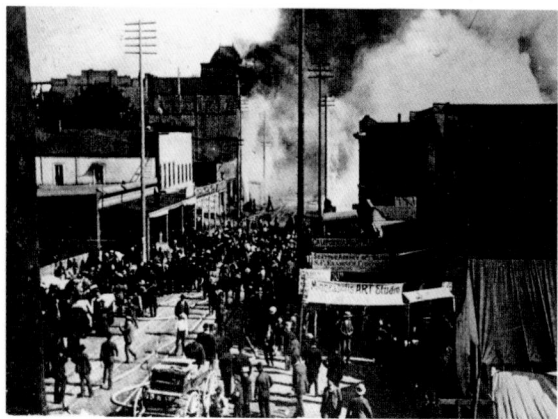

ABOVE *The start of the fire at Front and Madison streets.*

LEFT *Looking north on Front Street with the Yesler-Leary Building on the left.*

OPPOSITE PAGE *Facades of burned-out buildings line Front Street and reconstruction has already begun at Second and Columbia.*

Yesler-Leary Building BURNED 1889

Seattle's original settlement was named after New York. But it was San Francisco that the pioneers really tried to imitate and better.

Architect William Boone designed the Yesler-Leary Building as a direct copy of the Phelan Block in San Francisco. Completed in 1882, its three stories rose above surrounding buildings, and the one-floor brick Victorian tower on the corner jutted above the city. It was visible from blocks away because Mill Street (Yesler Way) rose so quickly, and Front and Commercial streets (First Avenue and First Avenue South) did not meet directly.

John Leary, Henry Yesler's development partner, had a hand in all of Seattle's industries. He was owner of the *Seattle Post*, headquartered next to the Yesler-Leary Building. After acquiring several other papers he sold it as the *Seattle Post-Intelligencer* in 1884. Leary successfully invested in water utilities, railroads, streetcars, real estate, Mosquito Fleet steamers, and many other types of ventures. He was elected Mayor in 1884, just before Yesler's second term.

On June 6, 1889, as the Great Fire spread south from Madison, there was hope that it would be halted by the brick Yesler-Leary Building, and the stone and brick Occidental Hotel. But as they were engulfed it was clear to Seattle's citizens that there was no stopping the fire. It continued all the way to the water beyond King Street.

Albert Hansen leased space in the Yesler-Leary Building at the time of the fire. One of Seattle's earliest jewelers, Hansen also sold pianos as the regional reseller of Steinway and Knabe. His jewelry store was on the first floor along Front Street, and the pianos upstairs. Some of his jewelry was saved, but all of the pianos went up in the inferno.

The first news reports of the fire already described the opportunity to rebuild the city. It would be fireproof, raised up above water level, and the street grid would be straightened out. Mayor Robert Moran and other city leaders had one particular problem with the streets that they planned to address.

The site of the Yesler-Leary Building was condemned in days. As the streets were rebuilt, Front Street was directly connected to Commercial Street. Henry Yesler tried to fight to maintain his property, but to no avail. The space in between the old and new Front Street was turned into a trapezoidal park known as Pioneer Place. By the time the totem pole was added to the park In 1899, most of the city was already calling it Pioneer Square.

WILLIAM BOONE

William Boone was Seattle's most important architect before and just after the Great Fire. His buildings followed Victorian conventions, and were often direct copies of buildings in California. Some of his most famous works were the Yesler-Leary Building, Central School (#3), Yesler Mansion, and Broadway High School. Boone came to Seattle late in life. He gradually worked his way from Pennsylvania through Chicago to Minneapolis. He headed to California to find gold in 1859, and then went back to work in San Francisco during its boom. At age 50 he moved to Seattle in 1882. In 1894 Boone was a founding member of the Seattle branch of the American Institute of Architects. After 30 years practicing in Seattle, he retired in 1910. He passed away at his residence in Madrona in 1921.

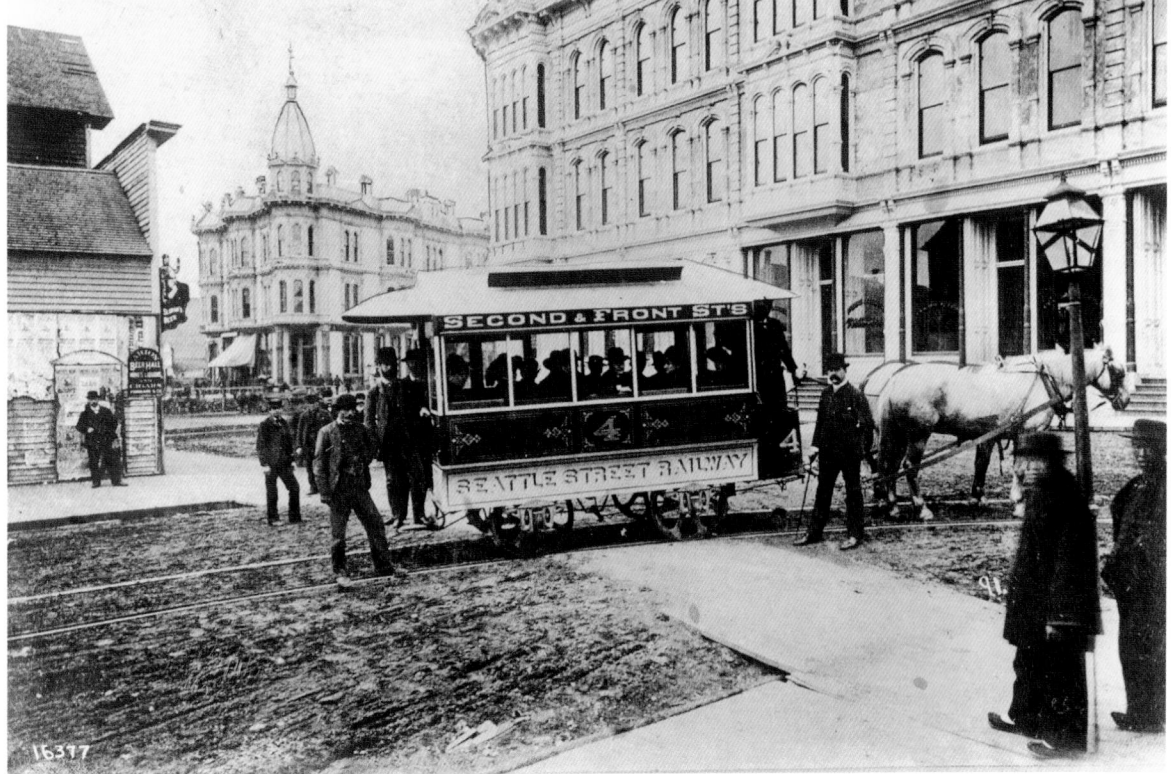

LEFT *The Yesler-Leary Building behind Seattle's first streetcar in 1884. The Occidental Hotel is at right.*

RIGHT *The cupola juts above Seattle's two- and three-story buildings. Seen in 1887 with Albert Hansen's jewelry shop on the right side.*

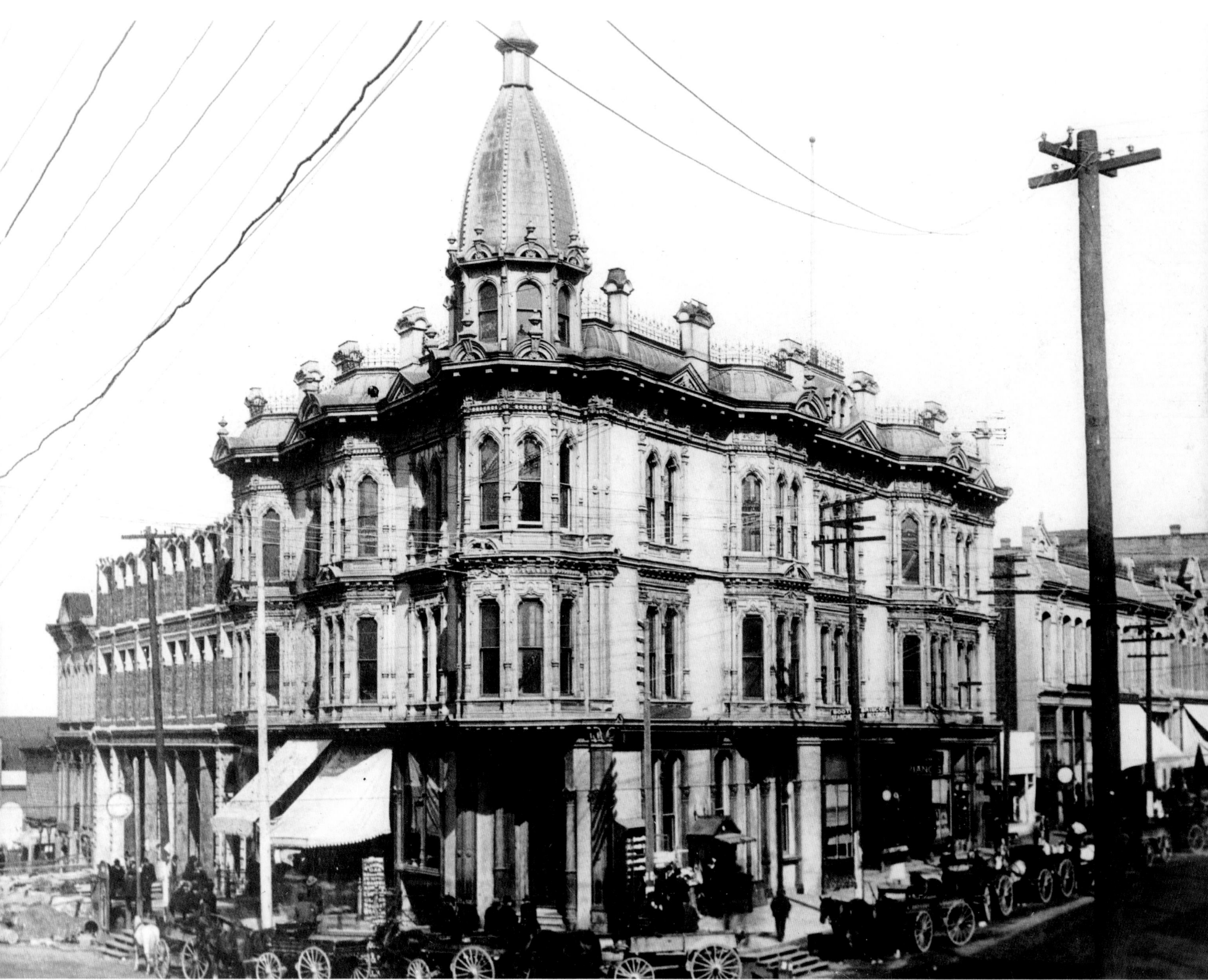

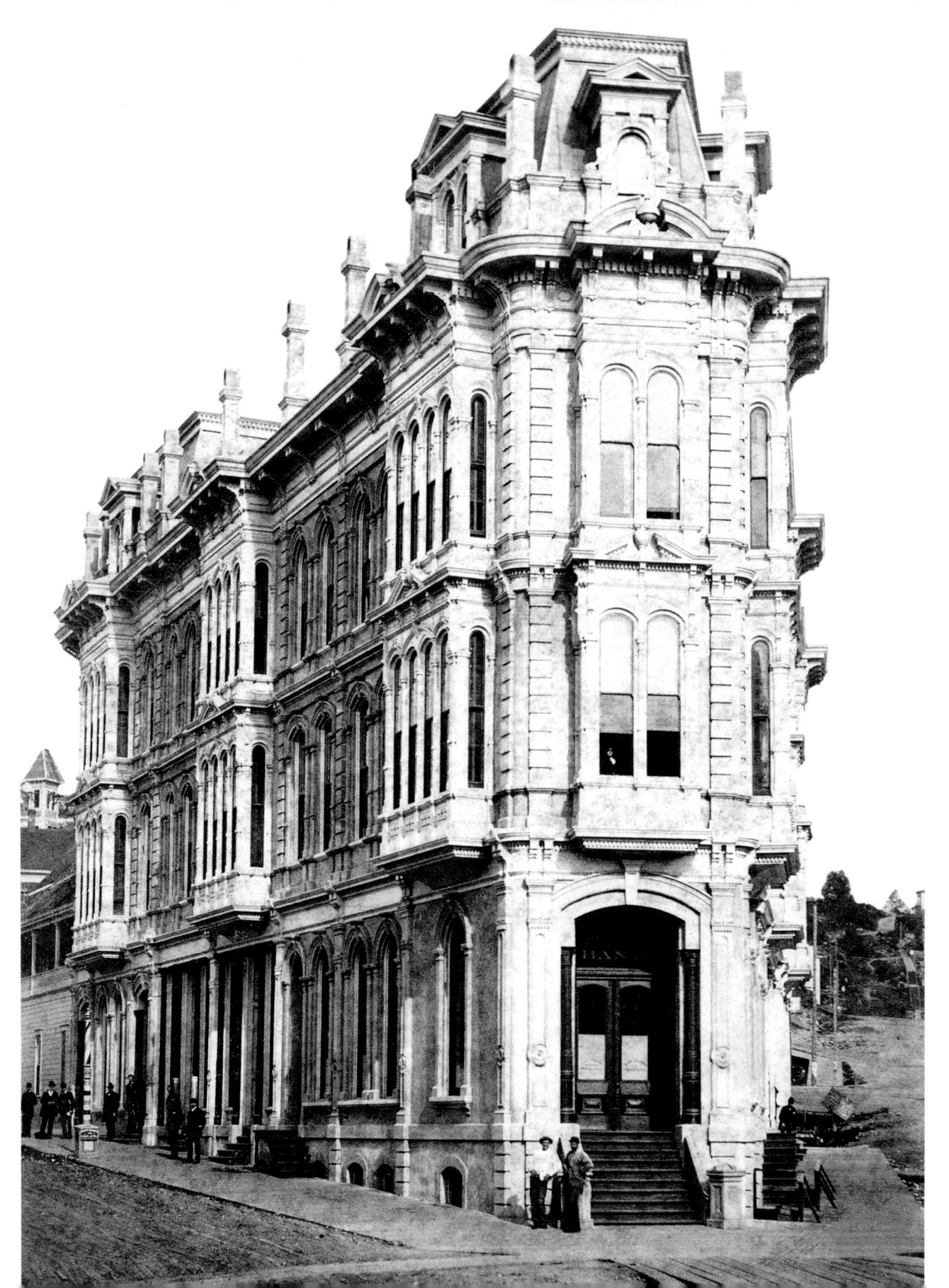

Occidental Hotel BURNED 1889

The wedge-shaped Occidental Hotel was Seattle's best travel hotel. Built in 1884, it was the largest hotel north of San Francisco and a fitting replacement for the old wood Occidental Hotel.

The original was opened 20 years earlier in 1864. The next year John Collins, friend of the owners, took a one-third share of the hotel. In 1867 he purchased it outright and moved from Port Gamble to operate it himself. Collins would go on to become one of Seattle's most prominent citizens.

The first Occidental Hotel was a wood building like all the rest in Seattle, two and a half floors high with rooms for 30 guests. It was pushed to the uphill half of the triangle, leaving the water side as an

LEFT *The hotel just after construction completed in 1884. The Puget Sound National Bank is open in the corner storefront.*

BELOW *After the Great Fire's devastation in 1889.*

open space called Occidental Square. With a flagpole in the middle this served as Seattle's gathering place. The hotel's broad balcony provided a great place for public oration.

In January, 1883, the original wood hotel burned down on a Saturday night. Collins was determined to not have it burn down again. He hired architect David McKay to design a fireproof building, built of brick and faced with stone. But it still depended on a wood frame and floors due to cost and technological limitations.

The new Occidental Hotel was Seattle's first upscale hotel. It had the most rooms of any hotel in the Pacific Northwest and the best appointed. An array of dignitaries stayed over the years, such as Senator John Sherman in 1884, and his brother General William Sherman of Civil War fame in 1886. In addition, many single men lodged at the hotel long-term, renting rooms and walking to their nearby businesses.

The first floor contained a number of retail spaces. They were anchored on the west tip by the Puget Sound National Bank, which a century later merged with KeyBank. Schoenfeld Furniture opened in 1887, and is still in Pioneer Square today. There was also the realty and bank office of L. H. Griffith, the promoter of early Fremont and several streetcars.

The Great Fire hit the Occidental Hotel five hours after it started, at 7:30 p.m. on June 6, 1889. The stone and brick facade crumbled after the wood trim and timber structure burned. While the rubble still smoldered, John Collins had a crew out excavating and preparing to build anew.

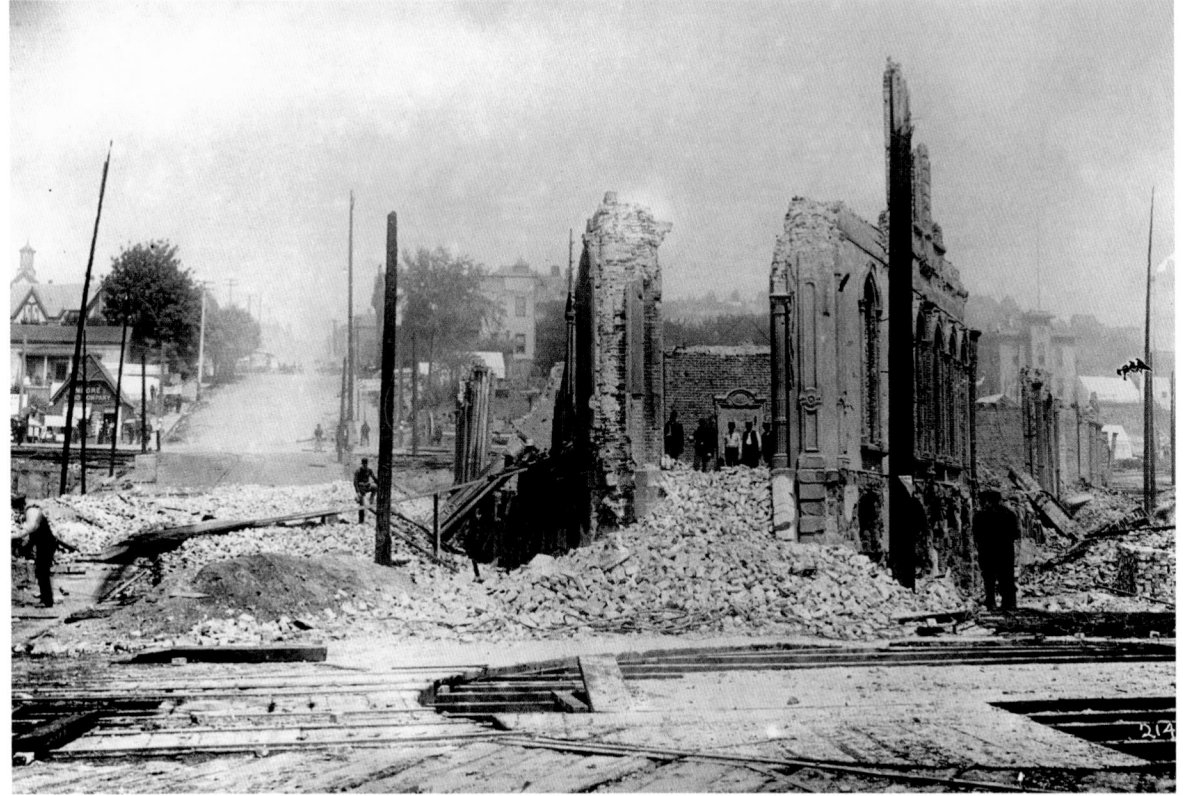

JOHN COLLINS

Born in Ireland in 1835, John Collins moved to the United States at the age of 10. He learned the lumber business in New England, and then sailed to San Francisco and entered the employ of Puget Mill Company. For them he ran the mill and hotel at Port Gamble. After the Occidental Hotel drew him to Seattle in 1867, Collins branched out into many other businesses. He worked with James Colman in the 1880s on the Seattle & Walla Walla Railway and the Cedar River Coal Company, two important industrial ventures. Collins also owned predecessors to the two newspapers that ruled Seattle for a century. His *Daily Telegraph* was sold to the *Post Intelligencer* in 1894, and his *Press Times* was sold to the *Daily Times*. In the early years Seattle's business leaders were also the political and civic leaders. John Collins proved successful at governance and grew beyond city government. Collins helped write the city charter and then was elected to the City Council in 1869. He advanced to Mayor in 1877. And then five years later he was elected to the Territorial Council, equivalent to the State Senate, in 1882. At his death in 1903 Collins had amassed one of the largest fortunes in Seattle.

Territorial University MOVED OUT OF TOWN 1895

The Territorial University of Washington, as it was originally known, was founded in 1861 before Washington was a state and as Civil War broke out between Union and Confederate states.

In 1860 Seattle was a tiny mill town with less than 300 residents. The pioneer founders were proud of Yesler's Mill and they didn't discriminate against any commercial activity. Saloons, brothels, and gambling houses catered to the loggers, sailors, and laborers that passed through the port or stopped in on a break from rural areas.

Arthur Denny, Daniel Bagley and other civic leaders knew that if they could secure a major government institution there would be a flood of investment and jobs. Three facilities of Washington Territory needed to be sited: the capitol, penitentiary and university. Seattle's leaders sought out and surprisingly won the university despite having very few families.

Denny donated part of his land claim on a shoulder of First Hill over Seattle's business district, known as Denny's Knoll. Money was raised for an ostentatiously grand building with three floors, a row of cedar Ionic columns, and a bell tower on top. It was designed and built by Seattle's own John Pike.

In the early years the school focused on preparatory classes, accepting grade school children and even teaching algebra and other basic courses to adults. The university suffered from lack of funding, and was essentially an extension of Seattle's secondary school. As Seattle and the Puget Sound region grew, though, the number of students and quality of education expanded. Finally in 1876 the first collegiate degree was awarded, to Clara McCarty of Puyallup.

In 1889 the university building served as city hall after the Great Fire. Later that year Washington became a state and the school was renamed the University of Washington. Over the years Seattle's residential and then business districts had overtaken the school campus and the university reached 300 pupils and was still growing. The university searched for a new home and selected Montlake in north Seattle.

Classes transferred in 1895, and the new building rang in the school year with the bell moved from the original school. Back at the old campus a graduate law school and other classes targeted at professionals continued for a number of years. Space was rented to the Mount Zion Baptist Church, the Seattle Public Library, and other tenants.

It was demolished in 1908 to make way for the Metropolitan Tract, a new commercial district built on the University of Washington's leased land. The columns were moved to an outdoor theater at the new UW campus. The theater hosted commencement for many years, celebrating the school's maturation into a true university and its impact on the city.

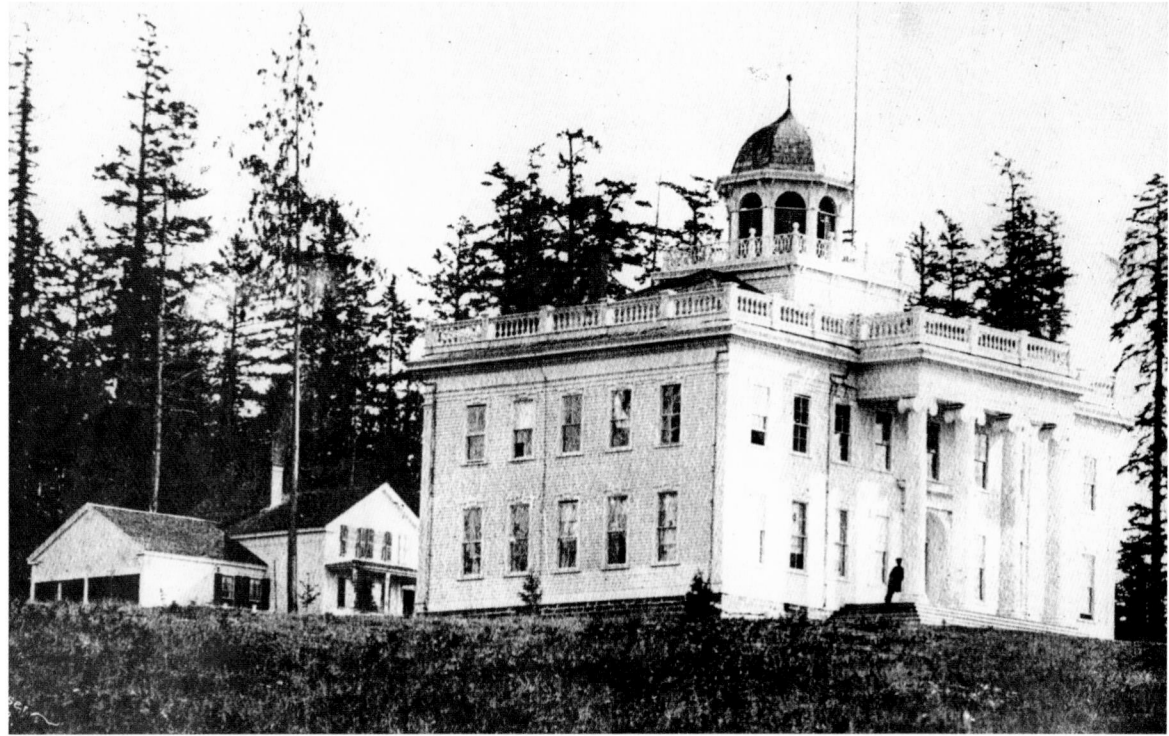

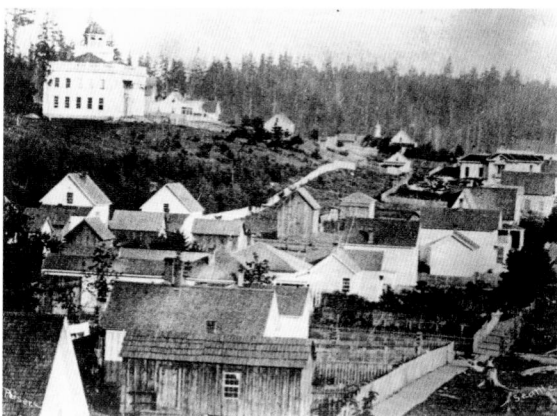

ABOVE *The university seen atop Denny's Knoll from about Third and Pike in 1878.*

LEFT *The university campus in 1864, a few years after completion.*

RIGHT *The university building in about 1905 while used as the Seattle Public Library.*

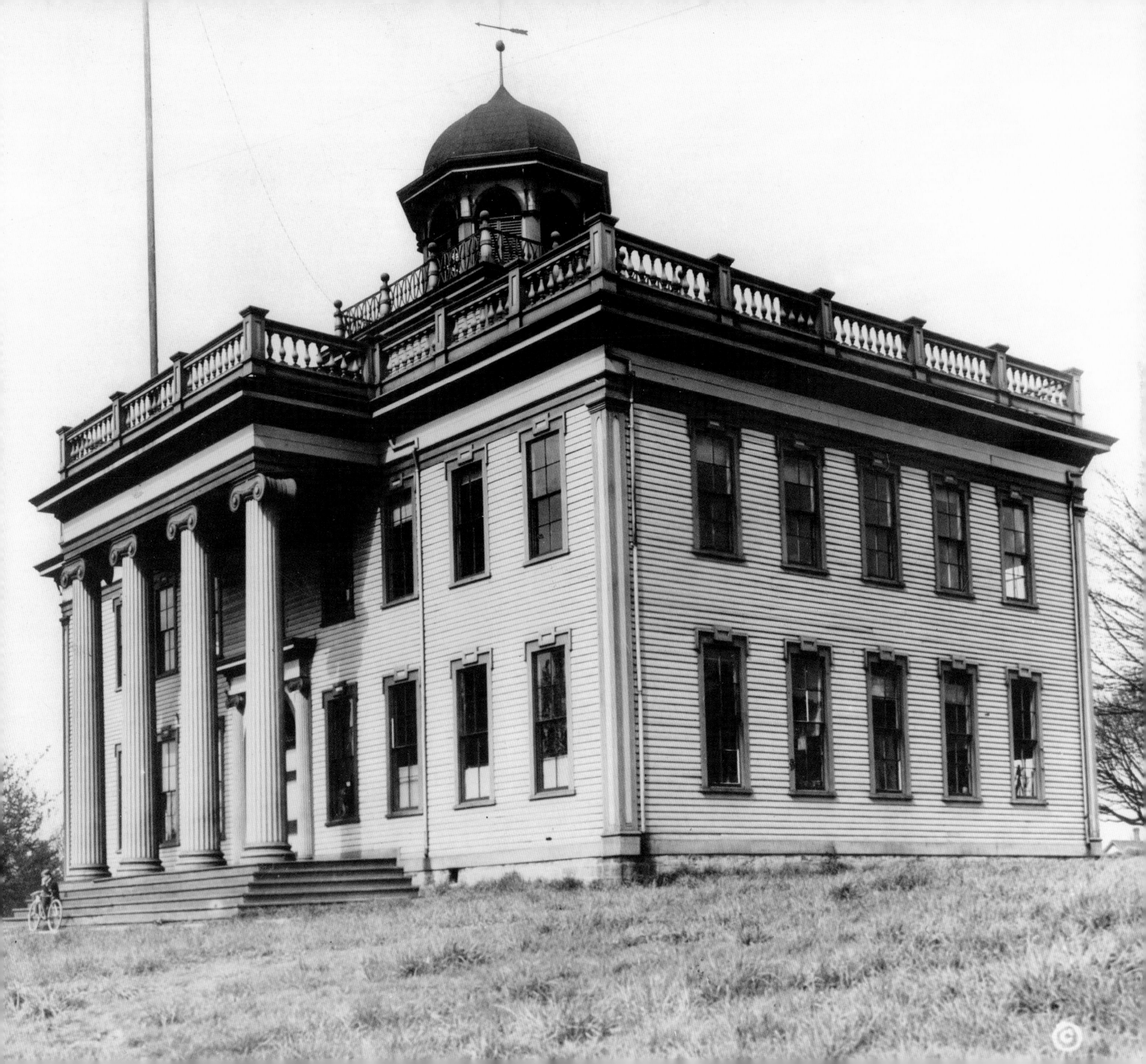

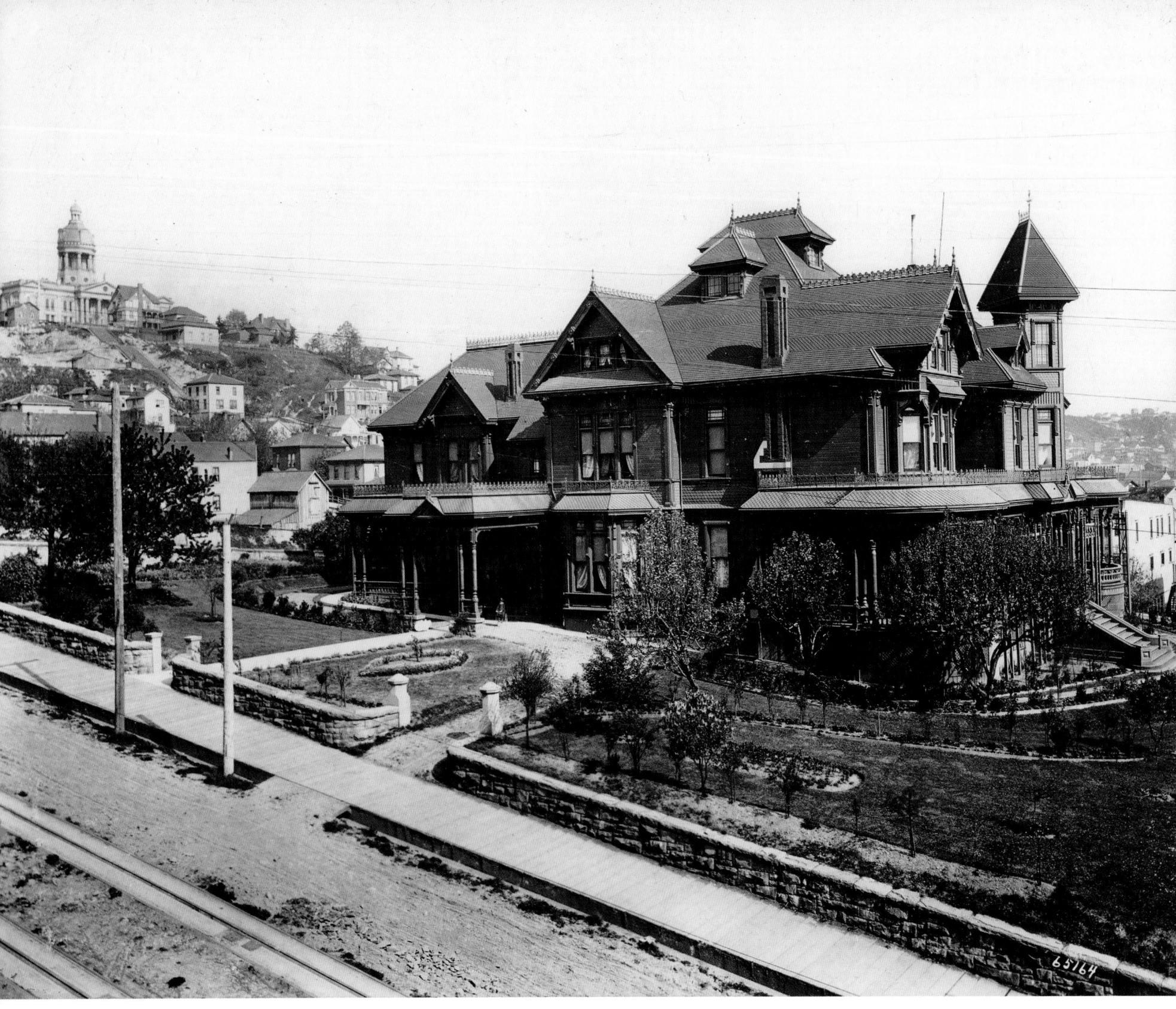

Yesler Mansion BURNED 1901

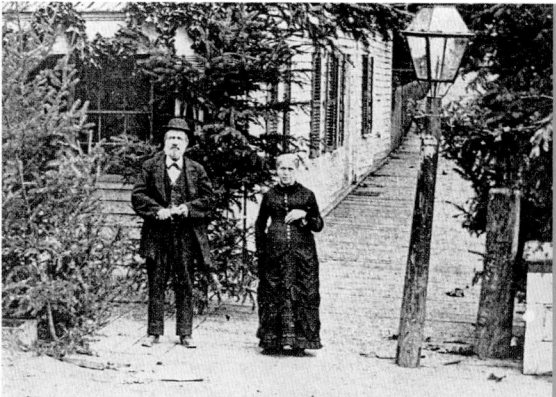

The 40-room mansion of Henry and Sarah Yesler was constructed over the course of two years, from 1883 to 1884. It had a short and tumultuous history as the grandest and most noticeable home in Seattle.

Despite their prominence and wealth, the Yeslers had lived in a nice but simple home across from their mill. After they blocked their own waterfront view with the Yesler-Leary Building, the Yeslers commissioned architects William Boone and George Meeker to design them a mansion. They asked for the most expensive home in Washington Territory.

The mansion was built uphill in the Yesler's orchard, facing Third Avenue at James Street. Like the Yesler-Leary Building, the Yesler mansion was a prime example of Victorian architecture, with multi-colored shingles on the roof, a porch that stretched from one side of the house to another, turrets, a staggered roof, and a variety of window styles. It was so large that the Yeslers rented rooms out as offices.

Sarah Yesler died in 1887, just three years after the ornate home was completed. Henry followed her in 1892. The city was promised the mansion to use as a city hall, but Yesler's will could not be found. Finally his estate leased the building to the city for the Seattle Public Library in 1899.

The library spread out in the airy mansion. A kitchen was converted into the bindery and one bedroom into the librarian's office. A dedicated children's reading room was established for the first time in a sun-drenched room overlooking a vine-covered veranda. The children even had their own library entrance.

Again the occupancy was short-lived, though, as the building burned down after midnight on January 2, 1901. Woken up by telephone at his home, Librarian C. W. Smith ran from Beacon Hill in the snow but was only able to save the records. The library lost 25,000 books, left with only the 7,000 items that were in circulation or in mobile collections.

LEFT *The Victorian mansion stood out from the surrounding box houses and commercial buildings.*

BELOW *The ruins of the mansion after it and the library's collections went up in flames in 1901.*

THE YESLERS

Henry and Sarah were wed in 1840 in Ohio. Henry left in 1851 to find riches in gold mining, and ended up starting a mill in Seattle instead the next year. Sarah finally joined him in 1858. In the intervening years, Henry fathered a daughter with Susan, who was the daughter of "Curley" Suquardle. Curley was Henry's mill foreman and a Duwamish chief. After Sarah arrived Henry found a foster family for daughter Julia and provided for her. As an adult she moved to Port Townsend and married, raising a family of her own. Upon arrival, Sarah took over the cookhouse at Yesler's Mill. As Seattle grew she was a leader among the early philanthropic community and women's groups. She helped found Seattle's women's suffrage society as well as the group that started the orphanage Children's Home. She also served as Seattle's first librarian in 1868, keeping the fledgling Library Association's collection of books at Yesler's Hall in a lending library. Sarah died suddenly in 1887 at age 65 and every flag in the city flew at half mast. In 1890 Henry was remarried to Minnie Gagle, who was both 60 years younger and his first cousin once removed. The newspapers whipped it into a scandal, and things got out of control after Henry Yesler died in 1892. No will could be found, and Minnie was sued by the City of Seattle for supposedly defrauding the public out of money Yesler had promised. After six months of courtroom fireworks, the parties settled and the case was dropped.

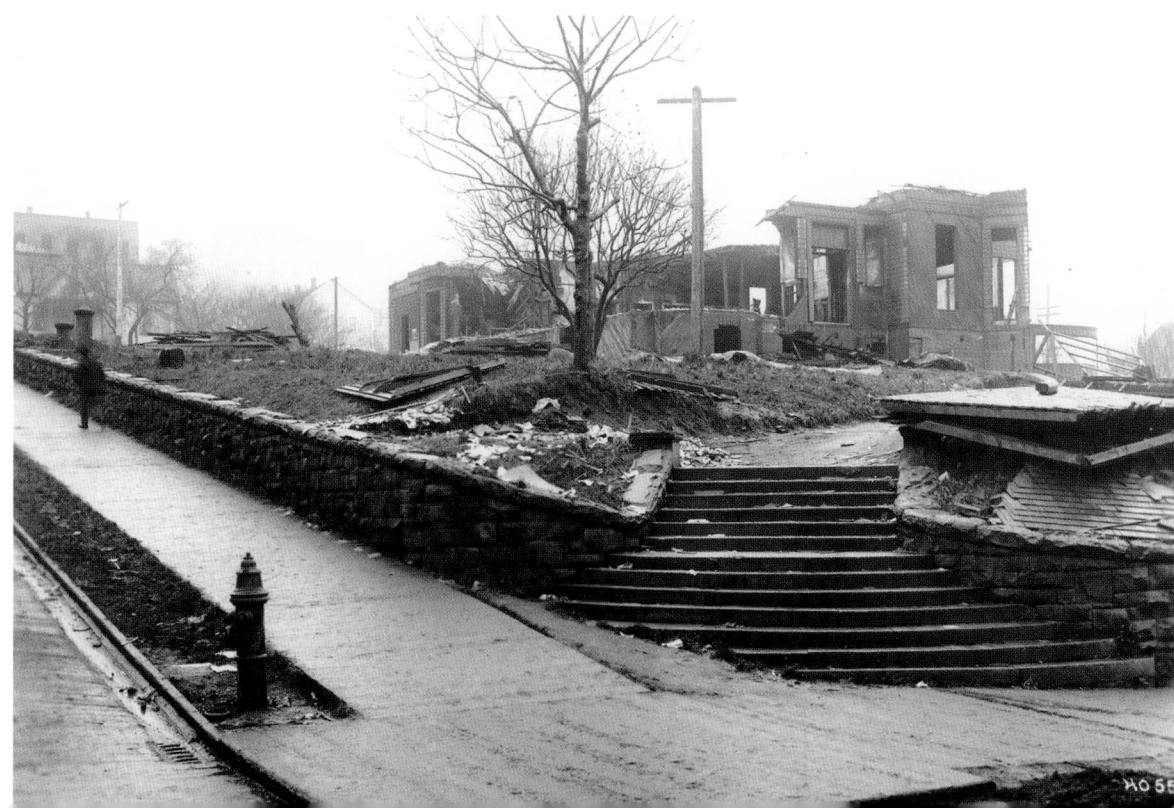

Moran Brothers Shipyard SOLD 1906

Moran Brothers took on the fledgling shipyards of Seattle and created Seattle's only battleship.

The first ship launched in Seattle was the stern wheel steamer *Black Diamond* in 1864. A variety of barges, schooners, barkentines, and side- and stern-wheel steamers were launched from the many shipyards that formed over the next decade.

Trained as a machinist in New York, Robert Moran moved to Seattle in 1875. Initially he found work as an engineer in a steamer on an Alaska route. In 1882 his mother and siblings followed him to Seattle. Together with his brothers Peter, William and Paul he opened the Moran Brothers machine shop and foundry next to Yesler's Mill. They repaired engines of steamers in the growing Mosquito Fleet. Robert Moran became such an established figure in the young city that he was elected to the City Council and then in 1888 was elected Mayor.

So he was both running the city and an important industry when he watched them both burn during 1889's Great Fire. Moran Brothers, like the city, rebuilt better than before. They decided to become a full shipyard, and relocated south on the waterfront next to Seattle Dry Dock and Shipyards, which Robert Moran was a part owner and Vice-President. He became involved in many other industries in the time after the fire, including the loan bank that later became WaMu.

The first boat that Moran Brothers built was the fireboat *Snoqualmie* for the City of Seattle. This was one of the many improvements to Seattle's readiness that Robert promised the day after the fire. Moran Brothers focused mostly on repairs until winning a contract to build the torpedo boat *Rowan* for the U.S. Navy in 1897. This was the first navy ship ever built on Puget Sound. At the same time they built the tug *Golden Gate* for the U.S. Revenue Cutter Service.

Because the Gold Rush started just a few months later, the increased capacity was perfectly timed. Three cargo ships for Alaska customers were launched later in 1897, and an astounding 32 in 1898. This included 12 mirror-image sternwheel riverboats produced simultaneously. When they were completed Robert Moran led the flotilla himself to deliver them to Alaska.

In 1900 Moran Brothers bid to build a battleship for the U.S. Navy, entering their most ambitious endeavor. Costs projected to more than the Navy had estimated, so wealthy citizens and businesses of Seattle raised $100,000 to cover the difference. The 440-foot steel hulled ship was launched in 1904 and after being outfitted the U.S.S. *Nebraska* was commissioned in 1907. She toured the globe with the Great White Fleet and took defensive position on the Atlantic coast. The *Nebraska* never saw combat, and her greatest service was transporting soldiers back home after World War I. She remains the only battleship to ever be built in Seattle.

Soon after the *Nebraska*'s launch, Robert Moran received shocking news that he had only a year to live. He began putting his affairs in order and he and his brothers sold their shipyard in 1906.

Robert Moran lived a long, healthy life and passed away in 1943 at the age of 86. The shipyard went on to build submarines and cargo ships for World War I, 50 destroyers during World War II and a vast array of commercial ships in the more than century after Robert Moran and his brothers sold it. Today it continues as a branch of Vigor Industries.

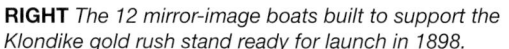

RIGHT *The 12 mirror-image boats built to support the Klondike gold rush stand ready for launch in 1898.*

LEFT *The hull of the battleship U.S.S.* Nebraska *launches in 1904.*

BELOW *The* Nebraska *at New York's Hudson-Fulton Naval parade in 1909.*

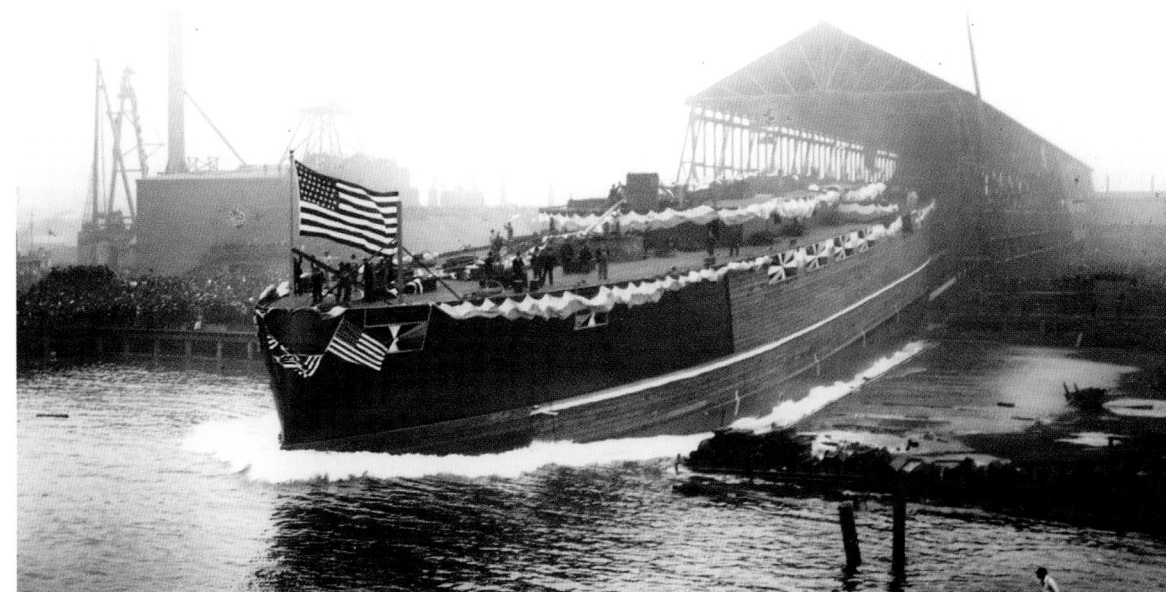

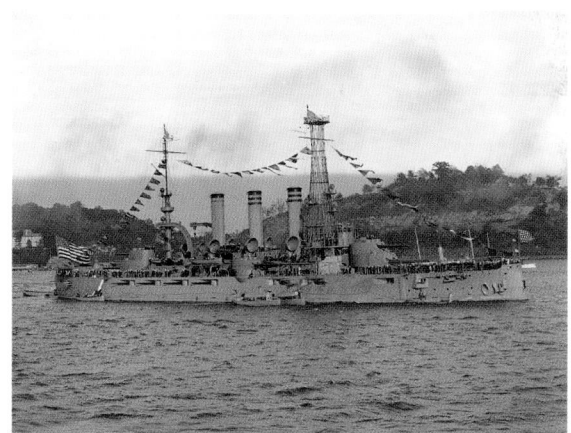

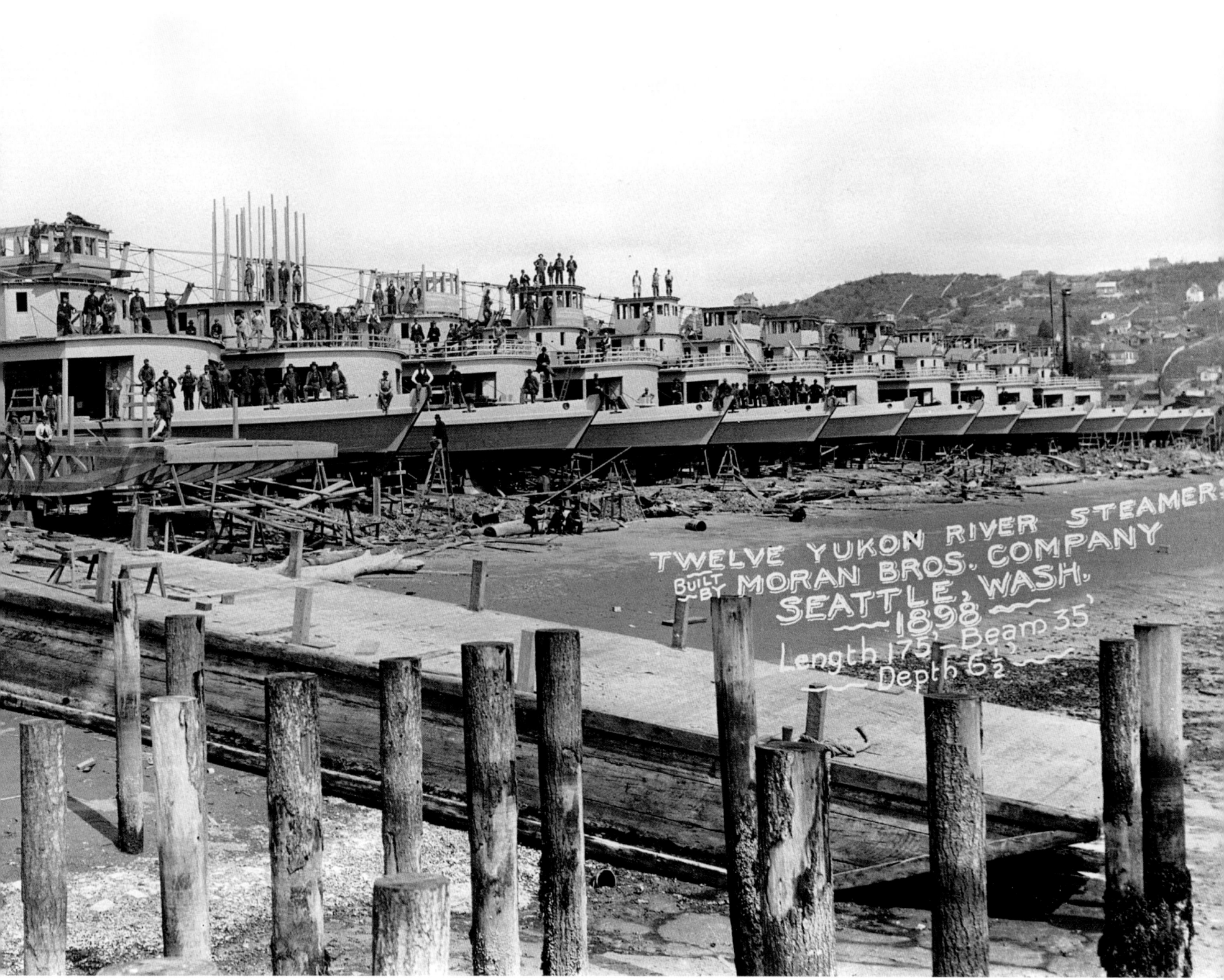

TWELVE YUKON RIVER STEAMERS
BUILT BY MORAN BROS. COMPANY
SEATTLE, WASH.
1898
Length 175' — Beam 35'
Depth 6½'

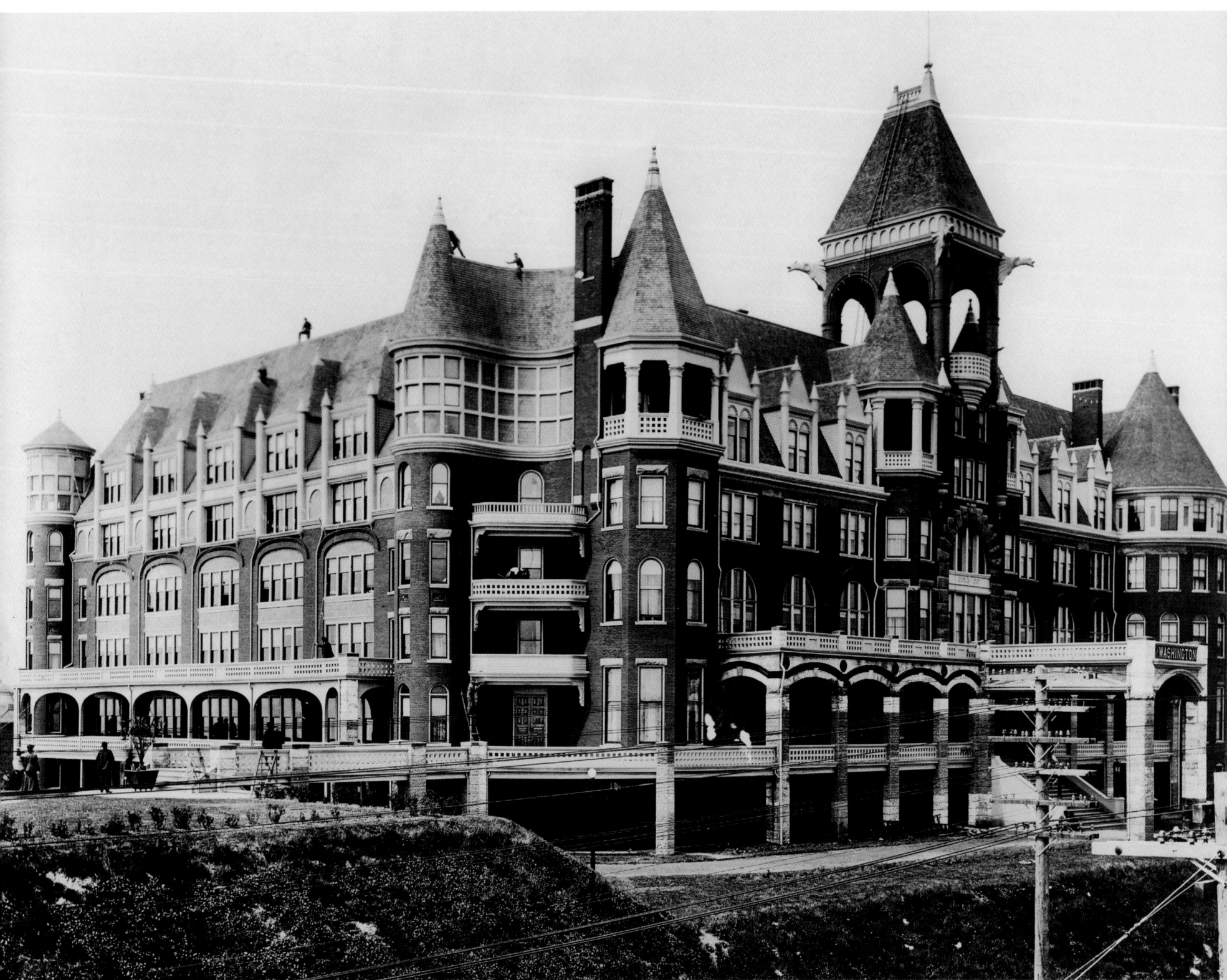

Denny Hotel DEMOLISHED 1906

The Denny Hotel looked down on Seattle unfinished for a decade. Just as it asserted its place as Seattle's iconic hotel it was destroyed in the first Denny Regrade.

In the 1870s and 1880s, Seattle continued to spread northward uphill from Pioneer Square towards Denny Hill. The hill's original owner, pioneer Arthur Denny, finally decided with a group of investors in 1889 to make a spectacular hotel with a commanding view near the peak of his property.

Work was slowed as construction focused on rebuilding Seattle's commercial core, but largely completed in 1891. The national economic crash of 1893 kept the doors shut awhile longer.

In 1900 the hotel still lay complete but unfurnished. However, disagreements between the boards of the owners kept doors shut for guests. Ownership was split between the Denny estate, the Dexter Horton Bank, and a manufacturing company in Iowa. The grand hall was rented out as facilities for meetings and balls in the interim, giving Seattleites a glimpse of the hotel on the hill.

In February of 1903, Seattle developer James A. Moore secured purchase of the hotel from the squabbling owners. First he rechristened it the Washington Hotel to escape its checkered past. Then he went to work furiously preparing the hotel to open by the end of May. He had his eye on the planned visit of President Theodore Roosevelt, and outfitted a special suite on the first floor for him. A thousand rose bushes were planted. Walls were papered, floors carpeted. Beds, chairs and a stuffed elk for the lobby were trucked in.

The hotel was immediately profitable, paying a tenth of its capital cost in the first six months. But by the spring of 1904, trouble loomed again for the hotel. City Engineer R. H. Thomson had been methodically flattening and widening Seattle's streets for years. In 1903 attention was on Pine Street along the south edge of Denny Hill below the hotel.

Next was Second Avenue in 1904, which cut deeply into Second Avenue and destroyed the base of the cable railway which led up to the hotel. Moore was fine with that, and planned to dig a tunnel under the hotel and build a large elevator to replace it.

Suddenly in April of 1904, talk began to include regrading Third Avenue, which the Washington Hotel straddled atop the hill. Spirits calmed briefly in 1905 as the conversation changed to placing a tunnel under the hill. But by the end of the year, it was decided that the entire hill needed to be removed. The Seattle City Council passed ordinances in November to level Third Avenue, right under the hotel.

On the evening of May 7, 1906, Moore and his wife hosted a grand ball as farewell to the hotel. The rooms were trimmed with roses, rhododendrons, and lillies. Women wore fine gowns of silk and lace. Demolition started the next day, and Moore's family moved to a new home in his Capitol Hill neighborhood. Structural steel was already on order to build the New Washington Hotel.

OPPOSITE PAGE *The hotel in 1903, after Moore opened it as the Washington Hotel.*

BELOW *The completed, ornate lobby in 1903, ready to accept guests. A stuffed elk stands beside the reception.*

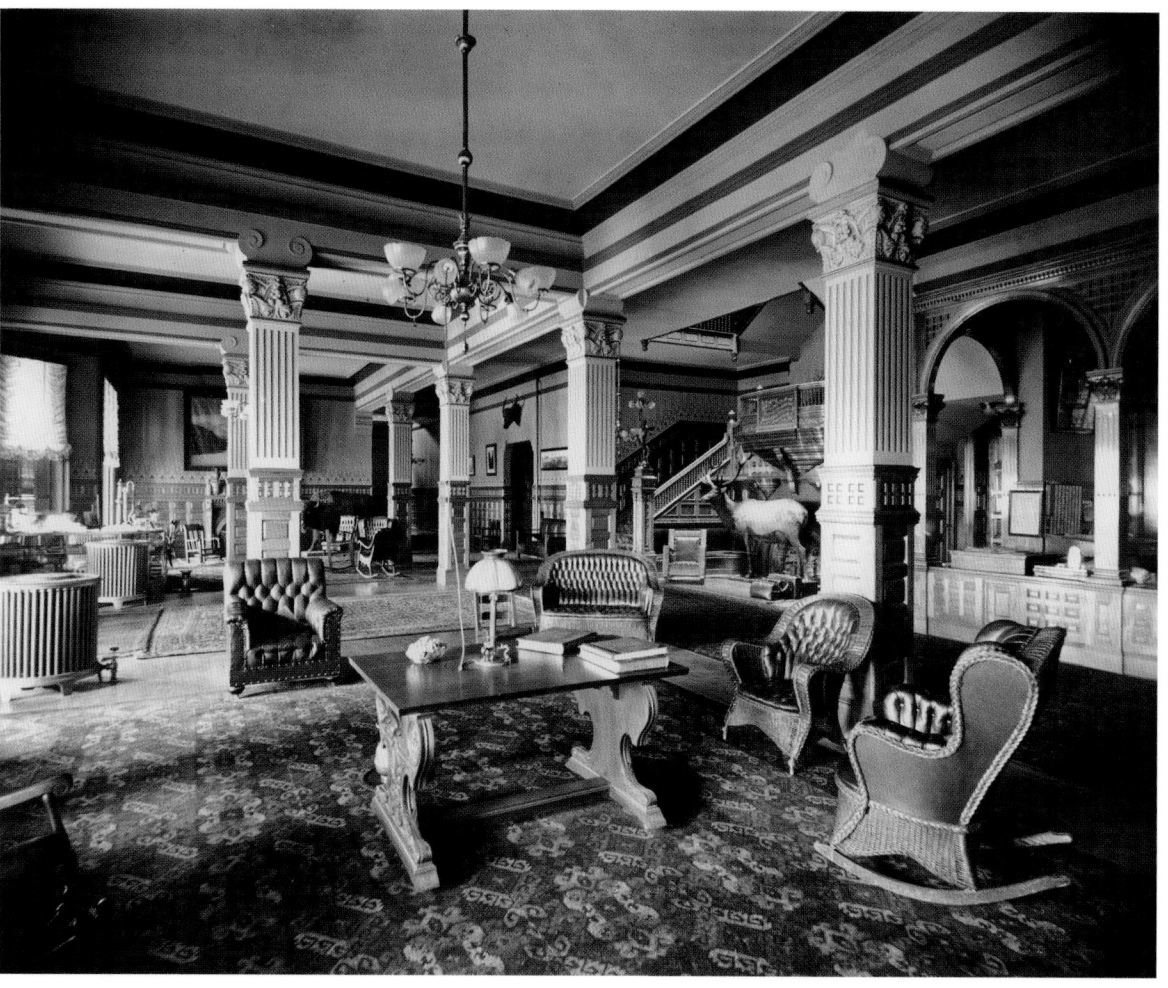

City of Ballard ANNEXED 1907

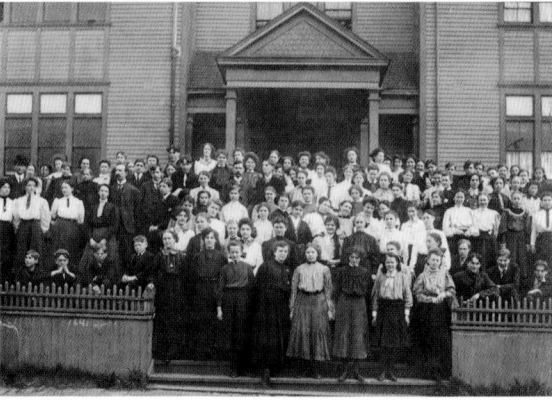

Present-day Ballard began as Shilshole, a village of the Duwamish people along Salmon Bay. After Seattle's founding, Shilshole chief Suquardle worked as foreman at Yesler's Mill and established a camp there for his people to work alongside him.

Intense logging of Salmon Bay began in the late 1870s, feeding Yesler's Mill. Much of it came from the land claims of the area's first settler, Ira Utter, and his neighbors along the bay's north shore. Judge Thomas Burke bought their land in 1882, subdividing it for sale as individual lots. Burke, Daniel Gilman, John Leary and others then partnered as the West Coast Improvement Company in order to develop the area. They got rich during the strong real estate market before the Great Northern Railway's 1893 arrival in Seattle.

The name Ballard came from their other major partner, William Rankin Ballard. Ballard moved to Seattle in 1868 to study surveying and civil engineering at the Territorial University. He surveyed the Yakima Reservation for the federal government and then in 1876 went to work with his brother on the Mosquito Fleet sternwheeler *Zephyr*. After his brother's death the next year he became captain and part owner with John Leary.

While working on the *Zephyr*, Captain Ballard began investing in the Salmon Bay area and opened a store with a partner, Captain Hatfield. Once a customer settled a large bill with a worthless parcel along the Sound, already cleared of its valuable timber. Later when the store was closed, the partners split the assets. Ballard lost a coin toss and was stuck with the land. Later in 1888 this became his share of the West Coast Improvement Company.

Captain Ballard and his partners encouraged industrial development on their land and had quick success. The first sawmill in Ballard opened in 1888. Later that year the Stimson mill opened, and Seattle Cedar followed in 1890. After the Great Fire destroyed Seattle's business district, Ballard's mills boomed. By 1902 there were 13 sawmills in town producing eight million shingles and 165 million feet of lumber per year. Ballard became famous for red cedar shingles in particular, and it was half-jokingly said that shingles were better than cash in Seattle.

By the start of 1890 a number of other industries complemented the mills. The desired residential development followed the jobs, and Ballard's 1,600

residents allowed them to incorporate a new city in April. The West Street Electric streetcar started that same year, connecting Ballard with Seattle. In 1905 an interurban from Ballard to Everett began slow construction, doing more to impact the rural areas than Ballard itself.

The population continued to explode with 10,000 people in 1904 and 17,000 in 1907. One factor was the swift rise in first- and second-generation Scandinavian Americans, who composed a full third of Ballard's residents. They were drawn from Midwest and Mountain West states by the Puget Sound's similarity in climate and topography to Scandinavia. Ballard was home to the mills and fishing fleet that let them use the same skills as back home.

There was only one thing that Ballard lacked: a large, steady supply of fresh drinking water. The wells dug above the saltwater line sufficed at first, but Ballard's growth quickly overwhelmed them. In November 1906 Ballard's voters chose to become part of Seattle. Access to Seattle's Cedar River pipeline and its fresh mountain water outweighed any benefits of remaining an independent city. Annexation took effect May 29, 1907.

ABOVE *Pupils at Ballard's Broadway School in 1891. Broadway was renamed Market Street after annexation.*

RIGHT *At 20th Avenue NW and Leary Avenue NW near the heart of Ballard, just after annexation.*

BELOW *Ballard's Carnegie Library. Built in 1904 and now a Seattle landmark.*

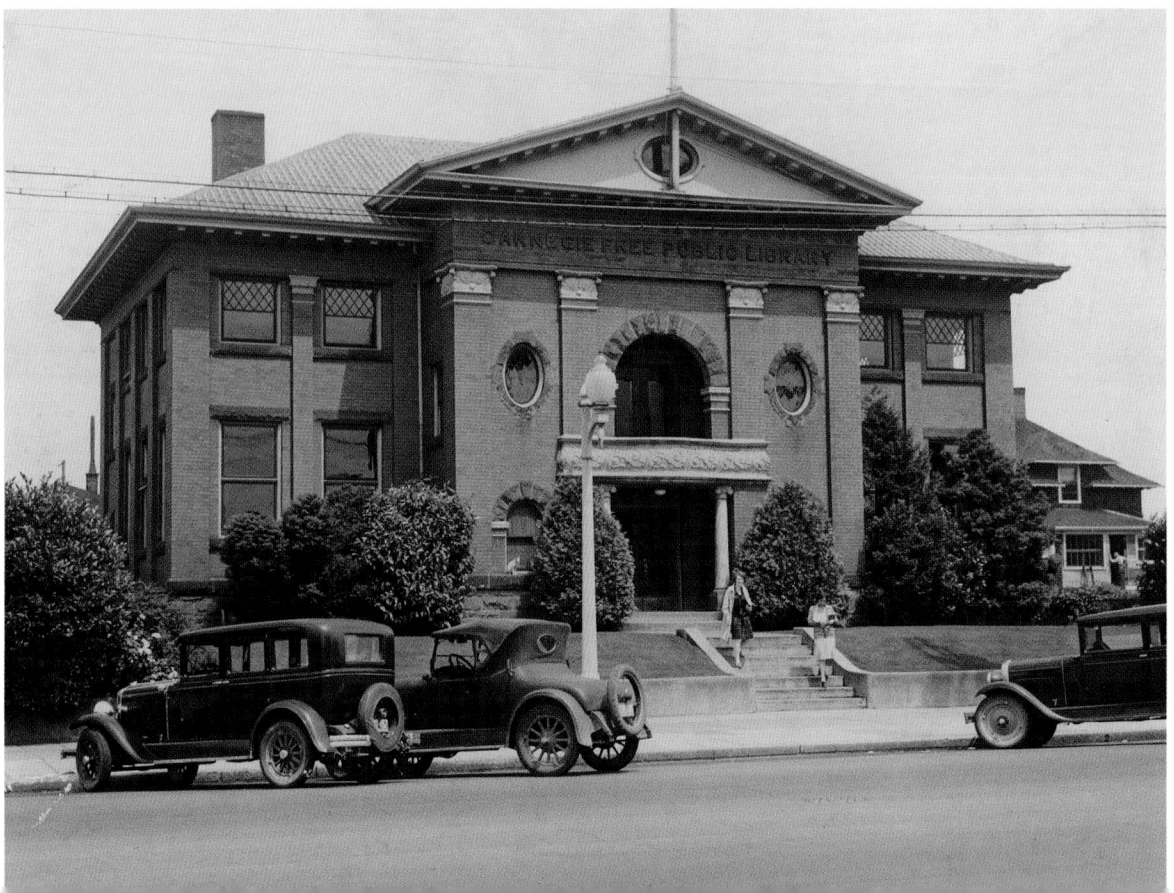

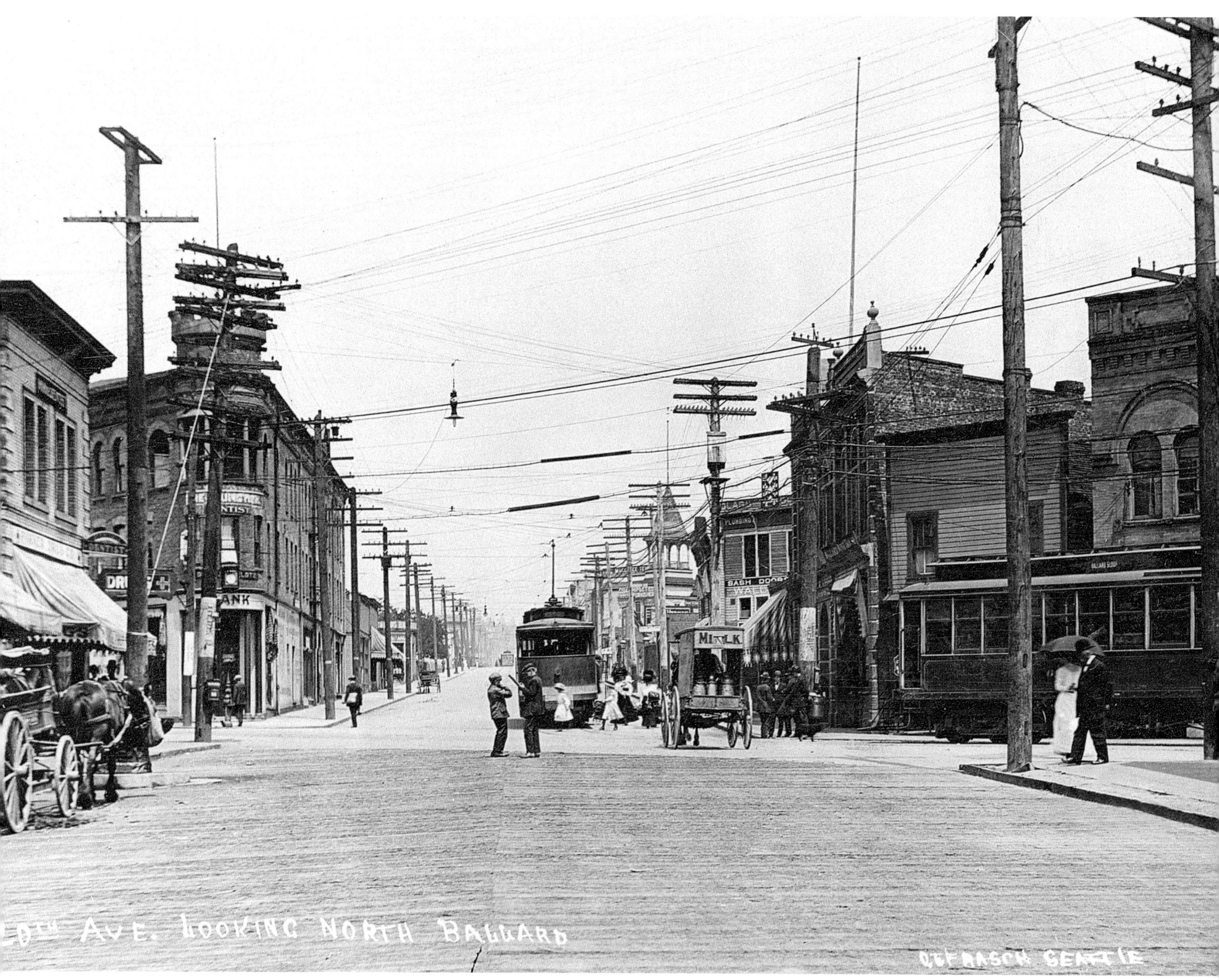

5TH AVE. LOOKING NORTH BALLARD

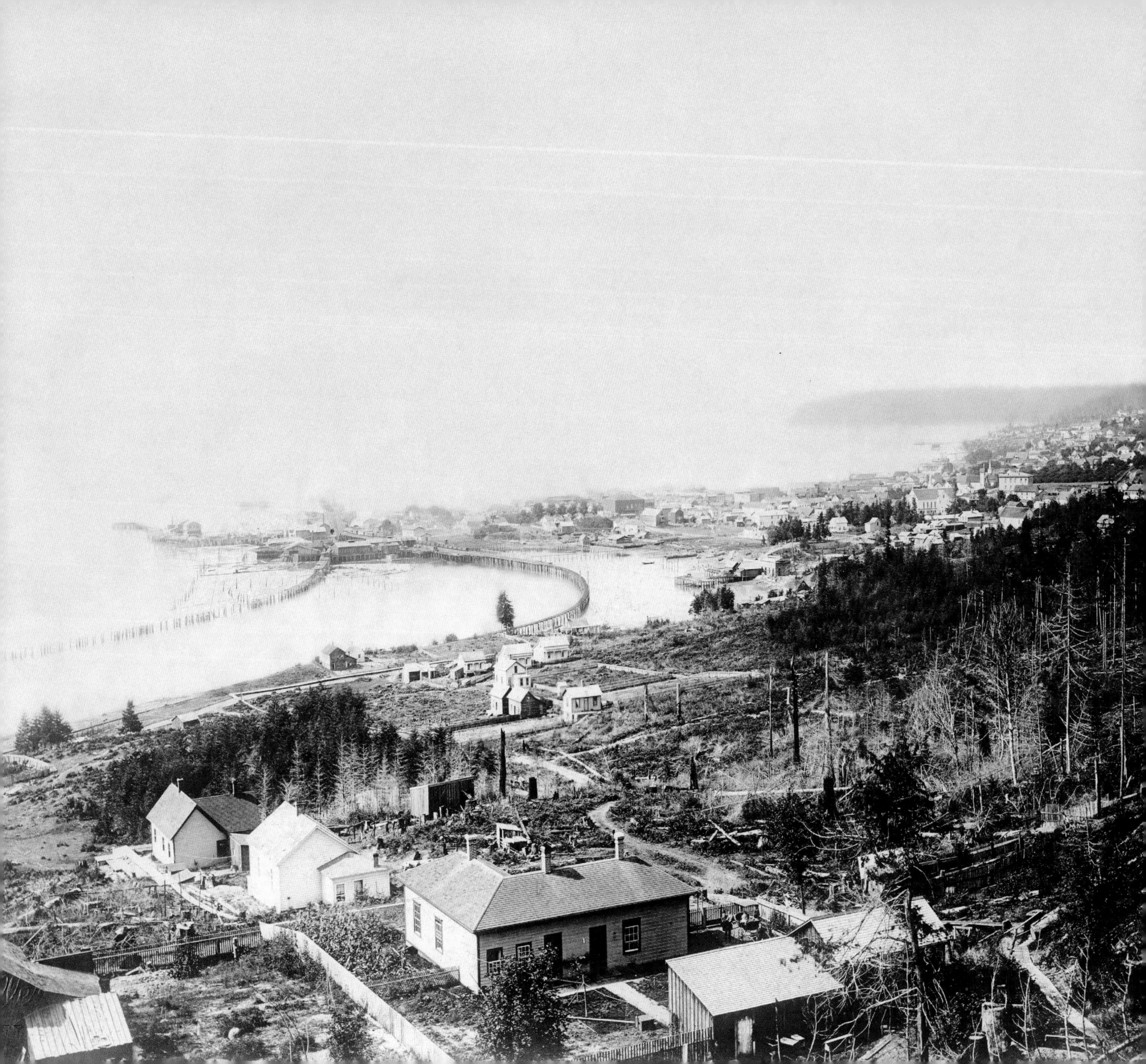

Jackson Ridge REGRADED 1908

Initially Seattle's engineers focused northward, leveling Denny's Knoll where the university had been, and Denny Hill while the hotel still sat on top. This opened up easy routes to Lake Union, Queen Anne Hill, and Ballard. Next they moved east.

Seattle was held against Elliott Bay by a ridge that ran north to Portage Bay at the new university site and south to Renton at the Black River. Three cable car lines were built over the ridge, all on First Hill. The Yesler Way cable was first in 1887. The Madison Street cable followed in 1890. And the James Street cable in 1891. These cable cars opened up the "out back of the city," a wild country full of deer, cougar and bear.

The James Street cable was part of a system known as the Union Trunk Line. It was unique in that it ended at Broadway and connected with streetcars running in each of the other cardinal directions. The southern car ran over a narrow, slide-prone ridge to Beacon Hill known as Jackson Hill or the Jackson Ridge.

The ridge had 15 to 20 percent grades on Jackson, King and Dearborn streets peaking around Tenth Avenue. Because of inaccessibility, the number of people living just a half-mile to the southeast of Pioneer Square was as low as those eight miles north.

After City Engineer R. H. Thomson took down the 100-foot Denny Hill, he knew he could just as easily level the thinnest part of the eastern ridge. Work would proceed from either side: first on the north end at Jackson Street along First Hill in 1907; then on the south at Dearborn Street to round off Beacon Hill in 1910. The dirt was flushed towards the bay, raising the area east of Fourth Avenue South with 40 feet of fill.

But before that could start the neighborhood needed to be cleared. Three hundred homes were moved from the 68 blocks of the Jackson Street regrade, most on the north end near Main Street where Japanese immigrants were establishing the residential districts of Japantown. Another 40 homes and an orphanage made way for Dearborn Street's cut.

Hoses sprayed 24 million gallons of water each day to wash the four million cubic feet of dirt from the ridge away into the tide flats. The deepest dig for the first regrade was at Tenth Avenue South and Jackson Street: 78 feet of dirt was removed. Dearborn Street was sluiced more than 150 feet down at 12th Avenue South, cutting Beacon Hill off until a bridge could be built.

This left a deep chasm with many buildings in precarious positions, particularly on Washington and Main streets. In the midst of the earth moving, the Nippon Kan Theatre and Japanese Baptist Church were built just beyond the edge of the regrade at Maynard Avenue South and Washington Street. Landslides pulled the new church in, though, forcing relocation. Similarly, a house at Tenth and Jackson slid 25 feet down an embankment with a family inside. Luckily no one was hurt.

Even when the neighborhoods were gone and the regrades were over, the ridge echoed on for decades with landslides regularly taking out buildings and streets.

OPPOSITE PAGE *Looking west past sparse settlement on the northwest side of Beacon Hill to the tide flats south of downtown that were filled with the ridge.*

BELOW LEFT *From the Jackson Street wharf looking east at the ridge in 1882.*

BELOW *Hosing away the ridge in 1908.*

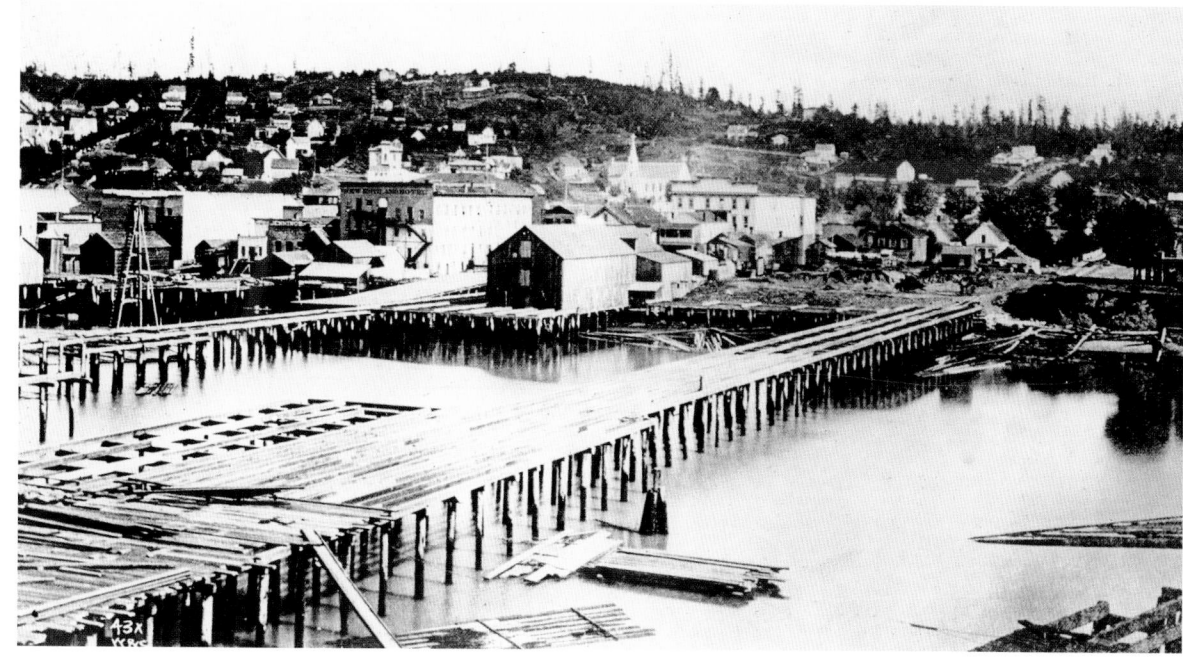

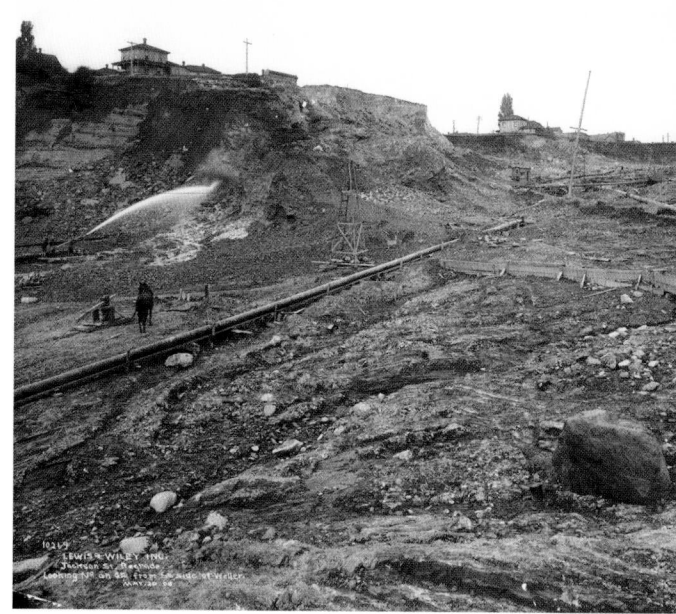

First Chinatown RELOCATED 1909

Seattle's Chinese community has gradually shifted and spread southwest as the city has grown. The first Chinese immigrants arrived when just about everyone was a newcomer, around 1860. Seattle had about 300 people and they were centered around Yesler's Mill at the junction of Commercial (First Avenue South), Mill (Yesler Way) and Front (First Avenue) streets.

That's where the first Chinese business in Seattle was located. Chen Cheong's 1867 cigar company was just south of Mill on Commercial. He was soon joined by Chin Chun Hock, who opened a dry goods store Wa Chong nearby on Mill Street and Post Avenue. Chin diversified as a broker between construction firms and Chinese laborers.

The first Chinatown developed, though, after Wa Chong moved into new quarters on Washington Street between Second and Third avenues in 1876. Other businesses, such as Mark Wing Long Company and Quong Tuck, opened nearby, and hundreds of Chinese workers and laborers filled apartments and houses.

Seattle's founders considered Chinese to be partners, just as they did the local Native American population. But the second wave didn't see it the same way, and felt wronged by the low wages that the immigrants were willing to tolerate. It came to a head in 1886, when the Knights of Labor instigated anti-Chinese riots. Judge Thomas Burke, Henry Yesler, "Doc" David Maynard and others tried to defend the Chinese, preventing serious bloodshed at least. But half of Seattle's Chinese population had already left town before the riots, leaving only a few hundred. The rioters forced all but a few dozen onto ships to San Francisco.

With the rest of downtown Seattle, the mostly vacant Chinatown burned in 1889. Over time Seattle's Chinese population recovered from the riots, and Chinatown grew again. It spread eastward up Washington to Fifth Avenue.

By the early 1900s Chinese New Year was again a spectacle, drawing Seattleites of all backgrounds to enjoy the fireworks, music, dances, and brotherly love in the form of free cigars. Two Taoist temples were the center of festivities, located in an alley off Washington Street between Fourth and Fifth Avenue South. One belonged to the Chinatown Masons, Chee Kung Tong, and the other was at Hip Sing Tong's headquarters.

The old Chinatown was finally destabilized by cheap land. Starting in 1907, the ridge connecting First Hill and Beacon Hill was cut down. Jackson Ridge had held Seattle against the tide flats, with the first Chinatown at the south end between the business district and water. Suddenly the gap from Jackson to Dearborn released the pressure, and Chinese businesses spread east into the empty land. More hotel rooms meant lower prices to compete with Portland and San Francisco for migrant laborers to board in the offseason.

Wa Chong and Quong Tuck instigated the first Chinatown. They also led the exodus to what we now know as Chinatown: east of Fifth Avenue South and centered on King Street. The offices that they moved to in the Kong Yick buildings are now the home of the Wing Luke Asian American Museum.

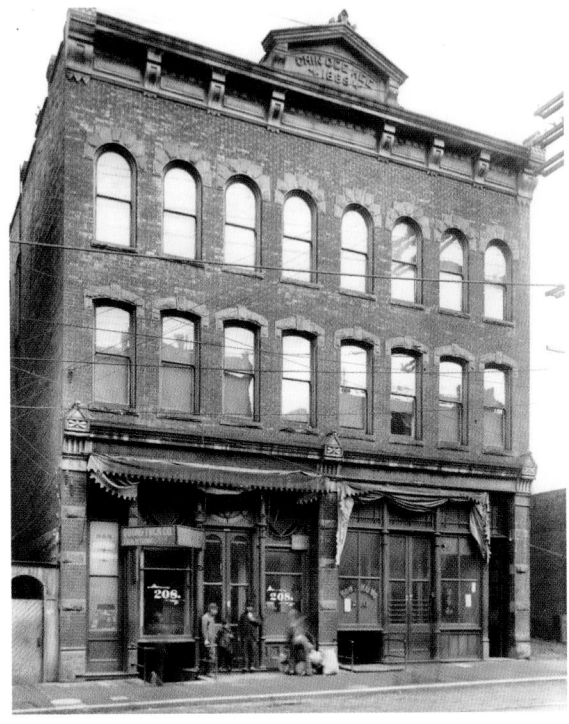

ABOVE *Chin Gee Hee building in 1904 with Quong Tuck on the left.*

RIGHT *Canton Building filled with Chinese businesses and lodgers in 1907.*

LEFT *After the move east of Fifth Avenue.*

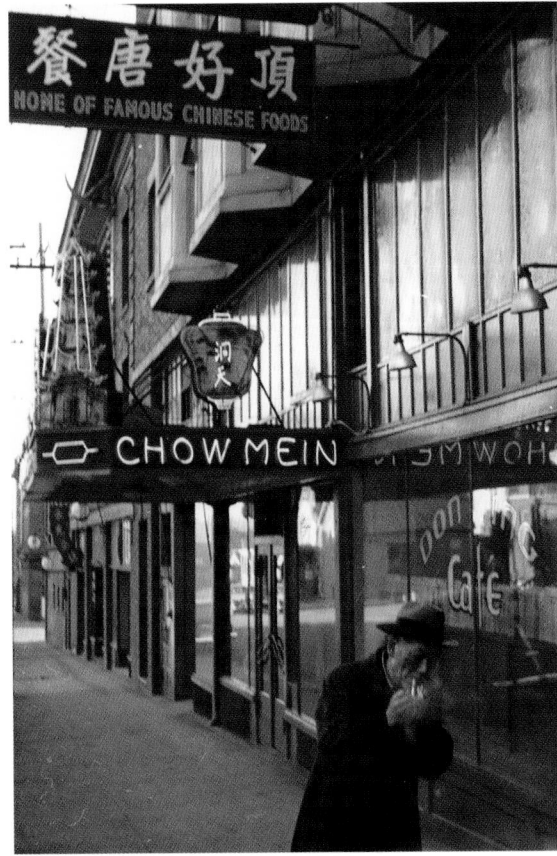

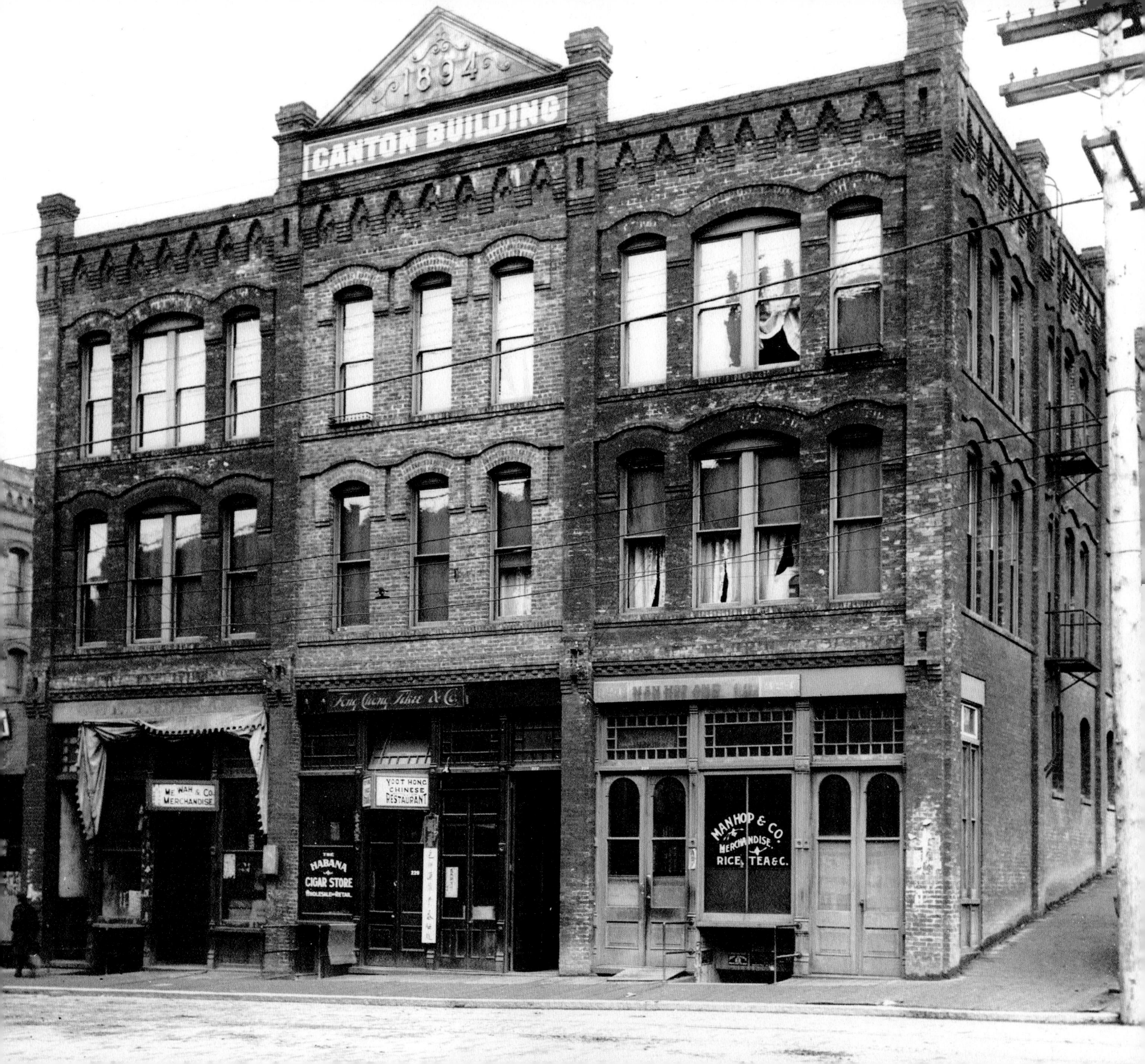

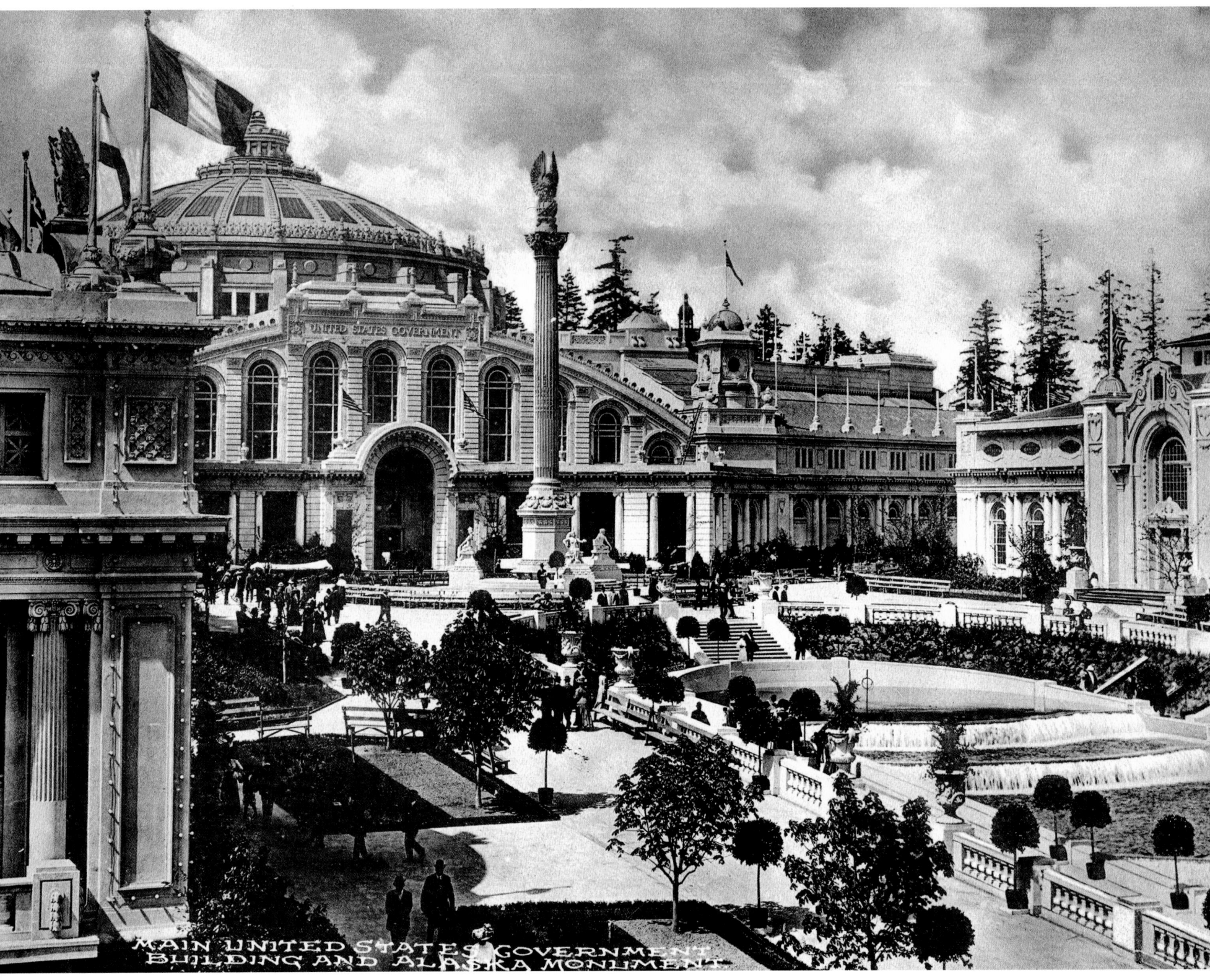

MAIN UNITED STATES GOVERNMENT
BUILDING AND ALASKA MONUMENT

Alaska Yukon Pacific Exposition CONCLUDED 1909

Seattle's first World's Fair was held from June to October of 1909. Although initial plans called for permanent buildings, about half were destroyed immediately after the fair. Only a few exist today.

The event was intended as the 10-year anniversary of the steamer *Portland*'s 1897 arrival from the Yukon with two tons of gold. That event catapulted Seattle from a port town to the pre-eminent city of the Pacific Northwest, second only to San Francisco on the West Coast.

The idea took off quickly. It was first raised by Godfrey Cheandler, who mentioned it to prominent Seattleites on his way from Alaska to Portland for the Lewis and Clark Exposition in 1905. Only one World's Fair is officially approved each year, and 1907 was reserved for the 300th anniversary of the settlement of Jamestown. Seattle settled for 1909.

As planning picked up steam, organizers decided to broaden the fair. It would celebrate both gold rushes: in Nome, Alaska and Klondike, Yukon Territory in Canada. Seattle's domination of trade with Asia and the Pacific islands was added to draw in more exhibitors and provide a unique flavor to the fair. It was given the cumbersome name of the Alaska Yukon Pacific Exposition.

After examining several possibilities, it was decided to site the fair on the new grounds of the University of Washington. The university completed several fine buildings, but most of their property was still wild and unused. It provided a blank slate for the fair, but also presented the opportunity to landscape the campus and leave new buildings for the growing university.

Olmsted Brothers, America's leading landscape architecture firm, was brought in to layout the fairgrounds, create water and plant features, and arrange the building locations. The large central buildings were arranged around a fountain forming the Central Court, facing south towards Mount Rainier. On opposite sides of the fountain were the Oriental Building and European Building, near mirror images of each other and designed in French renaissance style. At the head of the fountain stood the massive United States Government Building. With more than 90,000 square feet of display space this was the crown of the fair. Along with the Alaska Building, Mines Building and other main buildings they were built out of brilliant white plaster and all destroyed at the end of the fair.

A handful of buildings had life after the fair until demolition. Of those, the first to be destroyed was the Oregon Building, which the law department used until 1917. The Forestry Building housed the Burke Museum until rot was discovered in its load bearing logs in 1923. The Administration Building was used for offices and classes until 1937. The New York Building, a copy of Senator William Seward's New York mansion, served as the president's residence until 1927 and then housed the music department until 1950.

The Hoo Hoo House was used until 1959 as the faculty club, when it was replaced with a modernist building. The Auditorium was renamed Meany Hall and survived until earthquake damage required its demolition in 1965. The Washington State Building briefly housed the university library, then the state museum. It was used for classes until it was demolished in 1988.

Despite these success stories, there was a clear difference after the fair. In 1909 Seattleites entered a marvelous escape from their wood-and-brick world. Afterwards, they entered a collegiate campus with a set of buildings that rekindled their imagination.

OPPOSITE PAGE *The Central Court with the U.S. Building in center, European Building on left and Oriental Building on right. The Cascade Fountain fills the middle of the court.*

BELOW *Looking down the Pay Streak, the exposition's entertainment zone.*

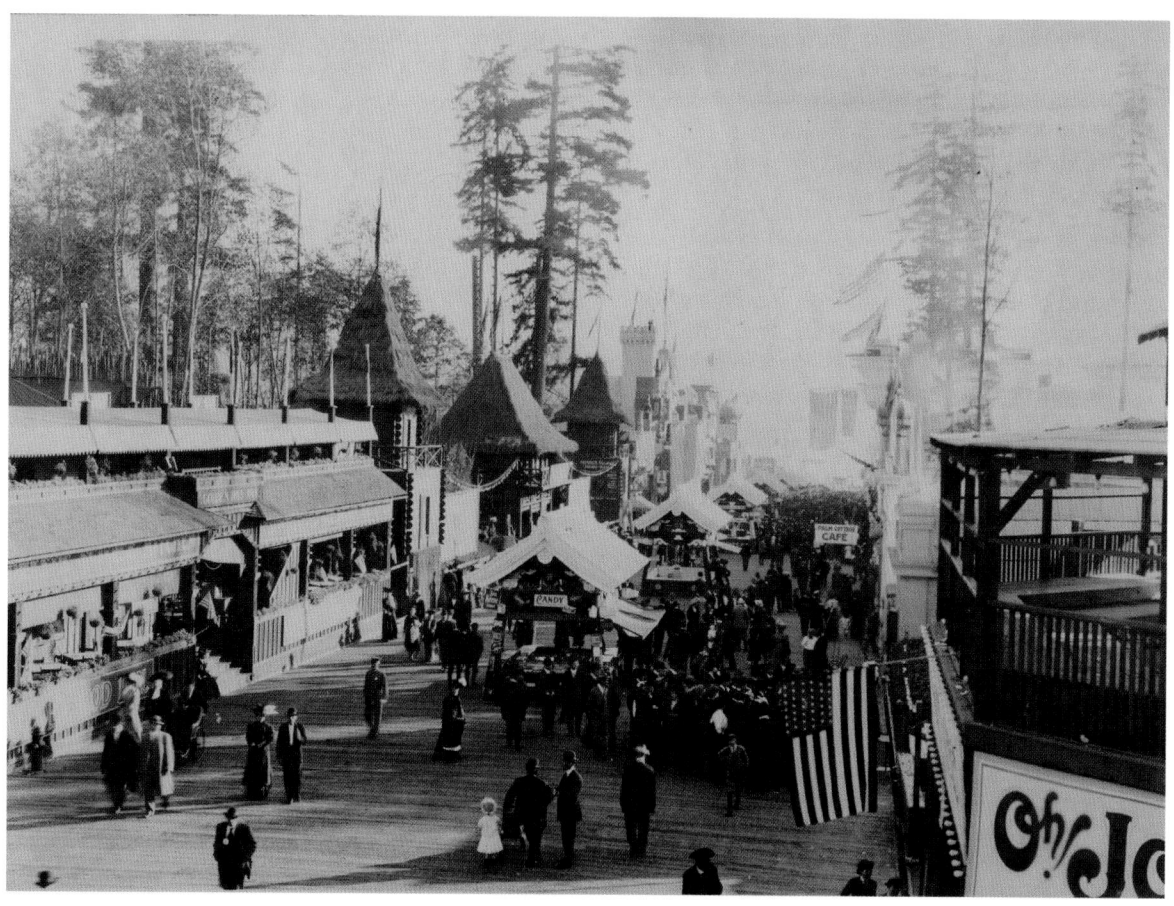

City of Georgetown ANNEXED 1910

Georgetown was settled in 1851 by Luther Collins, Henry Van Asselt and the Maple family. They landed a week before the Denny Party claimed Alki Point, and fared much better farming the Duwamish River delta.

Their agrarian approach led to much slower development than industrial Seattle, though. Any pretensions of a bucolic lifestyle were spoiled when the Seattle Race Course was opened in 1869 on part of Collins' claim. Saloons, brothels and other entertainment soon followed. In 1871 Collins sold another part of his claim to developer Julius Horton. Horton subdivided it and advertised home lots for a village he named Georgetown after his son George.

Georgetown became home to the newly formed Puget Sound Brewery in 1883. This brewery grew slowly at first, and then merged with two others to form the Seattle Brewing and Malting Company in 1893. They launched a new product, Rainier Beer, and eventually all brewing consolidated at the Georgetown plant. It grew to be the sixth largest brewery in the world.

The Grant Street Electric Railway opened in 1892, and was extended as the Puget Sound Electric Railway's interurban to Tacoma in 1902. The interurban started running just in time for the opening of King County's fairgrounds and racetrack at The Meadows in Georgetown. With customers no longer limited by the infrequent steam train service to Seattle and Tacoma, the floodgates were opened to Georgetown's saloons and gambling halls.

Georgetown was under siege, though. By 1900 the temperance movement was in full swing in Washington. They went after saloons, hoping to remove the social setting for most drinking. In many small towns the teetotalers were in control and blocked most licenses. When they lost, things could get ugly. In 1902 a saloon in West Seattle was blown up with dynamite after the Anti-Saloon League failed to block its license.

In 1903 they drafted a new state legislation called the "local option" to allow unincorporated communities to ban saloons just like the cities. County commissioners had a habit of approving all saloon licenses, including seven in Georgetown. Unfortunately for the Anti-Saloon League, Andrew Hemlich, the president of Georgetown's Seattle Brewing and Malting Company, also happened to be a state senator. He and his "liquor interest" allies rendered the bill harmless through amendments.

However, a complex power play by Governor McBride at the end of the 1903 session brought Hemlich in direct opposition with other King County legislators, and nearly caused passage of the local option. Fearing for the future of their company and the town it supported, Seattle Brewing executives quickly brought about a vote to incorporate a new City of Georgetown in 1904. It passed, and brewery manager John Mueller was elected Mayor.

In 1904 Seattle was in the midst of a crack-down on rampant vice, restricting it to the lava beds and making it difficult to make a dirty dollar. With its reputation as a beerman's town, Georgetown became a magnet for the crime fleeing Seattle. Georgetown attempted to control the wave of new gambling enterprises and prostitution, but Mayor Mueller soon threw up his hands. He let the entertainment district spread through downtown and let roadhouses pop up at will.

One of the city councilmen captured the prevailing sentiment: "Now we have a chance to get revenue from gambling, the saloons, etc. Georgetown is not a religious town and never will be. It is a brewery and saloon town and will be as long as men want to drink. Georgetown needs the money and this is one way of getting it." When it seemed like there weren't enough hours in the day to profit on vice, Georgetown's saloons just

RIGHT *Ninth Avenue South with the Seattle Brewing and Malting Company on the right and saloons advertising their Rainier Beer on the left.*

BELOW *Workers at Seattle Brewing and Malting Company pose with steins and kegs of beer.*

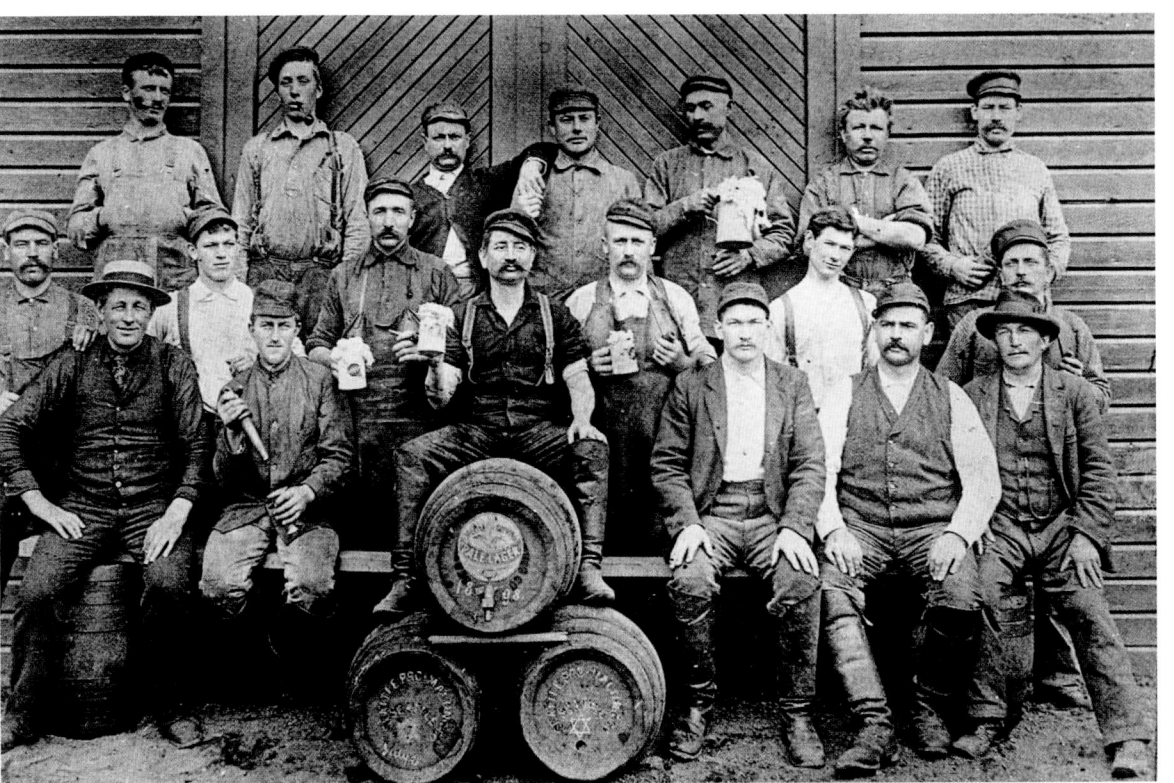

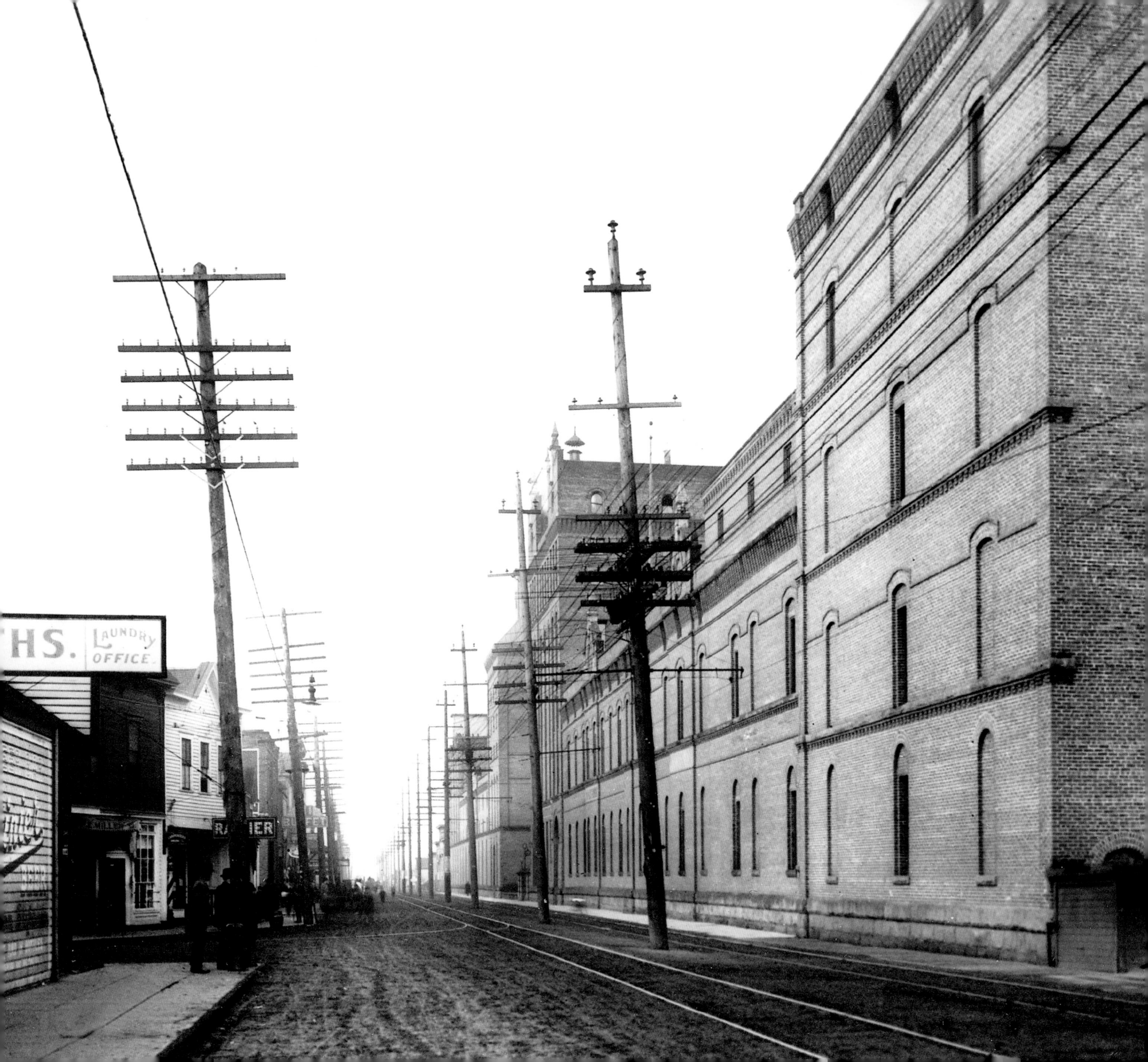

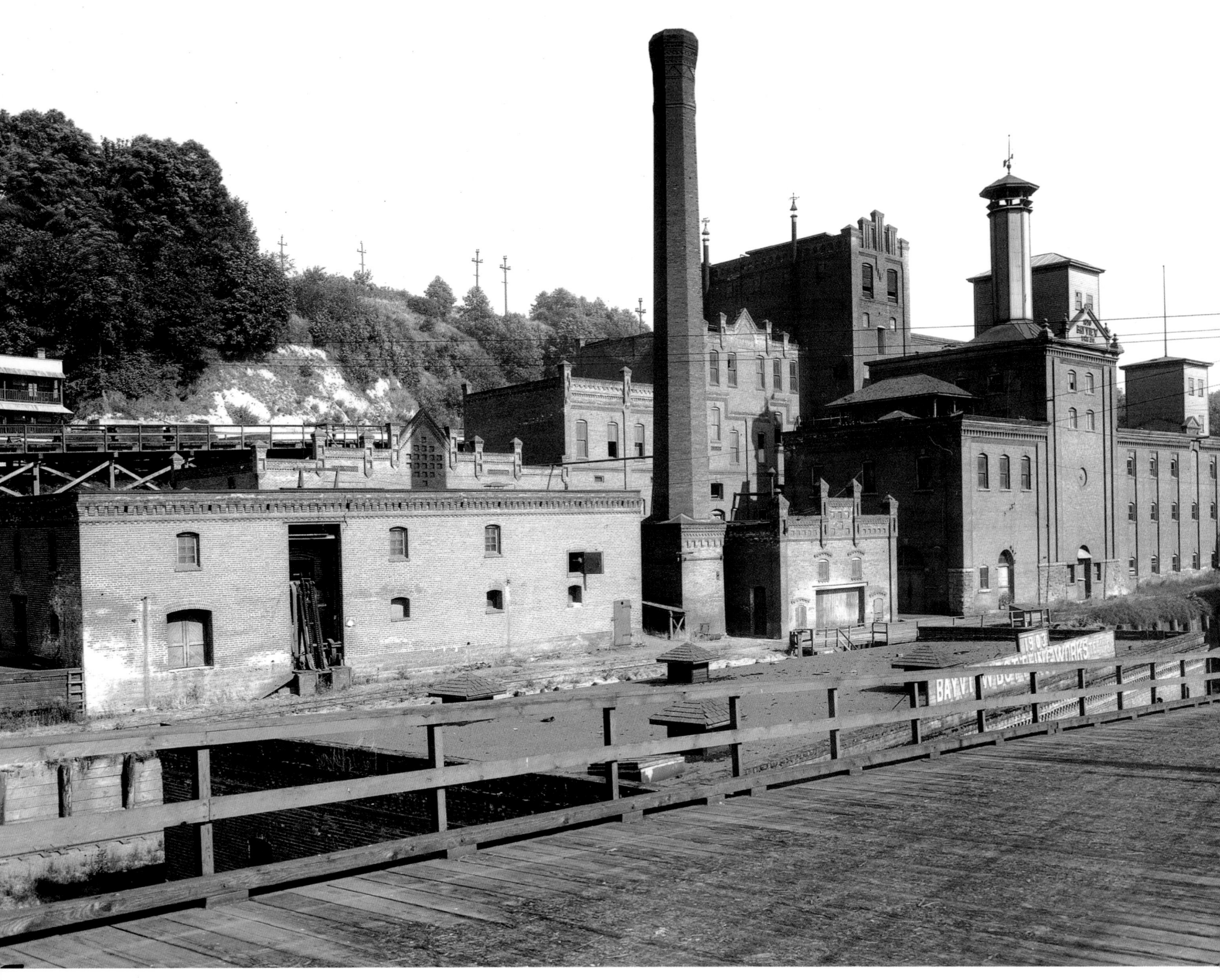

decided to stay open round the clock and seven days a week, in violation of state law.

The enterprise in debauchery was a success, with city expenses paid almost entirely by saloon and gambling licenses and fines for lawbreaking assessed to visitors. By 1909, though, annexations by Seattle had caused Georgetown to be completely engulfed by its larger neighbor. The Anti-Saloon League started another political battle at the state capital. They organized a group of residents in the Oxbow neighborhood to threaten secession. The Georgetown city council finally agreed to allow an annexation vote.

Georgetown's biggest problem was the same as Ballard: it lacked a clean source of water. But really it was a dysfunctional city. Garbage was heaped on the bank of the Duwamish River. The school had no water. There was one police officer.

On March 29, 1910, the little beer town voted for annexation, 329 to 238.

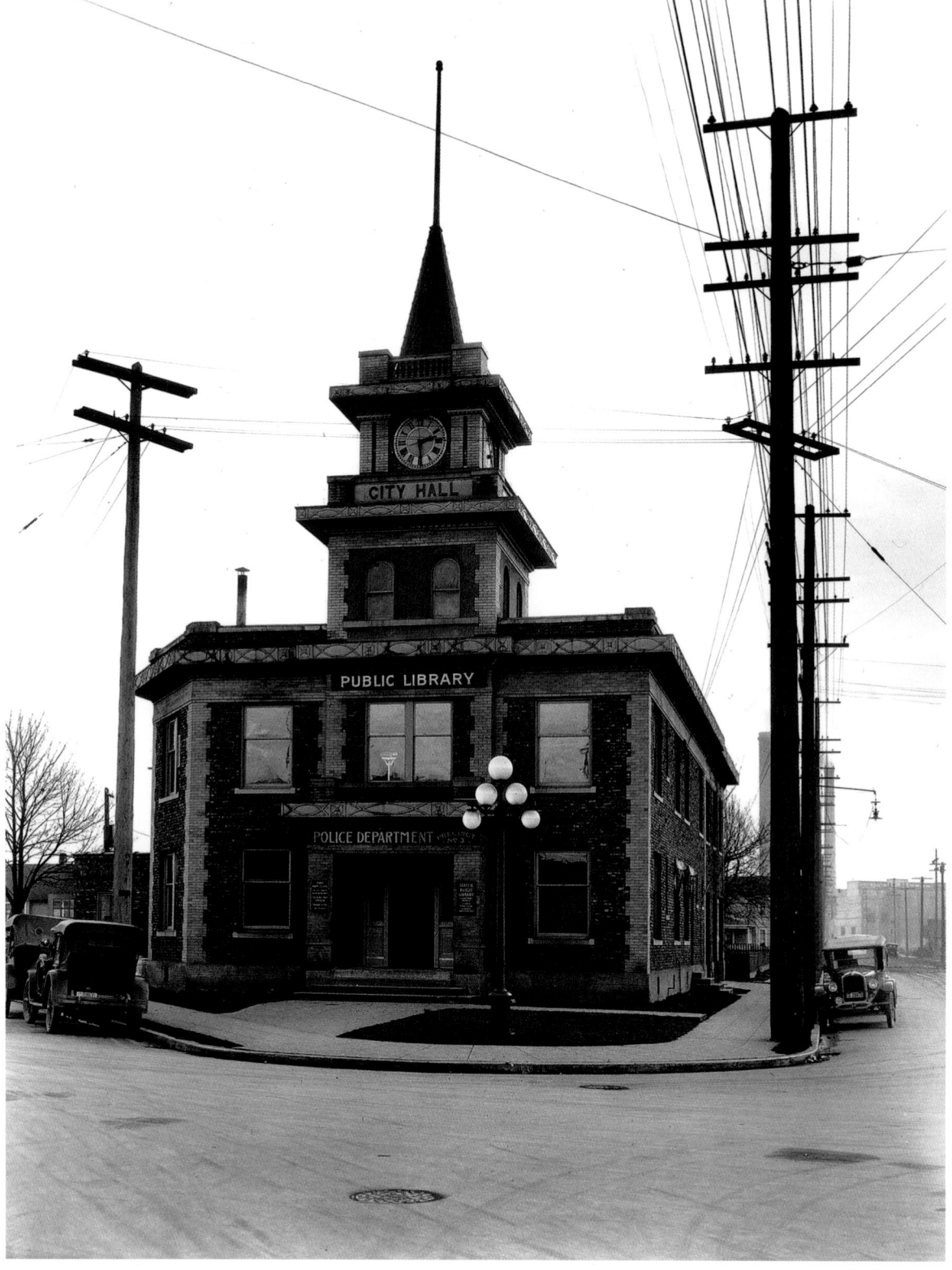

LEFT *Looking over the Bayview Bottling Works to the array of other Seattle Brewing and Malting Company buildings. Beacon Hill rises in the background.*

RIGHT *Georgetown's City Hall, also home to the city library, fire department and police department.*

Luna Park DISASSEMBLED 1913

Luna Park was Seattle's first amusement park. For seven seasons, Seattleites got a taste of Brooklyn's Coney Island.

In 1906 West Seattle was still its own city, separated by Elliott Bay and the Duwamish River from Seattle. It was most famous for the sandy beaches at Alki Point. But the waterfront all the way around the peninsula to the ferry dock was lined with summer cottages, campgrounds and private bath houses for changing into beachwear. For those who could afford to buy or rent, West Seattle was a wonderful escape.

Just before Christmas that year, the front page of the *Seattle Sunday Times* news section reverberated with the headline "Complete Coney Island Resort is to be Established at Duwamish Head." It announced that 10 acres of the northern

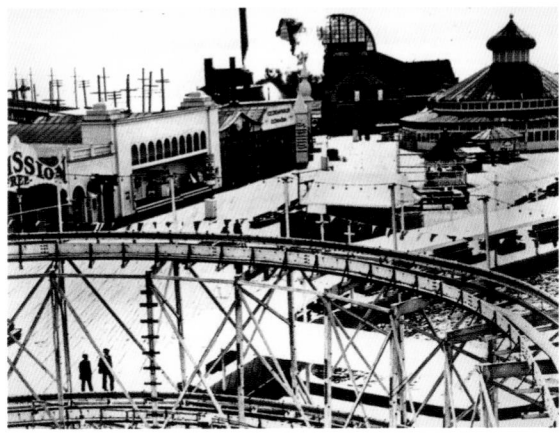

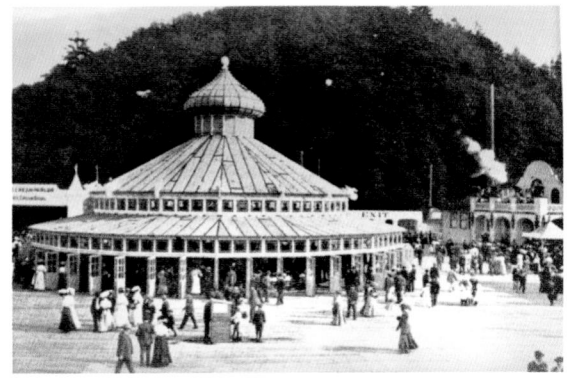

tip of West Seattle would lose a section of camping, cottages and the Mosquito Fleet shipyard King & Winge. In their place an amusement park with some of the best rides on the West Coast would be built.

Surveyors went to work immediately. In January of 1907 Charles Looff arrived from New York to oversee construction and then manage the new resort with his family. Concrete piles were driven into the shallow tideflats all winter long. A natatorium or saltwater pool was built first and then piers with a roller coaster, carousel, boat water slide, movie theater and other attractions.

Looff was one of the few artisans in America making hand-crafted carousels. From his workshop in Rhode Island he created dozens of merry-go-rounds with jewel-encrusted steeds featuring real horse hair. This became known as the Coney Island style after the carousel he installed there in 1876. The Seattle carousel was unique for its variety of animals including giraffe, lion, camels and dragons.

Looff ran a family business. His son William became an electrician, was Luna Park's master mechanic and also vice-president of the Luna Park Amusement Company. Son Arthur later in life designed roller coasters and likely designed Luna Park's Figure 8 coaster. Arthur also served as secretary of the Luna Park Amusement Company. Son Charles stayed behind in Rhode Island to operate the carousel factory. Dedicated to this new venture, the extended Looff family lived in a house across the street from the amusement park, looking out over Elliott Bay and the Puget Sound.

Luna Park opened in 1907 just in time for Independence Day and the beginning of camping season in West Seattle. It was an immediate success. Visitors had their choice of routes to the park grounds. A brand new ferry was put in service by the West Seattle Improvement Company. Seattle Electric Company ran a streetcar up from Spokane Street. In one of its last actions, the City of West Seattle built a new plank road along the water from Youngstown. Luna Park readied a covered parking garage to keep precious automobiles safe.

Business remained strong in 1908. In 1909 the Alaska Yukon Pacific Exposition brought tens of thousands of travellers to Seattle, which meant even more visitors than before for Luna Park. Things were going so well that in 1910 William was

left to run Luna Park with his young family. Charles and Arthur moved to Long Beach, California to open a new carousel factory and replicate the beach amusement parks of the East Coast.

The Looff family continued to invest in California, but before the 1912 season they sold the Luna Park Amusement Company to Chicagoan William Labb. Labb had extensive amusement park experience, including the design of attractions for White City in Denver, Colorado and the entire White City park in Dayton, Ohio. Unfortunately he did not find success operating Seattle's Luna Park.

In 1912 there were five deaths in eight weeks at the natatorium, which technically was a separate company. The public viewed them as one amusement park, though, and patronage dropped quickly. In 1913 Labb invested in new paint and other beautification and a new attraction called the Third Degree. But Labb's cash flow was upside down. Two months into the 1913 season, creditors sued for their money. The rides and attractions were sold at auction.

Luckily, the Looff family was able to purchase Luna Park's carousel. They shipped it to San Francisco for a new attraction at the Playland amusement park in 1914. Today that carousel continues to delight children and adults alike in San Francisco's Yerba Buena Gardens.

William Looff moved his family to San Francisco to manage the carousel attraction, and then to a new carousel at Santa Monica. Eventually his children returned to Seattle though. His son Dorrell went to work as a clerk at Washington Mutual in 1928 after graduating high school. When he retired in 1971, he was vice-president of the expanding bank chain.

LEFT ABOVE *The roller coaster Figure 8 is in the foreground.*

LEFT *Children ride the carousel inside its circus tent-like building.*

RIGHT *Luna Park's natatorium and hall are just above the steamer. The rides stretched to the west on the Elliott Bay side of the Duwamish Head.*

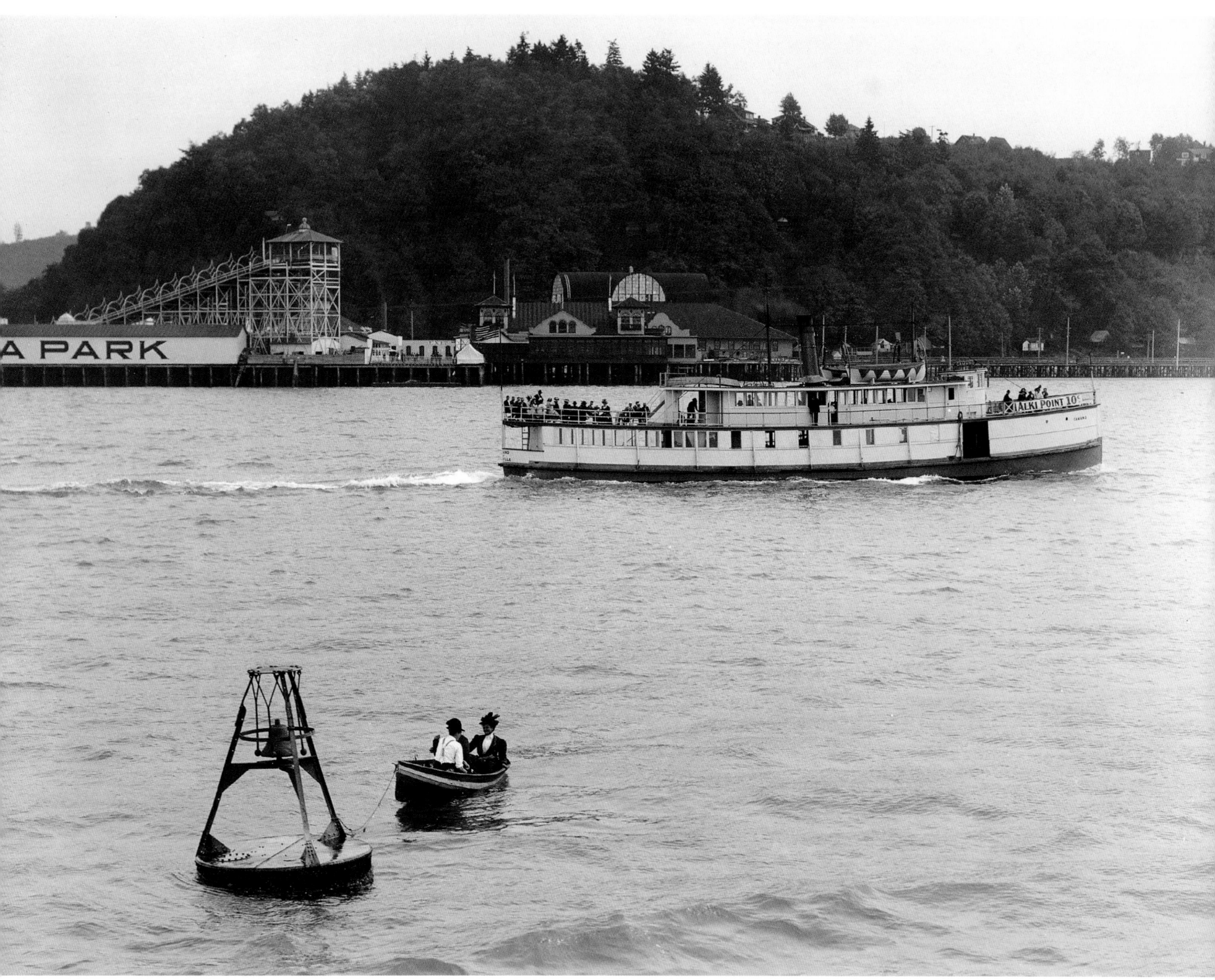

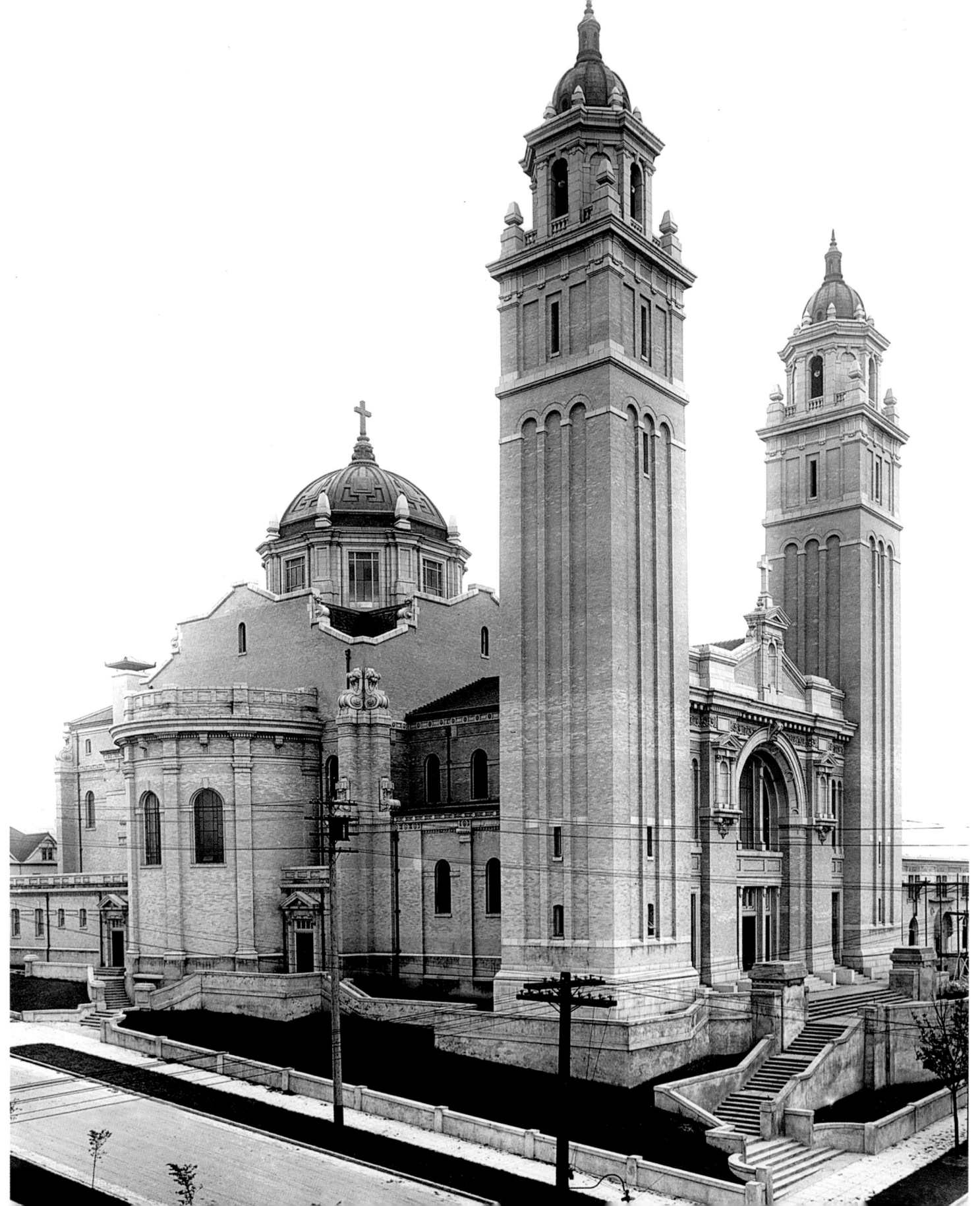

St. James Cathedral DOME COLLAPSED 1916

The cathedral of the regional Catholic Diocese on First Hill featured a dome until the 1916 snowstorm that blanketed the city. It was not replaced.

The Archdiocese of Seattle started first as the Diocese of Nesqually in 1850, two years before the Denny Party arrived at Alki. It was located in Vancouver, Washington, across the Columbia River from the Archdiocese of Portland.

In 1896 Father Edward O'Dea was appointed Bishop of Nesqually, and along with letters of congratulations he received overtures from Tacoma, Spokane and Seattle to become the new home for his see. Vancouver was clearly too close to the Archdiocese in Portland. Seattle's Father Prefontaine joined with business leaders to convince O'Dea that Seattle's growth would turn it into Washington State's most important city.

In 1903 Bishop O'Dea asked Rome for approval and moved his church to Seattle. Temporarily working out of Father Prefontaine's Our Lady of Good Help Church, O'Dea acquired property on First Hill for construction of a new Cathedral of St. James.

Construction of the Italian renaissance styled church began in 1905 and completed two years later. The building featured two 175-foot towers facing the waterfront and a graceful, copper-covered dome with lit cross. The dome let in light and because its weight was borne by the exterior walls there was no interior obstruction by pillars.

The cathedral was one of the last projects of architects George Heins and Christopher LaFarge.

The partners had 25 years experience designing churches across the country and Heins in particular was one of the world's experts on church architecture. They were famous for their work on New York's Cathedral of St. John the Divine and Washington, D.C.'s St. Matthew's Cathedral.

Their background made the problems with St. James Cathedral very concerning. From the day of dedication the acoustics of the chapel were awful, and the dome was at fault. Bishop O'Dea tried pulling a velvet curtain across the base of the dome, but it was no help. He suggested installing a stained glass window across the bottom, but the architects rejected that idea.

Unfortunately the dome had more fundamental, structural problems. In 1916 Seattle was hit by one of the worst snowstorms on record. Seven feet of wet snow, weighing an approximate 30,000 pounds, piled up on the dome. The walls below the dome held fast, and the dome's brick and terracotta distributed the weight. But on February 2 one of the four steel trusses gave way, sending the dome crashing into the altar below.

Designs for the replacement began immediately. A lower dome was debated, an idea which had been considered for years to improve acoustics. Finally it was decided to build a flat roof instead, designed by Seattle architect John Graham, Sr. The acoustics were finally fixed.

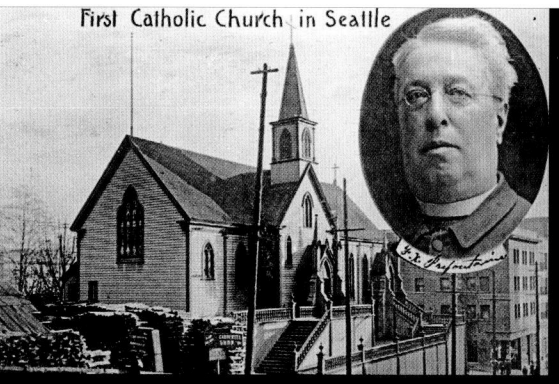
First Catholic Church in Seattle

FATHER PREFONTAINE

In 1867 young Father Francis Xavier Prefontaine moved to Seattle, bringing the first Catholic religious presence. There were 10 claimed Catholics in Seattle at the time, but Father Prefontaine's first mass was delivered to only two of them. He started from a small house at Third Avenue and Mill Street (Yesler Way) and built the Church of Our Lady of Good Help on nearby land at Third Avenue and Washington Street in 1870. The church grew steadily, with 600 parishioners by 1883. In 1905 a new Our Lady of Good Help was built at Fifth Avenue and Jefferson Street. During the Third Avenue regrade, the city decided to cut a new street through the old church block diagonally to Fourth Avenue. It was named after the pioneer priest, Prefontaine Place. Prefontaine was granted the title Monsignore but was ailing and already almost 70 when St. James Cathedral opened in 1907. When he passed in March 1909, the cathedral was filled beyond capacity for his funeral.

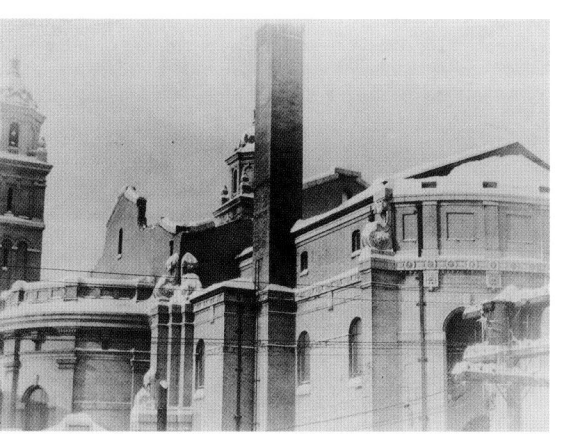

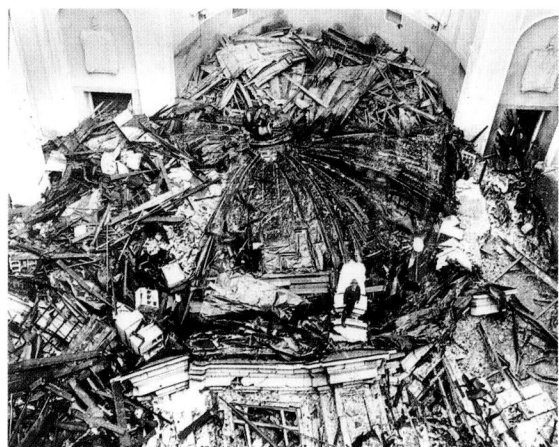

OPPOSITE PAGE *The full cathedral with dome, seen from Ninth Avenue and Marion.*

FAR LEFT *Soon after the dome collapsed, seen from the Terry Avenue side.*

LEFT *Viewed from above, the wreckage of the dome is strewn about the chapel and covering the altar.*

King County Courthouse CONDEMNED 1927

After Washington became a state in November, 1889, county governments were able to borrow money to build new facilities. King County consolidated its offices, court and jail atop Yesler Hill in a towered structure that was a Seattle icon for four decades.

The courthouse was architect Willis Ritchie's first work in Washington, and it was also the state's first truly fireproof building. He moved to Seattle within weeks of the Great Fire and brought with him experience with stone construction and public buildings. The floors were made of steel and concrete. No wood was used for any part of the structure, all completed in brick and tile. The foundation and outer walls were made of sandstone quarried near Bellingham and sandstone for the entry columns was quarried in Tenino near Olympia. The exterior was finished in cement stucco.

The first floor housed offices for all county departments, the second the courts, and the daylight basement held prisoners. With a broad imposing facade and tall clock tower, the building was one of Ritchie's only works in the neoclassical style. It quickly picked up the nickname "Tower of Despair."

The Tower of Despair earned its name in 1901. In August, the courthouse carpenter began erecting a scaffold in the tower's attic. It was used as a gallows for Charles Nordstrom, who was given the death sentence after shooting Will Mason while he sat in his dining room eating dinner with his family. It had been two decades since the last King County execution, and Nordstrom spent half of that time filing appeals. The gallows was used again in 1902 to execute William Seaton, who had been convicted of the murder of one man and attempted murder of a woman and two little girls, all with an axe. He only waited one year for the slipknot.

The prison was initially built with iron bars. After several attempts to escape by sawing through them the county constructed a new steel ward to house the most dangerous suspects. The strength of the steel and the double stone wall was tested in 1905. Jack Chesterfield was waiting transport to the state penitentiary in Walla Walla, arrested for imprisoning and repeatedly raping a young artist. He swore he would never leave King County and acted on that after his wife smuggled him contraband during a visit. First he set off two sticks of dynamite, blowing

a hole in the terracotta ceiling and knocking the lock off of the door. He pulled out a revolver and tried to shoot his way out but finally turned the gun on himself when it failed. The suicide attempt failed as well, as did several others over the years. He finally died at Spokane's insane asylum.

The courthouse was overcrowded in jail and office by this point. Discussion of where to build a new courthouse led to construction of a joint structure with Seattle's city government. When the City-County Building was complete in 1914, the courtrooms and all of the offices were moved into it. This left the 200 men and women in basement jail as the only tenants of the building.

In 1929 three separate forces led to the destruction of the courthouse. First, the building was slated to be left empty when a new jail began construction in the top floor of the City-County Building. Second, the county chose Yesler Hill as site for its new Harborview Hospital. Third, the city

pushed a never-realized plan to flatten Yesler Hill in a regrade. And as the need for jobs rose in 1930, sentimentalists and pragmatists lost the argument.

While emptying the building they found a frayed, weathered old noose in the clock tower. The sheriff remembered tossing it into a corner to save it from morbid treasure hunters. The courthouse was demolished starting January 8, 1931 and sold as scrap.

RIGHT *The clock tower and gloomy cupola gave the courthouse the nickname Tower of Despair.*

BELOW *Forcing lawyers to swear their way up the stairs gave it the name Profanity Hill.*

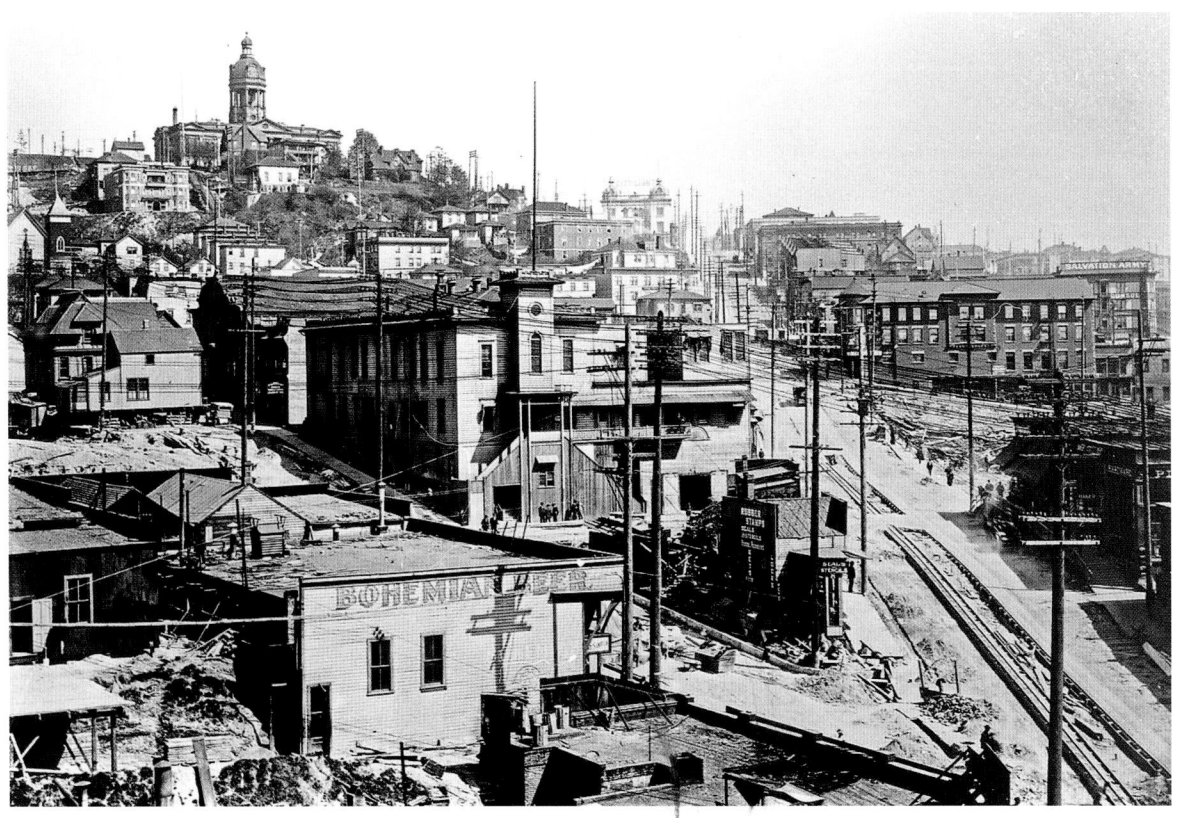

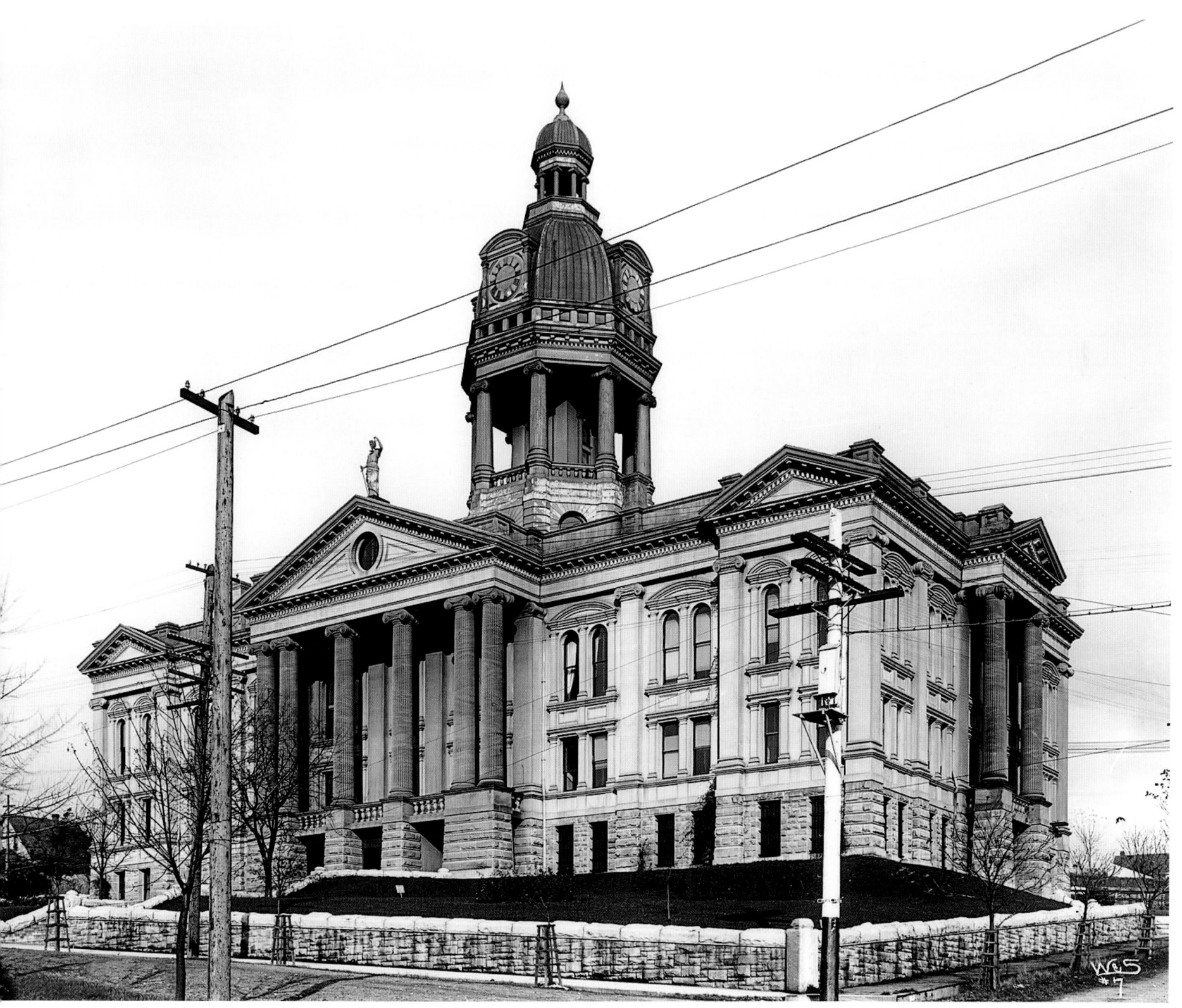

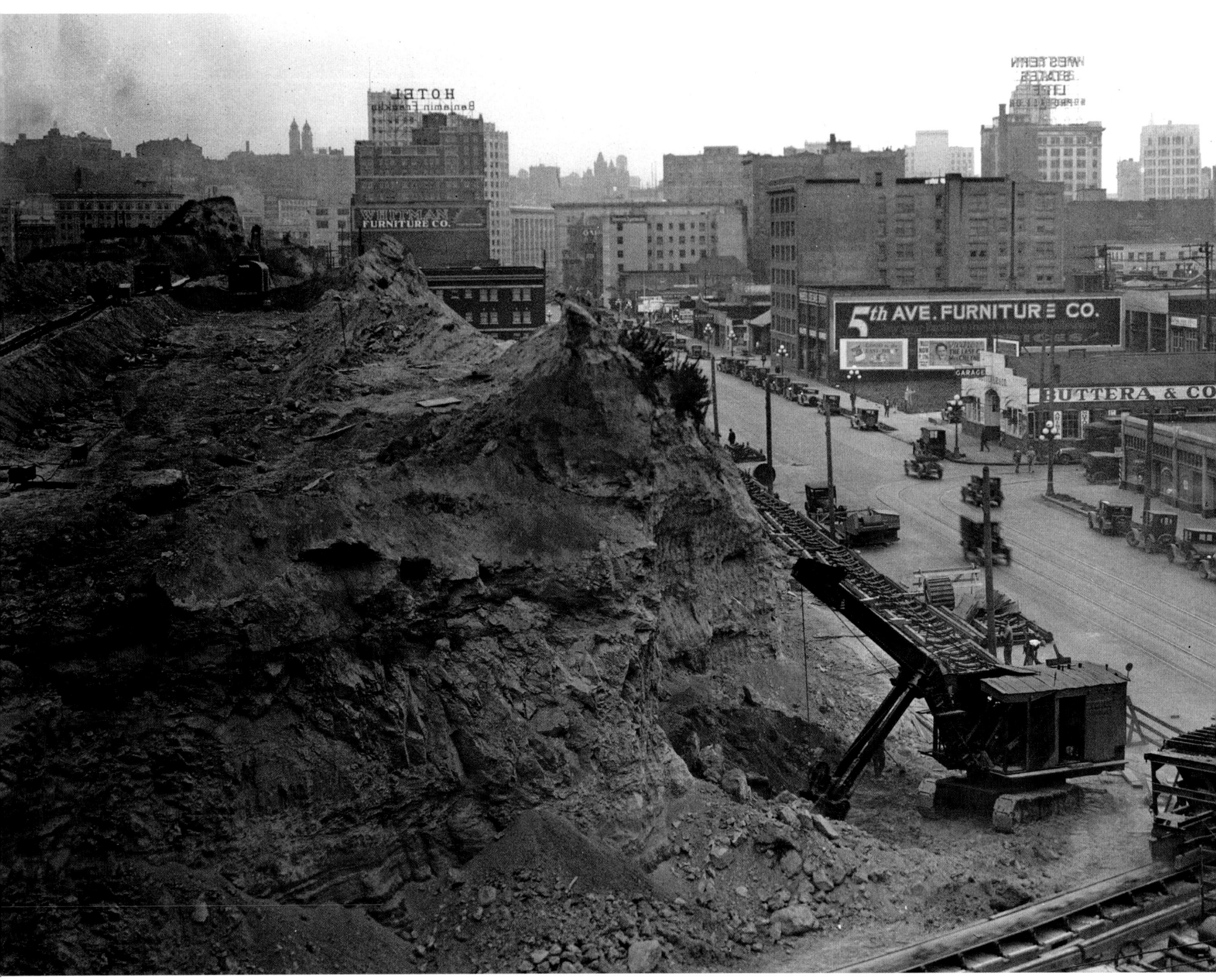

Denny Hill REGRADED 1930

Denny Hill was the most dramatic of Seattle's efforts to reengineer the landscape.

Seattle started on a small spit of land. The spit stuck out into the north end of mud flats pouring out of the mouth of the Duwamish River. Beyond the spit the shore narrowed along a steepening bluff. The shore widened again to a smaller mudflat between Queen Anne Hill and Magnolia Bluff.

Between Queen Anne Hill and the tiny town of Seattle, the bluff rose almost 200 feet from the waterline to Denny Hill. The land undulated with valleys, gullies and plateaus from Denny Hill north to Lake Union and east up the ridge.

After streets were run through, Denny Hill's peak was at about Third Avenue and Lenora Street. In 1884 horse-pulled streetcars began running on Second Avenue from the original settlement area at Yesler's Mill up the slope to the steepest part of Denny Hill at Pine Street. Despite the steep walk, the hill's views and seclusion drew wealthier residents. Robert Moran and his brother Peter moved into a home right at the top. They were still there when Robert was elected Mayor and when the brothers began their shipyard after the Great Fire in 1889.

Just before the fire, the Front Street Cable Railway was built parallel to the streetcar on First Avenue. The cable continued over the shoulder of Denny Hill to Depot Street (Denny Way). In 1890 the cable was extended halfway up Queen Anne Hill, through the developing community of North Seattle in the areas known as Belltown and Uptown today. By this time the horses had been replaced with electricity on the streetcar, and construction of the Denny Hotel was underway.

Further city investment in Denny Hill was paused by the 1893 financial panic. In 1898 city engineer R. H. Thomson flattened, widened and planked First Avenue. There was an immediate impact on real estate along the road, with new homes and businesses popping up in previously inaccessible spaces. By 1900, City Councilman W. V. Rinehart began publicly discussing the destruction of all of Denny Hill.

Thomson decided to take it slow. He cut at the south of Denny Hill with a regrade of Pike and Pine streets and at the west on Second Avenue in 1903. The Second Avenue regrade left a steep embankment on the side of the hill, leading precipitously up to the Denny Hotel. The edge of the hotel's lawn fell away several times. In the worst case several thousand tons of dirt buried the streetcar line on Second that had been hauling away the soil.

All of that dirt had to go somewhere. Luckily, Seattle knew where to put it. The shoreline and tide flats had been a dumping ground for waste dirt, rocks, building materials, and ballast from ship holds. It was used to fill in mudflats to the south of town and fill in all of the gullies and valleys north of town.

In 1905 Thomson won out, and the city decided to completely level Denny Hill. The project was too massive to complete at once. The first iteration ran from 1908 to 1911. This was the most famous of the Denny regrades, taking down as much as 100 feet of dirt. Many landowners fought the process and their homes were left on Badlands-like pinnacles of earth called spite mounds. Eventually the city successfully condemned their property and it all came down. This regrade ran from Pike north to Cedar Street, covering 27 city blocks.

As happened with Denny Knoll in 1901, the Municipal Plans League focused on the Denny Regrade for the site of a new civic center. In 1912 Seattle voters decided not to invest in the new government buildings along with the tunnels, streetcars, harbor improvements and street regrades that were bundled into the full Plan of Seattle.

The remaining chunk of Denny Hill languished as the city waited to finish it. Property owners knew the regrade was coming and so could not invest in new buildings, and only did maintenance that was absolutely required. Finally in 1929 the next iteration began. By 1930 another 37 blocks were leveled. All that remained was a small bump at First and Virginia that property owners had declined to remove.

OPPOSITE PAGE *Steam shovels carve at the last bits of the hill in 1929.*

BELOW *The New Washington Hotel rises in 1908 behind the remnants of the hill that held its predecessor.*

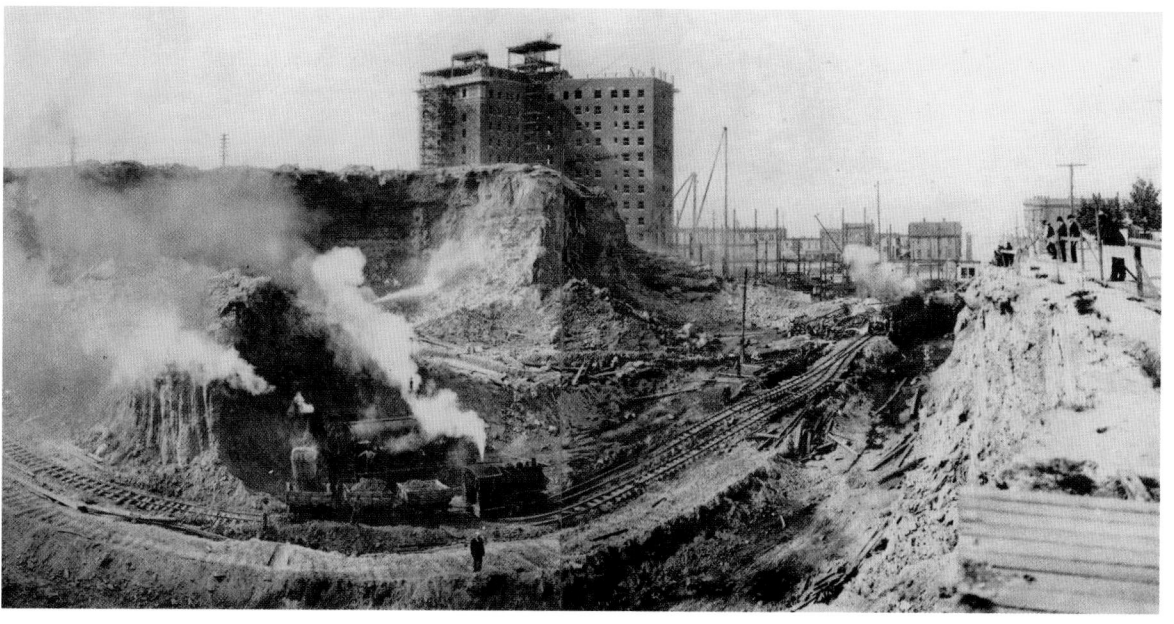

Production of Street Clocks EXPIRED 1932

Seattle was home to one of America's greatest street clock makers, Joseph Mayer.

Mayer came to Seattle at the age of 15 in 1883 and found work as a watchmaker. Joseph was joined by his brothers Albert and Markus, forming a manufacturing jewelry firm called Joseph Mayer & Brothers in 1897. With Seattle's rapid growth and the wealth of the 1897 Klondike and 1900 Nome gold rushes, jewelers proliferated. Joseph Mayer & Brothers supplied clocks, watches, diamonds, optical goods, tools and material to the jewelry trade.

By 1907 the Mayer brothers employed over 150 people. They made sterling silver tableware and souvenir spoons, cremation urns, memorial tablets and a variety of fraternal pins, medals, and loving cups as well as street car tokens for the City of Seattle. They designed and made the golden key surrounded by 22 nuggets from the original Klondike strike for President Taft to use from the Oval Office in opening the Alaska Yukon Pacific Exposition on June 1, 1909. This key was used by successive presidents for ceremonial openings up through John F. Kennedy who opened the 1962 Seattle World's Fair with it.

As the jewelers increased in number, the more high-class stores turned to street clocks as a way to differentiate themselves from the pawn shops and newcomers. Albert Hansen was one of the first, purchasing a clock in 1890 from Seth Thomas in Connecticut. These clocks were made of cast iron and weighed several tons.

Starting in about 1906, Mayer & Brothers brokered sales of street clocks for Boston's E. Howard Company. Howard was Seth Thomas's rival, and considered by many to be the foremost maker of street and tower clocks in America. Joseph began experimenting with modifications and enhancements to Howard's clocks.

In the 1910s Joseph Mayer & Brothers began selling a line of clocks designed entirely by Joseph. The cases were cast in local foundries, and eventually the Mayer brothers manufactured the clock works inside as well. Larger, more ornate cases followed. Several varieties of lights were available. Clock options included two dials, four dials, and even eight. Depending on the design, the center of the dials were 12, 15 or even 17 feet above the sidewalk. This put the top of the largest clocks at over 20 feet high.

Mayer sold dozens of clocks, not only in Seattle but all over the Northwest, adding to a few already in place from other manufacturers. By the late 1920s, Seattle became known as the City of Clocks. The area around the junctions of Fourth Avenue, Westlake

Avenue and Pike Street was densest with clocks and with jewelers, and picked up the nickname Diamond District. At its peak there were 16 clocks within a block of that intersection. They all originated with Joseph Mayer.

Then the Great Depression hit. New clock sales vanished. Mayer was hired by the city to remove clocks that were no longer functioning and violated city ordinances. His best clock business was reselling and relocating them as jewelers went bankrupt.

In 1937, under stress from ill-health and overwork, Joseph Mayer committed suicide at his Dexter Avenue factory. The new owners scrapped his clock castings and plans.

His clocks, though, live on. Seven still grace the streets of Seattle. The rest, more than 50 in number, are mostly in the Northwest but they have been found as far away as Illinois, New York State, and Puerto Rico.

RIGHT *L. W. Suter had a fantastic example of a four-dial in front of his Second Avenue store.*

LEFT *Burnett Brothers' massive clock started on First Avenue but spent many years across from Carroll's Fine Jewelry at Fourth and Pike.*

BELOW *This two-dial was at Caplan Jewelry on Westlake in the Diamond District.*

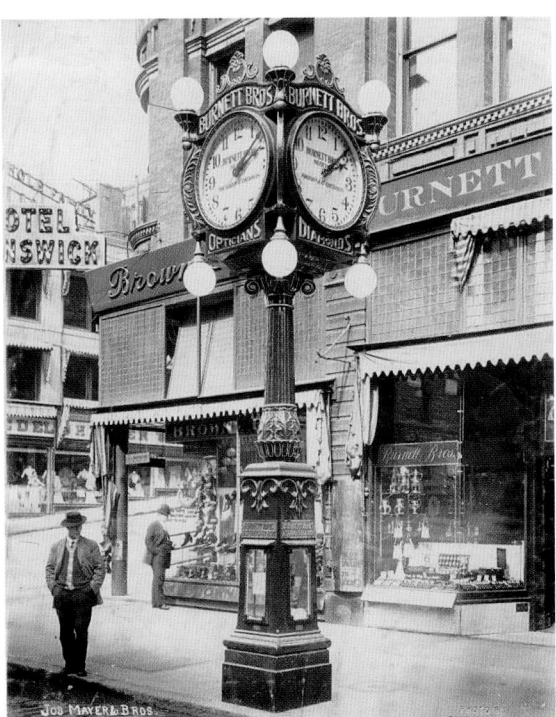

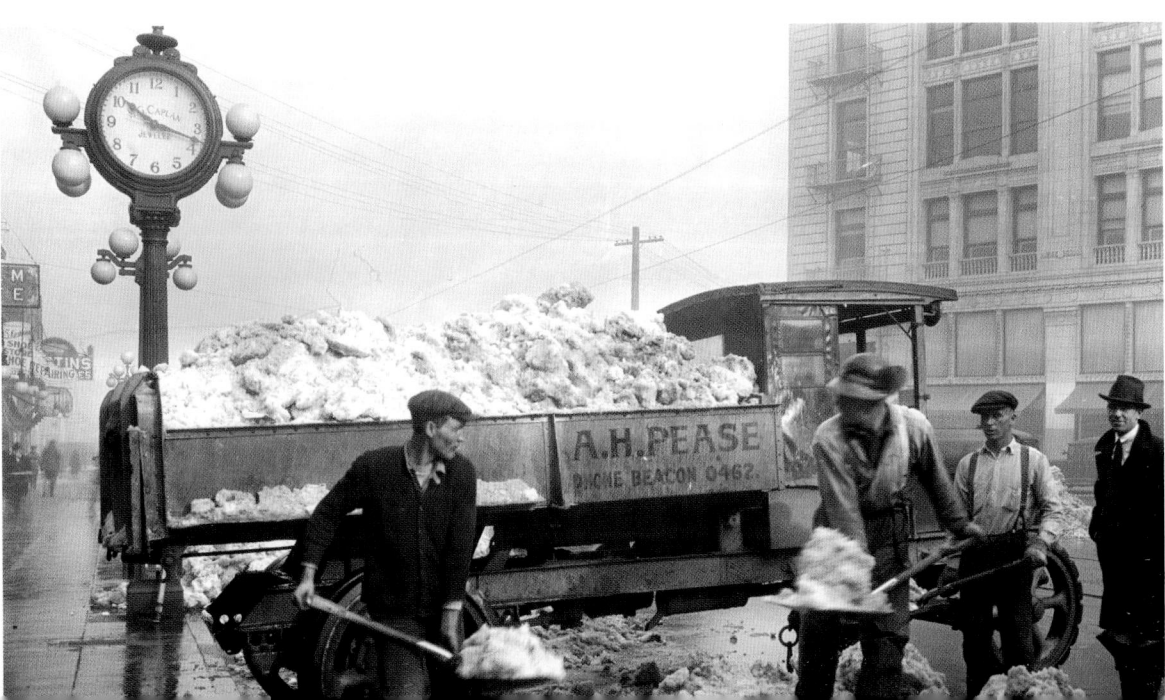

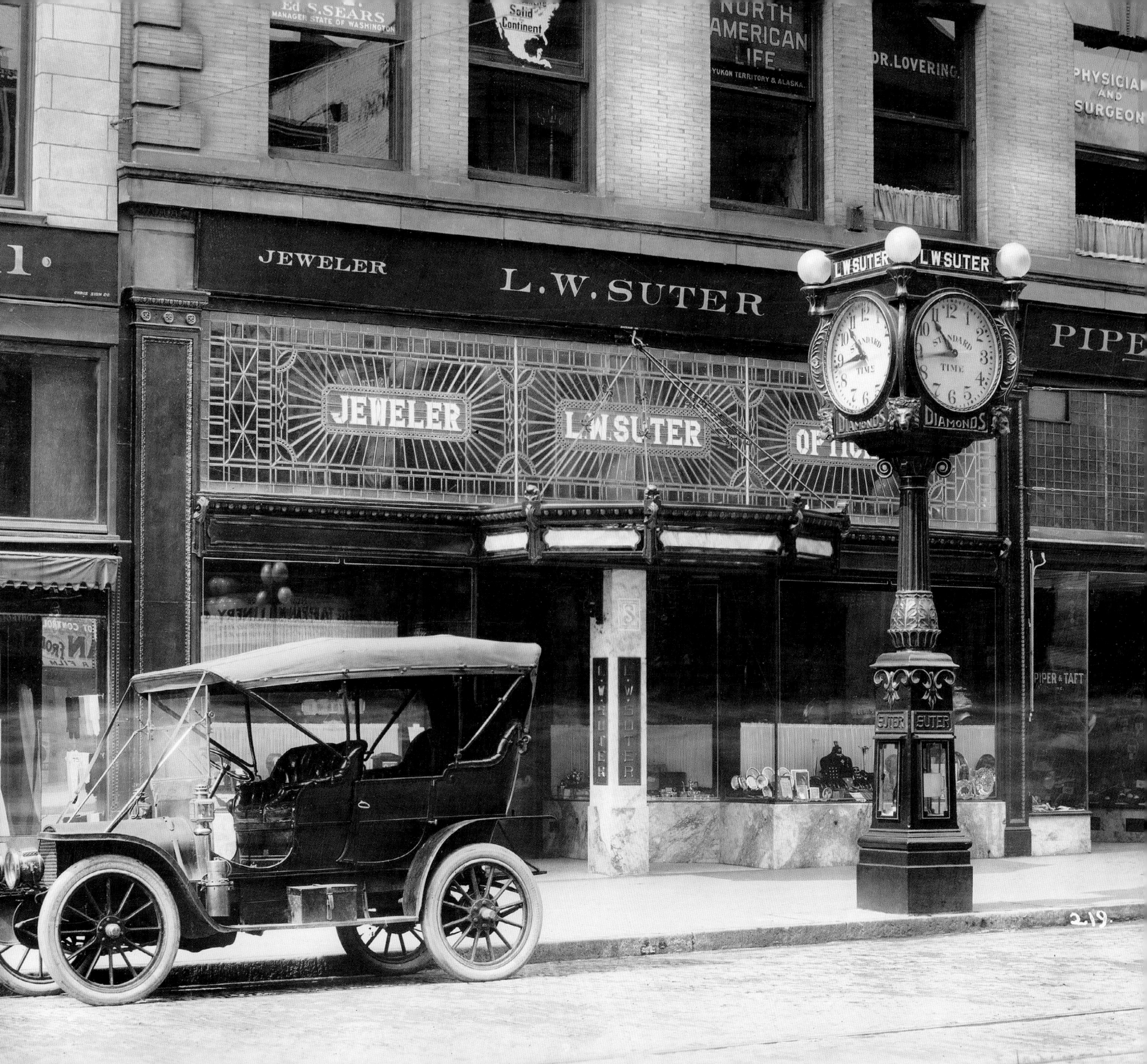

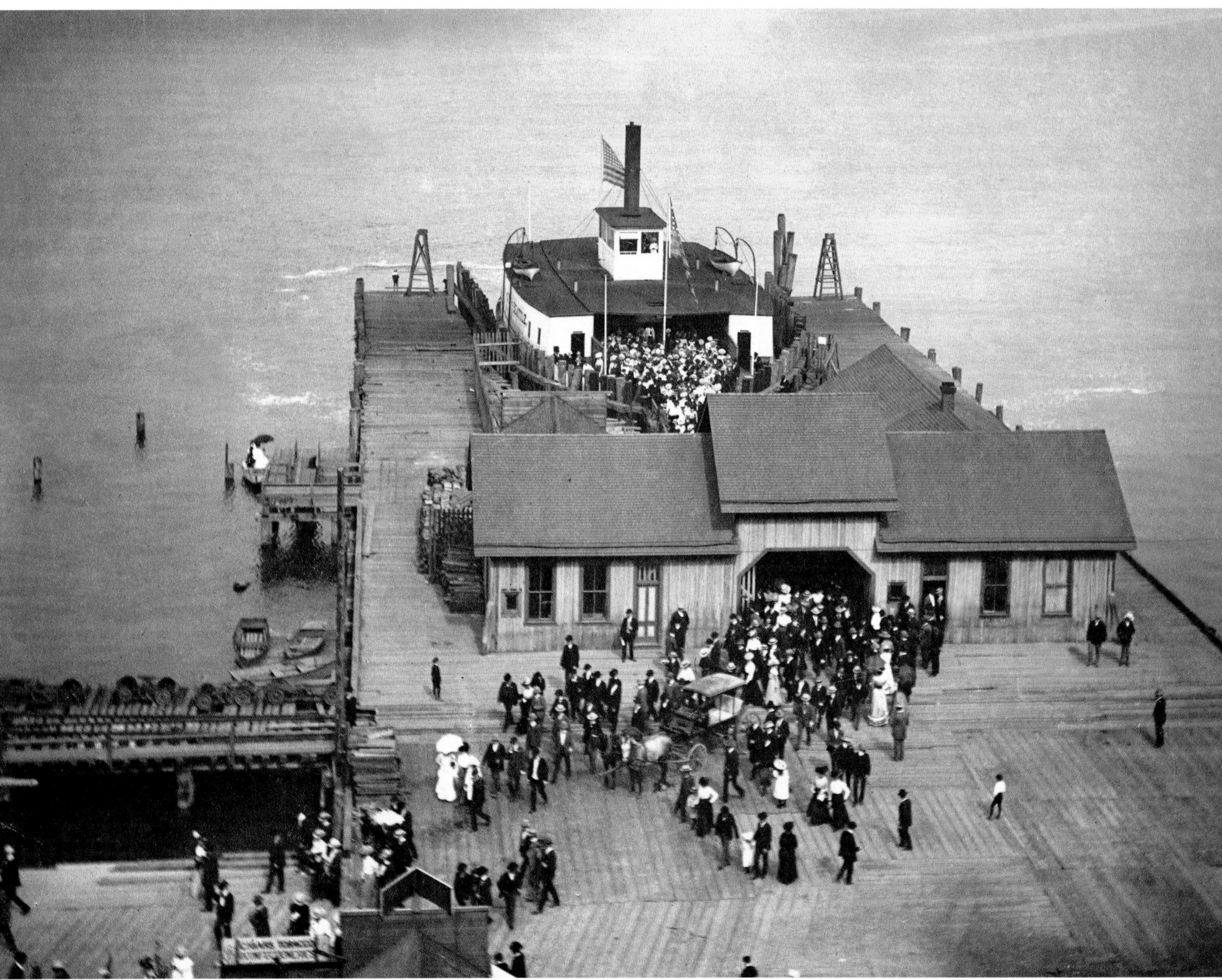

Mosquito Fleet REPELLED BY CAR FERRIES 1936

As communities grew around the Puget Sound and up the many rivers that empty into it, a fleet of small ships gathered to ferry people and light cargo. Compared with the massive ocean sailing vessels and steamships, these little steamers buzzed around like mosquitos. No surprise then that they became known as the Mosquito Fleet.

The first small steamer was the upstart *Fairy*, which began service in 1853, the year that Yesler's Mill started cutting wood. She was truly tiny though, and struggled on the rough winter waters of Puget Sound. At the end of the decade the stately *Eliza Anderson* and her side-wheels ushered in a new era of transportation. The 1860s saw many more

100-plus foot steamers enter service between Puget Sound's ports.

Seattle anchored itself as the center of the Mosquito Fleet in the 1870s, homeporting more of the light steamers than any other city. Eventually every dock along the waterfront would be used to tie up the vast array of vessels from a long list of companies.

Within hours of Seattle's Great Fire of 1889, steamers came chugging in with help and supplies. The *Quickstep* from Tacoma was first, and she and the *Clara Brown* made two trips each the first day. The *Fleetwood* came from Olympia, the *Fairhaven* from Bellingham, and the *T. J. Potter* from Victoria.

By the time the new Colman Dock opened in 1908, there were hundreds of small vessels crisscrossing the Puget Sound. They competed with railroads and interurbans, and opened new communities across Seattle's lakes and bays until streetcars were snaked out to them.

The small passenger and freight vessels of the fleet didn't survive long in the auto era, though. In the 1930s, Seattle's ferry companies began to acquire combustion auto ferries from San Francisco which were made surplus by the completion of the Golden Gate Bridge in 1935. Colman Dock was rebuilt to handle more and bigger cars.

On January 10, 1936 the passenger steamer *Verona* caught fire and was left to burn at her dock in Seattle after the nightly run to Bainbridge Island. It was a symbolic end to the Mosquito Fleet.

LEFT *The* City of Seattle *empties a load of passengers in West Seattle headed to Luna Park around 1910.*

BELOW *The sternwheeler* Skagit Chief *was built at the end of the fleet's era in 1933. It lasted, out of place, only 20 years.*

BOYES MONORAILS

In 1910, William H. Boyes brought the first monorail fever to Seattle and the Puget Sound. Boyes proposed to link the Mosquito Fleet ports to inland destinations via a light, elevated monorail. In contrast to the monopolistic railroads of the day, it was the rail equivalent of the small steamers. Boyes had patented a monorail which he hoped to turn into a Coney Island amusement park ride in 1908. After meeting utopian city planner Edgar Chambless, his monorail became the spine for Chambless's linear city, named Roadtown. Roadtown also incorporated patented ideas from Thomas Edison and others. Even before the book *Roadtown* was published, Boyes arrived in Seattle in April 1910 pushing his technology. A test track was set up and investors bought shares in monorail companies linking Bellingham to Mt. Vernon, Port Angeles to Port Townsend, Port Townsend to Irondale, Seattle to Riverton and others. Seattle became headquarters to Alaskan, Canadian, and Mexican monorail companies. Boyes collected $15,000 in investments, but never expanded beyond short tracks at Smith Cove. He skipped town and was sued. But the investors believed the monorail idea had merit, and continued presenting plans until the 1930s.

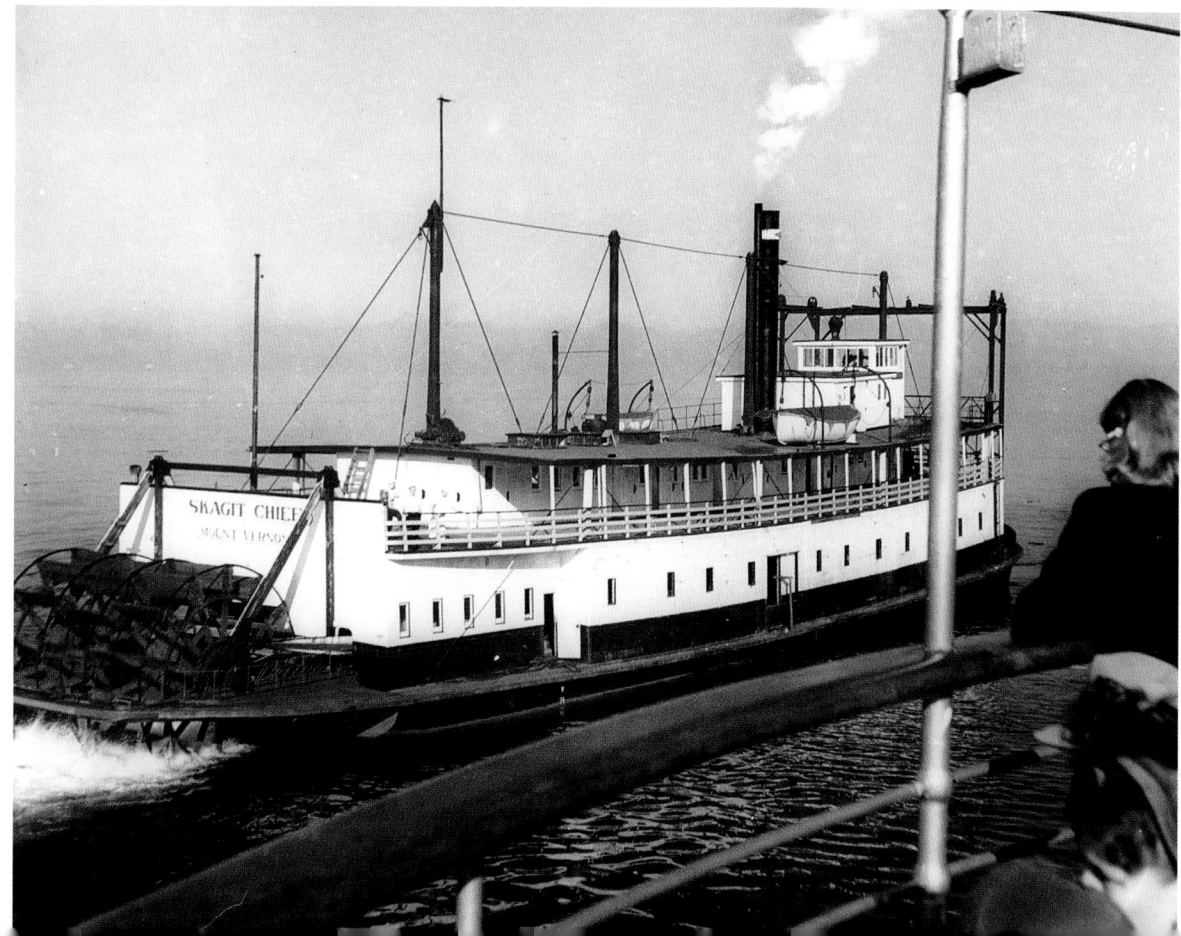

Colman Dock Clock Tower TOPPLED 1936

The clock tower was part of a 1908 redesign of Seattle's historic Colman Dock.

James Colman's original dock was built in 1882 next to Yesler's Mill, which he operated under lease. The dock was one of many that served Mosquito Fleet steamers: the Bellingham Bay Transportation Company's *Willapa*, *Bellingham* and *Dode*; Puget Sound Navigation Company's *Athlon*, *Telegraph* and *City of Everett*; and Port Orchard Company's *Mary F. Perley* were just a handful of the ships that frequented Colman Dock.

In 1908 Colman Dock was rebuilt as a "union wharf," where boats from six different steamship lines operated from a much longer dock. An elevated crossing was added to get passengers over the treacherous railroad tracks along the waterfront. Also an attractive domed waiting area with a restaurant was added. And at the end of the pier a tall, Spanish-style backlit clock tower showed the time to approaching vessels.

The waterfront was a dangerous place with boats hitting each other and the docks with surprising regularity. Just a few weeks after the new wharf opened, the steamship *Buckman* from San Francisco hit the dock so hard that the clock stopped. There was worse to come.

During the evening of April 25, 1912, the steel oceanliner *Alameda* was moving from the fuel dock to Pier 2 when an engineer mistook the order for full steam astern as full steam ahead. The *Alameda* plowed through the end of Colman Dock, severing the clock tower and sending waiting passengers into the cold, dark water of the Elliott Bay. The *Alameda* was hardly damaged, even after the clock tower fell on it and after ramming and sinking the steamer *Telegraph*.

The next day tugs hooked onto the clock tower, which was still floating in the bay. The glass of the clock face was shattered, but the E. Howard & Company clockworks were salvaged. It was restored and added to a taller 90-foot clock tower, which included a lit beacon flashing from the top.

It kept flashing until 1936, when the entire dock was torn down. In its place a modern, car-friendly Colman Ferry Terminal was built. It had a clock too, but it was built only facing inland.

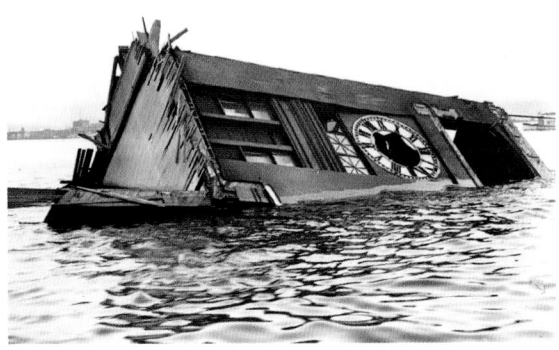

ABOVE *The tower floats after the* Alameda *accident in 1912.*

OPPOSITE PAGE *The taller, rebuilt clock tower in 1915.*

BELOW *After being discovered in a warehouse with chicken coops, the clock was restored and is now on display again at Colman Dock.*

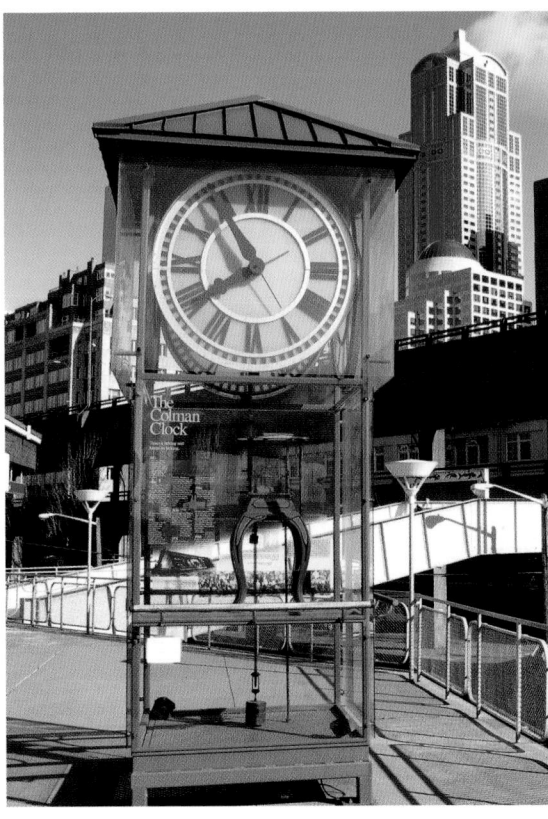

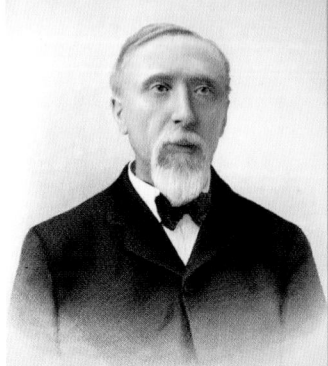

JAMES COLMAN

Born in Scotland in 1832, James Colman was a machinist and engineer before he emigrated to the U.S. in 1854. He moved to the Puget Sound in 1861, working at mills in Port Madison, Port Orchard, and Tacoma. Finally he arrived in Seattle in 1872, taking over management of Yesler's Mill for the company that leased it. Colman quickly became one of Seattle's leading citizens. He took financial and management leadership of the Seattle & Walla Walla Railway. Devised after the Northern Pacific chose Tacoma as its western terminus, the SWW was meant to cross the Cascades and meet the Union Pacific. Instead it only reached the coalfields at Renton, but it was profitable and forced the Northern Pacific to make a connection with Seattle. Meanwhile, Colman was building in Seattle. In 1875 he built Seattle's second brick building while in the midst of railroad construction. He used the money he made from selling the railroad to build Colman Dock, driving the last pile in 1882. After the fire he rebuilt the Colman Building into one of the top office buildings in Seattle, which housed federal offices and businesses such as Joseph Mayer & Brothers. Colman was involved in many enterprises and ventures, weathering fires and financial panics. James Colman died on December 13, 1906. Services were held at the family home at Fourth Avenue and Marion Street, led by the pastor of Plymouth Congregational Church where the Colmans were longtime members, leaders and supporters.

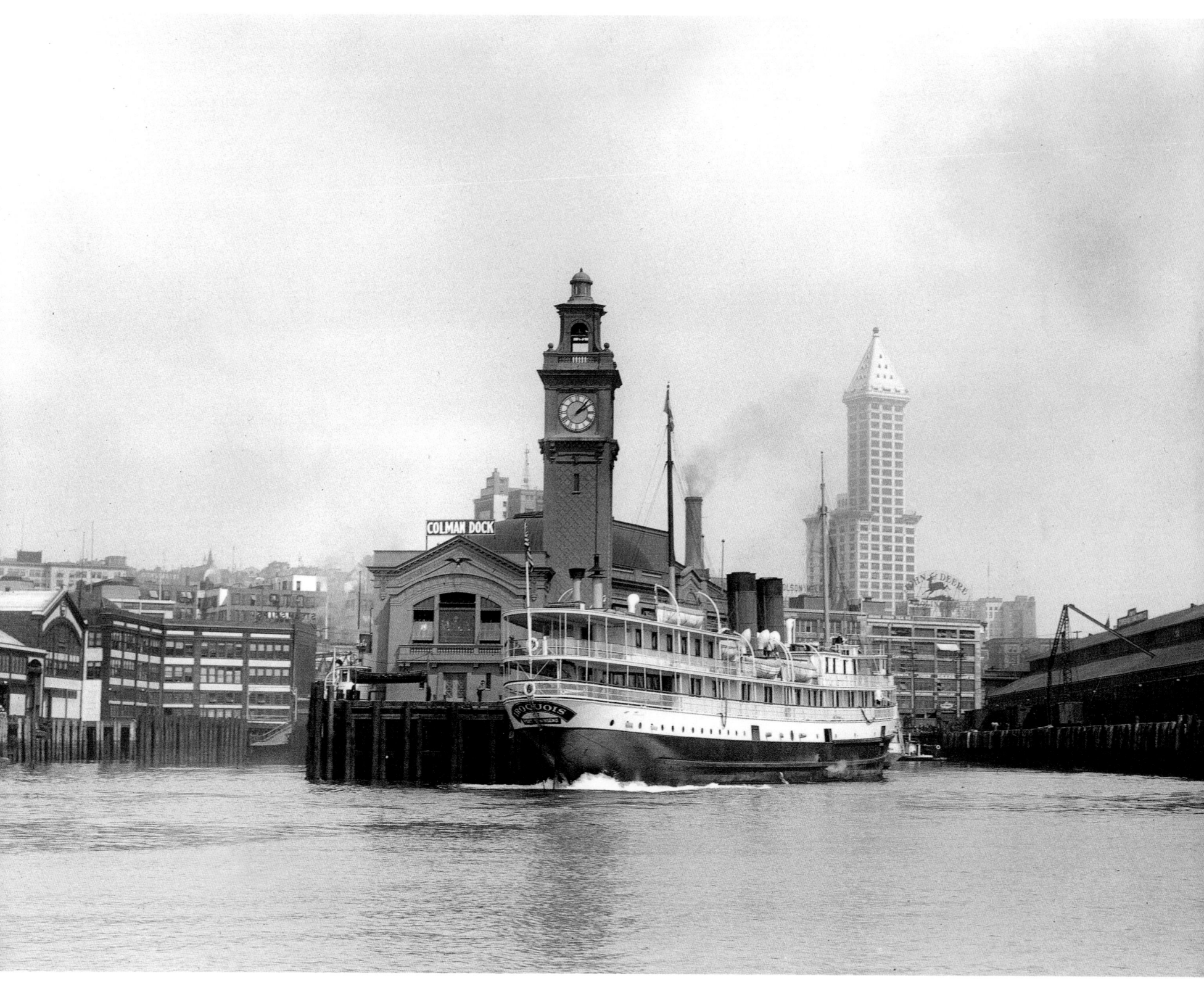

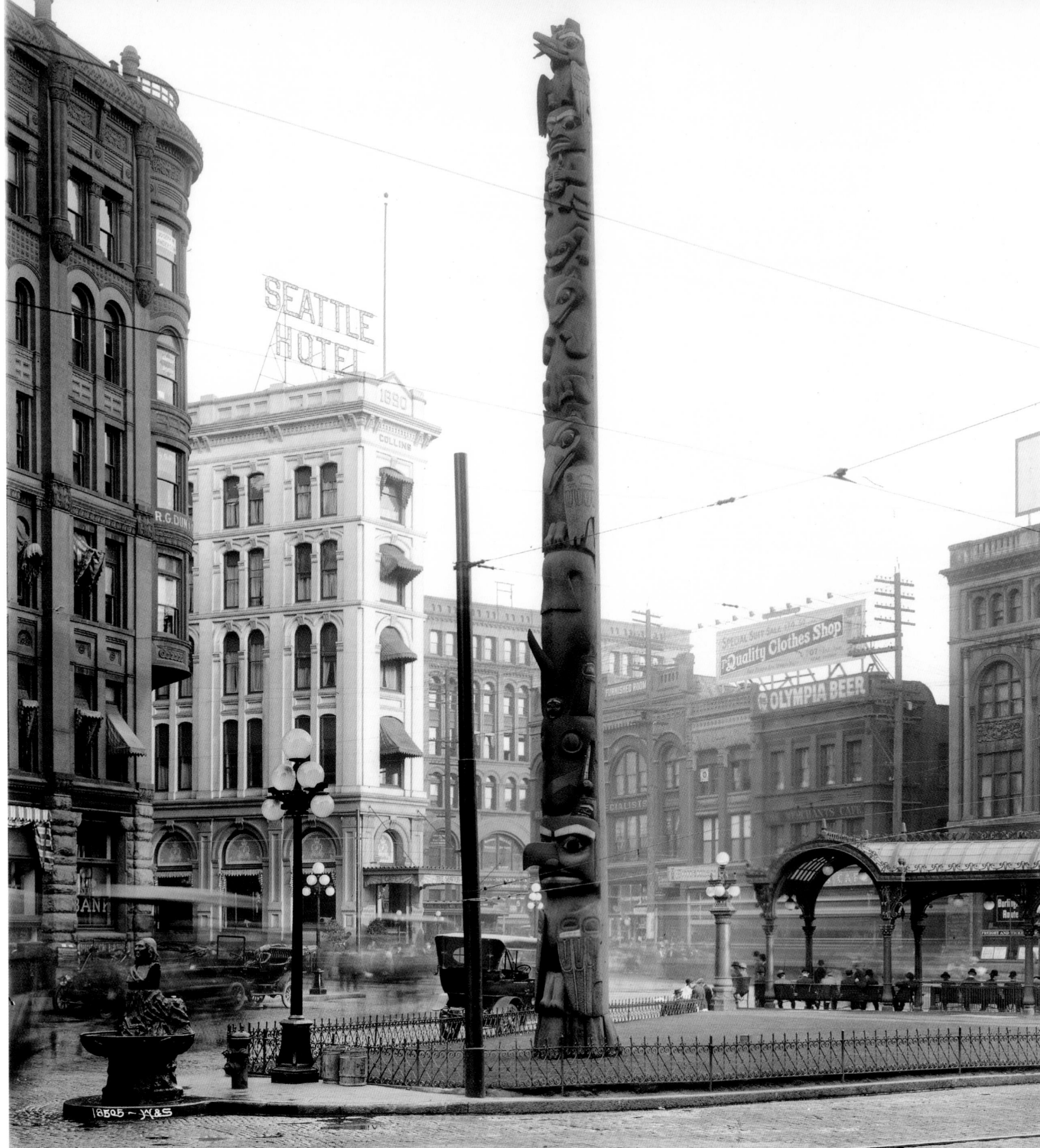

Pioneer Square Totem Pole BURNED AND RETURNED 1938

Thousands of years ago, the Tlingit people already populated the mouths of the rivers along what is now southeast Alaska. They developed a rich culture based on the land, the water, and the animals that inhabit it. Their stories, language and art helped them to pass on knowledge and skills from generation to generation. The totem pole is perhaps their best known cultural artifact. This is a story of one of those totem poles and how it came to stand in Seattle's Pioneer Square.

There was a woman named Chief-of-all-Women, who in about the year 1790 went to visit her sick sister. Chief-of-all-Women was from the clan Raven and lived on Tongass Island. To get to her sister she traveled across the Nass River, which Raven had created by spitting water out of his mouth. Raven had also shown her people how to make the canoe which Chief-of-all-Women used to cross the Nass, and taught them to fish, hunt seal, make fire and to do all of their daily tasks.

Raven also taught the Tlingit how to avoid accidents in the rapids of the rivers by not calling water creatures by their true names. This didn't work for Chief-of-all-Women on this trip. She was drowned in the Nass and did not make it to her sister's village.

Soon after, the Raven Clan carved a 60-foot totem pole to remember Chief-of-all-Women, and it stood outside of their longhouses at Tongass for more than a hundred years. In the interim, the nearby border of European land claims changed from Russian-British to American-Canadian.

In August of 1899, a group of 15 of Seattle's business leaders traveled to the southern tip of Alaska on an excursion. They included streetcar tycoon Jacob Furth, lawyer James Clise, historian Thomas Prosch and James Hoge, Jr., president of the First National Bank.

They decided to take home a totem pole to use as a centerpiece for their town square. They visited Tongass and cut down Chief-of-all-Women's pole while the town was away fishing. In October they raised the pole in Pioneer Square while Seattle rejoiced.

The totem pole became Seattle's emblem. It stood as a symbol of the riches extracted from Alaska during the gold rushes. The Duwamish, Lummi, and other Puget Sound Salish tribes had a carving culture as well, but it had not included totem poles. They embraced this new form both for financial and artistic purposes.

The 15 Seattleites were immediately indicted in federal court for the theft. They tried to pay damages to the Tlingits for the pole but handed the money over to the wrong people. The charges were dismissed in June 1900 by a friendly judge on consideration of additional money paid to the Tlingit.

In 1938 an arsonist set the pole on fire. It was severely damaged, and stood precariously. It was doomed. The city debated simply removing it, tying it with steel bands or copying it in concrete. Finally it was decided to have a replacement carved. Bids came from the Squamish, Makah, and Queets—including Joe Hillaire, who later carved Kobe, Japan's pole for Seattle. Anthropologists from the University of Washington intervened, though, and convinced the city to only work with Tlingit carvers.

The original, scarred pole was finally returned to its rightful home. In return, the Tlingit carved an exact replacement.

From his perch at the top, Old Nass Raven continues to watch over Seattle, with the moon in his beak.

OPPOSITE PAGE *The totem pole stands alongside the pergola cable car shelter within the newly completed Pioneer Square park in 1910.*

BELOW LEFT *Joe Hillaire's story pole after installation in Kobe, Japan in 1961. He did much of the carving in Pioneer Square park.*

BELOW *Erection of the stolen Tlingit pole in 1899.*

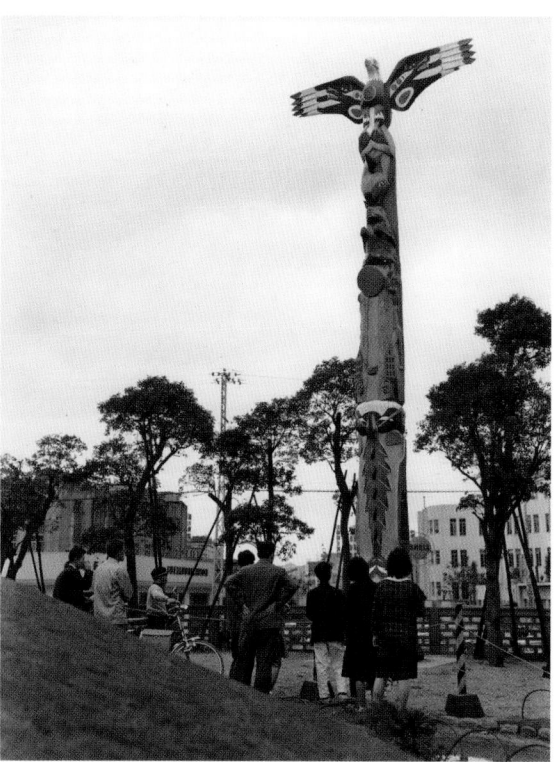

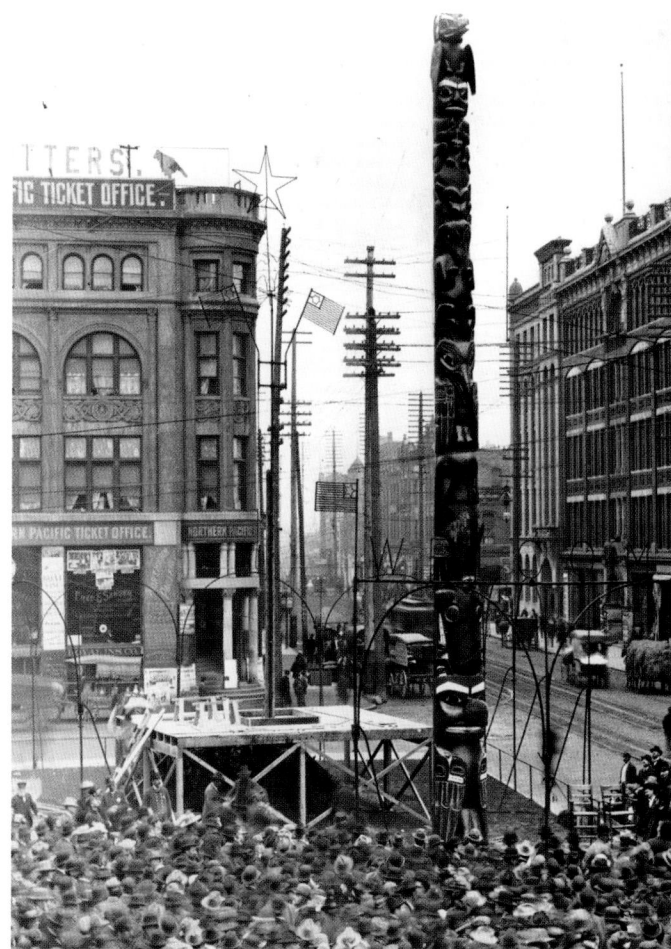

Interurban Railways RIPPED UP 1939

Interurban railways were electrified passenger trains that linked communities inland of the Mosquito Fleet steamers. Interurbans ran for decades but were eclipsed by the automobile and early highway construction. There were three lines from Seattle: Renton, Tacoma, and Everett.

The first to be built was the line through the Rainier Valley to Renton. Construction began in 1889 to haul wood from a mill to rebuild burned-out Seattle. The route would later become Rainier Avenue, but at the time it was still little more than a trail used by the Lake People to travel through the dense forest around the south end of Lake Washington to Elliott Bay. It was built on private land and followed the topography rather than the city's cardinal lines. The rail line's owner, Walla Walla financier James K. Edmiston, converted it to an electrified interurban in 1891. And at its end he platted out the community of Columbia in unincorporated King County southeast of Seattle. It was in a rich, fertile, wild valley but isolated by hills and bluffs from Seattle, the Duwamish River and Elliott Bay.

Edmiston's venture sold plots and tickets until the nationwide financial panic of 1893. The interurban was foreclosed by his debtors the next year, and he lost all of his remaining property. Things got worse for Edmiston. While he was visiting his insolvent bank in Walla Walla, an angry depositor shot at him several times and he miraculously escaped unharmed. With a long, angry line of creditors after him, Edmiston skipped out of the country and worked off his debt from Victoria, B.C.

The line was pushed a bit further while under bank management, and finally Frank Osgood stepped forward in 1895 to purchase the route. It was renamed the Seattle, Renton & Southern and constructed past Rainier Beach to Renton. With dense settlement by Italian immigrants to farm the valley and work in Renton's mines, the Rainier

Valley soon picked up the nicknames Garlic Gulch and Grappa Valley.

The interurban to Tacoma was the next to get rolling. The idea of connecting Seattle and Tacoma was so attractive that it brought investors to two rival corporations. The Seattle Tacoma Railway was the brainchild of Tacoma's "Colonel" Frank Ross and Seattle's Fred Sander. Ross had already tried making one railroad to Seattle. In 1892 he began laying tracks from Tacoma across the reservation of the Puyallup Tribe. He had the tribe's permission, but not the overseeing United States government. Federal troops came and got in a fist fight with his workers. That night Ross had the officers arrested

by Tacoma police. He was victorious and earned the nickname Colonel. Sander was involved in many of Seattle's early engineering projects such as the Union Trunk Line system, the Seattle Central Railway cable car, and the narrow-gauge Grant Street Railway to the new city of Georgetown. Sander and Ross secured rights of way in King County in early 1900, and by the end of the year they had determined the full route to Tacoma.

Just after Ross and Sander's plan was leaked to the press, the Seattle-Tacoma Electric Railway suddenly announced their presence. Its president was John Collins, two-time Mayor of Seattle and publisher of two newspapers. Judge Henry Bucey

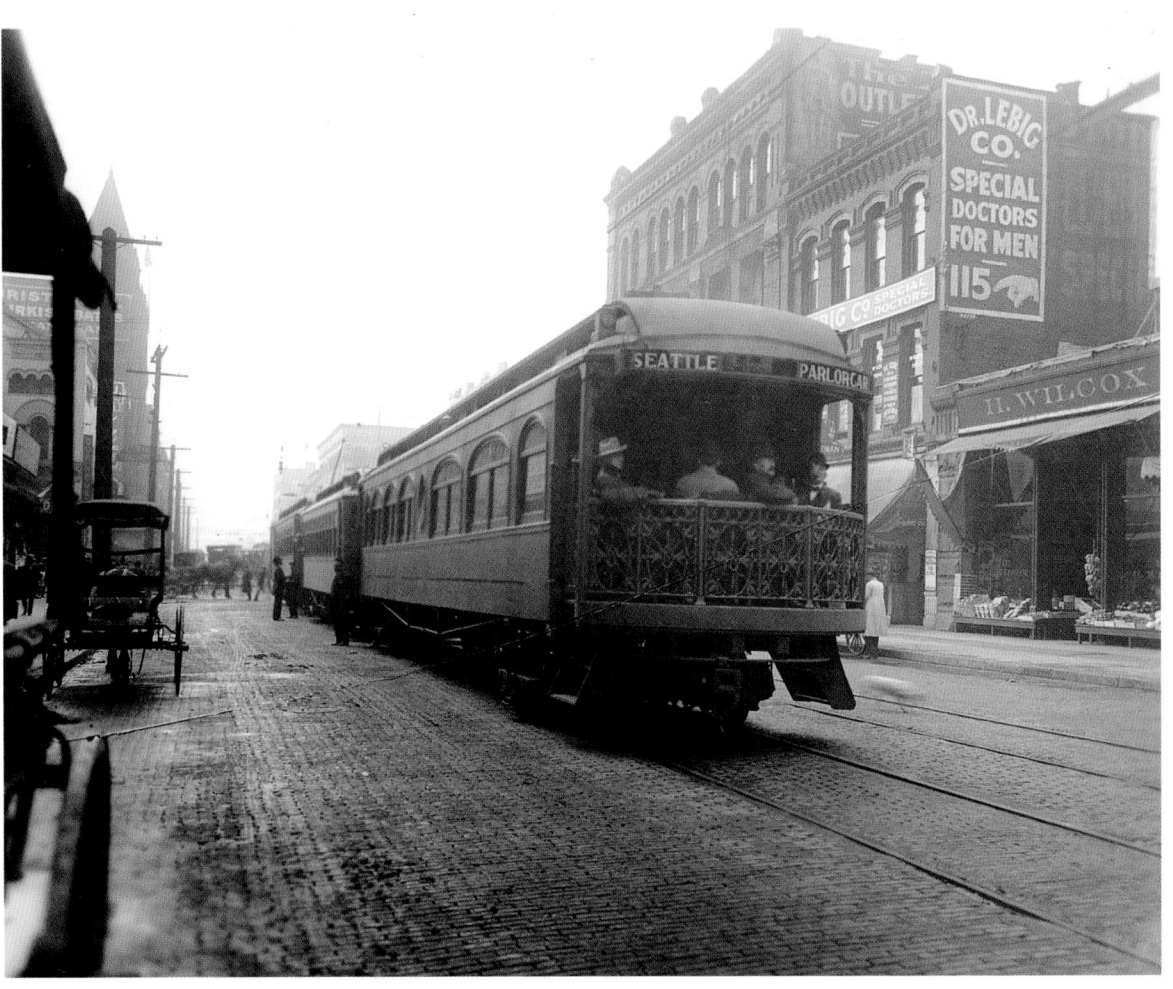

RIGHT *Passengers wait at Occidental and Yesler to head to Tacoma in the fancy parlor car around 1910.*

OPPOSITE PAGE *Riders from Bellingham needed to take a bus from Mount Vernon to Everett before they could make it to Seattle.*

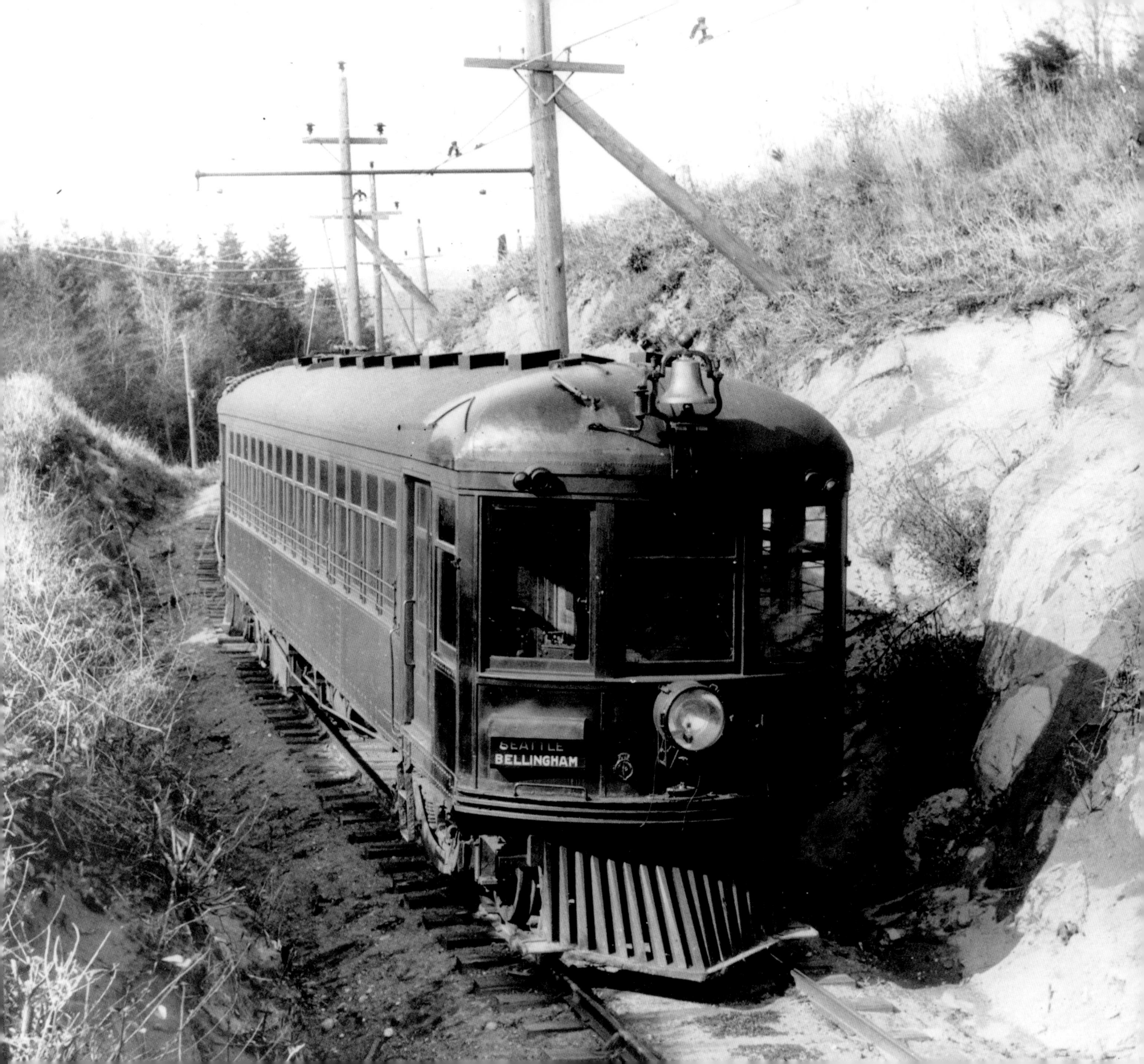

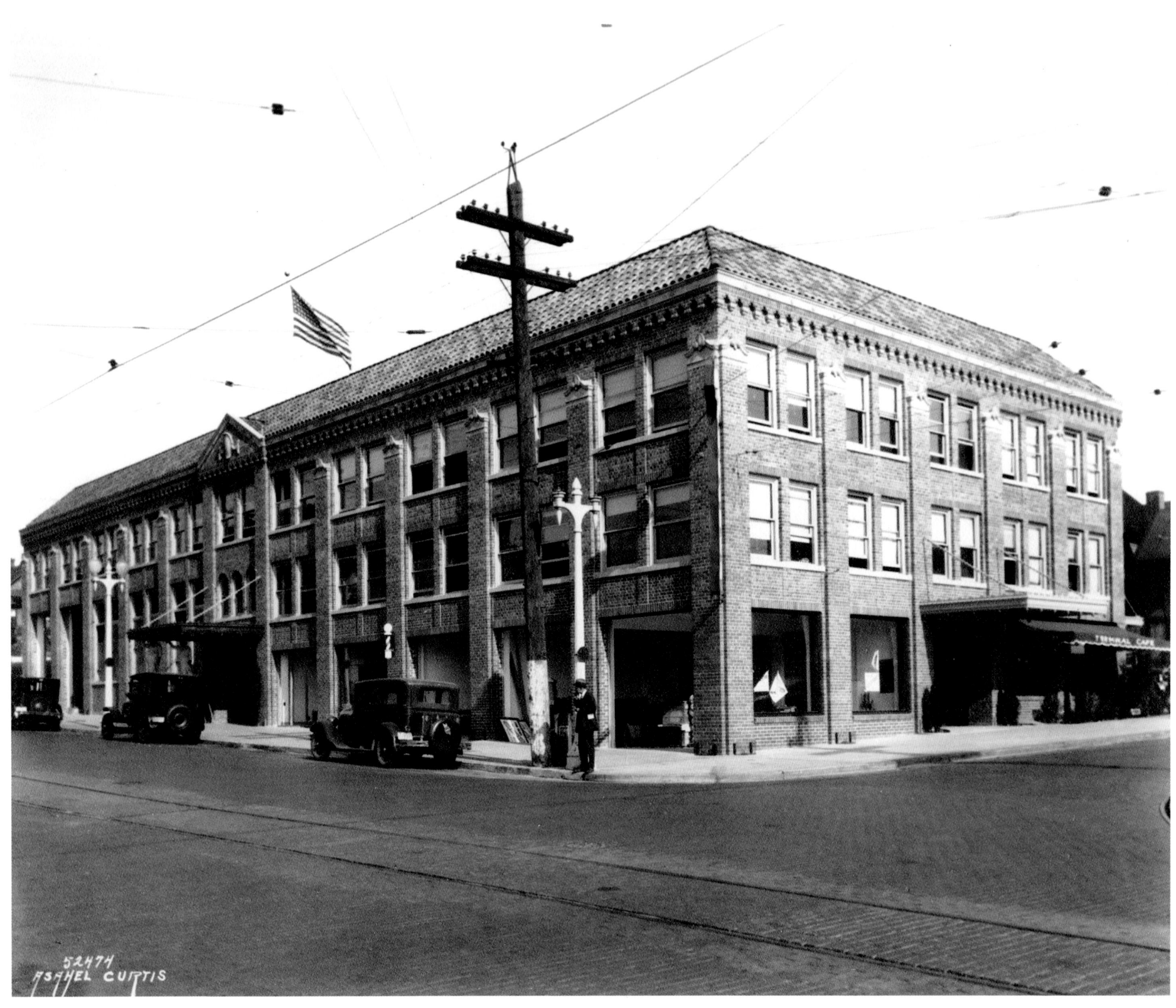

of Tacoma worked as manager, toiling behind the scenes for three years to gather capital and rights of way. Just before their announcement, Seattle developer James Moore threw his weight behind the enterprise. They had a head start with six miles of unused tracks headed south from Seattle.

The fight between the two companies was resolved by the national power and rail conglomerate Stone & Webster. All of Tacoma's and Seattle's streetcars had already been acquired by Stone & Webster, including Sander's Grant Street Railway in 1900. Looking to connect their two municipal systems, Stone & Webster first bought the celebrity-backed Seattle-Tacoma Electric Railway. Ross and Sander's Seattle Tacoma Railway quickly followed suit, and became the route of Stone & Webster's interurban. It passed through the Duwamish, White, Stuck and Puyallup river valleys and linked the agricultural communities of Kent, Auburn, and Orillia (today Tukwila) to the two cities.

The last interurban to start construction was the route to Everett, in 1905. The Seattle-Everett Interurban Company was also headed by Fred Sander. Initially the route was planned from the City of Ballard, with the idea of transferring passengers to Seattle. Request for a franchise from the City of Ballard was made in 1903, but it took more than a year for it to be approved. Finally cars began running halfway to Everett in March 1906, mostly carrying Sunday churchgoers and very light traffic otherwise. Stone & Webster bought Sander out in 1908 and opened full service in 1910. They intended to link all the way to Bellingham, and eventually Vancouver, B.C. to the north. But tracks never made it beyond Everett.

Soon the Renton interurban was the only independent railway line in the city. It changed hands several times, but Stone & Webster never stepped in to acquire it. The City of Seattle even tried to buy out the line in 1911 but had the price raised at the last minute. Seattle went on to buy all of Stone & Webster's railways in the city limits instead.

The interurban to Tacoma continued under Stone & Webster ownership, named the Puget Sound Electric Railway. It gave the Mosquito Fleet steamers fierce competition for long-haul passengers and created its own community rider

base as well. The interurban stopped running in 1928, though, defeated by the newly completed Highway 99 between Seattle and Tacoma.

The Renton interurban collapsed financially in 1937, at the depths of the Great Depression. The Everett interurban on the other hand remained viable, and the economy began to improve. But Seattle had decided to abandon its streetcar system, and the Everett interurban depended on Seattle Municipal Railway tracks and power from the northern city limits to downtown. With the writing on the wall, the Seattle-Everett Interurban's last run was February 20, 1939.

OPPOSITE PAGE *Seattle's Central Stage Terminal on the north end of town served interurbans to Everett as well as a number of bus lines.*

BELOW *The Seattle, Renton & Southern leaves the valley at Rainier Beach, stopping near a few houses before heading back into the wilderness. Rainier Avenue was later built along the tracks.*

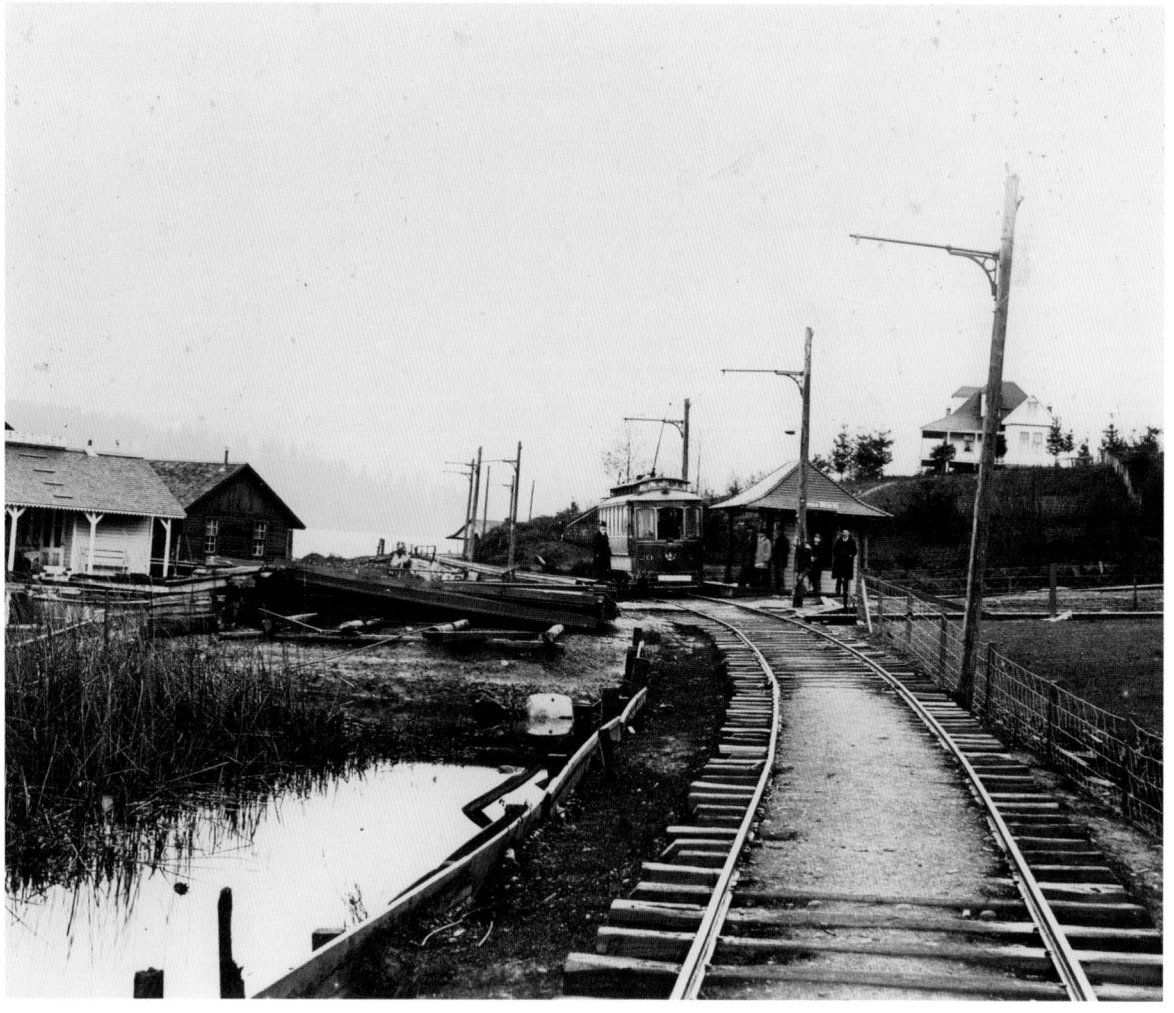

Cable Cars TAKEN OUT OF SERVICE 1941

With Seattle's hilly topography, cable cars were an efficient way to get out of Pioneer Square's bog and over the ridges.

Based on the success of cable cars in San Francisco, the Lake Washington Cable Railway was formed and opened Seattle's first cable in 1888. Seattle was only the fourth city in the world to run cables. It began right at Yesler's Mill and headed up and over First Hill and Second Hill, and down the back side to Lake Washington. Polished wood seats ran the length of the car facing out, sending children sliding from one end to the other as the car went up one steep side of the hill and down the other. Later this would become known as the Yesler cable car.

The Front Street Cable opened in 1889 from Yesler up Front Street (First Avenue) to Pike Street. It was rebuilt after the Great Fire and eventually extended south to King Street and north to Queen Anne Hill. It was ripped up for a streetcar in 1900; the steep grade of Queen Anne Avenue was conquered with a counterbalance, a dead weight hooked to the streetcar to pull it up.

Another cable was run to Lake Washington on Madison Street to complement the Yesler line. The Madison Street Cable Railway opened in 1890. It ended at Madison Park, a cluster of small cottages surrounding a park that had been a secluded part of the city. In 1911 most of the route was replaced with a streetcar, but the cable continued to operate from First Avenue up over First Hill to Broadway.

The shortest lived line was over in West Seattle. It opened in 1890, built by West Seattle Land Improvement who developed real estate and later leased land for Luna Park. In 1897 the line was shut down. The shortest length line in Seattle was the Union Trunk Line, which began operating in 1891 on James Street from Front to Broadway on the top of First Hill. In 1909 the Pioneer Square pergola was built at the end of the cable line with seating for waiting passengers and also covering a staircase that led down to underground bathrooms.

The James Street and Madison Street cables came to a halt in April 1940. Interviewed by a *Seattle Times* reporter, one of the conductors simply requested "Please say that I will miss the people. I have seen some of them grow up from babies to big men."

The Yesler cable route got a temporary reprieve until construction on a new Lake Washington Bridge through Mercer Island to Beaux Arts was completed in July 1940. Then the ferries to the island, Kirkland and Medina were abandoned, the cable cars were scrapped, and the cable itself was pulled out and dumped in the lake. With Seattle's 50-year-old cable cars gone, San Francisco became the last city in the world operating them.

OPPOSITE PAGE *Two Madison Street cable cars pass near the First Avenue terminus around 1900.*

RIGHT *The James cable meets Broadway streetcars in the early 1890s.*

BELOW *The last day of the Yesler line, August 9, 1940.*

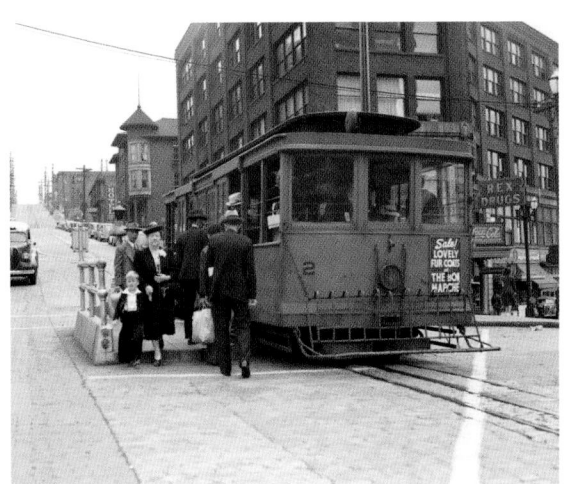

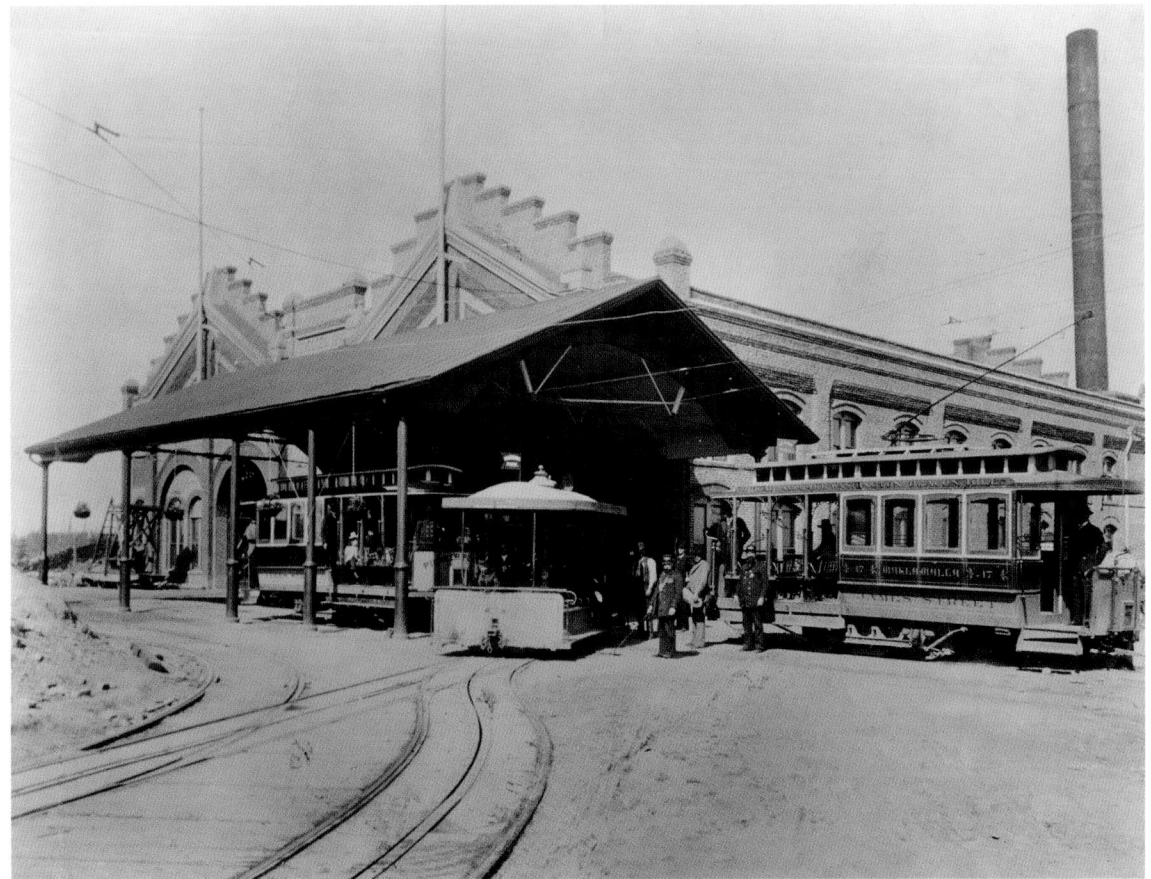

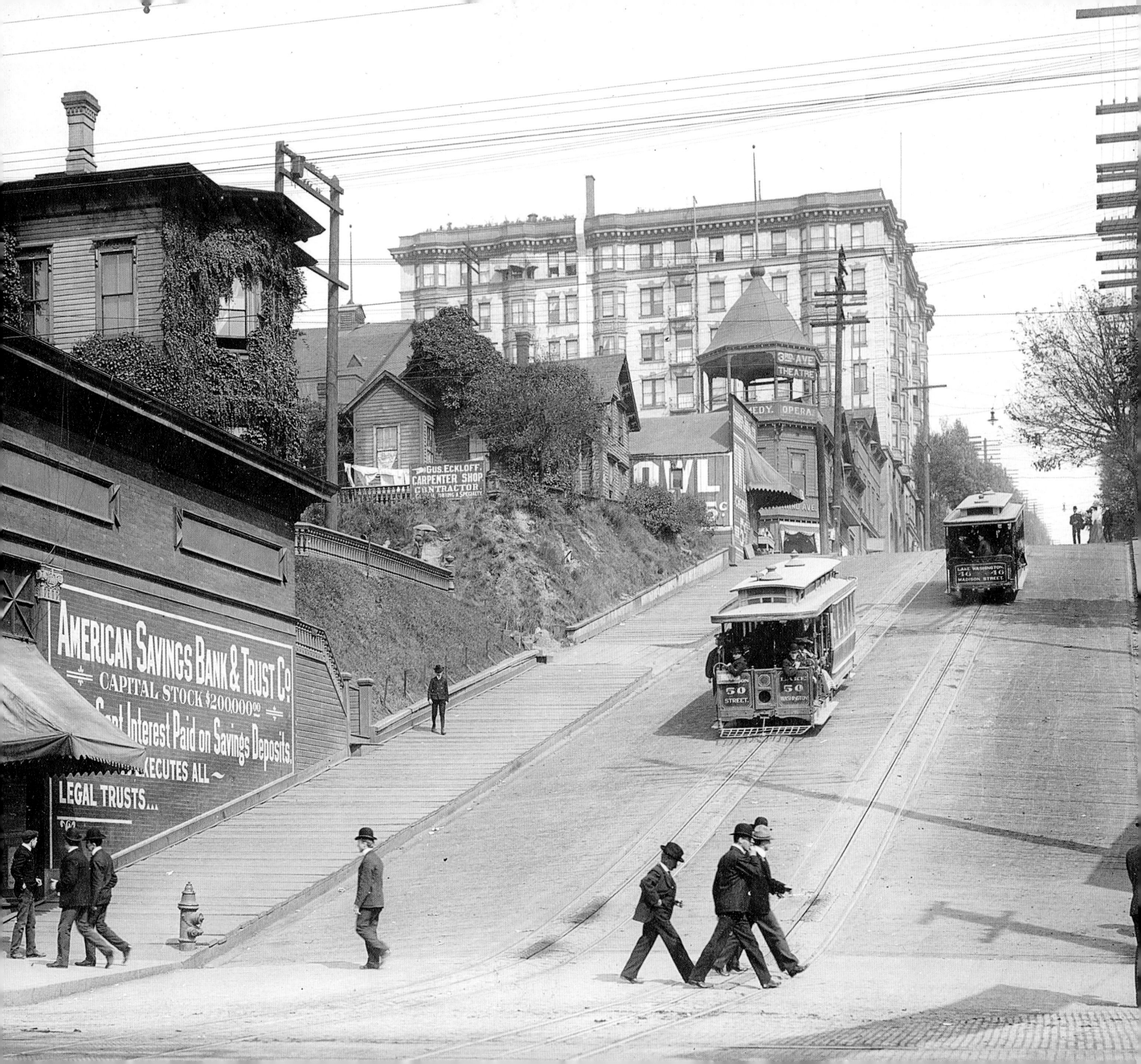

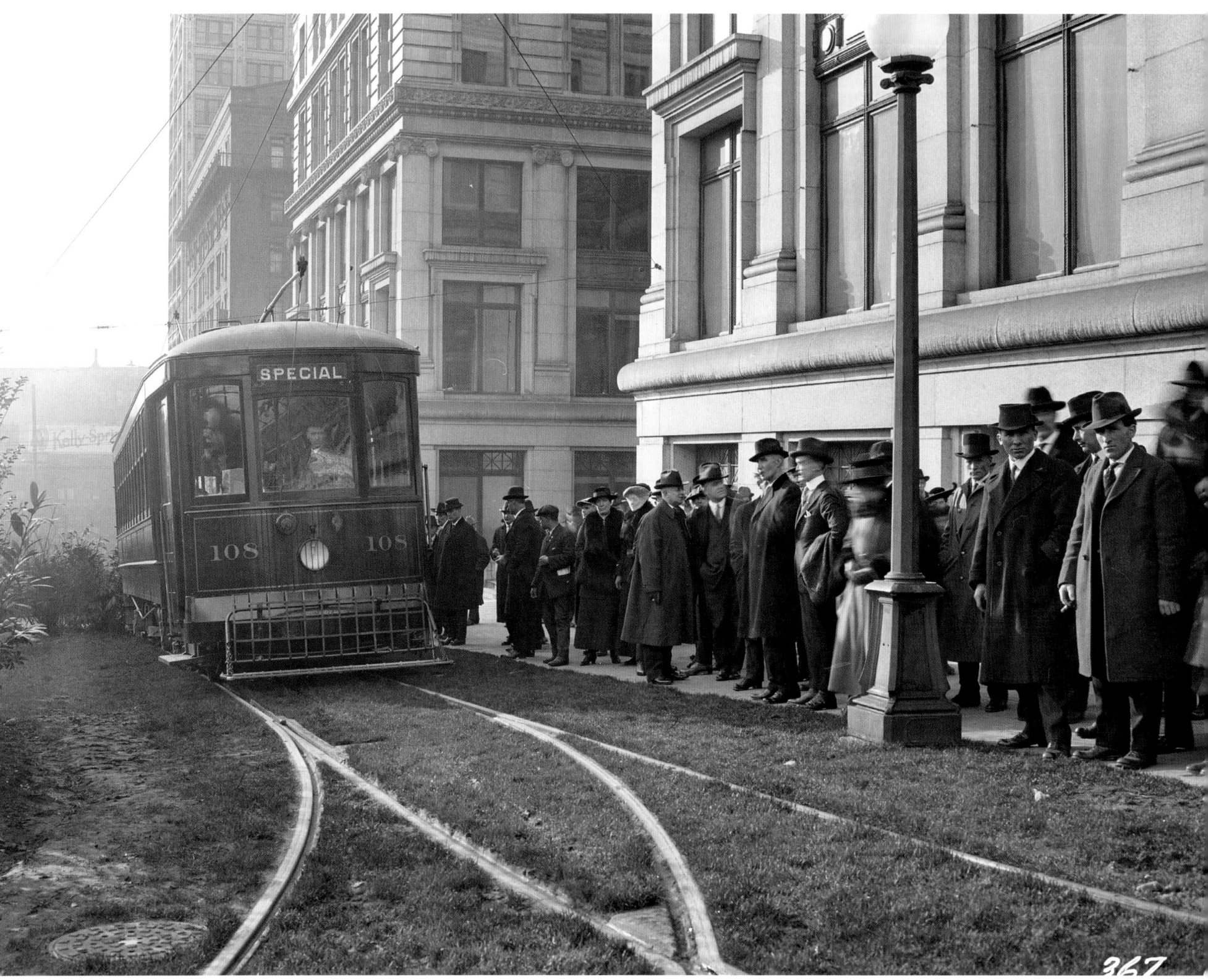

Streetcars SCRAPPED 1941

Seattle got a late start with streetcars. The first one ran on horse power in 1884, 50 years after they were running in New York.

Seattle was small and new, but with rapid growth at the end of the 19th century urban experimentation was perfectly suited. In 1889 the horses were replaced with electric traction, just a year after the first trolley service started in Virginia. Electricity was so new that Seattleites were afraid that it would arc uncontrollably from overhead lines to passersby and buildings, would magnetize pocket watches, and knockout horses that touched the rails.

By 1892, just three years later, 10 different lines snaked out into previously unsettled land. They ran out over trestles, paralleled streams, hugged the bottoms of hills and glided atop ridges. Like streetcars in other cities, they were funded by investors hoping to sell property.

For example, the West Street, Lake Union and Park Railway was built in 1890. It went down the bottom of the valley on the east foot of Denny Hill north to Lake Union and on trestles at the edge of Queen Anne Hill along Lake Union to the real estate venture at Fremont. This line was famous for being built to Lake Union in less than two weeks in order to beat out an extension of the Front Street cable on Westlake. The cable also gave up on their effort to reach Fremont over Queen Anne Hill. Electricity was the victor.

In 1898 Seattle's streetcar landscape changed forever. Jacob Furth, a major investor in many lines in their early days, began negotiating to purchase them outright. He consolidated almost all of Seattle's street railways under one new corporate umbrella, the Seattle Electric Company, completing acquisitions in 1901. The men behind the curtain funding him were Charles Stone and Edwin Webster, two MIT-trained engineers who ran an electricity management and consulting firm in Boston. Stone & Webster were careful to not hold direct ownership of SEC, hoping to avoid federal oversight. Instead, SEC paid the Boston firm for management services. The same shady arrangement took control of Tacoma, Everett, Bellingham and Olympia. Stone & Webster used the same loaded deck in cities across America.

It didn't take long for progressives in Seattle to get tired of the new monopoly. The first actionable plan came from James Moore in 1905 when SEC dragged its feet serving his real estate. He proposed creating a completely new system which would serve undeveloped areas of Seattle. The city council took the baton later in the year, challenging City Engineer Thomson to present a plan with a real price tag.

Thomson rolled it out in 1906, a new network of 40 lines along newly regraded and accessible

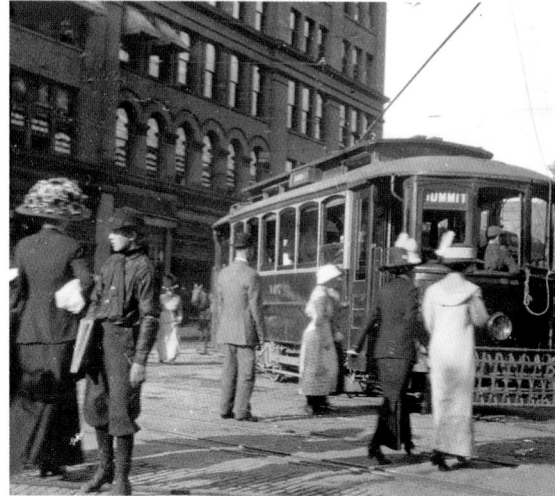

OPPOSITE PAGE *Inauguration of the first municipal line at the City/County Building in 1918.*

RIGHT *A car turns onto Pike Street on its way to Capitol Hill.*

BELOW *Guy Phinney's streetcar stands in 1891 where the south entrance to the Woodland Park Zoo is today.*

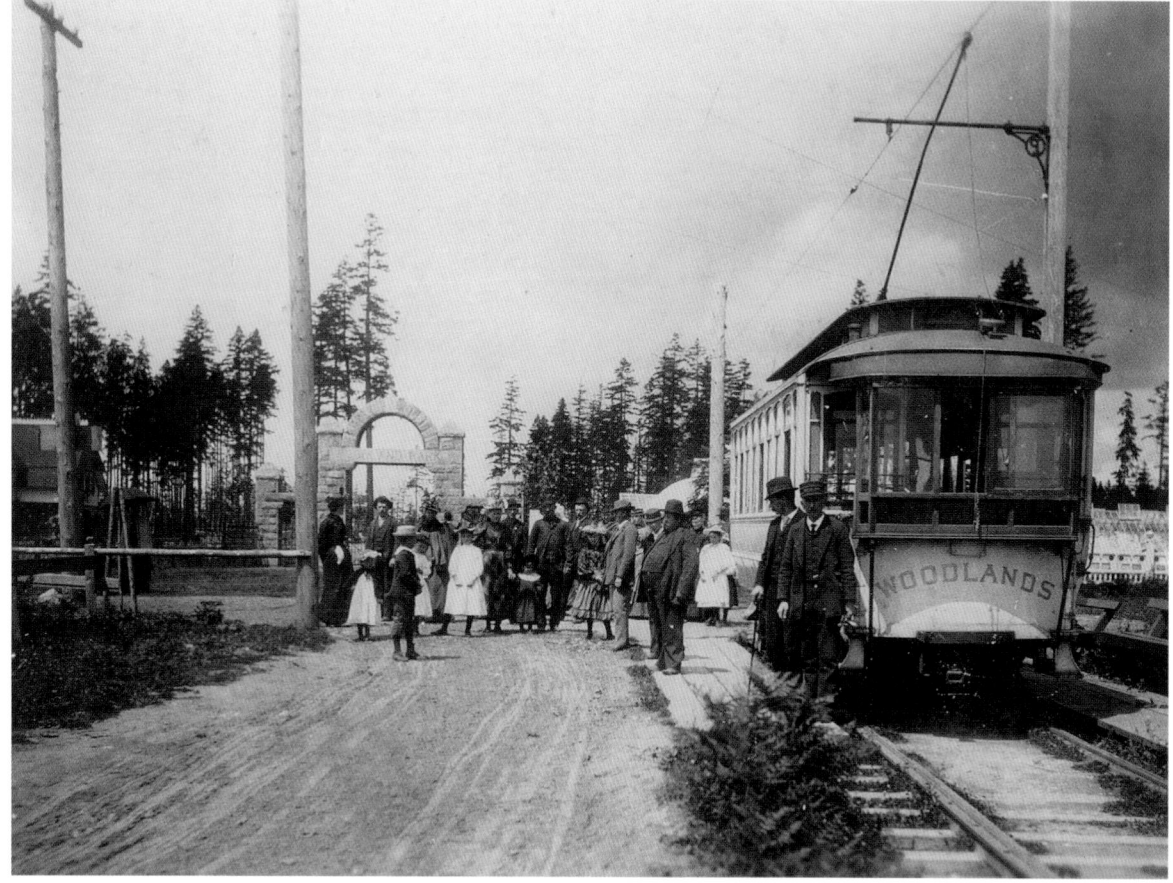

streets. An elevated viaduct would carry cars along the waterfront. Two hundred miles of railways spread like a web across the map.

The plan failed at the polls after an aggressive political campaign by SEC. The railway company took advantage of the free planning to put the public at ease with an array of new streetcar lines from 1907 to 1914. The seed was planted, though, and several attempts finally led to the City of Seattle purchasing the entire SEC system in 1919.

They paid too much. A grand jury found the Mayor guilty of stupidity but not conspiracy. The city was burdened with an incredible debt, forcing a choice between operating expenses and loan payments. By 1926 service was curtailed and all of the railway's bills and salaries paid in IOUs.

Things were bad in the Roaring '20s, and they became much worse financially in the 1930s during the Great Depression. The federal Works Progress Administration made funds available during the Depression for infrastructure construction. Seattle used it to concrete the street railway beds. But the city needed to remove debt.

Meanwhile, the auto industry was looking for revenue, and worked nationwide to get streetcar systems to convert to bus. Seattle citizens rejected the idea of conversion in 1937. But the Mayor worked out a deal the next year for the federal Reconstruction Finance Corporation to lend enough to pay off the remaining railway debt and also purchase a fleet of buses.

The final streetcar ran to Ballard on April 13, 1941.

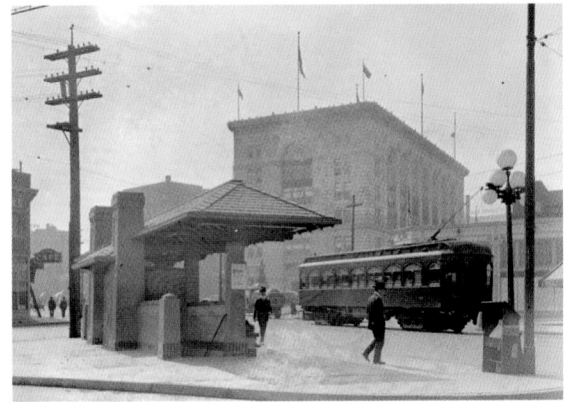

OPPOSITE PAGE *Two cars turn between the complex tracks at Second and Pike in front of MacDougall & Southwick.*

LEFT *A streetcar entering Times Square on Westlake passes the triangle's comfort station.*

BELOW *The raised tracks at Youngstown carried cars to West Seattle at about the same spot as the West Seattle Bridge today.*

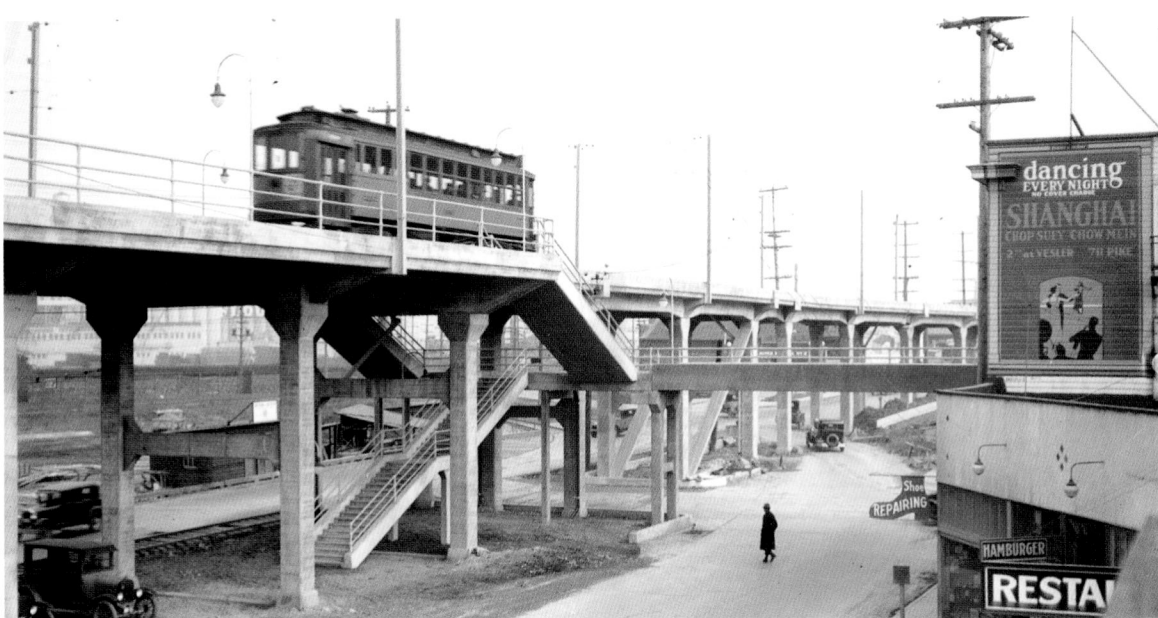

WATERFRONT STREETCAR

George Benson's streetcar ran for 20 years on Seattle's waterfront. No one can quite figure out why it's not running now. Benson grew up in Minneapolis in the 1920s and 30s infatuated with streetcars. He moved to Seattle in 1938, three years before the city scrapped rails for buses. But it was the worst of the Great Depression. Benson's job at G. O. Guy barely paid for food. Streetcars were a luxury that he could not afford, so he walked everywhere. Thirty-five years later, George Benson was a successful pharmacist and newly elected to the Seattle City Council in 1973. He still loved streetcars and immediately tried to convince Metro Transit to consider building a new streetcar line. The idea picked up the dismissive name "Benson's Folly." But he moved quickly, and by 1977 the pieces were in place. Northern Pacific agreed to let the city operate streetcars on an unused rail line along the waterfront from the Colman Dock ferry terminal to Elliott Bay Park (now Myrtle Edwards Park). Historic cars would come from Melbourne, Australia. Money came from the federal government, the city, and Metro Transit. After a few road bumps with financing, streetcars began running on May 29, 1983 amid great fanfare. The city named car 518 after George Benson. He named car 482 after his friend Robert Hively who gave him the idea for the streetcar. Of course no one was satisfied with the streetcars staying on the waterfront. Before the day was out there was already talk about a loop route to the Seattle Center. A short extension was built in 1990 with stops at Main Street in Pioneer Square and Fifth Avenue in the International District. Further extensions were studied to take the line north to Ballard or east to the Central District, with frequent public outreach for planning sessions. Suddenly in 2005 it was announced that the streetcar's maintenance building must be destroyed. It stood in the path of the Seattle Art Museum's Olympic Sculpture Park. Today the cars remain wrapped in plastic in a Metro warehouse.

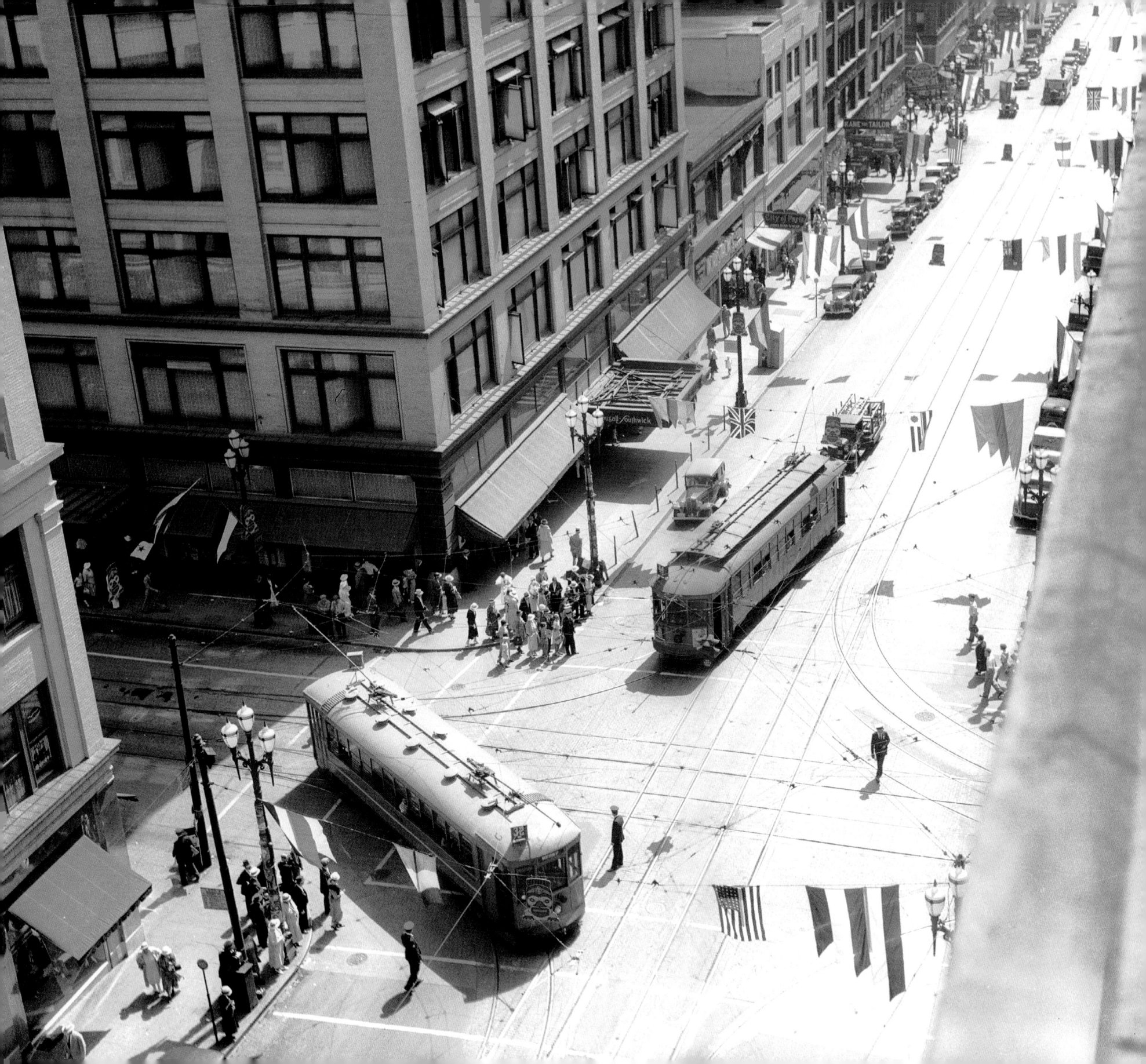

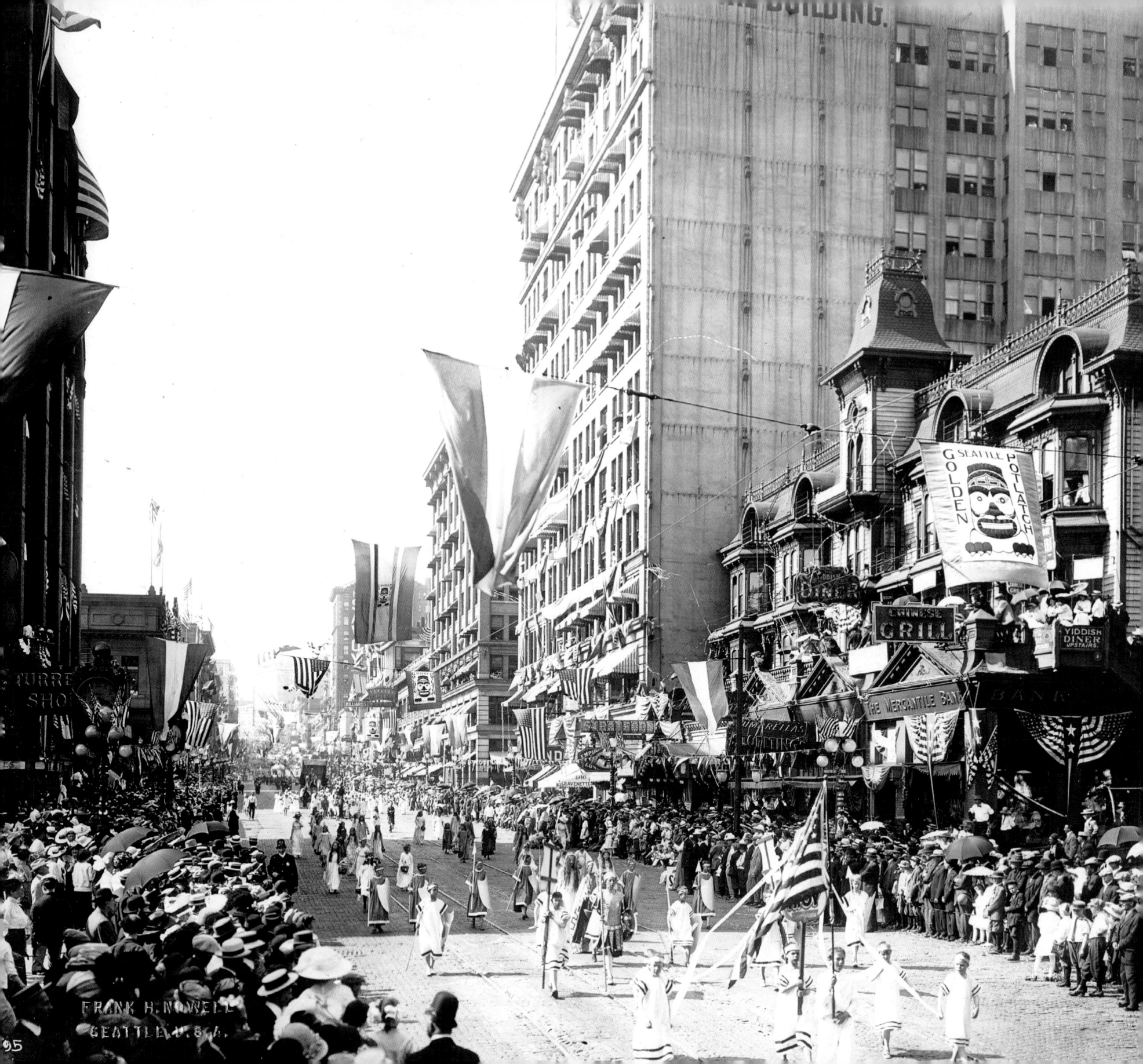

Golden Potlatch GOT TARNISHED 1941

Golden Potlatch was Seattle's summer festival in the early 1910s and late 1930s.

The term potlatch refers to a festival where the host invites all nearby peoples to join his celebration. It is a Chinook word and practiced by the Salish, Haida, Tlingit and other people who live in the coastal regions of Washington, British Columbia and Alaska.

The Golden Potlatch was born from the success of 1909's Alaska Yukon Pacific Exposition. In 1910 Seattle had no summer event while Portland held its fourth annual Rose Festival and San Francisco began the Portola Festival to showcase recovery from the 1906 earthquake. Like AYPE, Golden Potlatch would celebrate the gold which brought Seattle prosperity, differentiate Seattle through reinterpreted symbolism of native cultures, and invite people of nearby cities and towns to have fun.

The first Golden Potlatch in 1911 opened with the arrival of the steamer *Portland*, the vessel which carried two tons of gold into Seattle in 1897. It featured a float plane airshow by Curtiss Aeroplane, a display of Navy ships of the Pacific Fleet, and sailboat, cutter, and motorboat races. There were diving and canoeing competitions. And of course there were fireworks and a grand parade.

The festival grew in 1912. The Navy had created a new Pacific Reserve Fleet, leaving a number of ships permanently stationed at Bremerton on Puget Sound. These ships traveled across to Seattle for the five-day party. The Elks Club sponsored the first day of the event and major businesses from Broadway Auto to the New Washington Hotel funded publications and functions. The parade and all advertising featured a contrived totem pole-like costume that they called a Tillikum.

Things took a turn for the worse in 1913. On the first evening a fight broke out between a crowd of civilians on one side and three Fort Flagler artillerymen and two Bremerton-based sailors on the other. Thinking that socialists were to blame, a group of 70 sailors and soldiers gathered the next night and rioted across Seattle. They destroyed headquarters and meeting halls of the Socialist Party and the Wobblies. They shattered windows, broke down doors, and made bonfires out of books and pianos. A few month later Congress issued an apology and paid for the damages.

The Golden Potlatch was pared down to car and boat races and then forgotten during World War I.

Navy fleet visits began again after the war and were redefined in 1923. In that year the USS *Seattle*, homeported in Bremerton, became the flagship of the US Navy. Every summer party was rescheduled to coincide with Fleet Week, and more were added. The Elks held a party on the street outside their club building each night. The Naval Air Squadron put on an air show from Sand Point and President Warren Harding visited. The most odd spectacle was Americanus, a massive musical pageant depicting the history of America.

Seattle turned to the Golden Potlatch again during the Great Depression. In 1932 the Tillikums returned to Seattle, leading the parade at Fleet Week. The name Potlatch was used again to describe the summer festival: 1934's summer festival was the International Potlatch; 1939 was the Golden Jubilee Potlatch; and 1941 was the Aviation Potlatch.

After Japan forced America into World War II, the Potlatches were cancelled permanently.

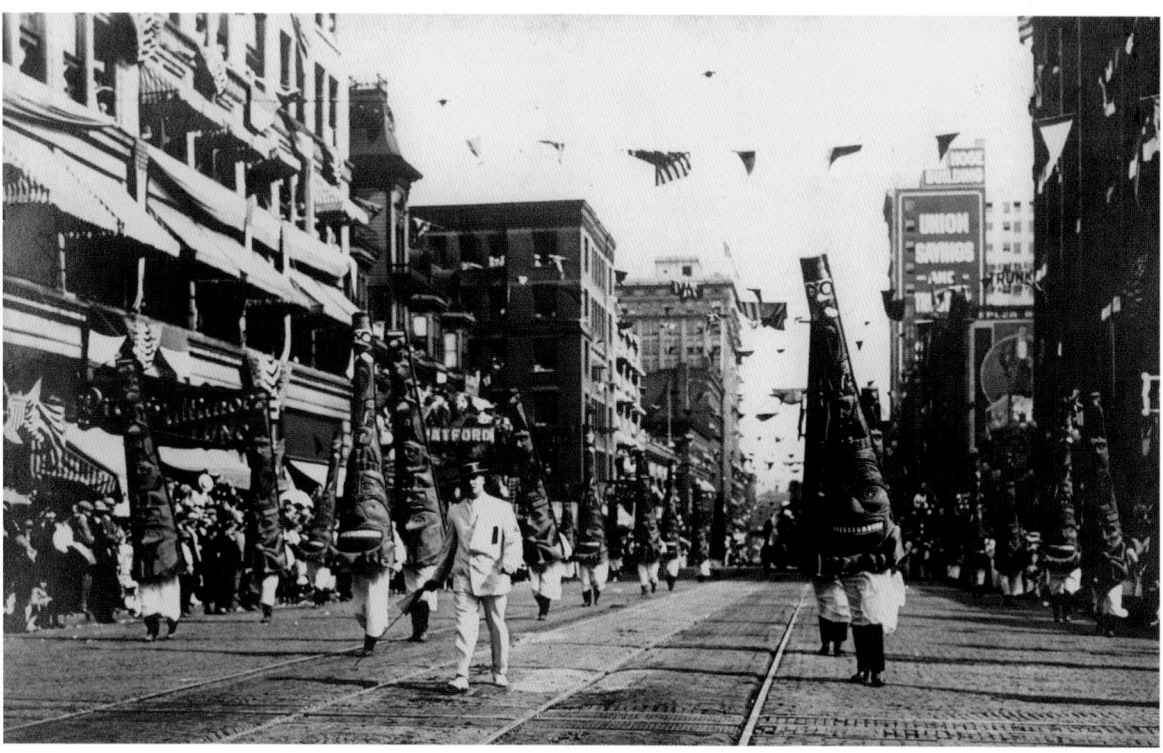

ABOVE *A float in the 1933 Potlatch parade after the name was brought back.*

LEFT *Children in playground units pass the Burke Building at Fourth and Madison in 1912.*

RIGHT *Festival officials don the Tillikum suit in the 1912 parade.*

Japantown WIPED OUT 1941

In 1888, Kyuhachi Nishii leased the Star Café and became the first recorded Japanese to settle in Seattle. Although they left no direct evidence, his kinsmen were already streaming into Seattle, filling the labor and service gap after Seattle's Chinese were run out of town. Nishii was displaced by the Great Fire, but the remaining Japanese population expanded quickly. There were just over 100 Japanese in 1890, and almost 3,000 by 1900.

By late 1891 local churches were holding Bible study classes mixed with English lessons. It was a win-win situation as the churches fulfilled their commitment to local mission work, and the Japanese learned English, built a support network, and often found jobs through fellow churchgoers. As the Japanese members of each church grew, they spun off their own congregations in Japantown. Eventually this included Baptist, Presbyterian, Episcopal, Methodist, Congregational, and Catholic churches among others.

The number of Japanese ballooned after 1896 when Japan's Nippon Yusen Kaisha Line began a freight shipping service from Yokohama to connect with the Great Northern Railway in Seattle. Early immigrants often intended to get rich quick and return to Japan after they'd saved enough money to set up businesses of their own. A noticeable portion of those that returned ended up back in Seattle again after their ventures failed, though, creating a sense of impermanence in every departure.

Japantown started inside the first Chinatown. Nishii's Star Café was located on Second Avenue South between Main and Washington. Another early merchant was Masahiro Furuya, whose store started at Third Avenue and Yesler Way in 1892 and moved into his own building at Second Avenue South and Washington Street in 1900. Along with Furuya's Japanese Commercial Bank, a number of businesses anchored the west end of Japantown in the area near Pioneer Square.

But as the community grew it spread up the side of Yesler Hill. After the Jackson Regrade began in 1907, new institutions like the Nippon Kan, Japanese Baptist Church, and Panama Hotel appeared around Sixth Avenue South and Main Street. Sixth and Main already had the miniature white castle that housed Maneki Restaurant. The intersection became the heart of Japantown, hosting Bon Odori festivals and other events.

Eventually it spread up Main Street across the south faces of Yesler Hill and First Hill all the way to 16th Avenue. Japanese in Seattle were unable to buy or rent in most parts of the city, so the majority lived within Japantown. Due to onerous immigration laws the flow of newcomers stopped in 1924, and the community population peaked at 8,500 before whithering during the Great Depression. But in its heyday during the early 1920s the community was a bubble of Japan landed in Seattle with men in yukata, women in kimono, smells of simmering broth or grilling mackerel, and the sounds of hundreds of businesses conducted in Japanese. The Japanese language newspapers, the school rooms, and the churches rang with the same group solidarity and community ethics that powered neighborhoods across Japan.

Japantown's difference in character from the rest of the city revealed itself through the ratio of self-employment. In the 1930s, almost half of Japanese in Seattle owned a small business or private practice. Only 6 percent of all Americans did so. In Japantown there were banks, jewelers, bakeries, barber shops, theaters, hotels, bathhouses, law offices, candy stores, physicians, dentists, tailors, general stores, and many other types of businesses. It was an entrepreneurial and service-oriented neighborhood.

Many of those business owners lost everything when the Japanese Commercial Bank went bankrupt in 1931. By the mid-1930s, the west end of Japantown was filled with vacant frame houses. The scattered tenants were mostly prostitutes calling to passersby with a rap on the window. City government wiped out this area in 1941 to create the Yesler Terrace housing project. Bigger changes were yet to come.

In February, 1942, Seattle's residents of Japanese descent were forced from their homes and businesses. The United States government's actions are varyingly referred to as internment, expulsion, imprisonment, or concentration camps. For three years these U.S. citizens and residents were held against their will.

When they were freed, there was no community in Seattle to return to. Some went home regardless, but many decided to begin new chapters of their lives in other neighborhoods or cities. Those that returned to Seattle felt compelled to prove their patriotism and suppress the traditions which made them stand out.

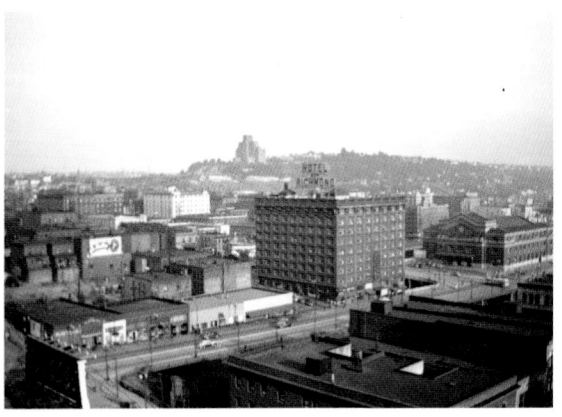

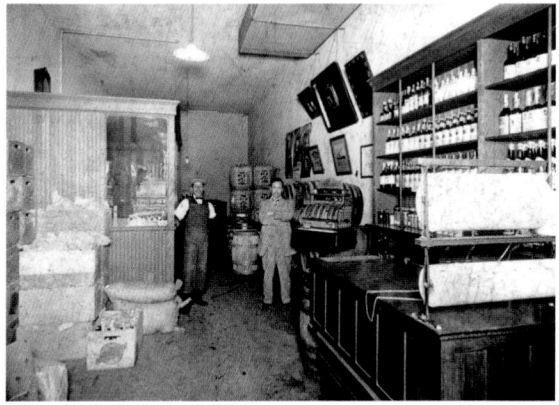

RIGHT *The Kanemoto family barbershop in the former Hotel Fujii at Maynard and King. The Kanemotos sent their children to live with relatives in Hiroshima during their formative years.*

FAR LEFT *Japanese businesses and housing mixed with Chinese and Filipinos in the gap between First and Beacon hills.*

LEFT *K. Setsuda Importers, near Sixth and Main.*

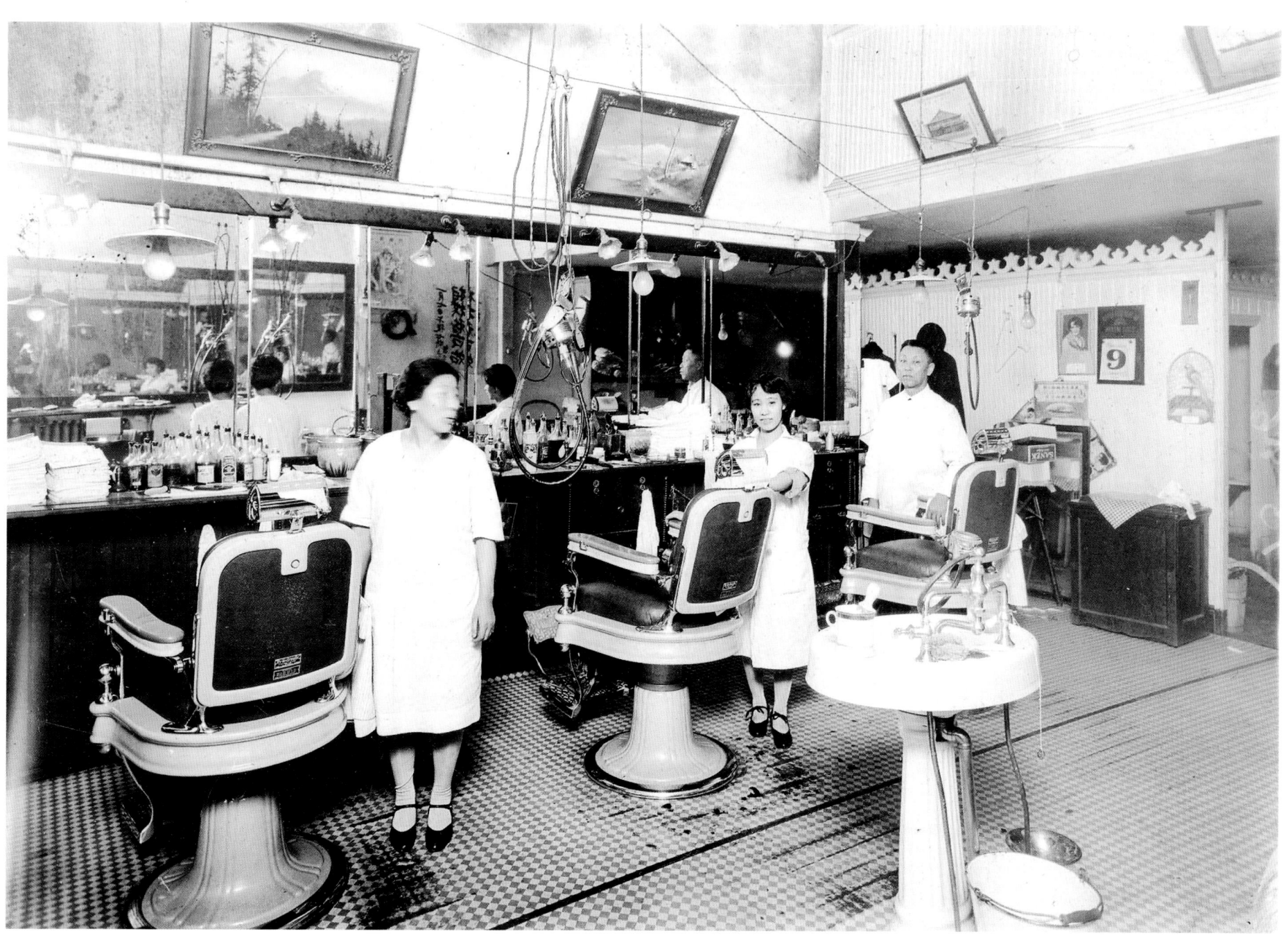

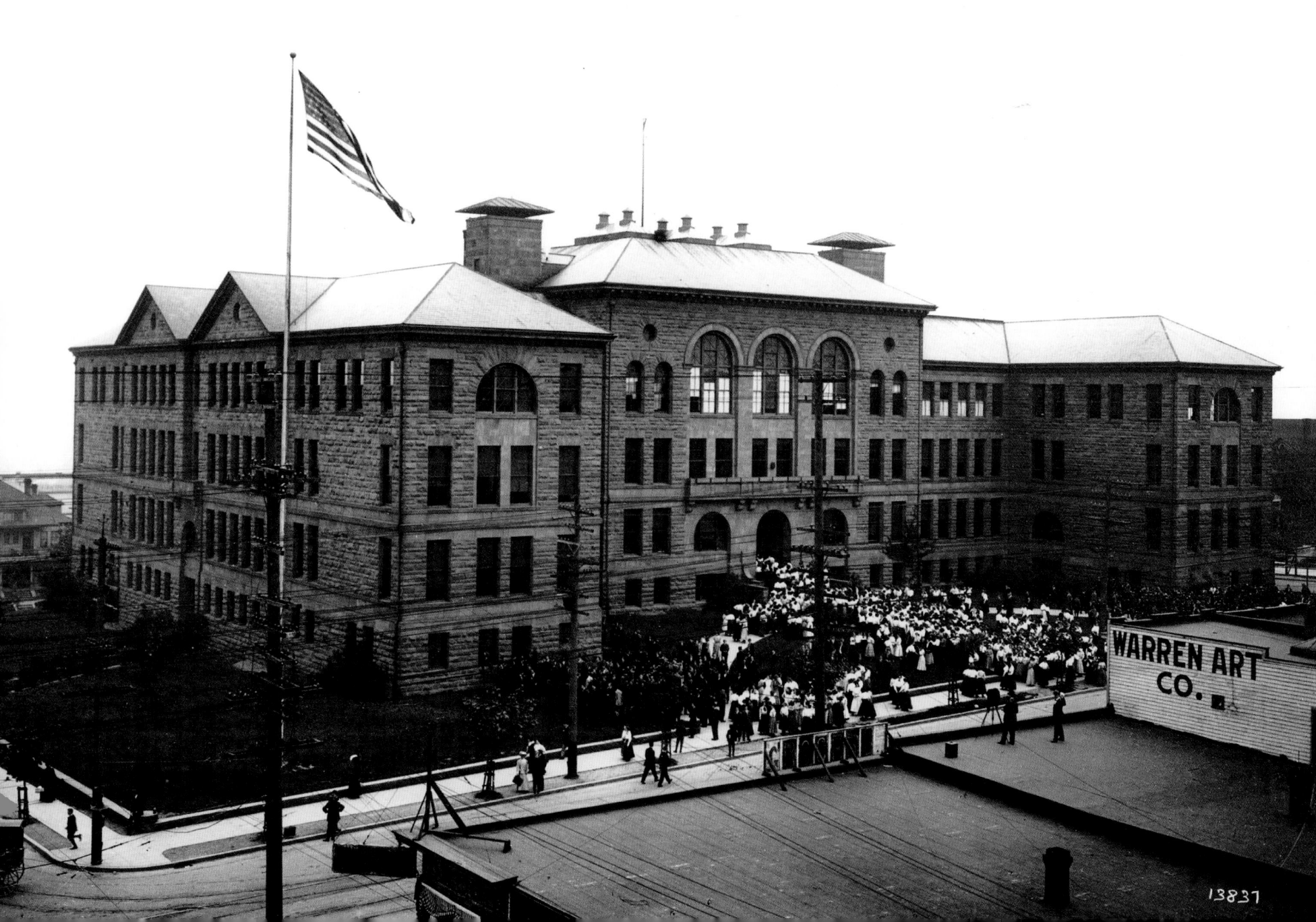

Broadway High School
GRADUATED 1946

Broadway High was Seattle's first dedicated high school. As Seattle grew, its children grew up too. The first high school classes were held at the Territorial University in 1876. Classes met in the Central School's second and third buildings in the 1880s and 1890s. But demographic data and Seattle's constant annexations indicated that a large, special-purpose high school building would soon be needed.

In 1902 Seattle High School opened on Broadway, between Pike Street and Olive Street. It was soon renamed Broadway High as high schools opened in growing communities from West Seattle to Wallingford.

Evening classes were added in 1920 for young adults to complete their high school diploma. A new building was added to expand the shop, electrical and mechanical programs in 1921. In 1930 these were folded into the new Edison Vocational School, which offered skills training to adults searching for a new career in the Great Depression.

One quarter of the high school's population disappeared in 1942, when Japantown's residents were forced into secluded prison camps. Adult training expanded at Edison though, as the War Department needed workers to replace military draftees and to fill expanding industry.

As veterans returned from the war in mid-1945, Broadway High began offering catch-up classes for G.I.s hoping to get their free college education. This

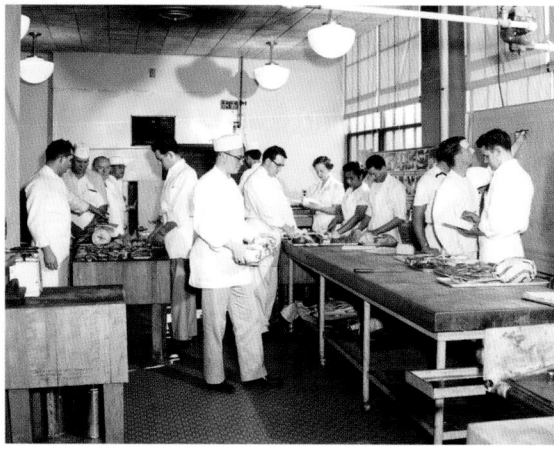

was so successful that the following May administrators announced that Broadway High would close and the building would be dedicated to veterans' and vocational programs.

The Capitol Hill community joined Broadway alumni, current students and many other groups to fight the change. But in the fall students were transferred to Garfield, Lincoln and Queen Anne high schools.

Eventually Seattle Community College replaced the technical school. In 1974 all buildings but the 1911 auditorium expansion were torn down.

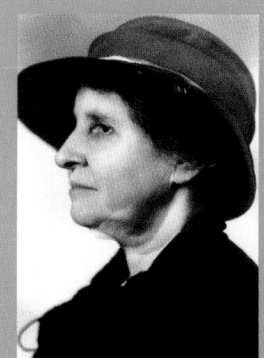

ADELE PARKER

Broadway High School's civics and economics teacher was representative of the school's energetic and progressive staff. Adele Parker came to Seattle with her parents in 1886 at age 17. Her father was a lumberman and land developer, and also involved in progressive politics. While teaching high school Adele Parker graduated in 1903 from the University of Washington's new law school. Of course she used this new expertise to improve her curriculum. But she also was an active member of Seattle's women's suffrage movement and an activist for good government. She campaigned for women's voting rights for 20 years leading up to the successful 1910 election, including writing articles for a regional magazine. Parker also wrote the Seattle city charter amendments for initiatives, referendums, and recall. Recall was used in 1911 to kick out Mayor Hiram Gill and clean up his corrupt cronies. In 1921 she resigned from Broadway High and set off for Moscow in Soviet Russia, where she hoped to write a book describing the economic and political experiment as it unfolded. She planned six weeks to arrive there, but it took more than a year of travel through Siberia and Russia including two deportations. Along the way she married one of her fellow travelers, hydraulic engineer Kay Bennett. Back in Seattle, Adele Parker Bennett was elected as State Representative for King County in 1935.

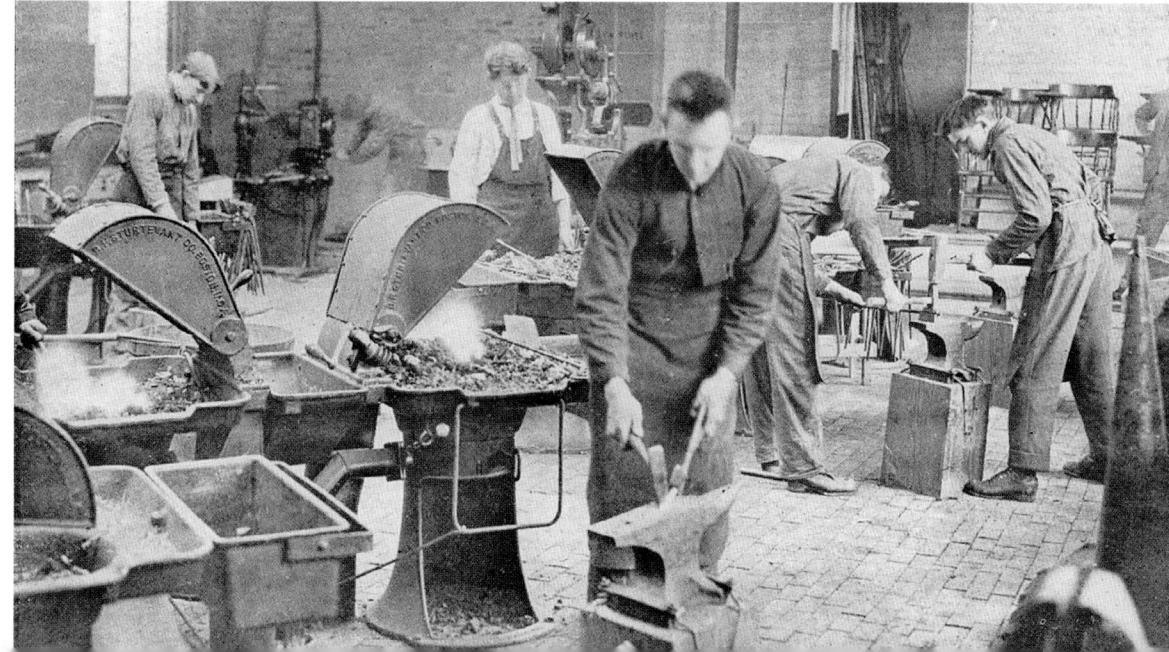

ABOVE LEFT *The culinary program at Edison in 1955.*

LEFT *High school students learning blacksmithing in 1919.*

OPPOSITE PAGE *Students pour through the high school's Broadway front doors.*

Firland Sanatorium RELOCATED 1947

Firland Sanatorium was Seattle's first public tuberculosis hospital, located in a bucolic setting north of the city.

The effort to treat tuberculosis in Seattle got started in 1907, with the death of Sarah Loretta Denny. Denny was the sister of Seattle founder Arthur Denny, and joined his family after they had established themselves on Elliott Bay in the 1850s. Over the years she accumulated quite a portfolio of real estate holdings for herself while donating her time and energy. In her will Denny left funds for a long list of causes, including $10,000 to establish a tuberculosis hospital. In 1908 the Denny Pulmonary Hospital was built south of Seattle on a bluff above the Duwamish River at the town of Riverton.

The Riverton hospital was private and only

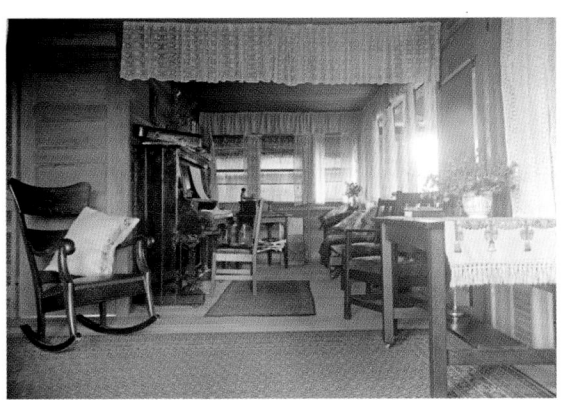

served wealthy patients. Soon after it opened a movement began to create a public hospital. The King County Anti-Tuberculosis League was founded for this purpose, with local banker H. C. Henry as its president. Henry's son suffered from pulmonary tuberculosis, making the issue personal to him.

The League secured use of a plot of land on the west side of Queen Anne Hill and in early 1909 began preparing supplies and tents to run their summer hospital. When nearby residents learned of the coming hospital, they were up in arms. Protests were lobbied, pamphlets were printed, and eventually a troop of women went to personally harass and block the wagons delivering the first load of goods for the hospital.

The Anti-Tuberculosis League regrouped, deciding not to continue the dispute. They put on a display at the Alaska Yukon Exposition to raise awareness and hoped to win over their fellow citizens. That winter Henry's son Walter died of the disease and Henry took immediate action.

OPPOSITE PAGE *The Walter Henry Administration Building.*

LEFT *A lounge with piano and phonograph.*

BELOW LEFT *Most patients had private rooms but communal rooms were used at times.*

BELOW *The children's hospital in Josef House.*

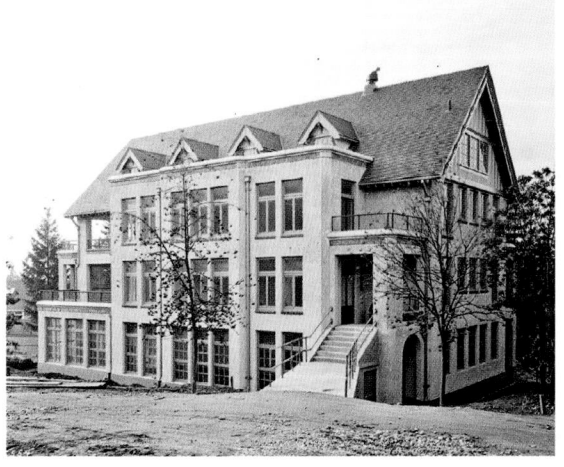

In 1910 Henry donated his own land near Richmond Highlands, 14 miles north of Seattle, and donated $25,000 in the memory of his son Walter. A successful political campaign led to more than 80 percent of Seattleites voting to fund the hospital. In 1911 it opened briefly as the Walter Horace Henry Hospital, and then changed its name to Firland in 1912.

State funding followed in 1914, paying for operations in the growing complex of buildings. Replacing temporary cabins, the buildings were all designed by Seattle's City Architect Daniel Huntington in English Tudor style. The Walter Henry Administration Building had the kitchen, surgery and living quarters for nurses. The Detweiler Building was the main hospital. A small children's building was created using funds raised by Seattle's school children selling flowers. The city also created Jenner Hall, which replaced the Beacon Hill isolation hospital for very infectious diseases. Separately, a small hospital was built for prostitutes with venereal diseases.

In 1927 a 50-bed supplement to the children's building was constructed, named Josef House after patient Josef Hansen. Hansen's tuberculosis had already reached an advanced stage when he was brought to Firland. A childless fisherman, he had accumulated some savings and property. He found the play of the children at the hospital both charming and saddening. Because he knew that he would never recover from his own illness, he asked his estate be used for the children's benefit.

Firland provided much of the needs for the kitchen from onsite farms, including eggs, chicken, and pork. The Henry Building featured an industrial bakery allowing the hospital to provide its own bread. Each day patients ate a morning meal of fruit, cereal, eggs, toast and milk. Dinner was served before noon and included meat, potatoes, vegetables, bread, and dessert. A light supper was served at four.

By 1946, Firland boasted 250 patient beds for adults and children. Firland was moved south to a former Navy hospital in 1947, merging with two King County tuberculosis hospitals. The hospital took a turn for the worse after departing from its rustic setting. It became one of the most aggressive hospitals in the nation in the use of confinement, forced hospitalization and forced elective surgery.

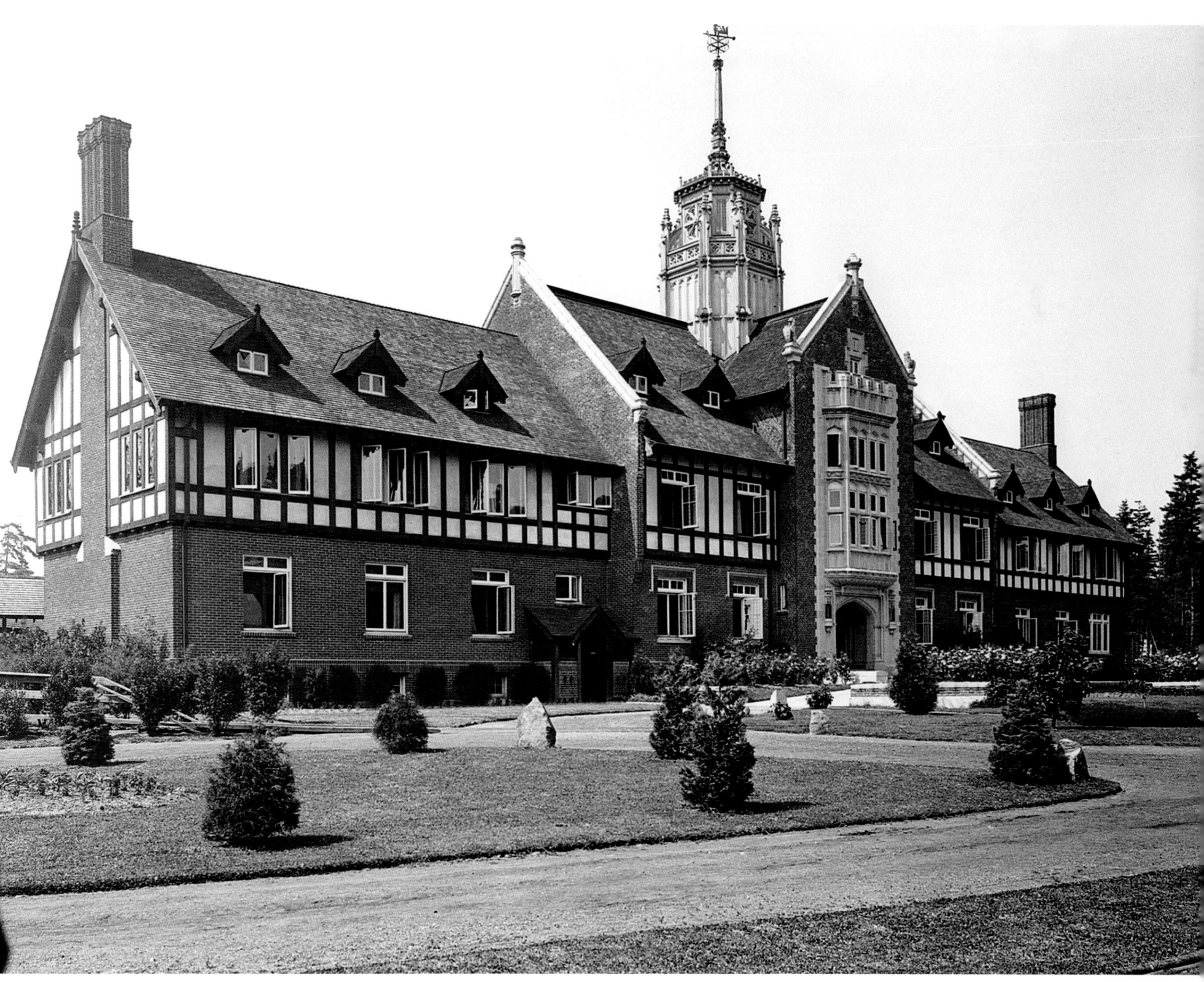

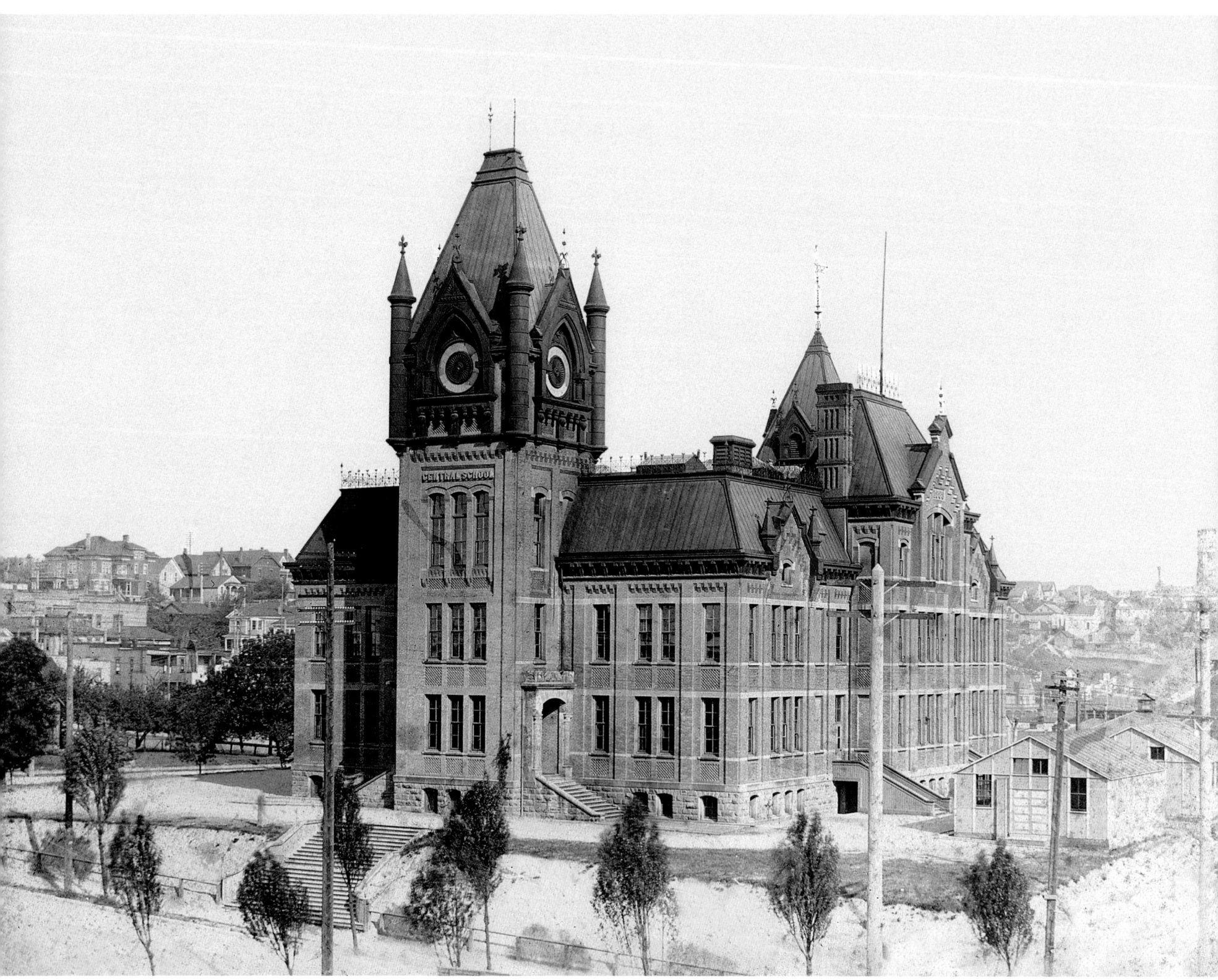

Central School SHAKEN LOOSE 1949

Seattle School District's Central School stood watch over downtown from its perch at Sixth Avenue and Madison Street for 60 years.

In early 1888 the second Central School was destroyed by fire, and its replacement was built entirely in brick. It taught an important lesson to Seattle. While the third Central was finishing construction, the Great Fire ravaged the business district below it.

The schoolhouse held elementary school students on the first two floors and high school students on the third floor. Despite being the biggest of Seattle's handful of schools, it still wasn't big enough. Vacant churches, synagogues, and meeting halls across downtown were rented as annexes for classes. Many students got to experience a new building each year. To make space for some of the annex classes, the school district moved the high school students to their own school on Broadway in 1902.

The building boom after World War I began to reduce enrollment at Central, a trend that continued for two decades. Families moved to the suburbs as offices and hotels replaced homes downtown and on First Hill. Finally in 1938 the Central School was closed, and it became a branch of Broadway's Edison Vocational School.

In 1949 a major earthquake shook Seattle. The Central School building was hit hard and two large chunks of brick cornice fell to the earth. One of them crashed through a neighboring portable. Fifty children had just gone outside to play, narrowly avoiding a disaster. The old school building was demolished soon after.

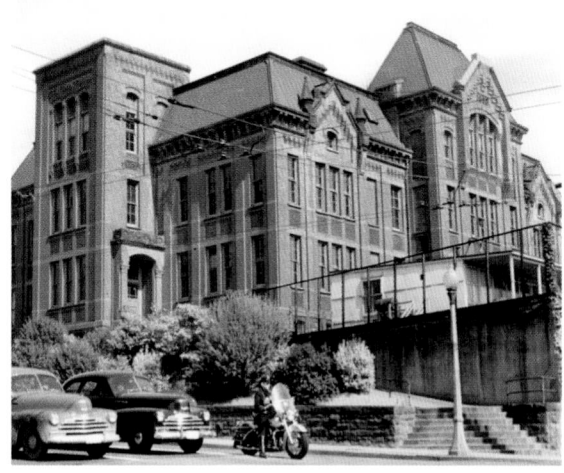

PRINCIPAL JOSEPH WIDMER

One fixture of the Central School was principal Joseph Widmer. He was from Eugene, Oregon, oldest of four children of German immigrant farmers. His parents worked hard and put all of the children through school at the University of Oregon. Joseph obtained his bachelor of arts in 1890 and continued for a M.A. in 1893. Joseph moved to Seattle after graduation and took the position of principal of the Latona School in 1893. His sister Margaret joined him after finishing her degree in 1898 and taught at a variety of Seattle schools for a decade before heading to California. Another sister, Gertrude, joined them in 1900 and also took a teaching position with the school district. Joseph transferred to principal of the Central School in 1902. For 30 years he watched over each recess with kindness. He engaged with the students and took an interest in their lives. By 1931 he had become very involved with the community of his Japanese students. The parents pooled money and funded a trip for Joseph to visit Japan, where he would lecture on American schools and also learn firsthand about the heritage of his students. Two dozen students stood in kimono at the pier waving flags as principal Widmer set off on the steam liner *Hikawa Maru*. Tragically, Joseph Widmer died of a heart attack in Kyoto in the final days of his trip. Despite caring for so many children, neither Joseph nor his siblings had children of their own. Each of them left their estate to the University of Oregon. They are all buried with their parents at the Odd Fellows cemetery in Eugene.

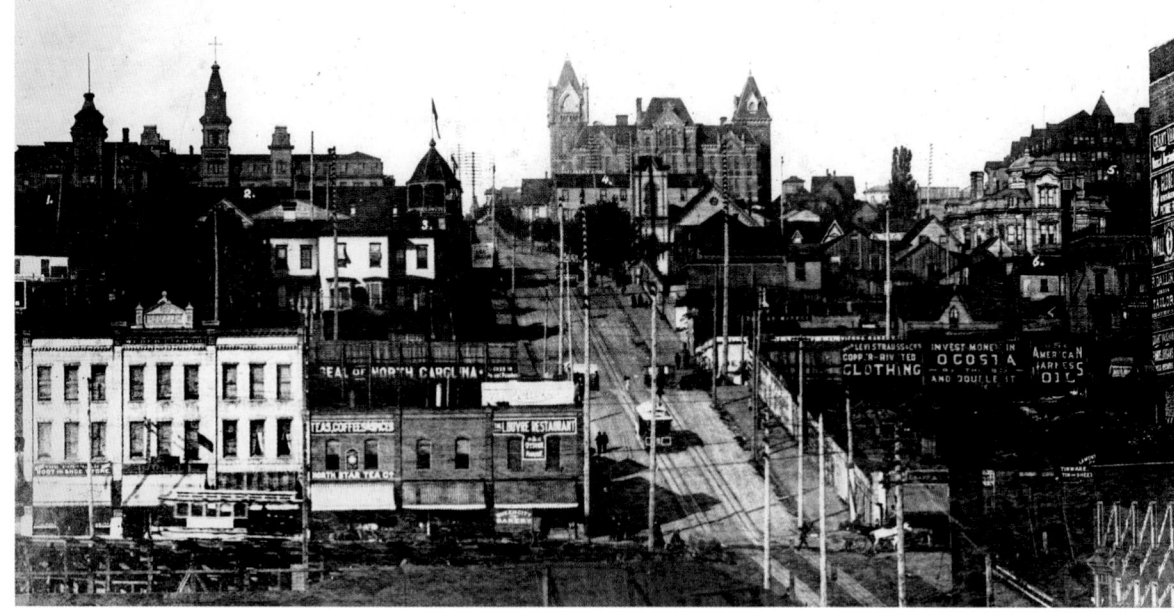

ABOVE LEFT *The building in its final days with the clock towers removed.*

LEFT *The school stood above downtown, seen here in 1895.*

OPPOSITE PAGE *Looking south over Madison Street the school is seen at its best.*

Carnegie Central Library REPLACED 1957

The Seattle Public Library's rented home in the former Yesler Mansion burned down in the early morning of January 2, 1901. Four days later, the *Seattle Post-Intelligencer* announced that Andrew Carnegie would donate $200,000 for a new building.

In 1886 Carnegie began purchasing library buildings for towns and cities around the country. He was one of the richest people in America, but had grown up in a working-class family. His life was changed through access to books, and he wanted to provide the same opportunity to others. He decided that he could best do this by creating libraries throughout the country. Any community in need would contact Andrew Carnegie to fund a new building.

The speed of Seattle's funding was due to a courtship between Carnegie and the library board which had been going on for almost two years. When the library began renting the Yesler Mansion in 1899, it was clear that they needed a permanent, purpose-built home. Librarian Charles Smith was first to contact Carnegie through friends of friends. Then library supporters began contacting Carnegie directly. Correspondence with his secretary suggested that Seattle target $50,000 for their request, based on the city's relatively small population.

On the morning of January 2, 1901, library supporter and *Seattle Post-Intelligencer* editor Joseph Pyle sent a short telegram to Carnegie informing of the dire situation and asking for Carnegie to fund a replacement. And he asked directly for $200,000, much more than previously discussed and more than the $2.00 per person formula that Carnegie used as a limit for funding libraries. Carnegie was reluctant at first but was won over by arguments of Seattle's fast growth and by the large operational budget that was promised. Eventually he would add another $20,000 as the project went over budget.

Within weeks of the fire, the library temporarily moved into the Territorial University which the Seattle Art League vacated for them. After funding was announced from Carnegie, many ideas were considered for the new library building. James Moore suggested reusing the old university grounds to build a City Beautiful cluster of civic buildings, including a new post office, city/county

building and museum. The university site proved off limits, but the idea of colocating the city hall and library persisted for more than a year. Finally the library board took unilateral action and purchased the block between Madison and Spring, Fourth and Fifth to build their new home.

After construction difficulties, the new neoclassical, Beaux Arts building finally opened in December of 1906. The luxurious building greatly expanded the library's functions and offered several new capacities. It was designed to circulate like an office building rather than a residence. The open shelf reading room expanded to 25,000 volumes. The library bindery, already an essential function after almost a decade of service, expanded its capacity to binding more than 60 books per day. Newspaper and magazine reading rooms were lavish and met the library's mission of providing a place for people to come and read who may not have had the opportunity elsewhere. An art gallery on the top floor presented paintings from the collections of prominent citizens like Fred Sander.

The building served Seattle for half a century. It was expanded, remodeled, and filled with more

than four million volumes. It added books for the blind, mobile services and a foreign language collection. During World War II, books were shipped from the central library to Seattleites of Japanese birth or descent imprisoned first in Puyallup's Camp Harmony and then in Idaho's Minidoka.

By 1948 the library board was convinced that the building could not last much longer. It was in extreme disrepair from lack of maintenance during the 15 years of the Great Depression and World War II. And it no longer supported the programmatic needs of a library which now spent most of its acquisitions money on films and records. It took time to secure funding. Finally in 1957 the library was moved to temporary quarters and the old Central Library was demolished for a new, modern structure.

RIGHT *The west facade on Fourth Avenue with fountain, stairs, and terrace added in 1910 after Fourth Avenue was dropped.*

BELOW *The library's bindery expanded significantly in the new building.*

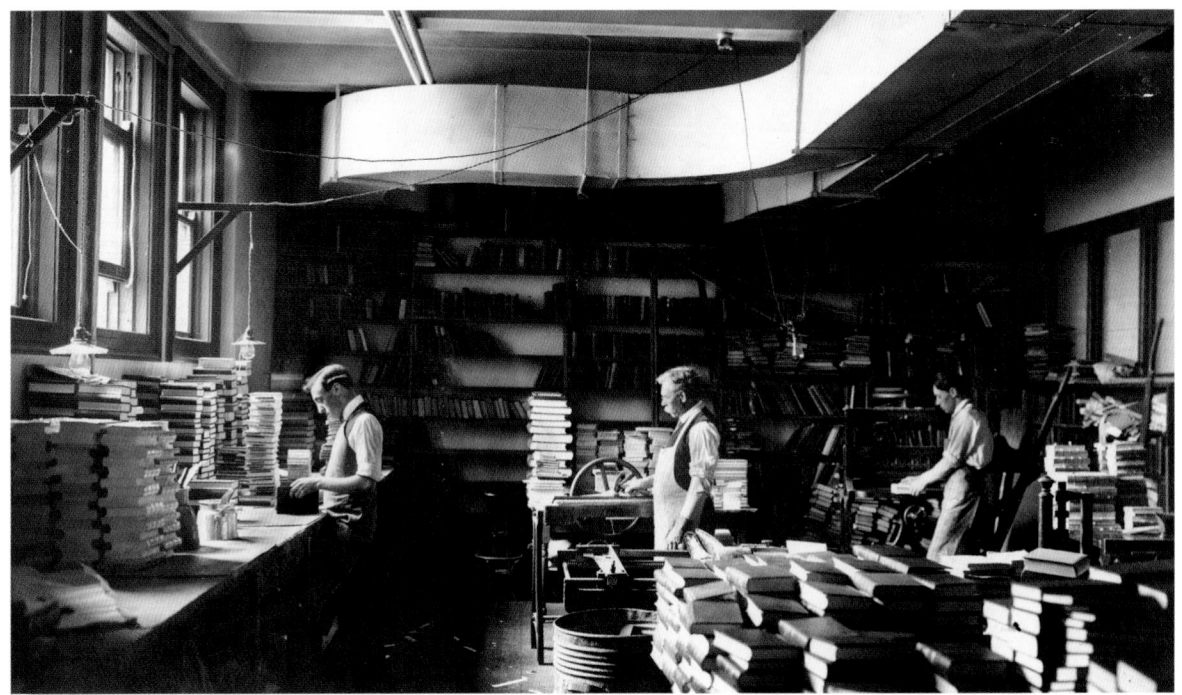

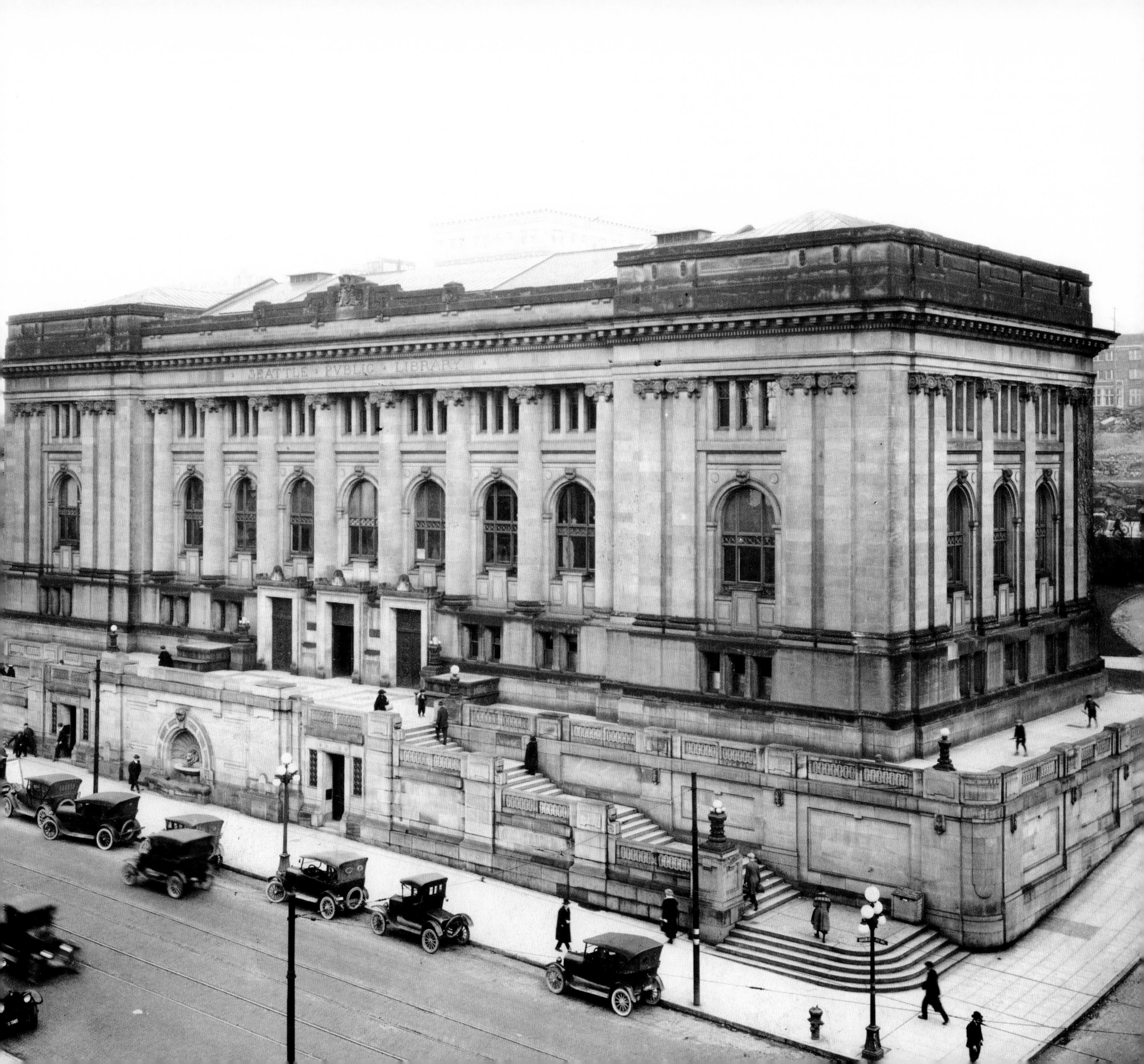

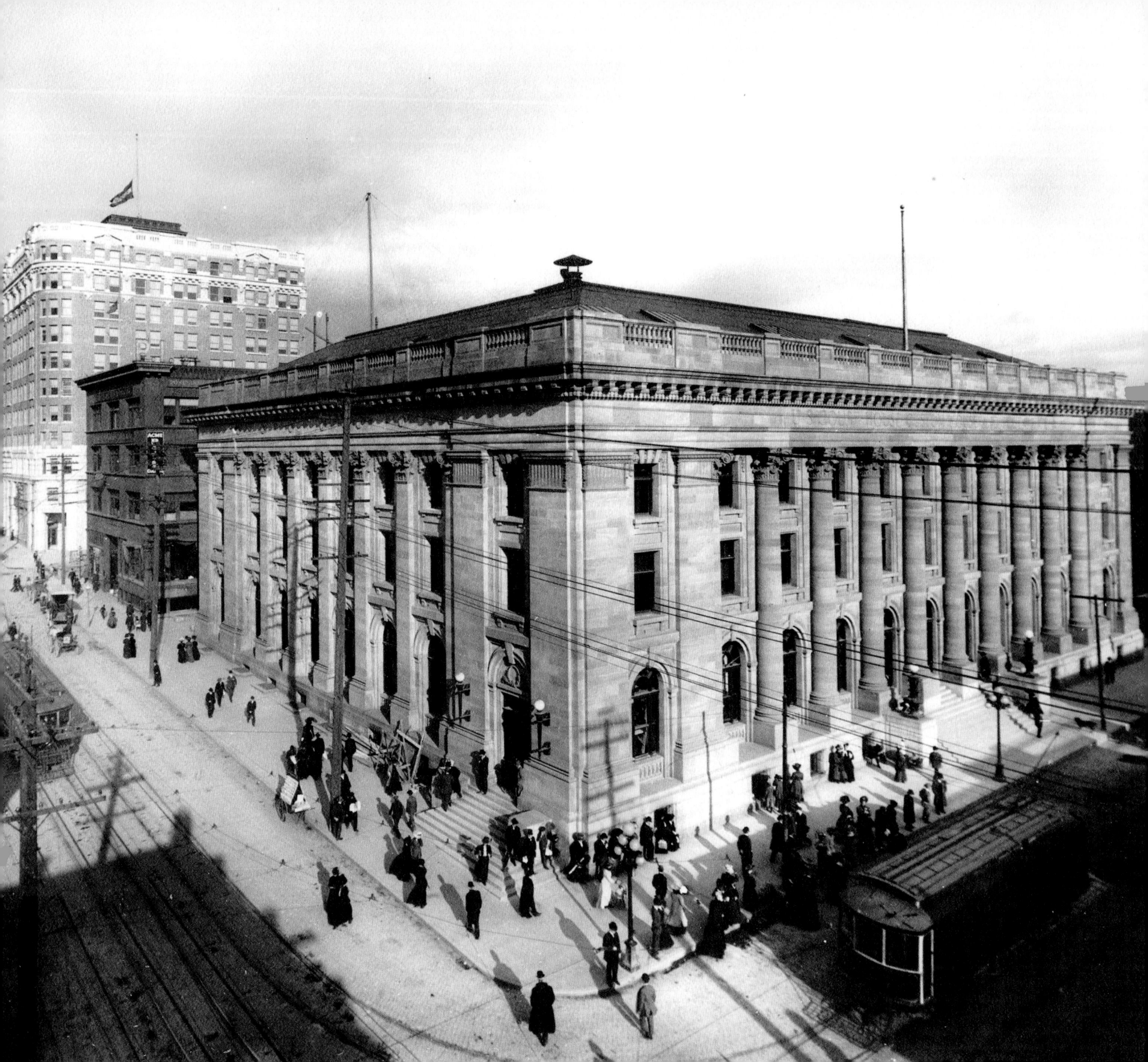

First Federal Building DEMOLISHED 1958

The first federally-owned building in Seattle was a Beaux Arts classical landmark at Third Avenue and Union Street.

Construction started in 1903, taking six years to finish. In the interim, Seattle's population more than doubled from 110,000 to 280,000. The first problems were with the stone contractor in Bellingham, because the quarried stone was initially too low quality. Then construction was paused to wait for the Third Avenue regrade. As interior work wrapped up, it became increasingly difficult to get marble from Vermont. All along, the Treasury Department architects kept changing plans, causing more delays.

In mid-November 1908 the Post Office opened, just in time for the Christmas rush. The Post Office occupied the first floor and basement, and for many employees it was the first time that they worked in natural light in more than a decade. The transition was a testament to planning and execution, as 300 employees flawlessly made deliveries and carried out their work on opening day.

The next week the Customs Department moved from the Colman Building to the second floor, but not every tenant got in so quickly. It took until April 1909 before the District Court was able to enter their space, and even that was forced. Along with it came the local U.S. Attorney and offices for the judges and other court workers. They were cramped into half of their space as piles of marble lay waiting to be installed.

The Post Office's facilities were overwhelmed by customers in 1909. The hundreds of thousands of visitors to the Alaska Yukon Pacific Exposition often stayed for days or weeks, and many told correspondents to simply address them in Seattle. Then they visited daily to see if anything new had arrived for them. The postmaster timed lines at more than 45 minutes to get from the sidewalk to the window.

Before the building was finished newspapers were already clamoring for larger facilities. The first crunch came in 1911, when the Justice Department opened a Seattle field office for the FBI. Several judges' offices were moved out to make space for them.

Departments were gradually transferred out of the building to make more space. In 1915 the Post Office opened an annex station for mail sorting near rail terminals. Located at Second Avenue and King Street, this facility received bulk mail bags from ships and trains. Many of these were already labeled for shipment to Chicago, Alaska, or other destinations for further sorting. Instead of trucking them to the main Post Office, they were routed closer to their source.

In 1923 the Passport and Civil Service Bureau moved out to make space for the District Attorney to expand. With no federally owned office space, they began renting. At that point the yearly federal rent paid in Seattle was $110,000. Congress was lobbied to expand the Federal Building to eight floors, but funds were not appropriated.

However, that effort did result in the creation of a new home for the assay office and immigration station, and for completion of a new Federal Office Building. Built in 1932 at First Avenue and Madison Street, it took in all departments except the post office and those affiliated with the district court. At the end of the Great Depression in 1940, a new Federal Courthouse opened at Fourth Avenue and Spring Street, Seattle's first modernist building. With no other government departments located at the original Federal Building, it began to be referred to simply as the Post Office.

In 1958 Seattle's main Post Office was demolished. A new, modern post office was built in its stead along with the 21-story Washington Building, first of the new developments on the Metropolitan Tract.

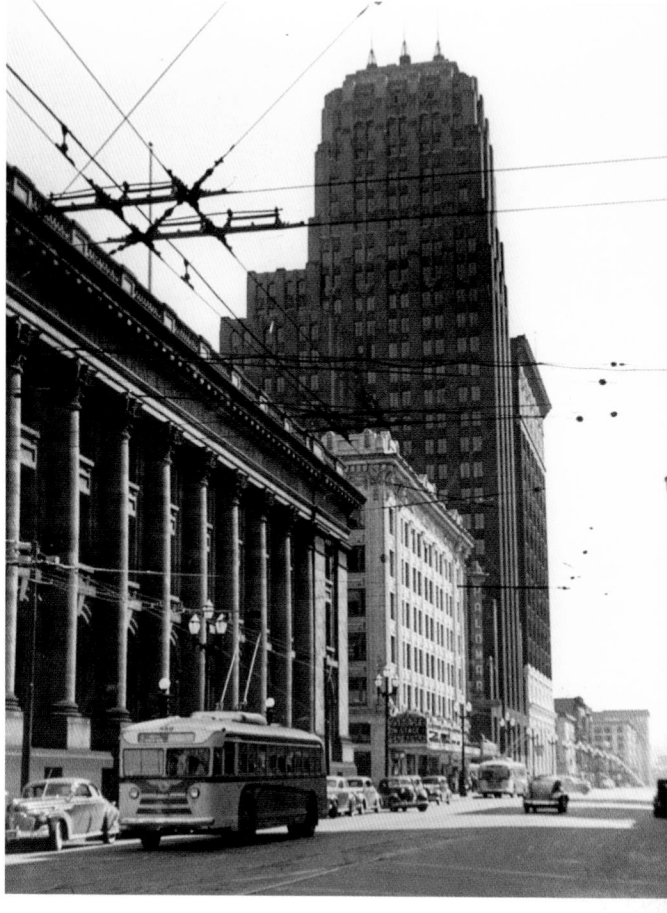

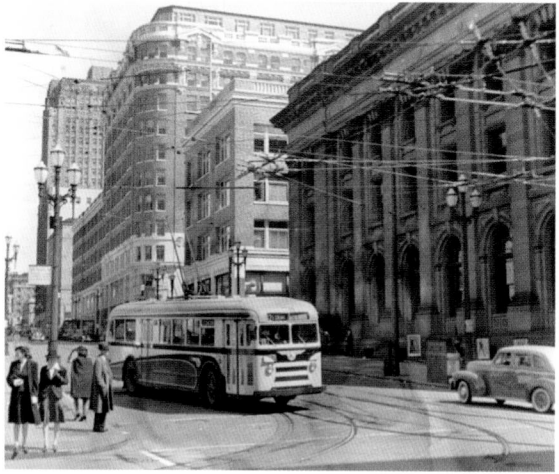

ABOVE *South on Third in 1949 with the Post Office on the left and New Pantages Theater next door.*

LEFT *East on Union at the end of World War II. The White-Henry-Stuart Building is two doors down.*

OPPOSITE PAGE *The Federal Building in 1909, with a crowd preparing to board the streetcar.*

Jackson Street Jazz Scene PACKED IT IN 1958

The musical roots of jazz are traced back into the 1800s through blues, ragtime, and African folk music tinged with Spanish influence in the Caribbean. But jazz became a nationwide cultural phenomenon in the 1920s during Prohibition, as Americans turned to semi-secret speakeasies to get beer and liquor. Bands played the intoxicating rhythms and burning melodies of jazz at these clubs, completing the edgy, illicit experience.

Surprisingly, Seattle got a head start. Prohibition became law in Washington State in 1916, four years earlier than the rest of the country. Seattle leveraged the old opium smuggling network to run rum for the rich and desperate. World War I packed troops into Fort Lawton, all new to Washington and expecting a drink.

Illegal clubs sprang up all over, but the police encouraged them south of First Hill and into the Central District. One of the first with jazz was the Dumas Club, a black social club at Fifth and Washington in 1917. That same year the conservative black paper *Cayton's Weekly* ran a full page editorial critiquing jazz and dismissing it as primitive, unmelodic and visual. The first documented jazz performance was in 1918 at Washington Hall.

The scene hubbed at 12th and Jackson grew quickly. Jelly Roll Morton's band arrived in 1919. The Creole pianist bounced into town from Vancouver and left again in 1920, soon after finding national fame. His clarinetist Oscar Holden stayed behind though, and became a fixture of the Seattle jazz scene for decades. Holden's style became Seattle's: technically precise, light on the Dixieland banjos and big horns, and in a four-beat rhythm later associated with swing.

Holden was a regular at Doc Hamilton's Barbeque Pit on 12th Avenue. The Dumas Club evolved into Seattle's hottest club, the Black and Tan. It was the center of Seattle's music scene when jazz eclipsed all other forms of popular music in 1928. That year jazz legend Joe Darensbourg

arrived in Seattle and later described it as other than New Orleans the only town in America with any character.

When Jelly Roll came to Seattle, saxophonist and trumpeter Frank Waldron was already teaching jazz. He lived atop Yesler Hill and ran his school in the middle of the Jackson scene. Working as a janitor during the day and playing speakeasies at night, he still found time to run his music school for decades. Many of his pupils became great jazz performers, though many were not heard of outside of Seattle. He taught the first two generations of jazz musicians in Seattle, which included a young Quincy Jones.

Quincy Jones was only a freshman in high school when he began taking classes from Waldron, and met Ray Charles the same year. Charles had a steady gig at the black Elks Club. Jones saw him there and introduced himself. They became fast friends, and Charles, only 16 himself, taught his younger friend how to compose music. Ray Charles recorded his first single and appeared

on TV and radio for the first time before leaving Seattle two years later. Quincy Jones wrote his first jazz composition for a jazz band at Seattle University. Jones left Seattle a year after his friend in 1951 to attend the Berklee School of Music in Boston.

While Jones and Charles spent key formative years in Seattle, Patti Bown is an example of a great jazz musician born and raised in the Emerald City. Walking home from school she peeked into clubs on Jackson and was hooked. In 1945 at 13 she secretly played jazz piano at the Officer's Club at Fort Lawton. Bown made her mother happy by studying straight piano at Seattle University during Quincy Jones's brief stay, and later studied at the University of Washington. At night she played the jazz clubs, but eventually skipped town in 1955 to join Jones in New York.

In 1958 the Seattle musicians unions desegregated. With black musicians able to work anywhere in town, they followed the money. The jazz scene on Jackson faded to a bittersweet end.

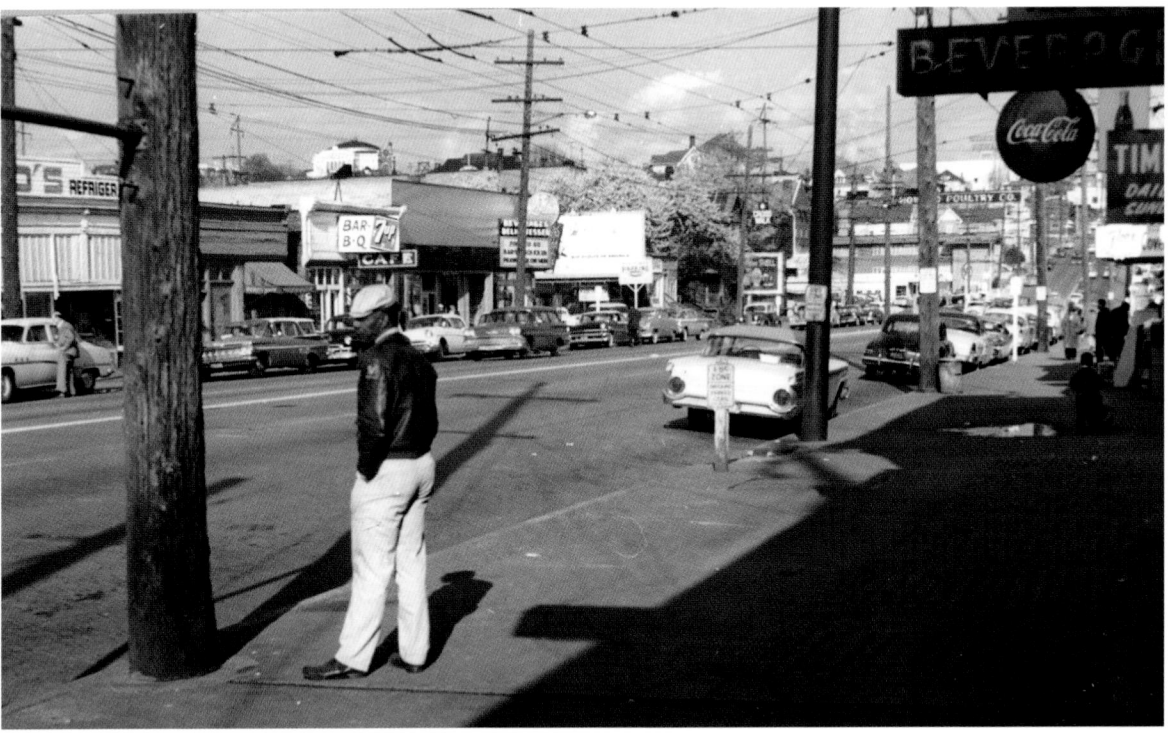

RIGHT *The heart of the jazz scene at 12th and Jackson, waiting for nightfall.*

OPPOSITE PAGE *The Question Marks, a band formed from World War II Navy performers who stayed in Seattle.*

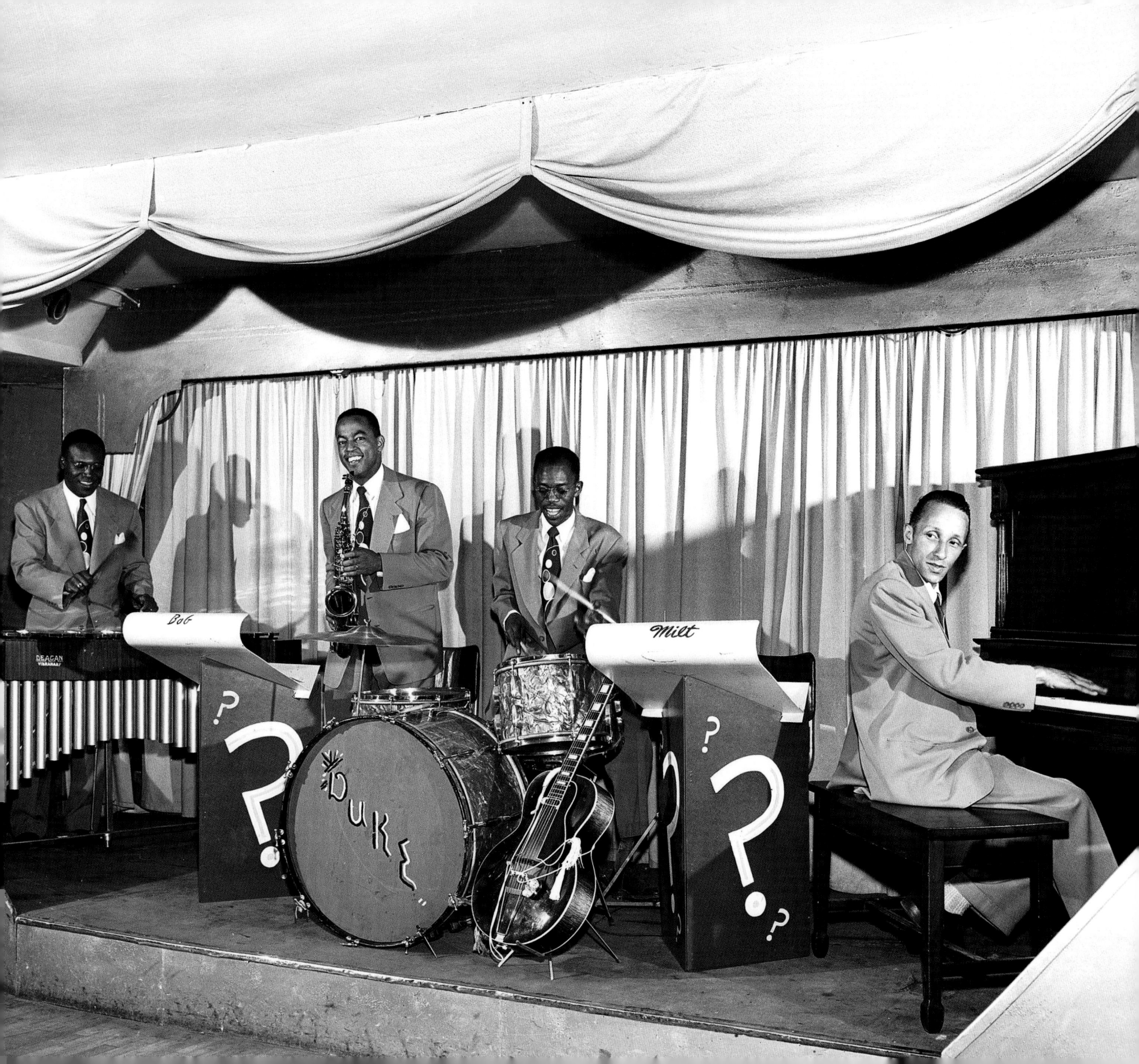

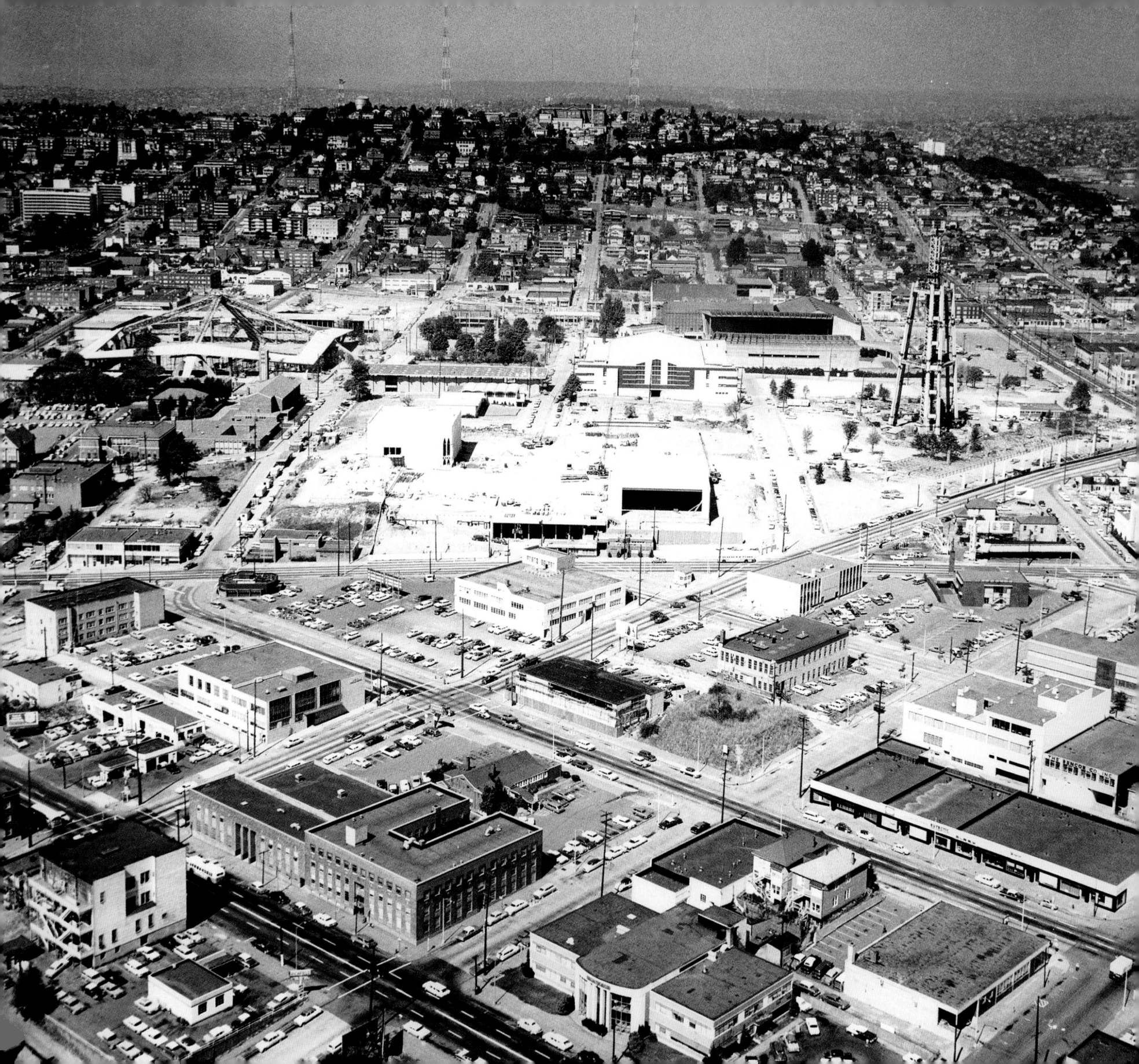

Warren Neighborhood CLEARED 1959

Warren was a neighborhood in the old North Seattle, the area settled by David Denny between Denny Hill and Queen Anne Hill. In 1890 the North Seattle Cable Railway was opened, extending the cable on First and Second avenues north from Denny Way to Highland Avenue on the south face of Queen Anne Hill. The part of the neighborhood to the west of First Avenue North became known as Lower Queen Anne (Avenue), and the part to the east as Warren (Avenue).

David and Louise Denny continued to farm on several blocks of Warren until they went bankrupt in the years after the 1893 financial panic. In 1898 the federal government leased their land for a horse and mule corral until Fort Lawton was completed. The neighborhood was finally able to breathe deeply when the hundreds of animals were no longer upwind.

In 1903 the west end of Denny's homestead was replaced with the Warren Avenue School and a field for Seattle's first professional baseball team, the Siwashes. The east part of the farm became a new streetcar yard for Seattle Electric Company.

Warren was built of simple wood frame houses and small, low-cost apartments. It followed the pattern of other Seattle neighborhoods, with wealthy residents on the hills and ridges and working-class families in the valleys and depressions. In 1920 Warren was one of several neighborhoods singled out for needing day care service because so many of the young mothers worked in nearby factories.

In 1939 the Seattle Housing Authority was formed to receive federal funding for the creation of low-income housing. Nationwide, slums developed during the Great Depression. Seattle's worst was a Hooverville of shacks in the industrial district. SHA focused instead on clearing out the dilapidated blue-collar neighborhoods. In 1939 Yesler Terrace was approved on Yesler Hill. In 1940, with additional funds from the Defense Housing Act to build homes for workers near military bases, SHA attempted to replace Warren. It was on the streetcar line to Fort Lawton. The City Council fought back and refused to agree to destroy another neighborhood without a clear need or unless Yesler Terrace proved to be a success.

In 1956 Seattle voters decided to turn the Warren neighborhood into a civic center for cultural, educational and recreational activities. The state legislature quickly took action, passing a bill to allow cities to apply for federal funding for urban renewal. Warren was tagged as a blighted area again in order to speed demolition.

The city and state were taking action in anticipation of federal sponsorship of a World's Fair in Seattle. In 1958 Warren was confirmed as the site of the upcoming World's Fair and demolition began.

One of the last buildings to go was the Warren Avenue School, which finally closed after the 1959 school year. The school's charter had changed significantly over the years. Portables with wheelchair access provided a groundbreaking program for children with cerebral palsy. Additional tailored classrooms served blind students and the hearing impaired. The students were transferred to other schools throughout the district.

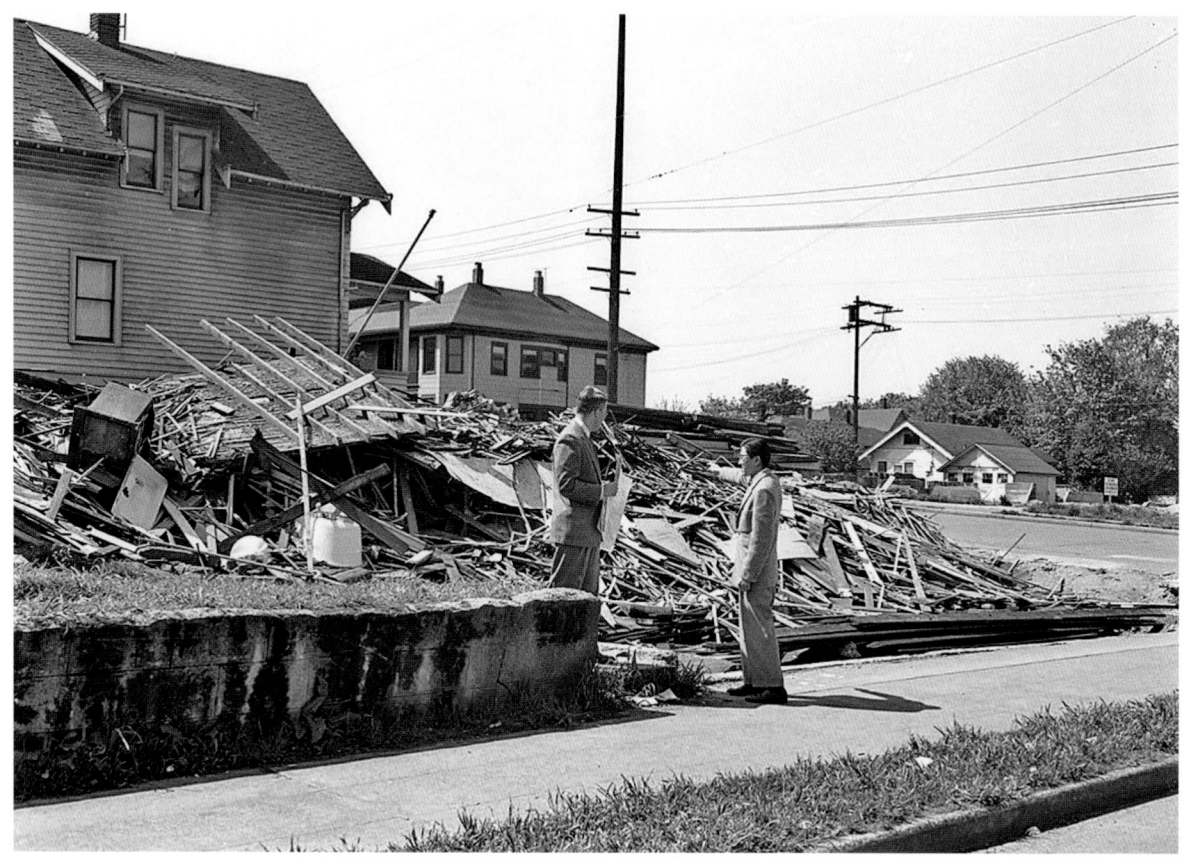

LEFT *Neighborhood demolition underway in 1959.*

OPPOSITE PAGE *Looking north over the former Warren neighborhood with the Coliseum and Space Needle rising amidst fair construction.*

Hotel Seattle DEMOLISHED FOR PARKING 1961

The Hotel Seattle was built above the rubble of the Occidental Hotel after it was destroyed during 1889's Great Fire.

Construction rushed to completion in 1890, making the Hotel Seattle the first luxury traveler's hotel to open after the fire. To that end, architect Steven Meany had designed a more restrained facade than its predecessor.

One of the first tenants at the hotel was Seattle's first official city library. It was located on the top floor from 1891 to 1894 until the reading room collection needed more space to grow. The hotel underwent periodic changes of its own. Over the course of 1909 and 1910 the 176 guest rooms were remodeled and the café was reopened. By the late 1930s, though, there were only 133 rooms.

At the start of 1941, Henry Takemitsu Kubota purchased the hotel from an insurance company that had been holding it. Within a year Kubota and his family of American citizens were herded onto rail cars and sent to internment camps. The Kubotas were lucky because Henry had powerful friends. Charles Clise, scion of Clise Properties, offered to manage the property while the Kubotas were away.

When they finally returned in 1946 the hotel still remained in their hands.

In 1960 developer Sam Rotenberg announced that the Seattle Hotel would be demolished for a parking garage, with an office building built atop it at some future date. He represented a group that had leased the property from the Kubota family. The announcement came as a number of groups were working to revitalize Pioneer Square and the triangle park. They were powerless to stop Rotenberg, though, and watched as the hotel was demolished in 1961. First the entire contents of the hotel were auctioned off in February, then the building was gutted in March, and finally the building was razed in April. Callous businessmen called it a renewal project.

ABOVE RIGHT *The hotel's new bus is full of guests for a tour or ride to the train station.*

OPPOSITE PAGE *The hotel is seen here around 1900, with the Yesler cable on the right and James cable on the left.*

BELOW *After demolition in 1961.*

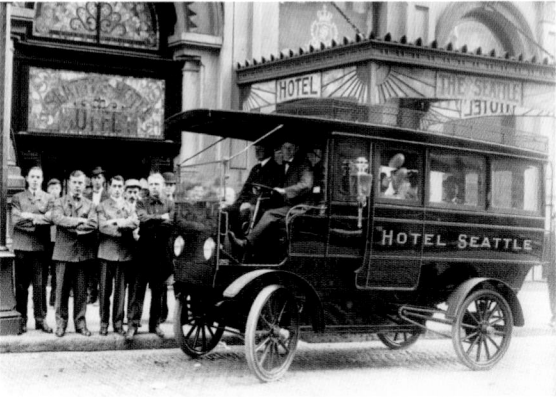

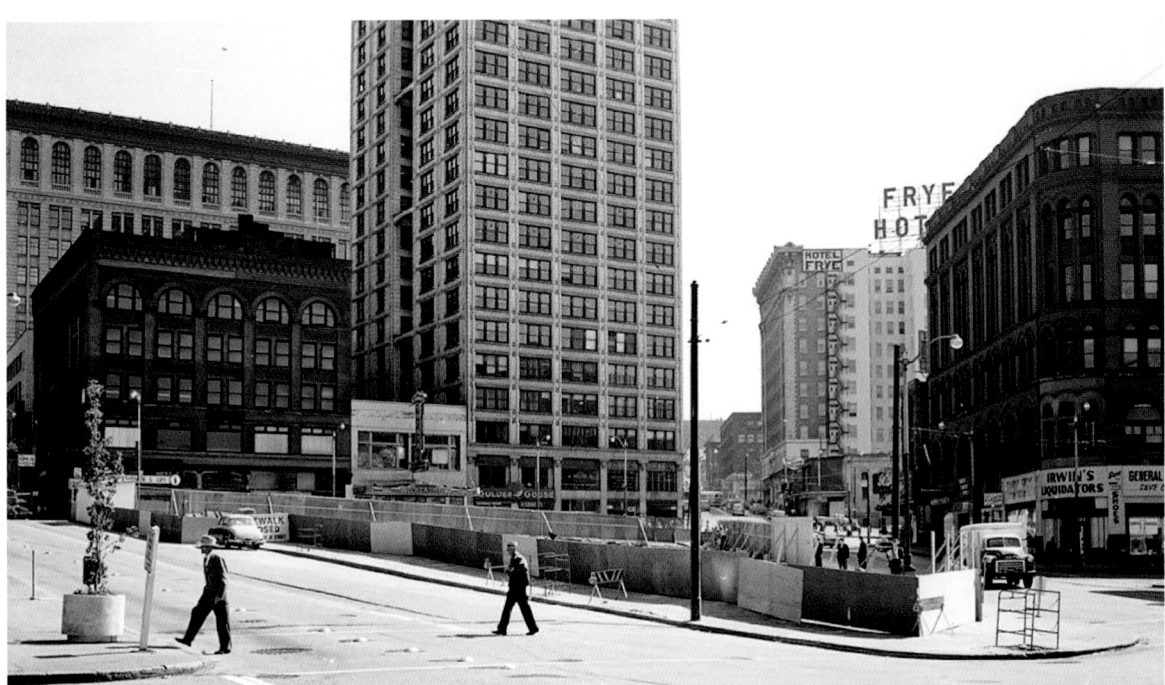

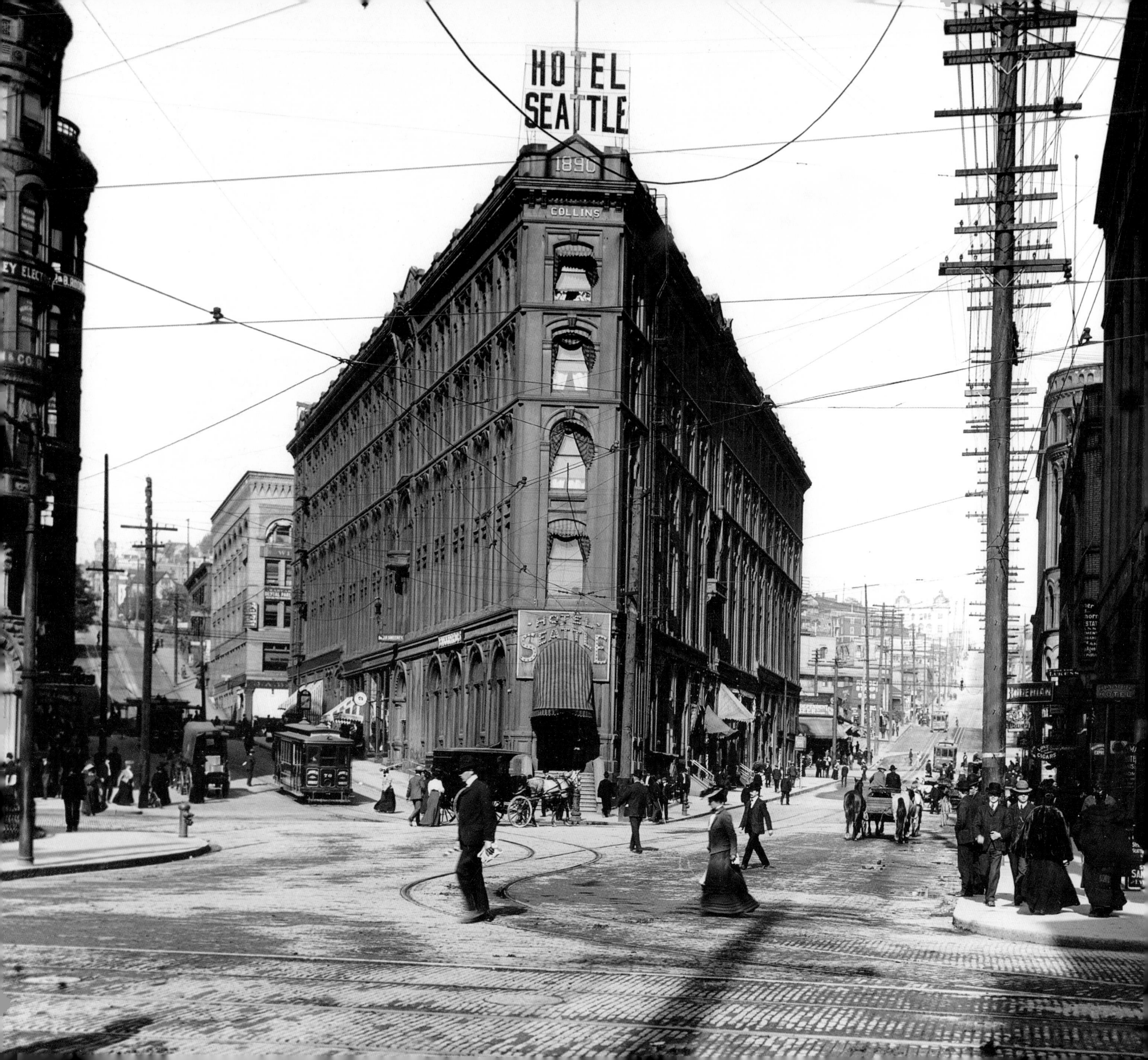

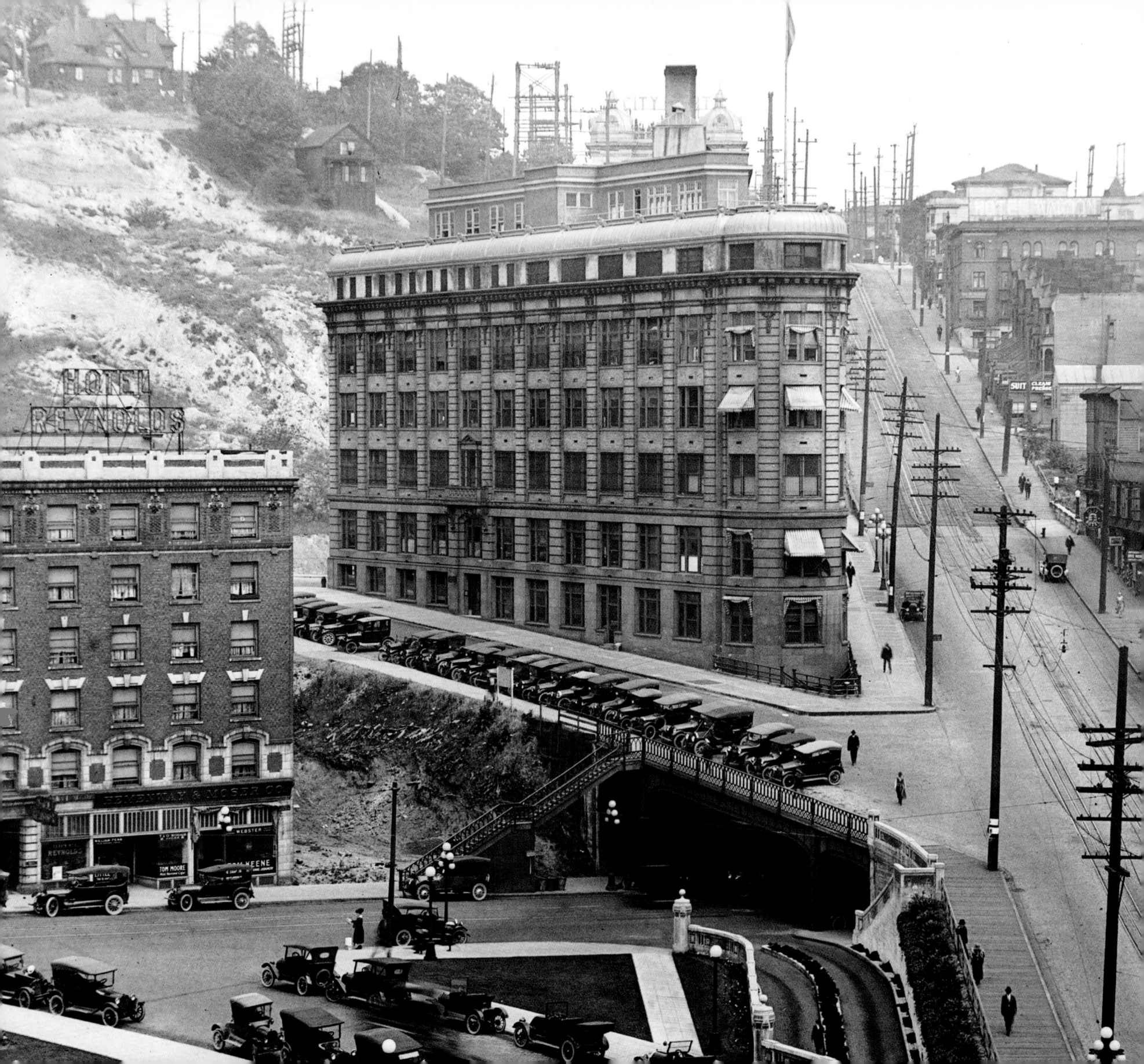

Yesler Hill LEVELED 1962

Yesler Hill was a subpeak on the Pioneer Square side of First Hill. A neighborhood clung to its slopes.

Although street leveling and massive hospital buildings have made it hard to see, First Hill's peak was still clear in the 1890s. It was at the intersection of Broadway and Summit, next to the James Street cable car powerhouse. It fell unevenly to the bay, with the Territorial University and the Central School on two knolls. But to the southwest of the peak, another shorter peak rose out of the ridge in between Jefferson and Terrace streets and Eighth and Ninth avenues, where Harborview Hospital is today. This subpeak and the neighborhoods on its west and south faces were Yesler Hill.

As Seattle spread up out of Pioneer Square, the west face was lined with small hotels, boarding houses and upscale homes. Wooden staircases took the place of streets and paths wandered with the slope through undeveloped properties. When the King County Courthouse was built near the top of Yesler Hill in 1891, lawyers were forced to walk up the stairs from their offices. Even if they paid for a short ride on the Yesler Cable they were still left with 80 feet of elevation to cover. As they cursed their way up and down the hill it picked up the name Profanity Hill.

Property owners like Charles P. Dose had other reasons to swear in 1912. He had fought city engineer R. H. Thomson's plan to regrade Fifth Avenue the year before. Maybe Dose got a bad feeling after Thomson moved off of the hill. Or maybe he watched the difficulty the city had removing the Jackson ridge on the south side of the hill. Either way, he lost his fight. He also lost his house after a landslide rolled down Terrace Street.

Any white person with money moved up on one of the hills: Capitol Hill, Queen Anne Hill, or the northern part of First Hill. The south slope of Yesler Hill was home to Japanese, Chinese and the lava beds. Brothels were the biggest business but there were gambling dens and after Prohibition hit Washington State in 1916 there were speakeasies mixed in as well.

In 1939 the city determined to clean up the area. It was tagged as a slum, and federal grants were used to level the entire area, replacing it with Yesler Terrace, a low income housing project.

The rest of the Yesler Hill neighborhood was eliminated in 1959. Interstate 5 was built through Seattle, decimating a line of houses, apartments, schools, and churches. Yesler Hill itself also fell to the shovels. The entire west face was gouged out to run the freeway through in 1962.

OPPOSITE PAGE *Yesler Hill rises behind the Hotel Reynolds and the triangular, former City Hall in 1920.*

BELOW *A patched and lifted 1880s home that survived on the slope of the hill until 1960.*

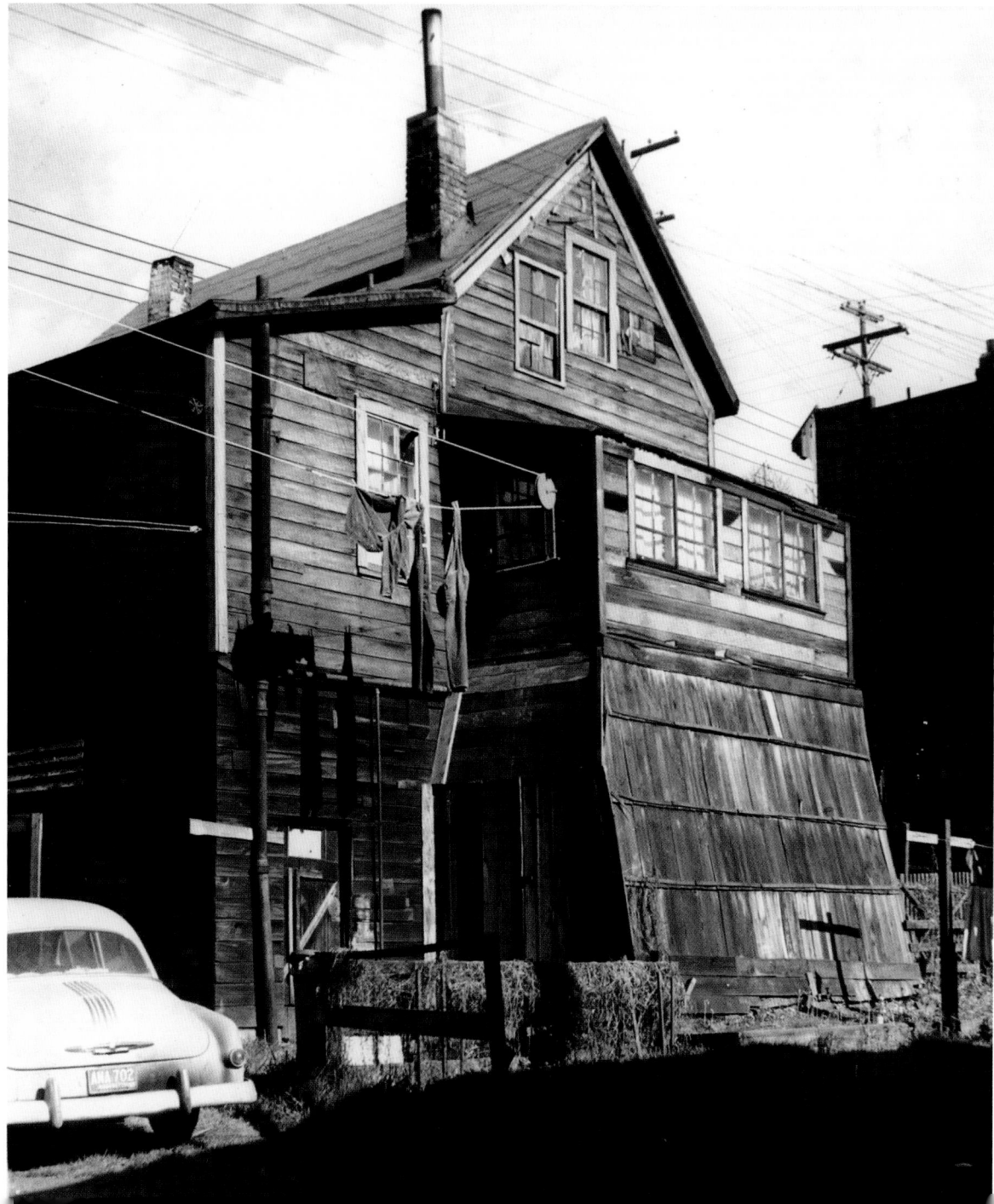

Century 21 Exhibits SCRAPPED 1962

Century 21, Seattle's 1962 World's Fair, was unique because of the number of permanent structures that were left behind. Seattle set out to give itself a civic entertainment center. Of course there were the Space Needle, Coliseum, International Fountain, and the United States Science Pavilion. Also the existing Armory was turned into the Food Circus, and the Civic Auditorium was transformed into the Opera House.

But in between the large, permanent buildings were many that were small and only needed for the months of the fair.

Several of the exhibits were model homes of the 21st century. Wood manufacturers, led by Douglas Fir Plywood, created the undulating Home of Living Light. Also known as the Plywood House, it was composed of circular rooms topped with quarter-ellipsoid skylight roofs. The ellipsoids were intended to be rotated to collect natural light and warmth in the winter, and avoid direct sun and heat in the summer. *Parade Magazine* sponsored a family to live in the house for a day and the six-year old proclaimed it to be "Fun... the kind of house I like." Many years later architects Liddle & Jones revealed that the exhibit was far from scientific. They spent 10 days designing and three weeks working with craftsmen on buildable drawings. The Plywood House was removed after the fair by barge to Olympia, Washington. Part of it served as an upscale restaurant until it was demolished in 2005.

Another plywood group, the United States Plywood Corporation, sponsored a very different model house titled the American Home of the Immediate Future. Called the space-module house by architect Robert Englebrecht, this home was made of modular, rectangular rooms which were prefabricated and bolted together on-site. The modules would maximize use of land and surround a central courtyard. After the fair the shell was purchased and moved to southeast Mercer Island, where hidden behind tall evergreens it is still used as a real home.

General Electric's Electric Living exhibit took an ordinary home from 1962 and filled it full of electric devices of the future. There was a projection television, a home computer, a digital video library, and even a personal fur coat chiller. One room was a disguised camper which could be simply hooked to a trailer hitch and taken on a solar-powered vacation. The building was designed by Seattle architect John Graham, Jr., and was destroyed soon after the fair.

Other free-standing exhibits showcased the infrastructure needed for modern life. Northern Pacific Railway's Transport 21 building featured an air cushion train and the future of rail transport. Bell Telephone's space included a Vanguard I satellite, solar batteries and touch-tone, push-button telephones. Run by Washington's electric utilities, the Pavilion of Electric Power cascaded a 40-foot wall of water past onlookers to impress them with the region's potential for dams.

Along with many other small buildings that weren't hauled away, these were all destroyed in the months after the fair ended. The dam was a pile of rubble by November, 1962.

John McFarland, head of the demolition company, expressed a reluctant peace with his role. "Over the years you develop an attitude towards this type of work. Certain structures have to be torn down when they are in the way of something good. You can't be too sentimental—but you can't be indifferent, either."

RIGHT *Exhibit buildings stretch out under the Space Needle's shadow.*

BELOW *The curved Home of Living Light, also known as the Plywood House.*

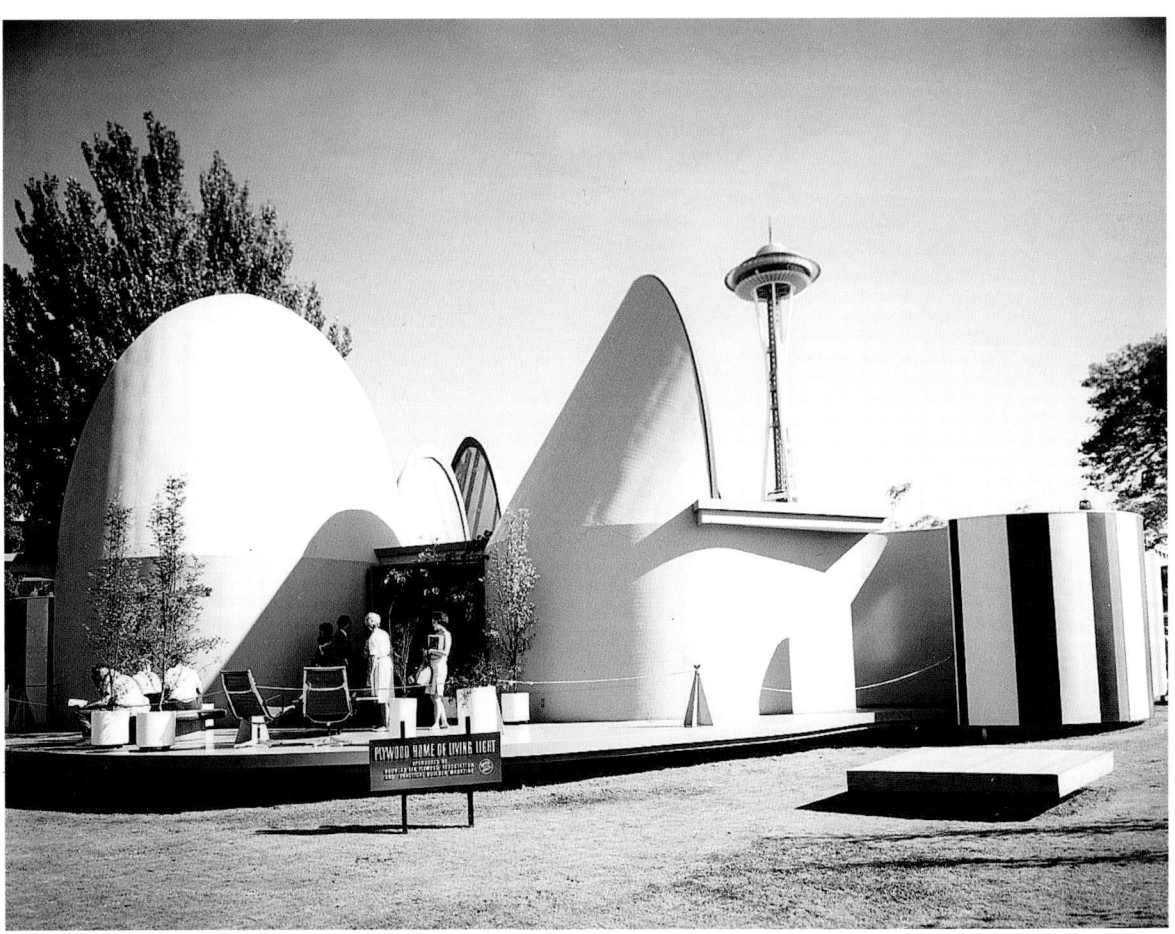

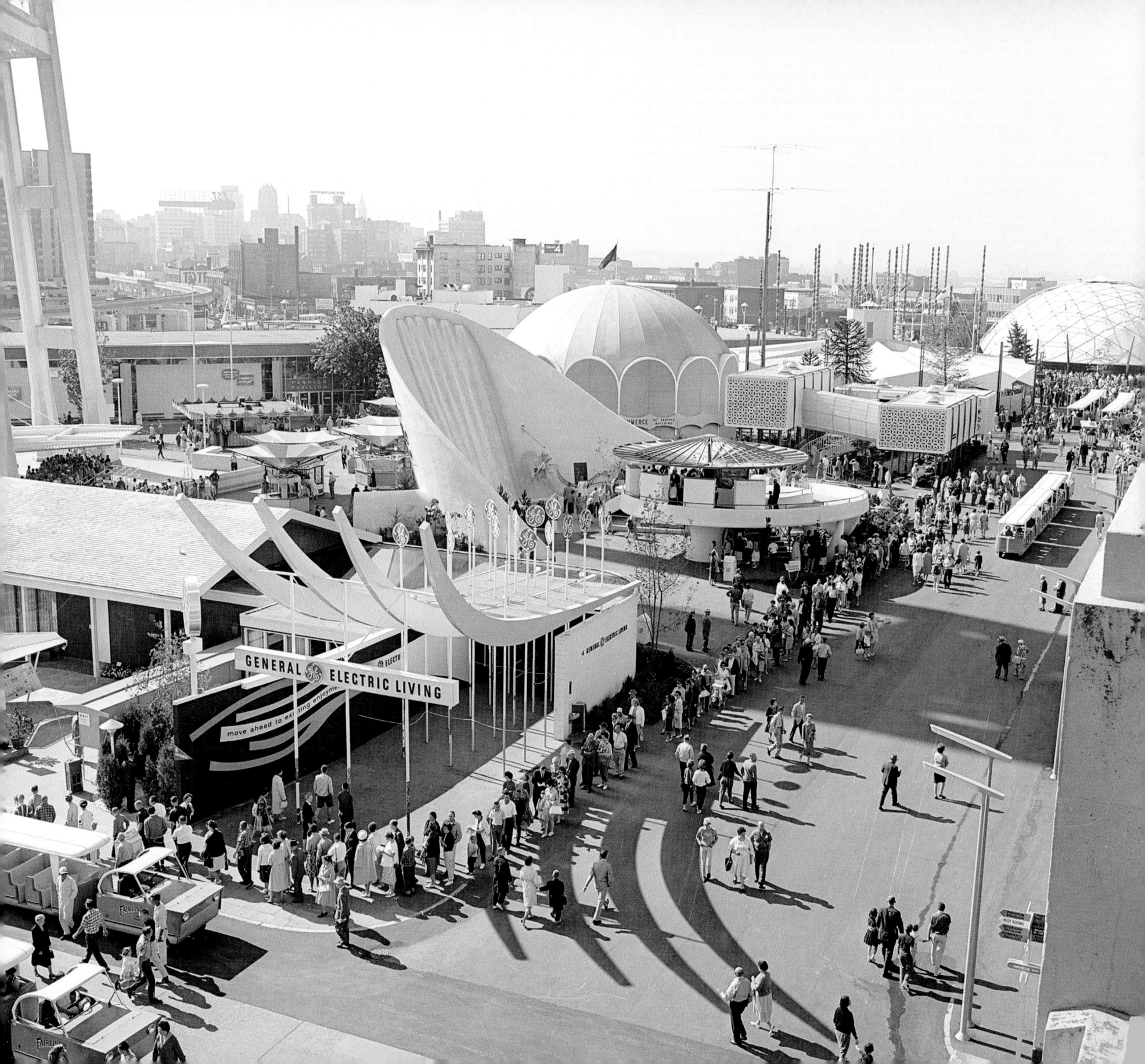

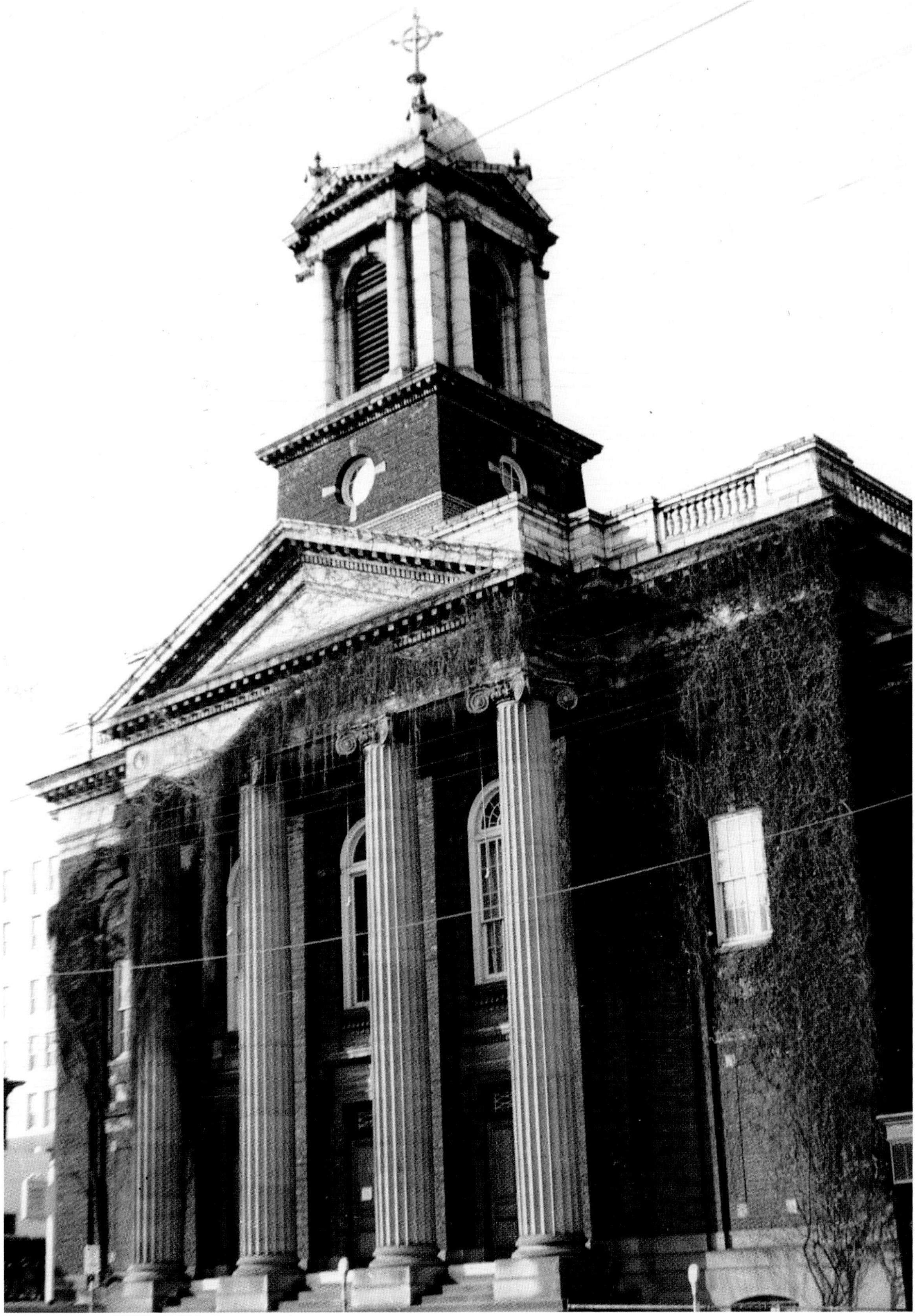

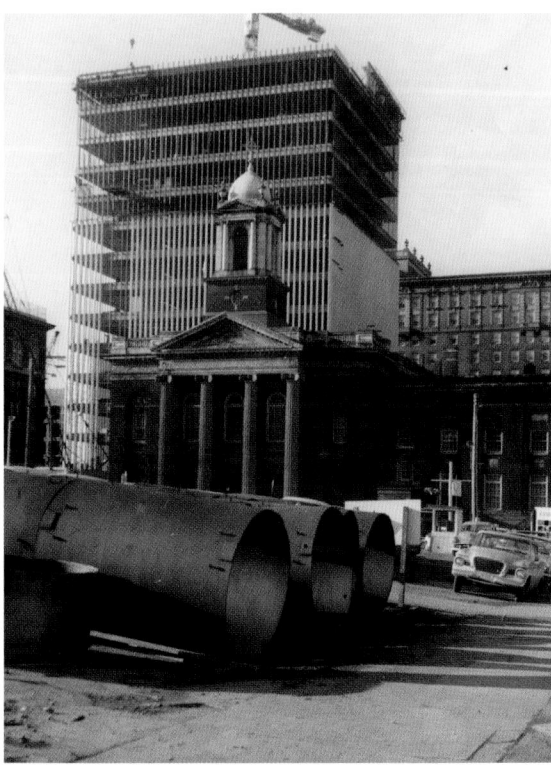

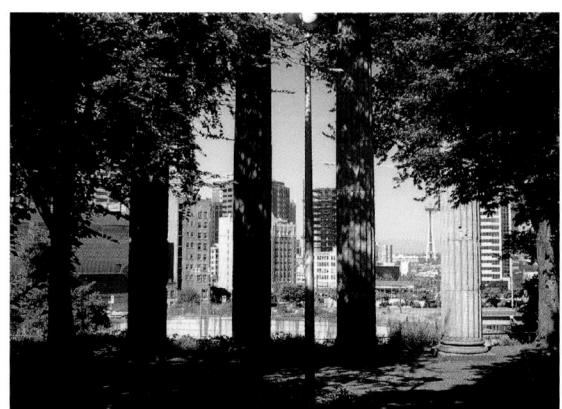

ABOVE *Pipes for Interstate 5 construction in front, and IBM Building going up behind in 1964.*

LEFT *Draped in ivy, the church stands tall in 1950.*

RIGHT *The view down University to Elliott Bay from First Hill is obstructed by the Olympic Hotel and Seattle Tower.*

BELOW *Plymouth ruins standing in Four Columns Park over Interstate 5.*

Plymouth Church **REBUILT 1965**

Plymouth was the sixth Christian congregation in Seattle, formed in 1869 when there were only a few hundred residents. Early services were held at a hall alongside Yesler's Mill.

The first Plymouth Congregational Church was built over Second Avenue at Seneca in 1873, backstopped by a stand of firs. The flock moved from this small wood building to Seattle's first brick church on Third and University in 1891 after the Great Fire.

In 1906 the church briefly but seriously considered moving to the far side of First Hill, following the residential pull into Capitol Hill. Property was purchased and a gothic building designed. Instead another space was chosen a few blocks uphill on the edge of the old Territorial University grounds at Sixth and University. The old church was vacated after Easter in 1911.

The new building was a departure for Seattle, a classical Georgian Colonial design by John Graham, Sr. It was occupied in stages as construction completed. After the new organ arrived the main hall finally held services in May 1912.

Parishioners entered up a flight of stairs through four massive columns. Three doors opened on an auditorium filled with mahogany pews. Marble pillars held aloft the balcony, and a glass dome capped off the ceiling. Twenty classrooms adjoined a second hall used for Sunday school. The kitchen was fit for a first-class hotel and the expansive dining room was rented out for public events.

By 1964 the church and its neighborhood had changed dramatically. The fellowship traveled from distant suburbs. Interstate 5 construction ripped up the hill right across the street. And the ice arena next door was replaced by the 20-story, modernist IBM Building skyscraper. So in June the reverend announced that the restrained but classical building would be demolished. Its replacement would be even more subtle, a modern building nestled at the bottom of the tower.

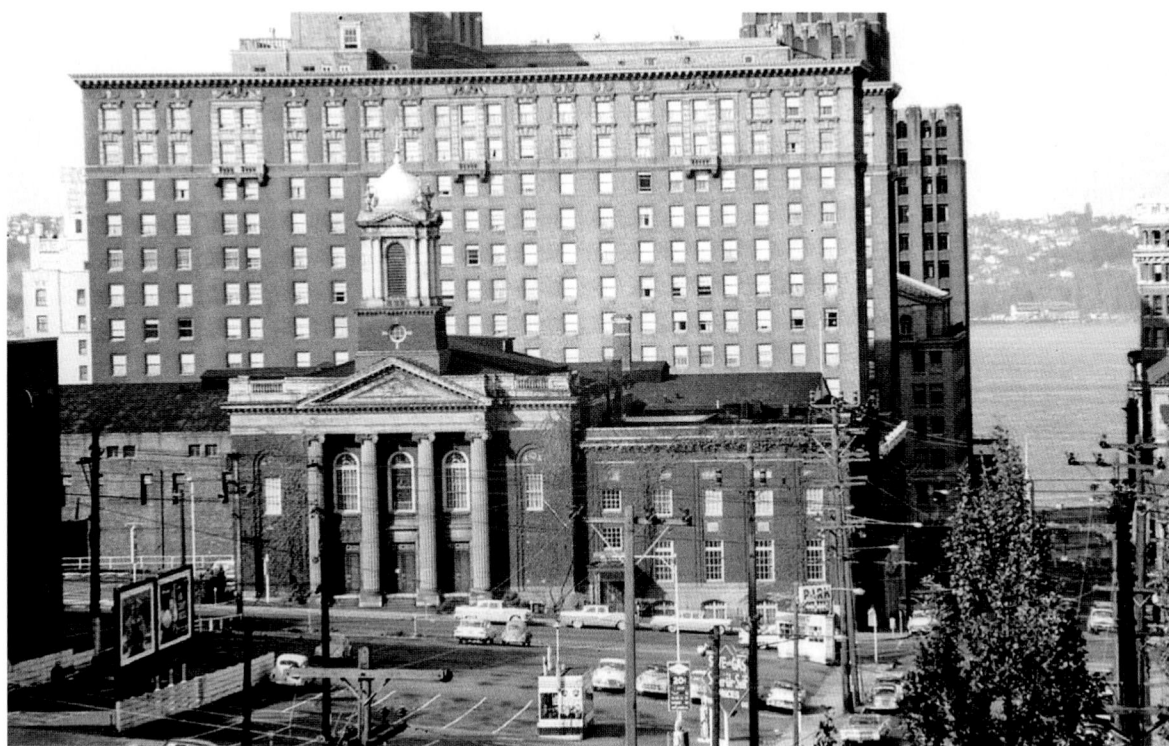

New Pantages Theater DEMOLISHED FOR PARKING 1965

The Palomar was the fourth and final of Alexander Pantages' theaters in Seattle.

In 1910 Pantages purchased the site of the Plymouth Church at Third and University, next to the new Federal Building. He was unsure what to do with it at first, considering a skyscraper or theater. After successfully collaborating with young B. Marcus Priteca on theaters for Portland, Oakland and San Francisco, Pantages decided it was time to build a new flagship theater and offices in Seattle. Priteca prepared the building and construction began in 1913.

Completed in 1915, the New Pantages was lauded for its ivory and rose colored French renaissance interior, in particular the decorative plasterwork. It featured the same white terracotta facade that hung on the nearby Jacob Green Building at Fourth and Pike. The entrance was framed with marble, bronze and glass mosaic tiles. The 1,800 patrons sat on spring-cushioned seating made to Pantages' design.

Pantages filled his theaters by relentlessly searching for truly entertaining acts and avoiding the big, expensive names. In order to judge acts he worked out in the theater as an usher, spoke with employees about their opinion, or sat and watched as a patron. He ran affordable shows that appealed to audiences in Seattle and in his growing chain of theaters across the West.

Although Pantages moved his headquarters to Los Angeles in 1921, Priteca stayed in Seattle. His offices were in the New Pantages from the day it opened through several name changes until the day it closed as the Palomar.

By the time the New Pantages opened, motion pictures were emerging as a force to rival vaudeville. In 1936 the Sterling Theater chain remodeled and reopened the New Pantages as the Palomar Theatre. It was primarily a movie house, although it still showed vaudeville as well. Over the years this would transition to plays and touring concerts with motion pictures as the mainstay.

By the mid-1960s, dynamics had changed downtown. The Seattle Center pulled away big-named musical acts. Movie theaters were smaller with more showtimes. And Interstate 5 poured cars into the city that needed a place to park.

On June 1, 1965 the Palomar was torn down to build a parking garage.

OPPOSITE PAGE *The New Pantages seen soon after opening in 1915 with the Federal Building to the left.*

LEFT *Demolition underway in July 1965.*

BELOW *Exuberant advertising for the film* Paris at Midnight *in 1926.*

ALEXANDER PANTAGES

Alexander Pantages was born in Greece as Pericles Pantages in 1896. He had grand ambition, and changed his name after hearing the story of Alexander the Great. Pantages had a hard journey before he entered his calling in theater management. He left home at age nine and took to the sea as a deckhand. He labored on the Panama Canal, worked as a waiter and tried his hand at professional boxing in San Francisco. Like every other restless man, he heard his calling when gold was discovered in Alaska's Klondike in 1897. Unlike the others he quickly realized that more reliable money was to be made from the miners than in the mines. He returned to Dawson City and found work as a bartender and helped the saloon owner add a stage to draw more patrons with music. After gold was discovered in Nome he moved there and tended bar for the first winter. But opportunity came knocking when the Klondyke Theater's owners failed to make ends meet. Pantages borrowed money from friends and opened his first theater, Pantages' Orpheum. Income and expenses were enormous. A violin string cost $40, but the theater charged $25 to see a show. Pantages arrived in Seattle in 1902 from the Klondike and Nome gold rushes. In Alaska he learned the basics of running a vaudeville theater. In Seattle he opened the Crystal. It was small, simple, and profitable. He leveraged profits to build the Pantages Theater, named after himself. After he married singer Lois Menhendall he built another for her to perform in 1911, naming it the Lois Theater. Alexander Pantages had no formal education and could not read or write. But he acquired a sailor and bartender's command of Greek, English, French, German, and Spanish. And he had an aptitude for mathematics which he used to control expenses and leverage investments to take new risk. Pantages was most often complimented for his unfailing memory and ability to find diamonds in the rough—or gold in the dust.

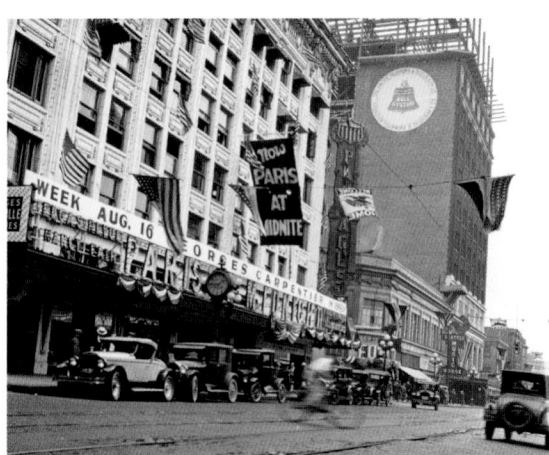

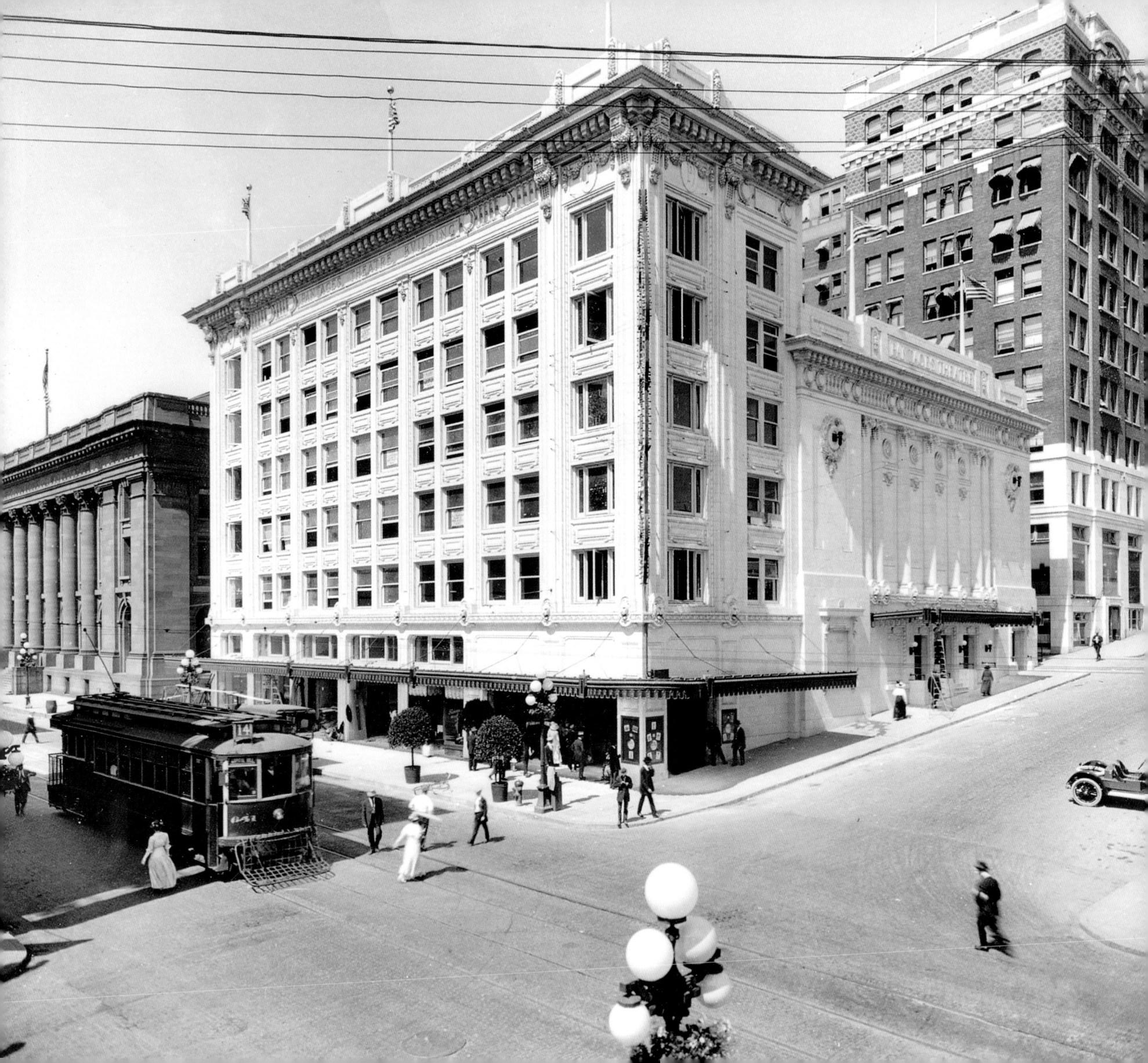

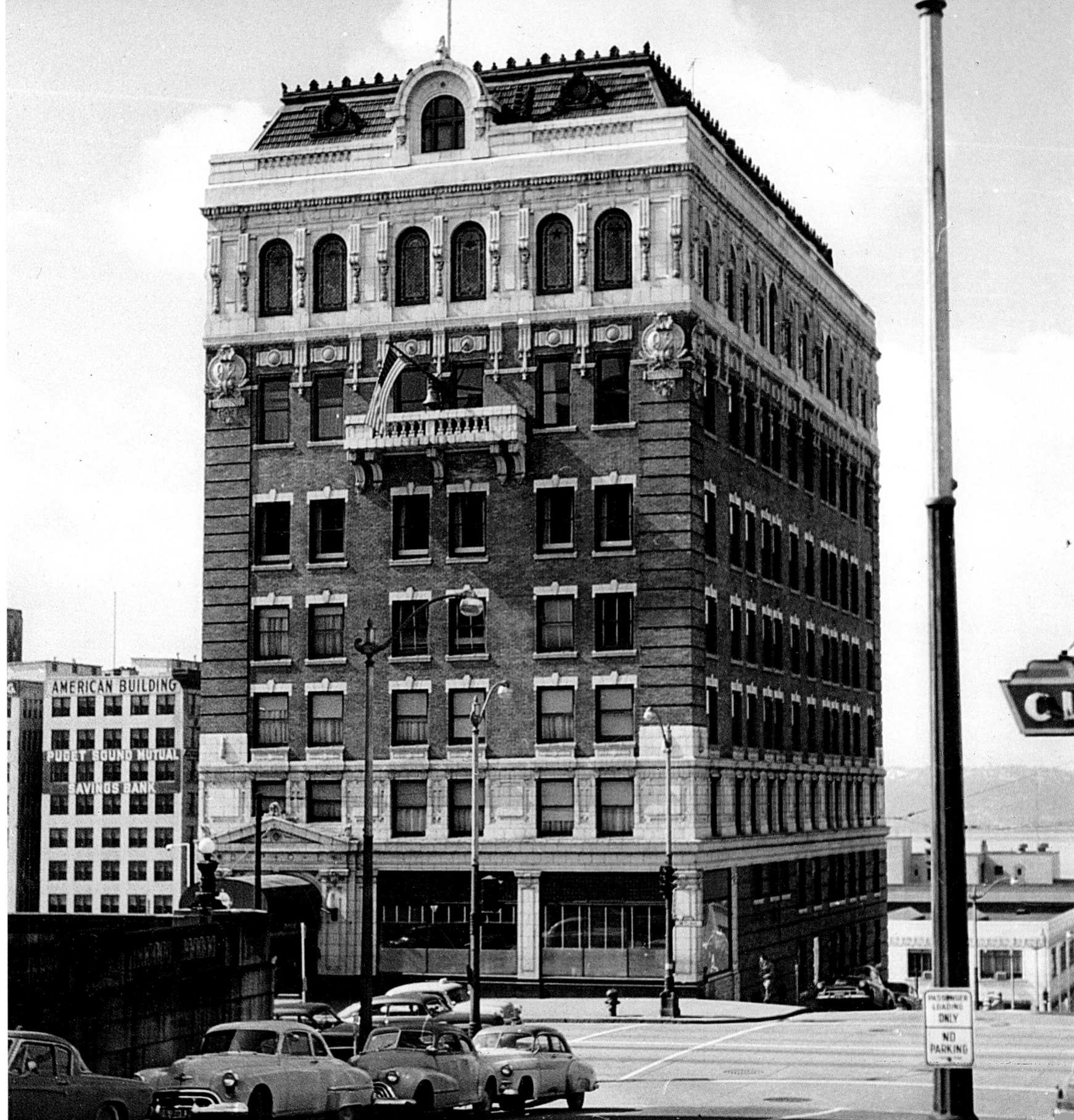

Elks Hall DEMOLISHED 1966

Their 11-floor temple represented the Seattle Elks' rise from obscurity to a power among local fraternal organizations.

Benevolent and Protective Order of Elks Lodge Number 92 was established in Seattle in 1888, one year before the Great Fire. They joined a crowded field of fraternal organizations serving the men of Seattle's 20,000 population. There were three Masonic temples, four Odd Fellows lodges, three Templars lodges, four Grand Army of the Republic posts, a United Workers lodge and a B'nai B'rith lodge. The Elks lodge moved quietly through its first decade.

After a successful carnival in Tacoma in 1901, the Seattle Elks secured free use of the old Territorial University grounds in 1902 for their own. The wildly popular festival, complete with elephants and blocks of booths, was repeated the following year. For their meetings and lodging, BPOE 92 rented the 13th and 14th floors at the top of the Alaska Building, the tallest building in Seattle.

During 10 years at the Alaska Building, membership rose from a few hundred to almost two thousand. After just a few years of tenancy, Elks leadership capped off a spectacular Considine & Sullivan vaudeville act at their auditorium by announcing that they had purchased property on the southeast corner of Second Avenue and Spring Street for their own building.

The building was designed by Seattle architect and Elk John Carrigan. He had experience with hotels, apartments, and industrial buildings. That was a perfect match for the nine-floor Elks lodge. It contained three floors of long-term hotel rooms for Elks members; pools, sauna and bowling alley in the basements; as well as an auditorium, gymnasium, and offices. A long dining room, cocktail lounge and rooftop garden provided ample space for entertainment.

The Elks Hall was opened in 1914 to great fanfare. First every member of the lodge packed the Alaska Building hall to close it out. Then they marched in parade around town before arriving at their new home. The opening celebration lasted three days and featured performances in every part of the building. The auditorium was used for a ball but also for boxing, wrestling, jiu-jitsu and kendo exhibitions. The bowling alley hosted a championship ladder with teams from local Elkdom

and the swimming pool held performances by expert swimmers and divers. All of the events were free.

In 1956 the Elks decided to downsize. Advertisements claimed that they had outgrown the building, but really the club no longer needed all of the internal facilities. Times had changed and Elkdom were more likely to just stay in a hotel when traveling. The champion hockey team was more important than bowling. In 1958 they sold their lodge building to the Jewish Community Center and soon after built a simple clubhouse over Lake Union on Westlake.

The Jewish Community Center only used the old lodge for a few years. Guest speakers, classes and other events were held regularly. In 1963 two major anniversaries were celebrated at the center. First was the 15th anniversary of the establishment of Israel. Second was the 50th anniversary of B'nai B'rith, the Anti-Defamation League. Panels discussed civil rights, discrimination, and other topics relevant to all people.

The next year Seattle-First National Bank bought the center and the rest of the block. They told reporters their plan to build a 50-story skyscraper. It would be the tallest building in the Pacific Northwest, taller than the Space Needle by 40 feet. That led to its nickname as The Box the Needle Came In.

On July 1, 1966 the Elks Hall went out just as it came in: with a party. The demolition crew painted a big "Pow!" on a bull's-eye on the side of the building, and lined up their wrecking ball. The bank set up bleachers for the crowd of onlookers. First

the chairman of the board gave a speech and a mass of balloons were released. Then a hovering helicopter dropped a smoke bomb. And finally the crane spun, sending the wrecking ball almost dead-center in the target.

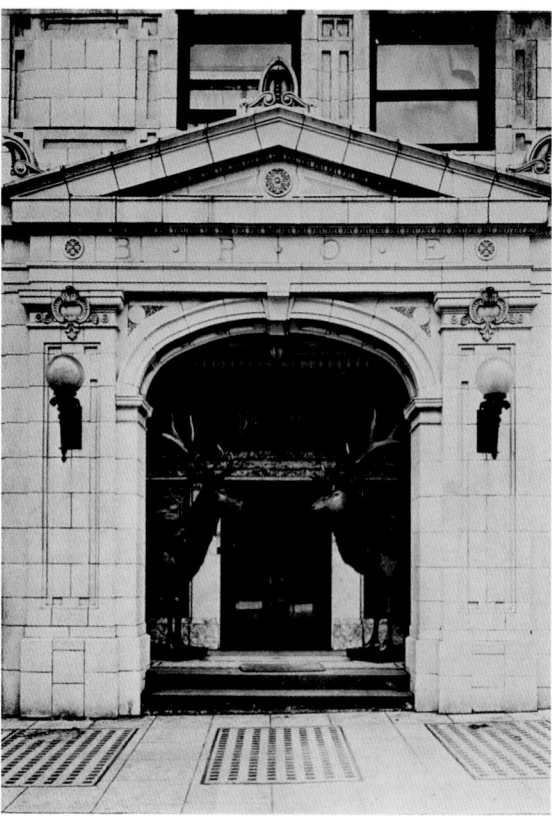

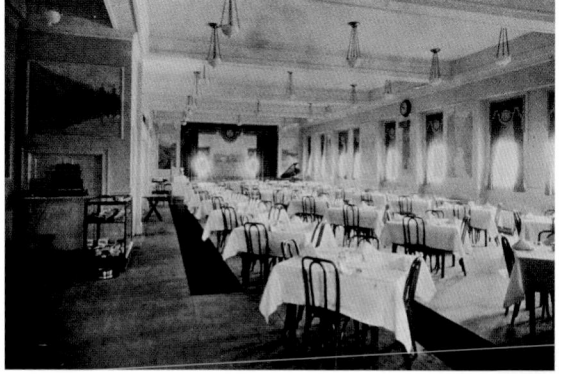

ABOVE *Two stuffed elk greet lodge members in 1914.*

LEFT *The dining room filled with tables, dressed for a gala event in 1914.*

OPPOSITE PAGE *Looking past the lodge in 1955 with Elliott Bay and West Seattle in the distance.*

MacDougall and Southwick QUIT BUSINESS 1966

By the time of its closure MacDougall's was the oldest retail establishment in Seattle.

The department store was started in 1874 by Paul Singerman, a new immigrant from Russia. Because he had been briefly in the Bay Area he named his shop the San Francisco Store. With his partner Ferdinand Toklas he expanded the store greatly in 1879. The next-door storefront was added and devoted to boots, clothing, and supplies for placer mining. They dug profit out of prospectors headed to Skagit County. Toklas stayed in the Bay Area as a purchaser, allowing them to undercut the prices of other stores in Seattle.

Their store became Seattle's classiest retailer. They were joined by James B. MacDougall as a third partner to run half of the retail. In 1882 they opened in new quarters with the largest showroom in Washington Territory. It had a second-floor wrap-around balcony, rounded counters, brass racks and large show windows.

The store witnessed a number of firsts. It was the first merchant to install a telephone in Seattle in 1883. It was at the terminus of the first streetcar in 1884. Management turned on Seattle's first commercial electric lights in 1886, five incandescent bulbs that lit the store to the amazement of the gathered crowd. In 1887 they incorporated Seattle's first elevator into yet another new building, the highest in Seattle. With each successive storefront or building the store had followed the northward pull up the regraded streets.

The San Francisco Store was destroyed in 1889, only a block from the source of the Great Fire. Store employees desperately tried to stop the fire from spreading to their building. By the time it was clear that they would fail, it was too late to save any of the merchandise. So over the next year the partners purchased new stock and rebuilt. At 3:10 p.m. on June 6, 1890, exactly one year to the minute from the time their store caught on fire, the new Toklas, Singerman & Company store was opened. It was five floors of varnished oak and ash, lit by arc and incandescent electric lights. It had more than an acre of floor space and the firm employed more than one hundred people.

After Singerman and Toklas retired in 1891, MacDougall added partner Henry Southwick and dropped the name San Francisco Store. MacDougall & Southwick prospered again after the 1897 Klondike gold rush, but they also found real competition from Bon Marché, Nordstrom and Frederick & Nelson. In 1908 MacDougall & Southwick moved to their final address, at Second Avenue and Pike Street, near their younger competitors.

The new building was a five story steel and concrete "skyscraper." Mahogany finish, soft colors, high ceilings and wide aisles with long views gave a very open and inviting atmosphere to customers. Pneumatic tubes transferred money from each department to the cashier's office. The second floor featured a room available to the public for women's committee meetings.

After opening the new store, MacDougall & Southwick quickly sold their interest to Mercantile Stores Incorporated, which owned dozens of other department stores. Mercantile struggled as Frederick & Nelson opened a much larger, more opulent store nearby in 1911, taking the crown as the high-end department store.

In the 1940s MacDougall & Southwick attracted customers and attention by implementing a Women's Day. Staff elected women to all executive positions in the store for one day only, and a variety of women's clubs took over each department to compete for highest sales. Of course they used the opportunity to feature new merchandise and run big discounts as well.

In January 1966 MacDougall's management suddenly announced that the three Seattle stores would close. The next door Penney's department store on Second Avenue took advantage of this by hiring key staff from MacDougall's, including the entire beauty salon.

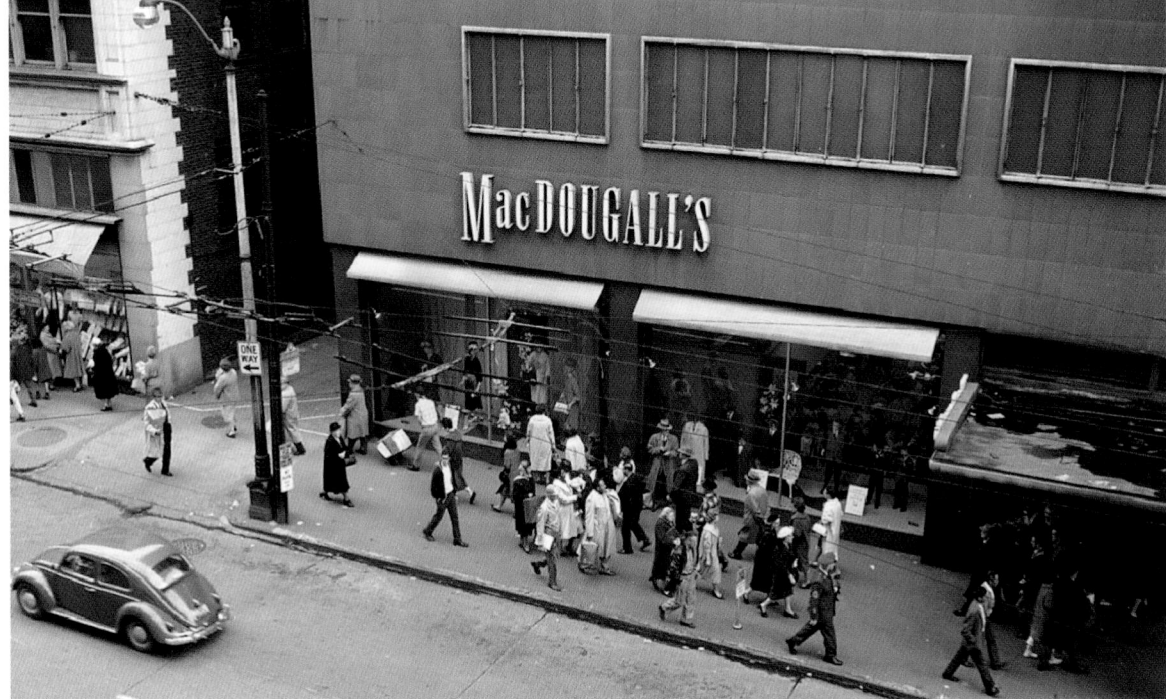

RIGHT *The store's female employees receiving instructions in 1912.*

LEFT *Spring fashions beckon passersby in 1961.*

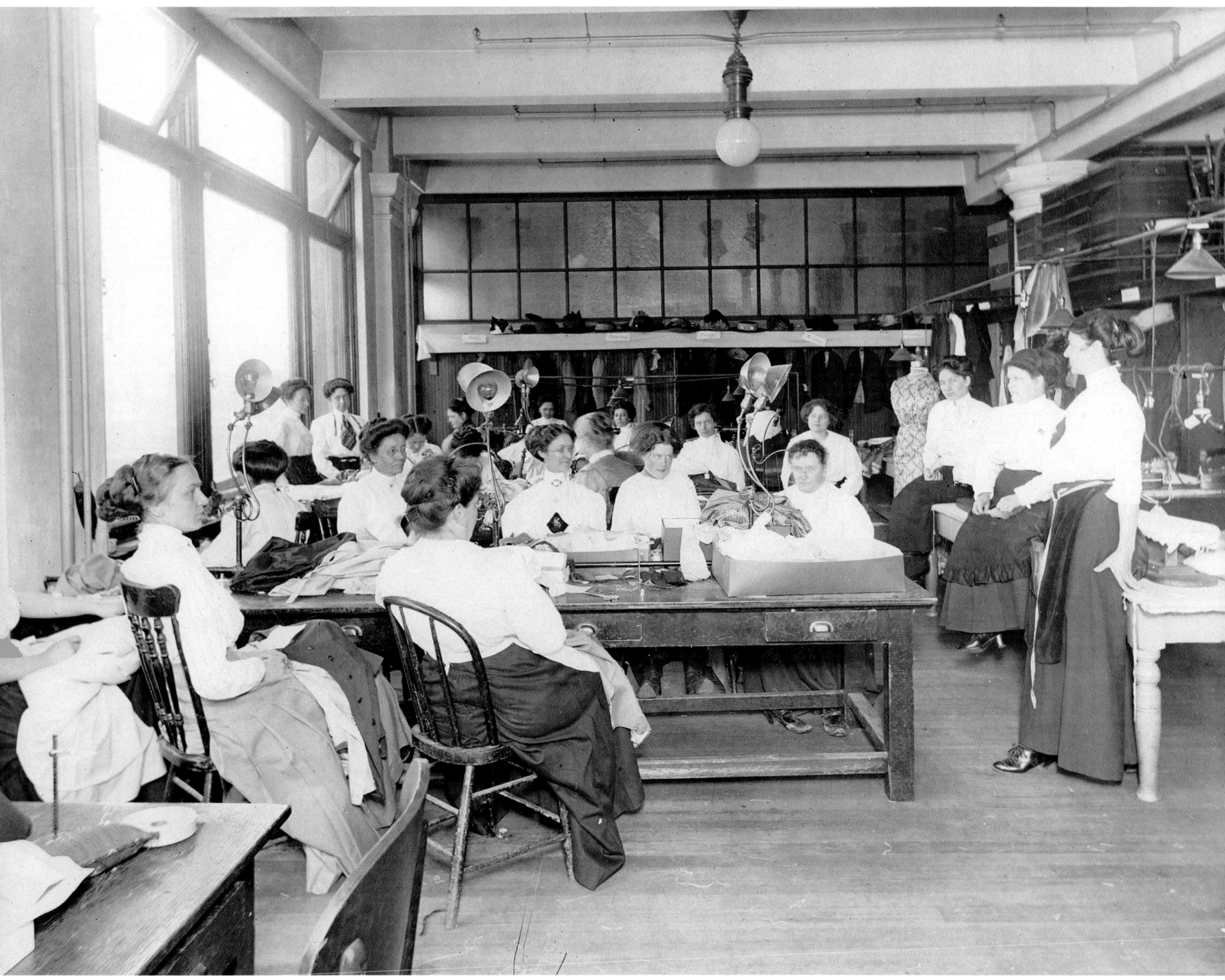

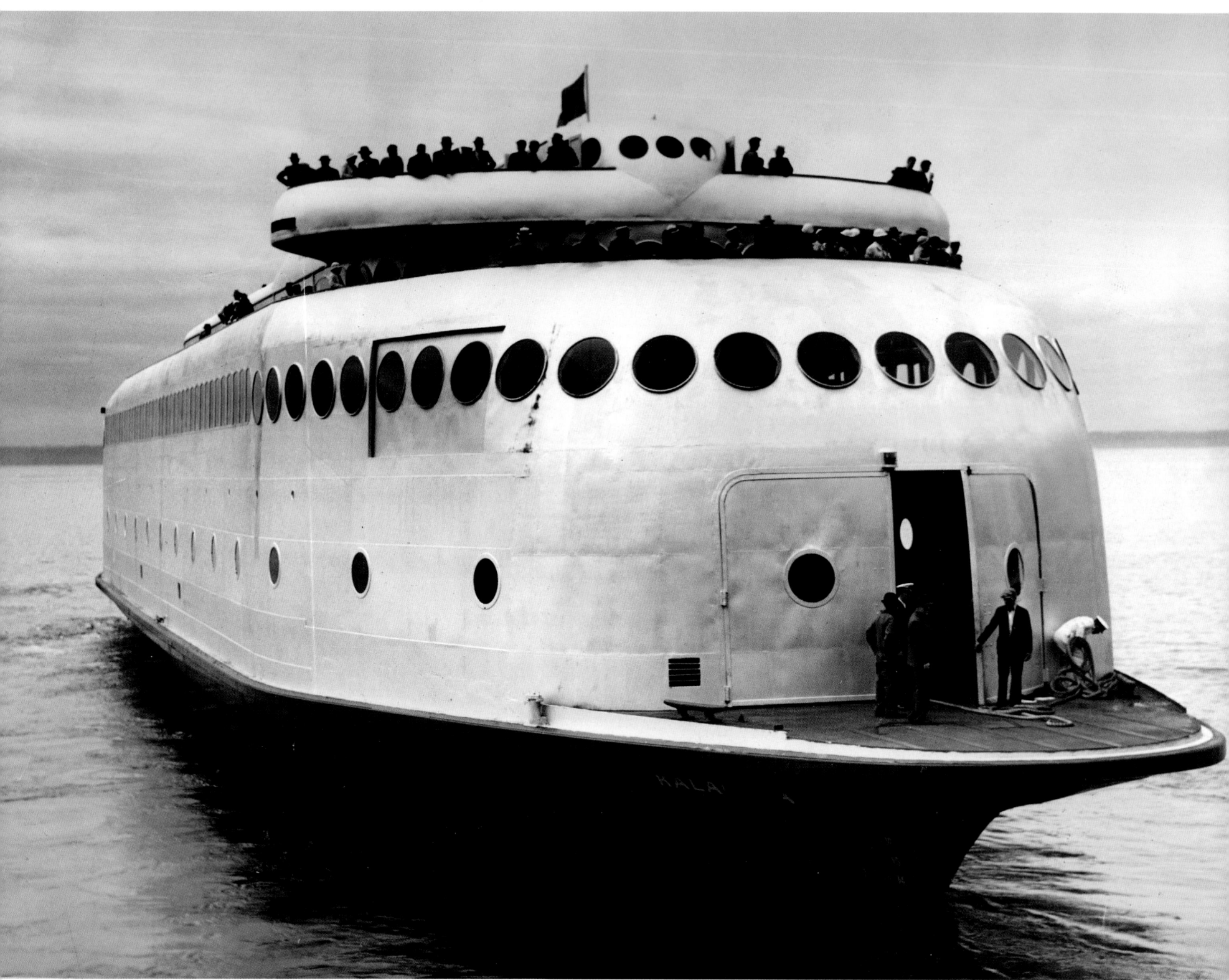

Kalakala **RETIRED 1967**

The *Kalakala* was the only Art Deco, streamlined ferry that the world has ever known. She entered service in 1935 at the height of the Great Depression, built from the hull of the burned-out MV *Peralta*. Her sleek, arc-welded lines earned *Kalakala* the title of the world's most photographed ferry until she was surplused in 1967 and towed to Alaska to be used as a shrimp and crab cannery.

She was built by the Puget Sound Navigation Company or Black Ball Line, who operated car and passenger ferries between the ports and islands of Puget Sound. The Seattle to Bremerton run was *Kalakala*'s main service but she also made excursions to Canada and spent time on the Port Angeles to Victoria, B.C. route.

Kalakala's name meant flying bird in Chinook jargon, the old trading language of Oregon Territory. Scandinavian immigrants thought it came from the Finnish for fish, which worked just as well. The ferry had a few other names. Tourists mistakenly called her Click Click, while Seattleites dubbed her the Silver Slug. The teeth-rattling vibration from the massive engine and crank shaft gave passengers a free foot massage and earned her the names Kelunkala and Klanks-a-lot.

The *Kalakala* provided a luxurious escape during the Depression years. Friday night cruises featured her Flying Birds Orchestra with three decks of dancing. Regular service included three observation rooms, a Palm Room with cruise ship-like outdoor seating, commissioned paintings, men's and women's lounges, and a tap room with food, beer and wine for sale at all hours. The interior decorations were hand-picked by Lilly Peabody, widow of Black Ball's founder, because she didn't trust the engineers and naval architects to get it right.

During World War II, the *Kalakala* became known as Puget Sound's Work Horse, carrying five thousand workers per trip from Seattle to the Puget Sound Naval Station in Bremerton on the Olympic Peninsula. She was built expressly for this purpose, with below-deck showers for the Naval Station employees. The loads were more than her luxurious appointments could bear, though. After rampant vandalism the famous bar was shut down, the showers turned off, and upholstered seats were replaced with steel benches.

The *Kalakala* continued workman-like for three decades, gradually adjusting to bigger cars and new technologies. She served alongside two new classes of ferries until the immense, fast Super Ferries finally rendered her obsolete.

She was beached in Alaska for a decade canning seafood, and then another as a derelict. Finally she was rescued in 1998 and returned triumphantly to Puget Sound. She's still floating but she's rusted, battered, and needs tens of millions of dollars of care to make her whole again.

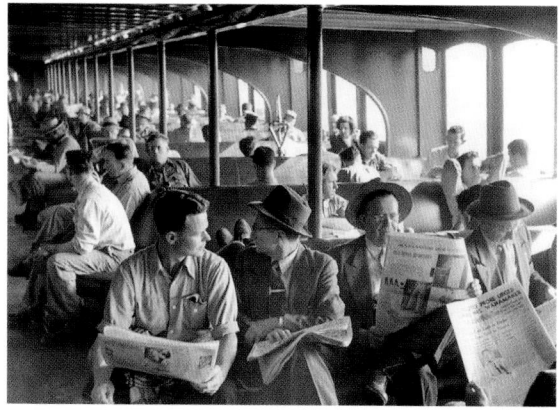

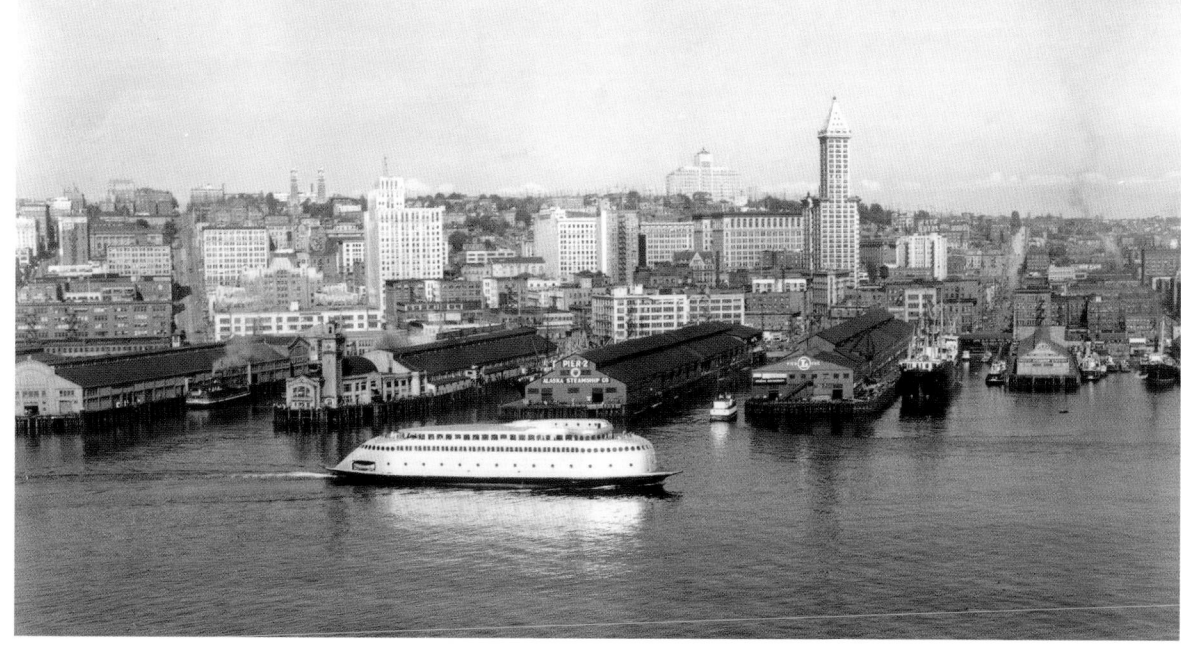

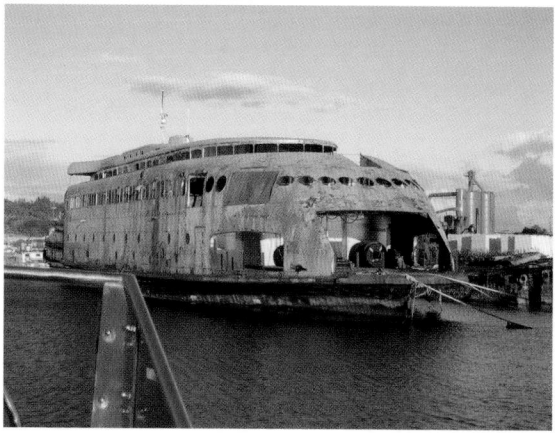

TOP *Passengers relaxing on the ride in the early 1950s.*

ABOVE *Derelict, the Kalakala is moored for now in Tacoma.*

LEFT *The Kalakala glides along Seattle's waterfront in 1935.*

OPPOSITE PAGE *Passengers watch as she comes into dock, and deckhands get the ropes ready.*

Orpheum Theater DEMOLISHED 1967

The Orpheum Theater was part of the Orpheum Circuit which toured vaudeville acts throughout the United States. The circuit started in San Francisco in 1886. But Seattle's Orpheum had different roots.

In the aftermath of 1889's Great Fire, John Considine moved to Seattle to open the People's Theater. It was located in the lava beds and made more money from the sale of liquor than from ticket stubs. The waitresses made more money turning tricks than from tips. After state and city laws banned the various parts of Considine's business model, as a last resort he turned to straight entertainment.

From Seattle Considine acquired a handful of theaters in cities across Washington and in British Columbia. He toured acts through them and in 1906 partnered with New York's Tim Sullivan to create a transcontinental vaudeville circuit. After success booking California's Orpheum Circuit in Seattle he took over all of their appearances in the Northwest.

Considine, already suffering because of the rise of the Pantages chain, met financial ruin in 1915. A business deal to sell all of his theaters had soured and left him with tremendous debt. The owners of the Orpheum Circuit purchased his theater in Seattle and then moved productions to the Moore Theater on a 10-year lease in 1917.

As the lease expired the circuit decided to build a new, dedicated Orpheum Theater. Opened in 1927, it filled the wedge from Fifth and Westlake halfway to Virginia, facing the new Medical-Dental Building on Times Square.

At 2,700 seats it was the largest house in the region. The unique Spanish renaissance interior included a Gothic dome, a massive chandelier and several types of marble in the foyer, all inspired by the Milan Opera House. The auditorium had twisted stanchions, intricate scrollwork and bronze grillwork.

The Orpheum had just a few exuberant years before the Great Depression began. For most of its years it showed movies, and it also housed the Seattle Symphony briefly.

After 40 years of shows it was demolished in August 1967 to make way for a new Westin Hotel. In the waning days all of the interior adornment was auctioned off. B. Marcus Priteca sat on the stage one last time in a prop throne and toasted his theater with a glass of champagne.

B. MARCUS PRITECA

Known to his friends as "Uncle Benny," B. Marcus Priteca came to Seattle in 1909 as a trained architect from Scotland. He worked for theater architect E. W. Houghton on projects possibly including Seattle's Majestic Theatre. Houghton had designed the Moore Theater in Seattle and was famous for theaters across the West. In 1910 at just age 21, Priteca was hired by Alexander Pantages to design his theater in San Francisco. Pantages was impressed both with the quality of the result and the low cost. He hired Priteca to design another two dozen theaters for him, including the luxurious Hollywood Pantages. The Hollywood was later used for the personal offices of Howard Hughes and hosted the Academy Awards for a decade. Priteca also did work for other theater owners, to the tune of more than one hundred theaters. Despite the large number of buildings and theaters that he designed in Seattle, very few survived the wrecking ball. The opulent Coliseum Theatre is among the survivors. In an interview just before his death in 1971, Priteca said that he wished Seattle would stop growing. He was proud of his theaters. The loss of the New Pantages and the Orpheum were particularly painful. His life, he said, was full of happy work.

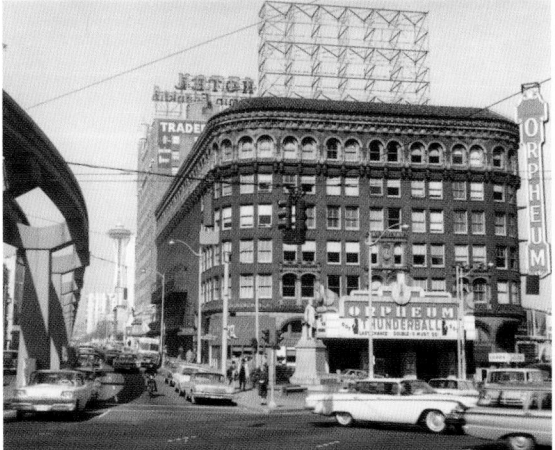

RIGHT *When it opened in 1927 the theater was on the north edge of downtown.*

FAR LEFT *The stage lays exposed as wrecking crews struggle to demolish the solidly built theater.*

LEFT *The monorail tracks and Space Needle are a sign of how much the area had changed by 1966.*

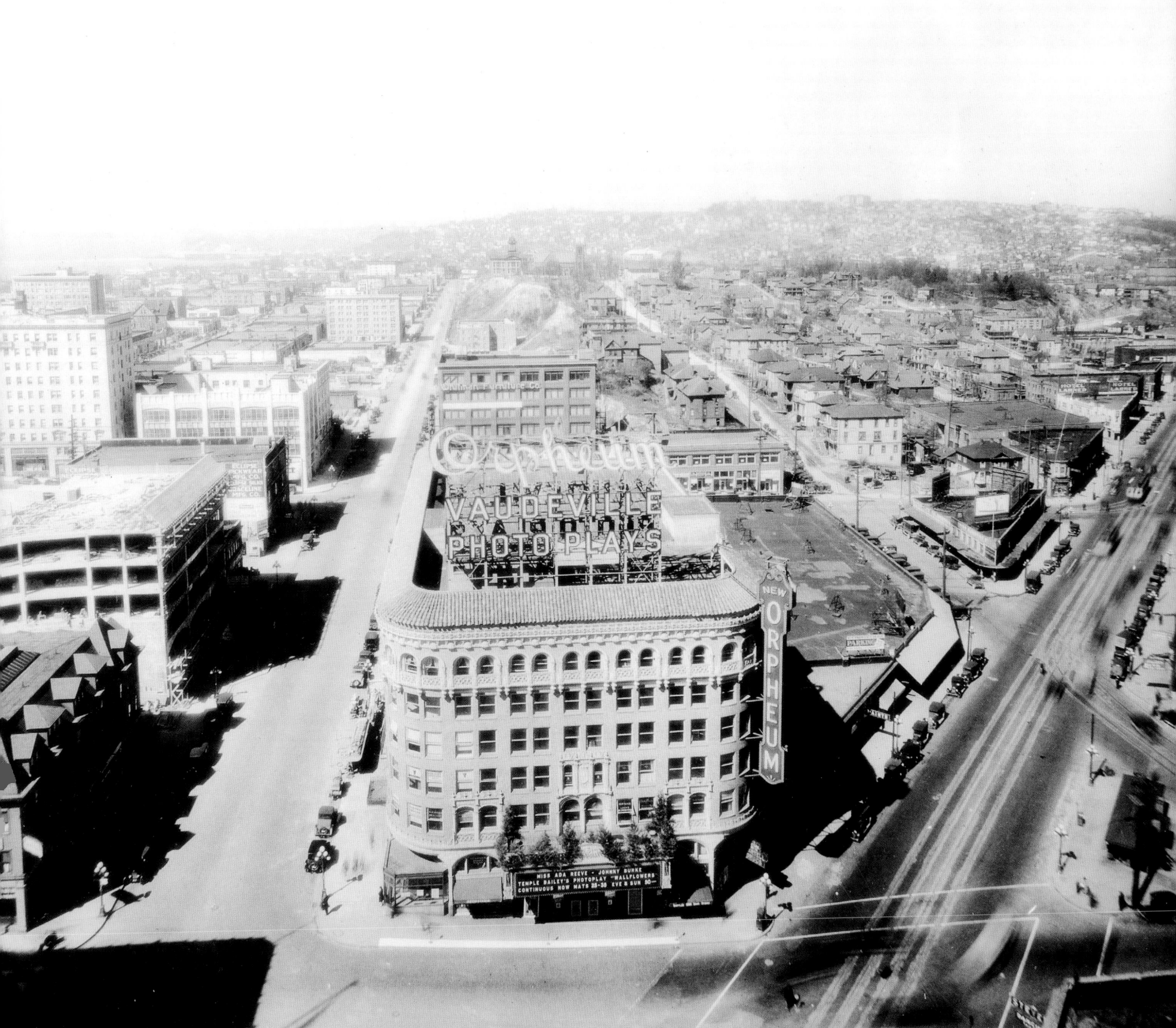

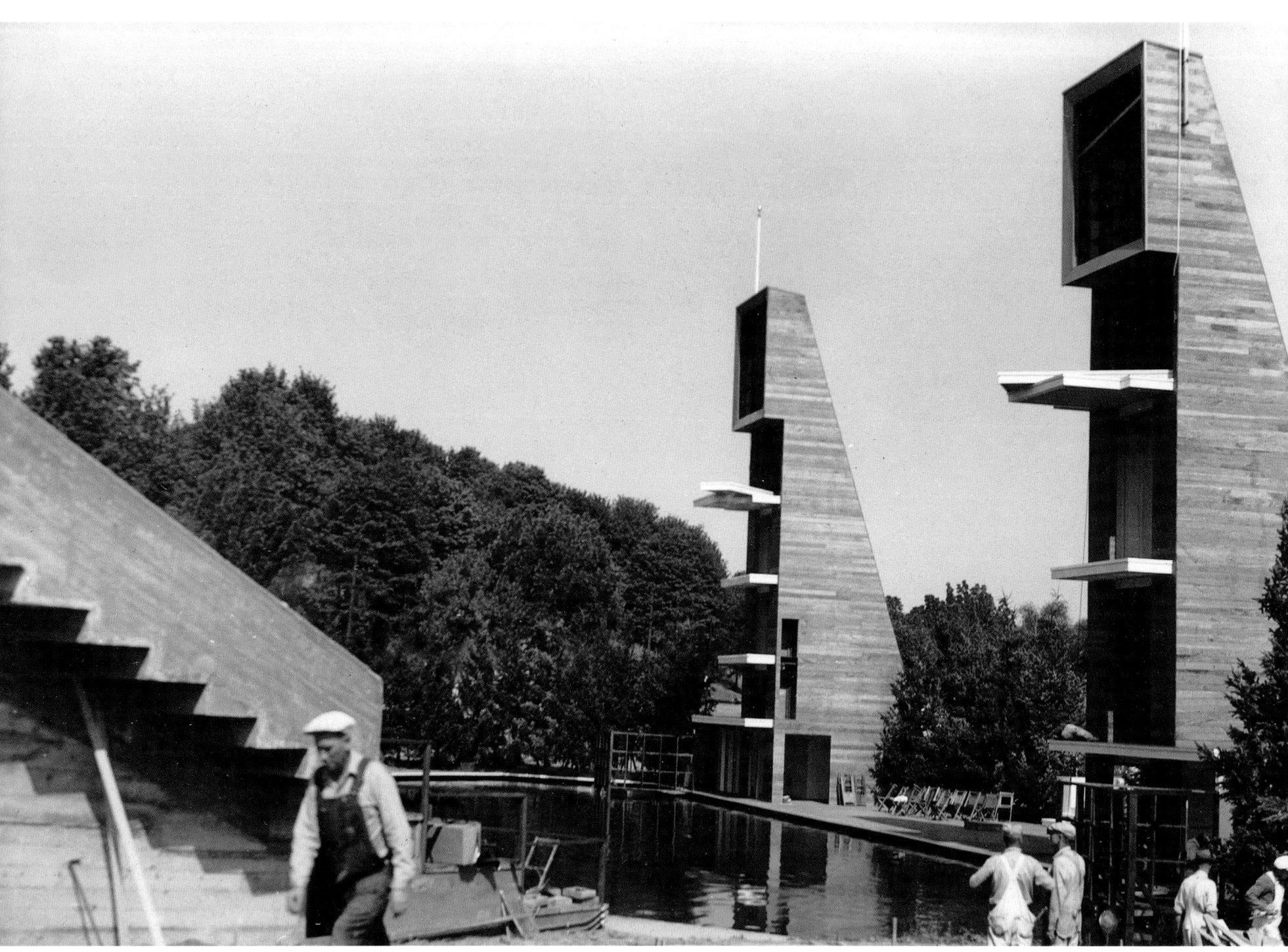

Green Lake Aqua Theatre DISMANTLED 1970

The Aqua Theatre was an outdoor aquatic stage on the south shore of Green Lake.

In 1903, the Olmsted Brothers landscape architecture consultants recommended that Seattle lower the level of Green Lake. The streetcar line and road around the lake hugged along the shallow shoreline, and the Olmsted Brothers' idea was to use reclaimed land to build a park. In 1911 the city did just that, creating 100 acres of parkland.

The lake's north, west and east shores were developed with bathing beaches, playfields, pools and other amenities. But the south shore was left largely unused.

In 1950 the organizers of Fleet Week and the Potlatches decided it was time to redefine Seattle's summer festivals. They hired the director of Minneapolis Aquatennial for his experience with water-based events. He planned 10 days of events on Elliott Bay, Lake Washington and Green Lake.

Green Lake would be the site of an aquacade, a series of swimming and diving performances along with comedic and musical sets. The water act was brought in from Minneapolis, where Al Sheehan's Aqua Follies had been a fixture of the Aquatennial from its beginning. His aquatic performance traveled occasionally for World's Fairs and summer events, so Van Kamp knew it would be a perfect addition to Seafair.

All they needed was an outdoor stage to host it. Seattle architect George Stoddard designed a concrete grandstand with two diving towers and a stage between the swimming pool and lake. Stoddard based it on the theater on Thomas Wirth Lake in Minneapolis, adjusted to the Green Lake

situation and allowing for year-round use by the Parks Department.

Formal request for the Aqua Theatre on Green Lake was filed in May. The City Council approved it June 1. Just 67 days later, on August 11, Seattle's first Aqua Follies opened at the start of the first Seafair.

In addition to the follies, a number of big-name music acts played the Aqua Theatre. Bob Hope was featured during Century 21. Sonny & Cher, The 5th Dimension, and other pop groups appeared infrequently. Operas, plays, orchestras and jazz concerts were held regularly by the parks department.

In 1964 the Aqua Follies were canceled in Minneapolis, and Seattle followed suit in 1965. The Aquatennial and Seafair management both cited rising costs and dropping attendance as the cause.

The theater had a brief revival in 1969. First up was Led Zeppelin opening for Three Dog Night in May for a sunny, early 2 o'clock show. Zeppelin had just released their first single and were on their second tour of the United States. They were so new that the next day's review still described guitarist Jimmy Page as "formerly of the Yardbirds." The confused writer for the *Seattle Times* also claimed that Three Dog Night outclassed Zeppelin.

Seafair put on a series of comedic, musical, swimming and diving performances again in 1969 with the International Water Follies troupe from Boston. It was a return to the theater's heyday with two weeks of two-hour shows.

A few days later The Grateful Dead and Jerry Garcia's New Riders of the Purple Sage rolled into town from their famous Woodstock performance. The planned August 20 show was canceled due to rain, so they went over and played in Ballard. They did the Aqua Theatre the next night with a mellow, meandering, psychedelic performance.

Fans at both the Dead show and Zeppelin climbed the diving towers for a better view. Fearing for public safety, the parks department had the towers torn down in early 1970. Other than an occasional outdoor religious service, it was the end of the Aqua Theatre.

OPPOSITE PAGE *Workers put on finishing touches for the first Seafair in 1951.*

BELOW LEFT *View of the stage from the completed bleachers.*

BELOW *Ruins of the theater still remain on the south edge of the lake.*

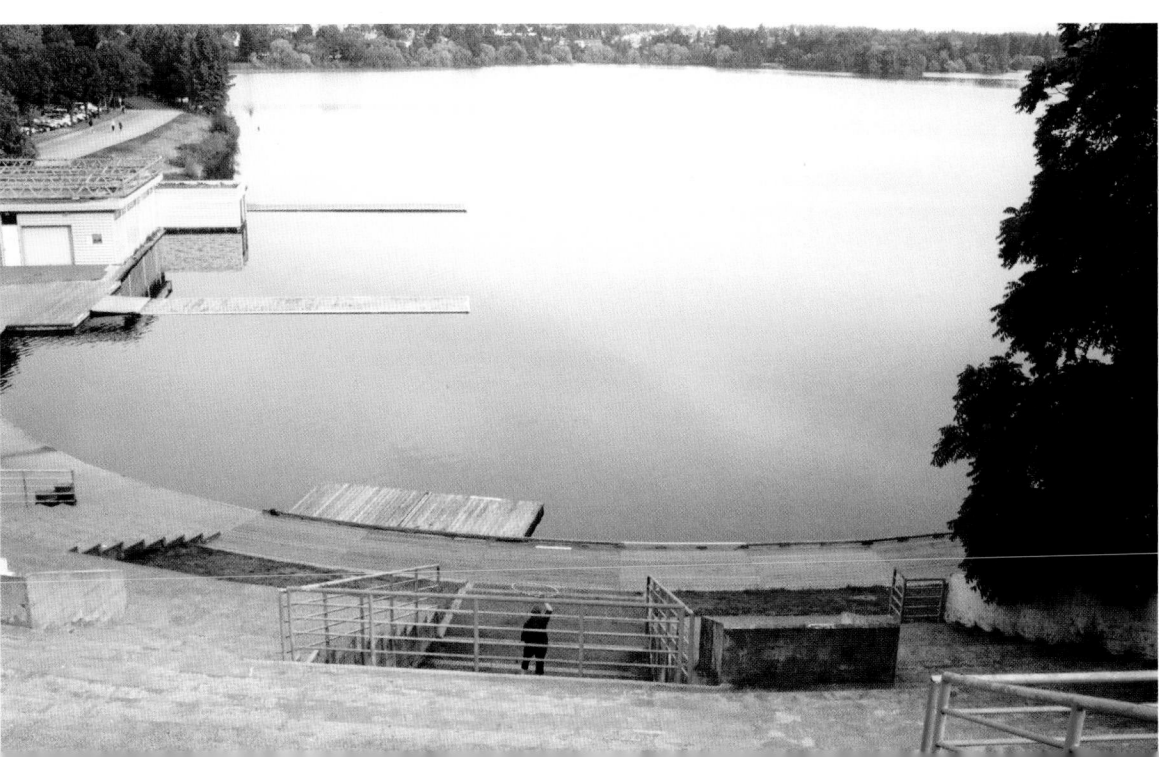

Burke Building RAZED 1971

The Burke Building was an office building developed by Thomas Burke. Burke was serving in the Washington supreme court and being courted to represent the Great Northern Railway in Seattle in 1889 when he decided to create a first-class office building.

It was designed by Elmer Fisher, commissioned in the months just before the Great Fire. The Burke Building along with his Pioneer Building established Fisher as Seattle's next top architect, supplanting William Boone. Because of the scarcity of materials after the fire and Thomas Burke's perfectionism, the building was not completed until more than two years after it was announced. Fisher designed nearly half of the office buildings created in downtown from 1889 to 1891, and the Burke Building was perhaps the best.

It was built on the northwest corner of Second Avenue and Marion Street, covering a quarter of the block. It stood six stories, U-shape fronting Second Avenue and open to the mid-block alley downhill. A lower floor had access to Marion Street and an additional basement accessed the alley because of the steep grade.

Fisher's initial designs were heavy with the Victorian elements that had been common in Seattle's architecture before the fire. But each time a drawing was published in the paper the building looked more like contemporary office blocks in Chicago. Stone gave way to brick and terracotta, peaked tower removed and cornice much simplified. The similarity to Chicago was intentional, as Thomas Burke repeatedly compared it to the Rookery office building which was the vanguard of that city.

The first floor of the Burke Building was done in gray stone, with a bank and storefronts along the street. The upper office floors were all red brick, with terracotta fired to match. Its relative simplicity of form and uniformity of color—along with its height—made the Burke Building stand out on Second Avenue for decades. Its form was easily recognizable from the bay in an approaching ship.

In 1894 Burke installed a steam-driven electricity plant in the basement of the building. In addition to powering businesses and elevators in the Burke itself, lines fanned out to do the same for surrounding buildings. It also provided power to the streetcars of the West Street railway to Ballard. The

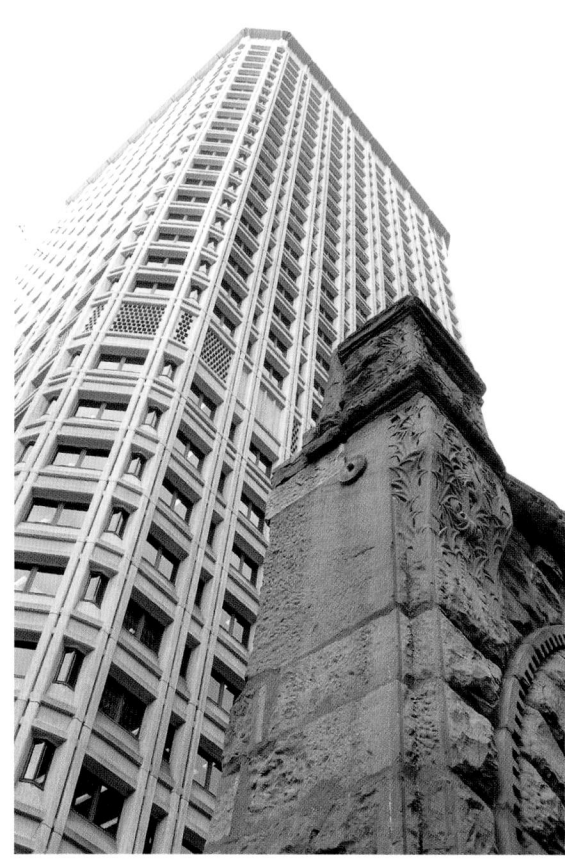

Burke Building Electric Company was the last independent power supplier acquired by Seattle Electric Company in 1900. They moved the equipment to Post Alley, where a new central facility supplied the city.

The office and retail space served businesses for six decades. It was demolished in 1971, though, to make way for a new federal office tower. The building was ransacked for salvage, and the feds decided to keep several artifacts scattered around their new campus.

ABOVE *Several remnants of the Burke Building now stand in the shadow of Seattle's third Federal Building.*

OPPOSITE PAGE *The Commercial National Bank occupied the corner storefront in the base of gray stone. Red brick and matching terracotta rose five floors above it.*

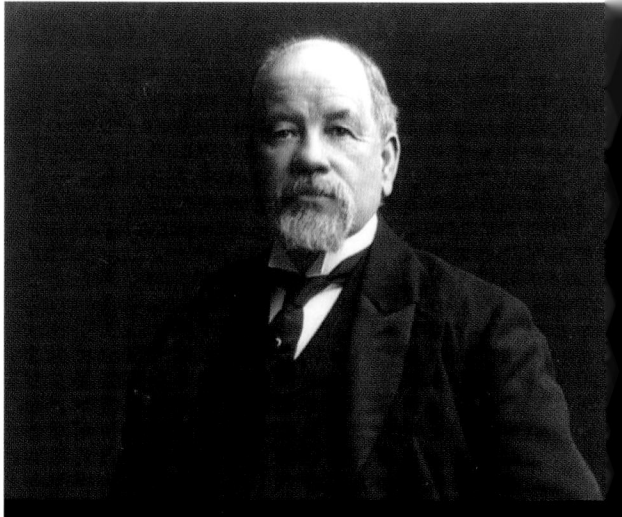

JUDGE THOMAS BURKE

Thomas Burke came to Seattle in 1875 when the population was still only 2,000. He immediately opened a law partnership, and was elected probate judge of King County in 1877. He acquired his honorific after being appointed as Chief Justice of the Supreme Court of Washington Territory in 1888. Burke had an unwavering confidence in the future of Seattle, and never had an idle moment or dollar. When a railroad, streetcar, business, or battleship needed funding, Burke was the first to contribute. Then he would hop on a train to New York to find capital to finish the job. Burke became corporate lawyer for the Great Northern Railroad and representative in the Northwest, convincing James J. Hill to end the transcontinental railroad in Seattle in 1893. Burke created the New York Block, Exchange Building, Arcade Building, and Empire Building. Burke also was involved in a surprising array of organizations. He was president of the Northwest Society of the Archaeological Institute, a member of the Japanese Society of Seattle, a charter member of the Seattle Chamber of Commerce, a director of the U.S. Chamber of Commerce, and even a trustee of the Carnegie Foundation. Judge Burke died while in the midst of a speech at Carnegie Hall in New York in 1925. He was speaking to the foundation about the need for peace and friendship between Japan and America.

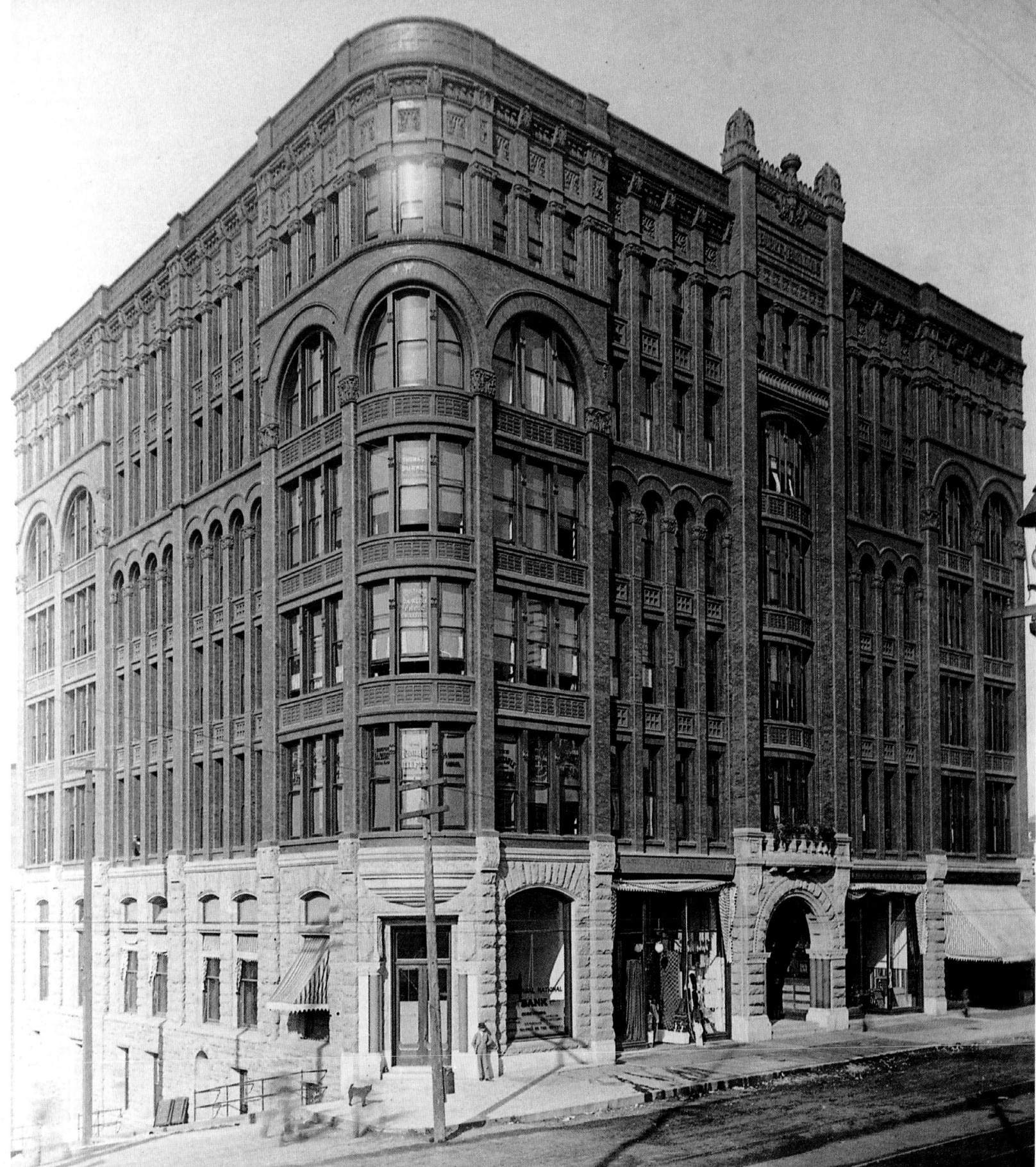

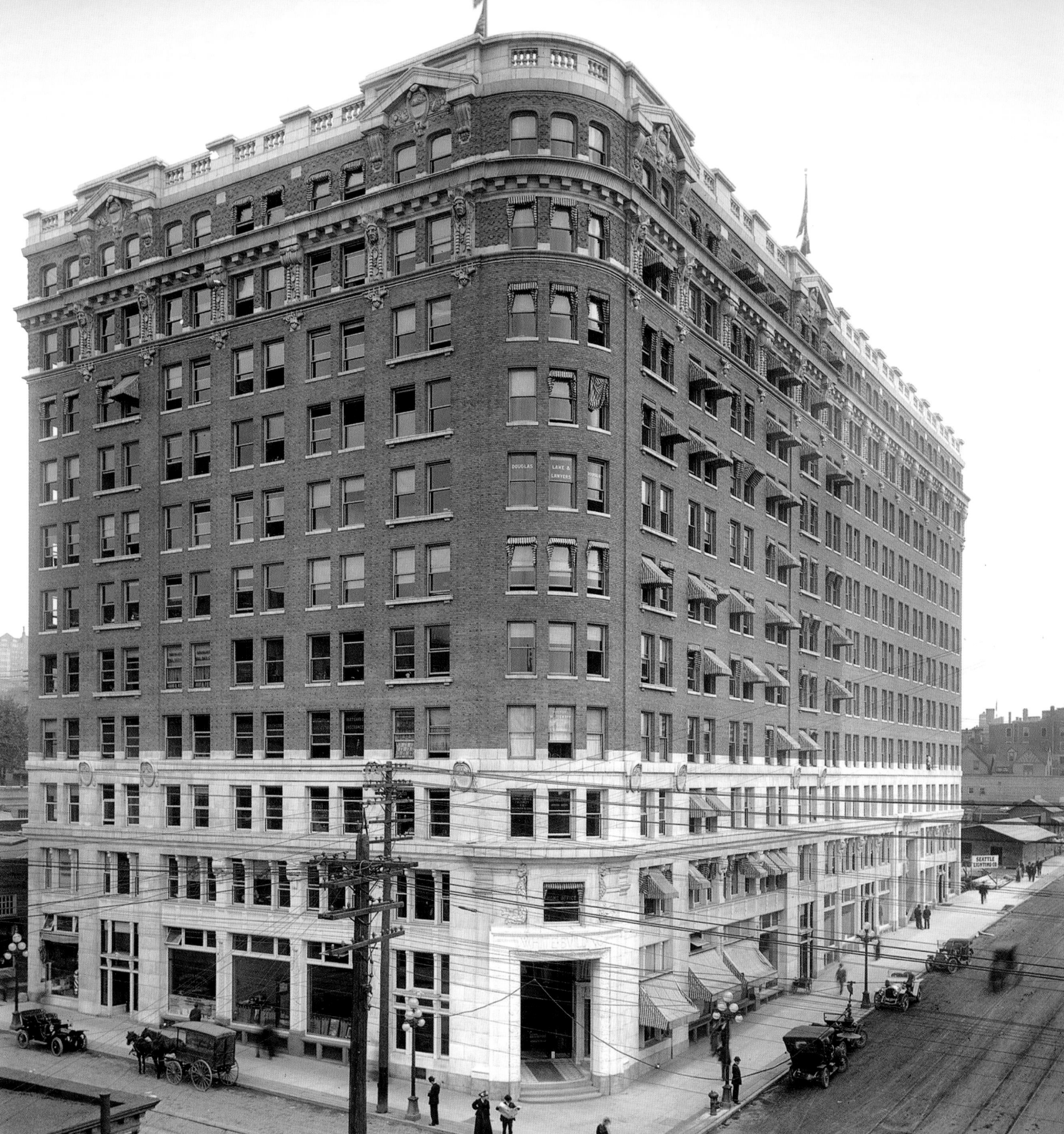

White-Henry-Stuart Building DEMOLISHED 1974

After the University of Washington moved to Montlake in 1895, they leveraged the old Territorial University and began developing their urban property. For a number of years the buildings were leased to a variety of tenants including the city library and the Central School. Then in 1907 Denny Knoll became the latest victim of Seattle's regrading. Twenty vertical feet of dirt—ten million cubic feet—were removed to bring the streets down to a constant grade across the campus.

The UW regents leased out the entire site to the Metropolitan Building Company. Plans for the Metropolitan tract called for a new "city within a city," following the tenets of the City Beautiful movement. Common elements and materials would unify the blocks with a consistent skyline and harmonious architectural experience.

Three of the buildings were so tightly integrated that they eventually lost their individual character. The White Building was completed in 1909. The Henry was completed later that year. The final of the trio, the Stuart, was completed in 1915. Later they became known simply as the White-Henry-Stuart Building. The entire tract was planned in a Beaux Arts style, and the trio featured a brick facade with white terracotta banding. Busts of Native Americans and other flourishes adorned the buildings.

The Metropolitan Building Company's lease with the university ended in 1953, and a new era began for the Metropolitan Tract. Eventually only the Cobb Building—stylistically identical to the White-Henry-Stuart—and the Olympic Hotel would remain. In 1974, the White-Henry-Stuart complex of buildings were demolished to make way for Minoru Yamasaki's Rainier Tower.

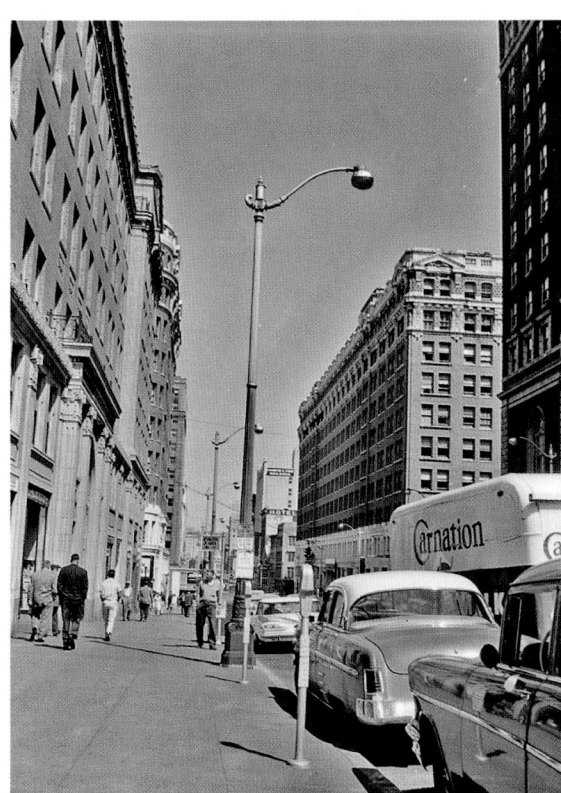

ABOVE Looking north on Fourth Avenue, the sharp corner of the Stuart Building at University stretches the complex the full block length.

LEFT The White and Henry buildings are complete, taking the complex to mid-block from Union to University streets in about 1910.

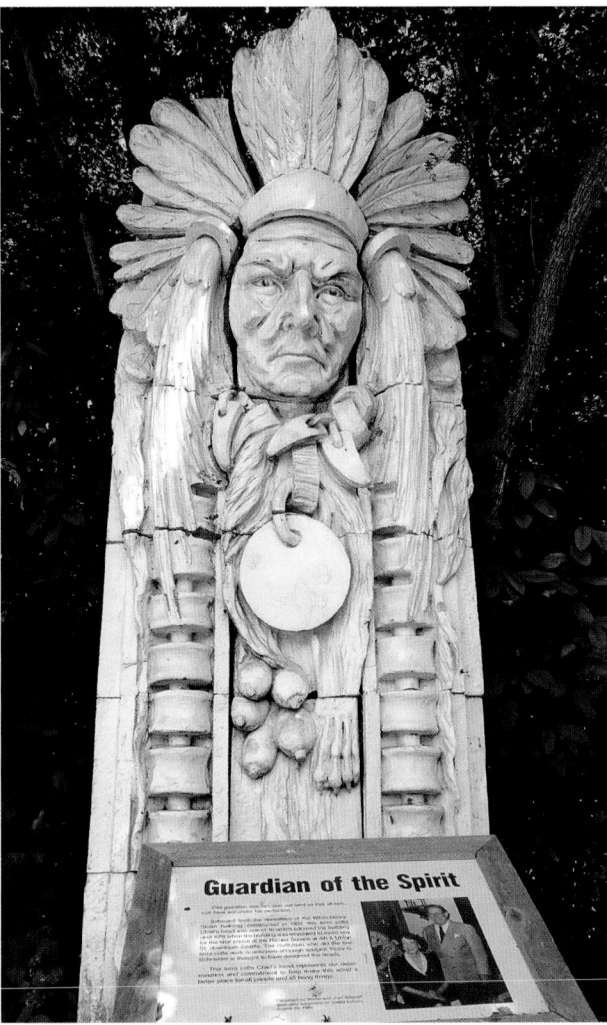

Guardian of the Spirit

EDWARD CURTIS

For the last hundred years the rumor has persisted that the complex's terracotta Native American chieftain heads were modeled from one of Edward Curtis's photographs. Edward began working as a photographer in Seattle as a teenager in 1887 to support his brother Asahel and widowed mother. Asahel joined him in 1892 but later struck out on his own, becoming a successful landscape and urban photographer. In 1898 Edward's photograph of Chief Sealth's daughter Kikisoblu or Princess Angeline won the National Photographic Society Grand Prize. The following year he joined the Harriman Expedition to photograph Alaska's native societies, and the next year joined an expedition to photograph the Blackfeet. Based on that experience, Edward began his life's work in 1906 and spent the next five decades completing his 20-volume photography masterpiece, *North American Indian*. He surveyed more than 80 tribes, took 40,000 photographs, and along the way cataloged the culture and history of the people he met. The "Indian Head" terracotta was reportedly a Sioux chieftain, but it has a strong resemblance to Little Plume, a Piegan chief that Edward photographed in 1900.

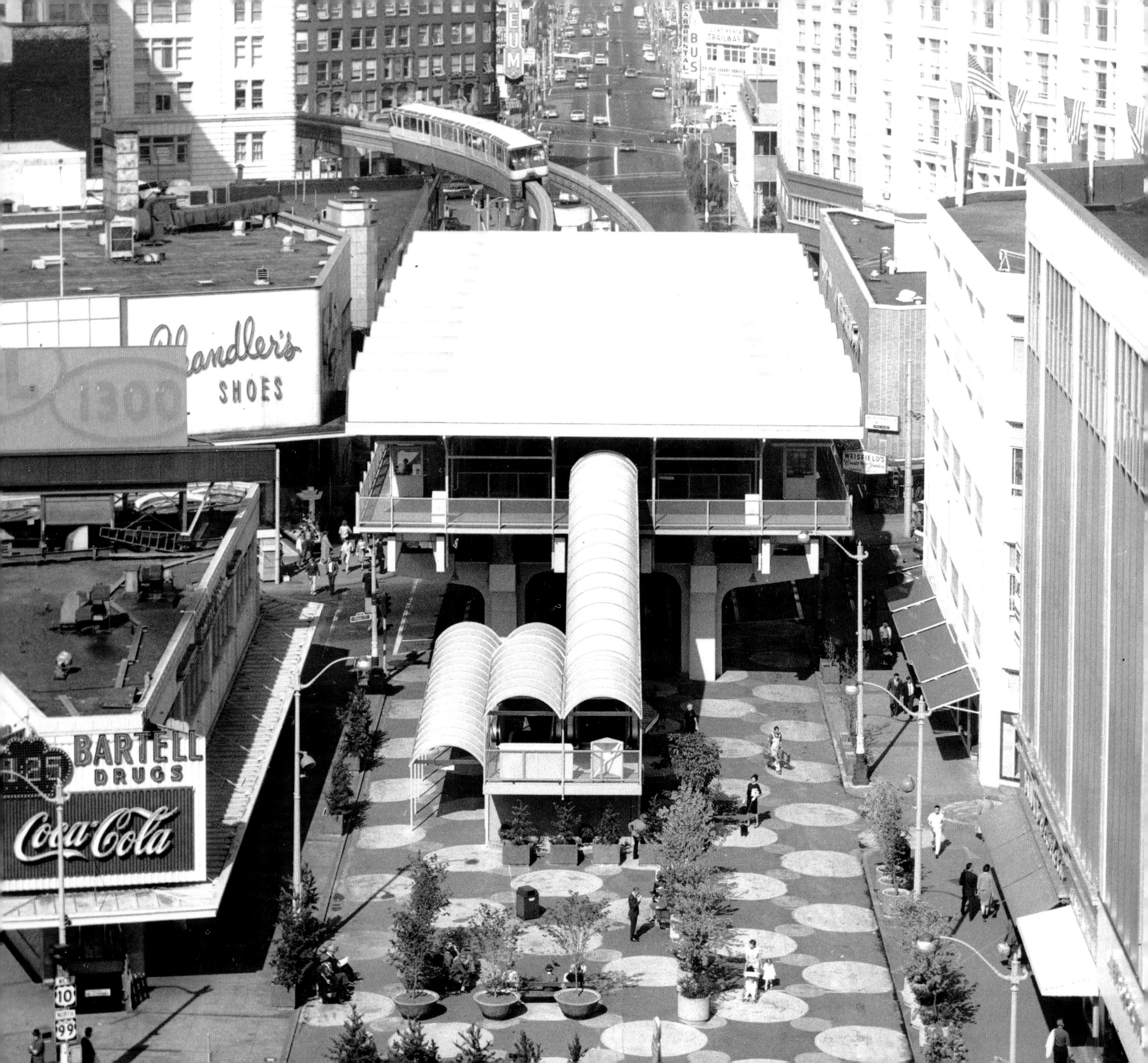

Westlake Monorail Station REPLACED WITH MALL 1986

The streamlined World's Fair Monorail was built for the 1962 fair in Seattle. The scene of it gliding on simple concrete tracks became an iconic, modernist image of Seattle. The monorail ride was very simple to understand for tourists: one stop at the fairgrounds, a two-minute ride, and one stop downtown at Westlake.

The monorail was built in 10 short months by West Germany's Alweg Corporation from May 1961 to March 1962. The entire project was a demonstration of excellence in engineering and execution.

The monorail traveled south on Fifth Avenue to Westlake Avenue, where it turned and entered a mid-air station. In order to build the station, Westlake Avenue was closed to automobiles from Olive Way south to Fourth Avenue. The station was suspended over Pine Street with access at either end. Ramps ended in Times Square near the Orpheum Theater to the north and the new Westlake Park to the south.

The Seattle Art Commission caused several alterations to Alweg's design for the station.

Supports for the station were narrowed. The station was moved from the area along Fourth Avenue to mid-air over Pine Street. The Commission was unable to convince Alweg to use space-saving escalators instead of switch-backed moving walkways or speedramps. As a compromise, the speedramps were one-way. The entrance was to the south of Pine Street, and the exit to the north.

The design allowed more than 10,000 people per hour to pass through the terminal, matching the maximum capacity and arrival rate of the monorails. It was needed, as 136,000 people rode the monorail in the first five days alone. There were more than seven million rides by the end of the fair. Nearly half of fair goers rode the monorail and went through Westlake Terminal.

The canopy over the speedramps and the station was light, porous, and unadorned, fitting the Modern design tenets of Century 21. It was formed by a series of shallow arches, supported by steel tubing and lit by large globes.

Debate about what to do with Westlake Park actually predated the monorail. Plans for the park

were put on hold because many people believed the monorail would be torn down after the fair. After it proved successful during the fair, the Arts Commission and other groups began arguing that the station should be pushed back closer to Olive Way.

By the mid-1980s, it was decided to build a new shopping mall with a monorail station at the top and a bus tunnel station in the basement below. A hotel tower capped the building at Fifth and Olive Way.

The station was torn down in September 1986.

SEATTLE MONORAIL PROJECT

Taxi driver Dick Falkenbury had an idea that he couldn't shake. Stuck in traffic, he could not understand why the monorail only had two stops. In 1996 he set out to collect signatures to put an initiative on the ballot. Voters would be able to consider an X-shaped system that reached the corners of Seattle. The initiative won, and the monorail continued to receive support through two subsequent elections. First voters agreed to fund planning of the system, and then in 2002 a razor-thin margin approved construction of the 14-mile Green Line, which would travel from West Seattle to Crown Hill. After reaching agreement with a developer, the monorail agency's financial situation fell apart. Tax revenues were far lower than expected. The agency returned to voters with a shorter line only to West Seattle in 2005. This time voters said no.

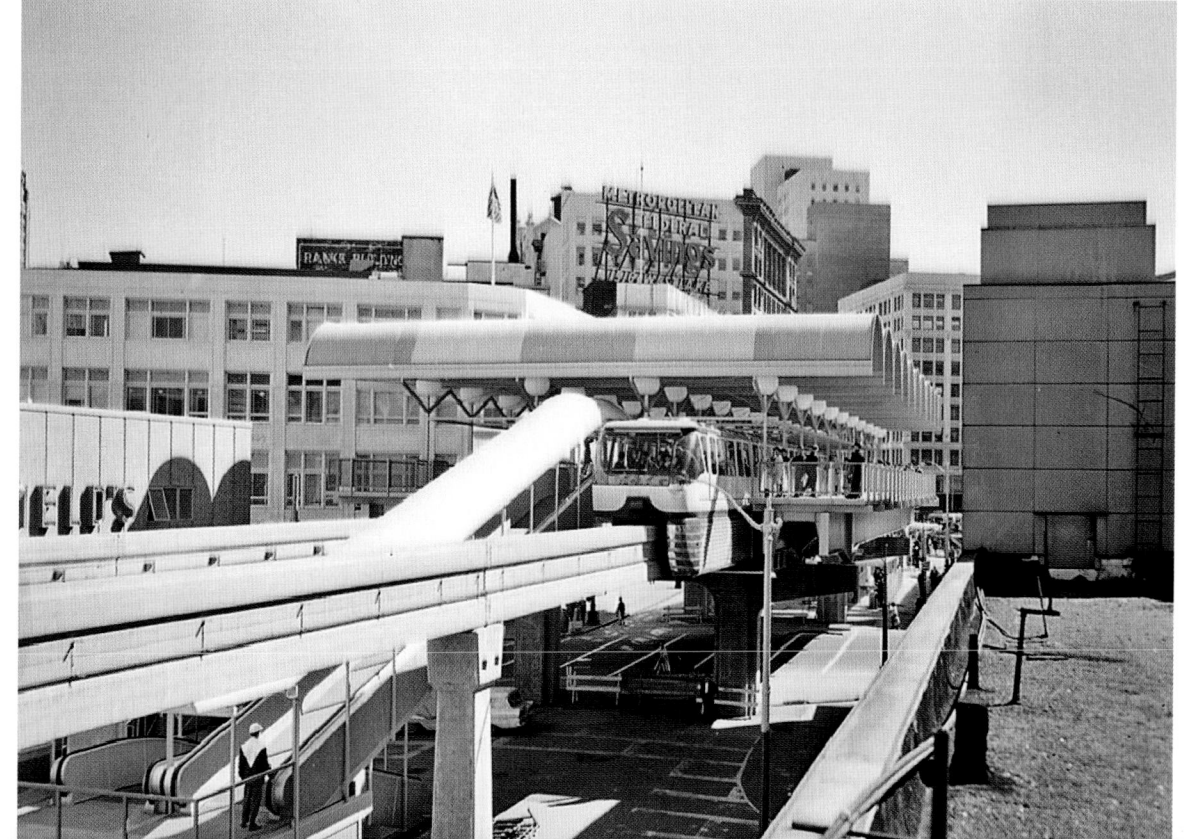

LEFT *Looking south through the station with moving walkways and Pine Street below.*

OPPOSITE PAGE *Looking north up Westlake with the Orpheum Theater ahead to the left and Frederick & Nelson to the right adorned with American flags in 1963.*

G. O. Guy Drugs REBRANDED 1987

George Omar Guy uprooted his family and drugstore in 1888 from Chicago and moved to Seattle. He was 14th in a steadily growing list of drug stores, but he had one claim to fame that differentiated him from the rest: G. O. Guy invented the ice cream float.

In 1872, Guy worked at a drugstore part time to gain experience while studying at the Philadelphia College of Pharmacy. One day while serving a vanilla soda to one customer and ice cream to another, he accidentally dropped the ice cream into the soda. He apologized profusely and was about to pour it down the sink when one customer charitably asked to drink it anyways. The man was pleasantly surprised and told his ice cream-ordering companion to order one as well. Two years later the drugstore owner, Robert Green, popularized the ice cream soda at Philadelphia's Centennial Exposition.

The float lore was enough to allow Guy to survive his store's destruction in the 1889 fire, and come back bigger. He had time to save much of the store before fire swept over, and he set up a first-aid station to treat victims of the fire. He ran his store out of tents during reconstruction, and then moved to Second Avenue and Yesler Way opposite the newly built Hotel Seattle.

Guy separated himself from the competition with opulent interiors. He paid for French-cut glass for his mirrors and oak display cases to be shipped all the way past Chile. He stocked the largest selection of herbs, barks, leaves and roots in the Pacific Northwest. There was no lock on the front door because the store was open 24 hours a day.

After George's death in 1927, his children began expanding the business. In 1929 over a million ice cream sodas were sold, and 1930 brought three new fruit flavors. There were White River Valley berry, Wenatchee cherry and Island Belle grape which used locally bred grapes from Olympia. By 1933 there were 11 stores around the city and G. O. Guy was Seattle's oldest drugstore.

As part of Pioneer Square's 1960s revitalization, George's grandson G. A. Guy remodeled their modernized store back to the style of the 1890s. What remained of the original furnishings were put back on display, including the colorful glass globes and old gold-lettered jars.

In the late 1970s the family sold G. O. Guy to Sam Rubinstein, who converted the larger suburban stores to his Bonanza 88 brand. In 1987 Rubinstein sold the six small urban Seattle G. O. Guy stores to Pay 'n Save. After several successive acquisitions and changes in corporate strategies, none of the former G. O. Guy drugstores remain in operation.

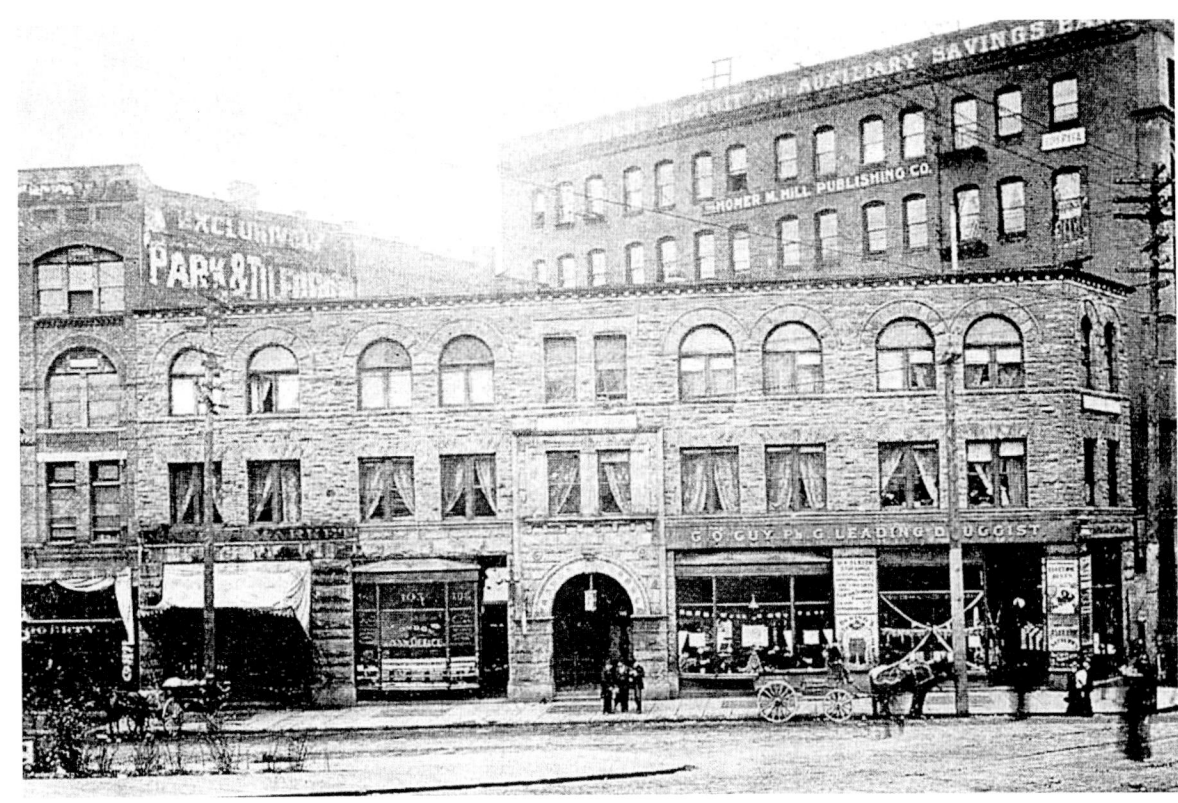

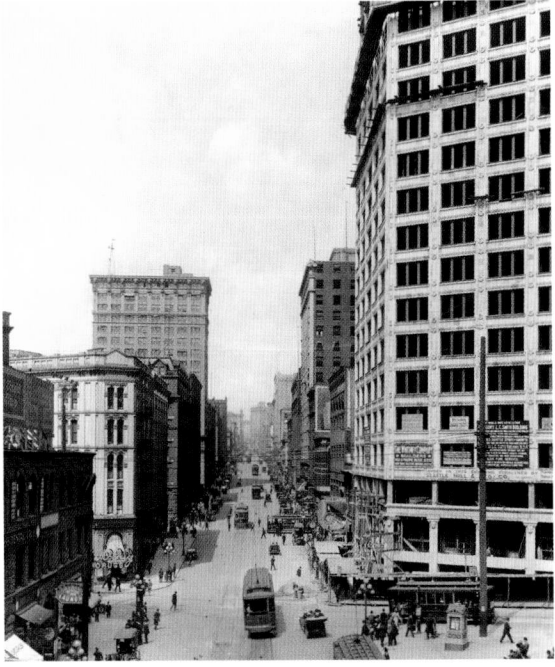

ABOVE *G. O. Guy is on the near left with the Smith Tower on the near right, looking north on Second Avenue.*

LEFT *On the right side of the Metropole Building on Second Avenue, his sign says "G. O. Guy Ph. G. Leading Druggist."*

RIGHT *Guy's soda fountain is decked out for the Alaska Yukon Pacific Expo, ready for a rush of customers.*

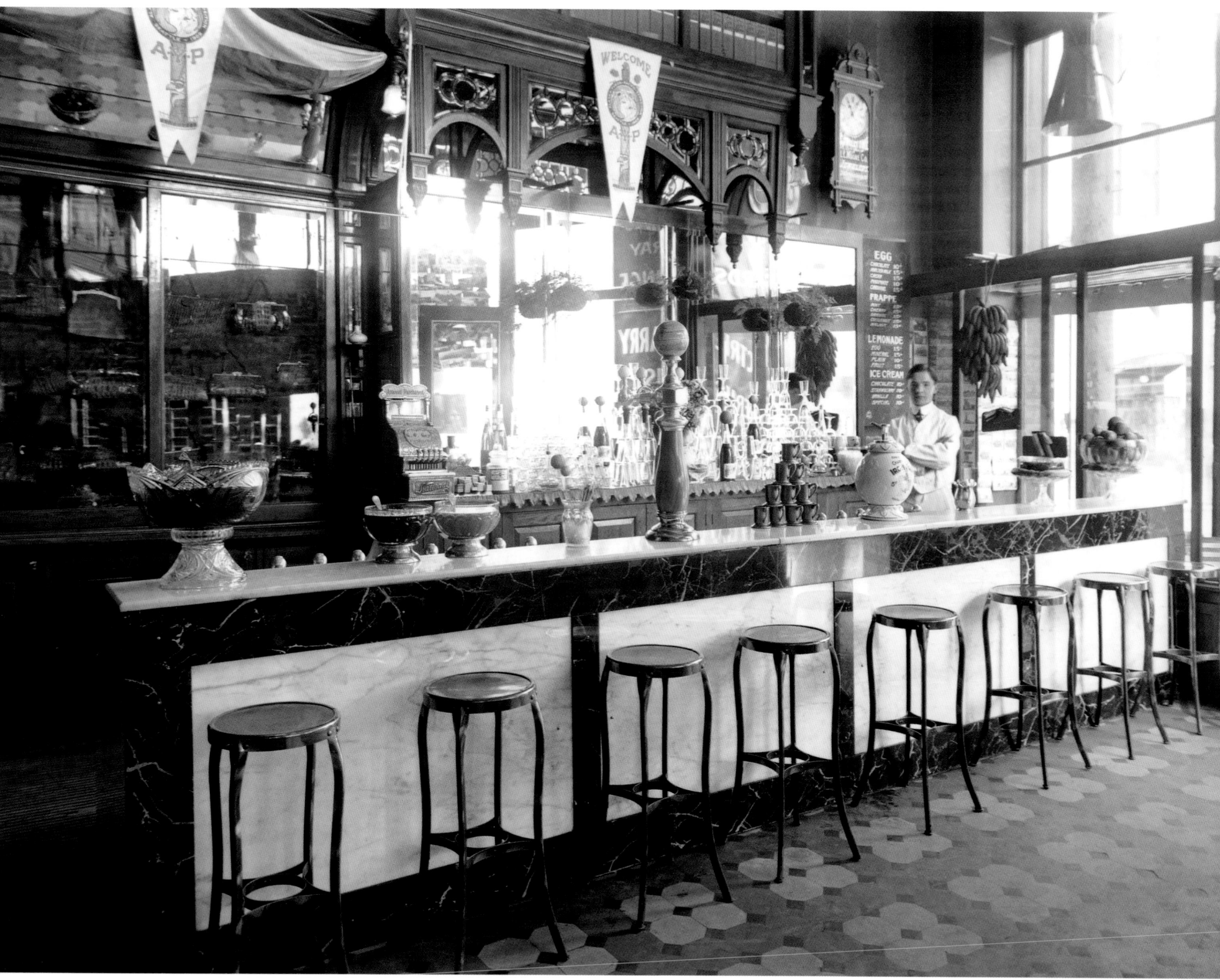

I-5 Ramps to Nowhere CONNECTED 1991

For three decades Seattle's skyline included massive aerial ramps from Interstate 5 that dramatically led to nothing.

When I-5 was completed in 1967, a major junction was provided near Dearborn Street south of downtown Seattle. The mid-air junction would be needed when U.S. Route 10 converted to Interstate 90 and connected all the way to the Alaska Way Viaduct on Seattle's waterfront. I-90 construction was already progressing rapidly to the east side of Lake Washington.

I-90 hit a snag when Seattle residents discovered that federal planning laws had been violated by the state highway department. In particular, the required evaluation of impacts on

OPPOSITE PAGE Two of the ramps to nowhere, later connected to I-90's exits.

RIGHT Two of SR-520's remaining ramps in the Washington Park Arboretum.

BELOW I-5 snakes south of downtown past Beacon Hill. Four flying ramps come to abrupt ends mid-air over the warehouses.

people, economy, and the environment had been completely skipped. After several appeals, federal courts ordered the state to complete the Environmental Impact Statement in 1972. It took them seven long years to write.

The ramps were emblematic of Seattle in the 1970s. Boeing entered a downturn in 1970, leading to 17 percent unemployment in Seattle. Demolition

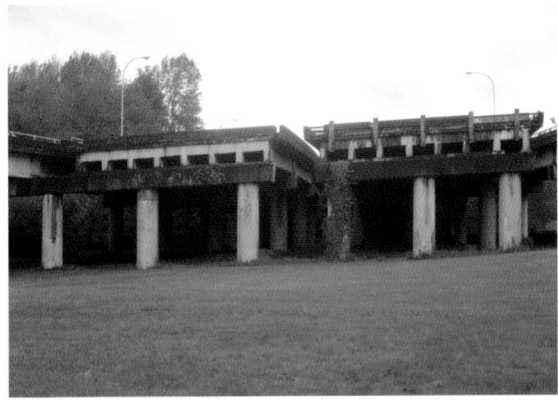

of old buildings downtown left empty holes with staircases leading to side entrances that no longer were there.

But it also represented a city that struggled with the brutalist ugliness of the new freeways and missed the landmark churches, hotels, and entire neighborhoods eliminated by I-5. Seattle's citizens revolted against leadership to stop the Bay Freeway through the Seattle Center and R. H. Thomson Expressway through another set of neighborhoods.

When the Kingdome was built, the ramps intended for a viaduct connection were instead turned into on- and off-ramps for I-5 at Royal Brougham. It took two more decades, but eventually I-90 moved forward and reached I-5. The entrances, exits and junctions were finished in 1991, putting an end to the ramps to nowhere.

520'S RAMPS

In early 2013 city and state leaders announced that Seattle's last remaining ramps to nowhere would be destroyed. State Route 520 heads east from I-5 to Lake Washington, crosses the lake on one of the world's longest floating bridges, and continues east into suburban cities. In the 1960s Seattle's planners were drunk on freeways. A grid of freeways were planned to cover the city. One called for the extension and upgrade of Empire Way (now Martin Luther King, Jr. Way) from I-90 to 520. The new road would be called the R. H. Thomson Expressway, named after Seattle's famous former city engineer. 520 construction prepared for the junction with a variety of ramps. But Seattle's citizens had seen enough with I-5. Neighborhood groups from Lake City to Judkins Park protested to the City Council. Finally the R. H. Thomson Expressway was canceled in 1970. The ramps have stood for two extra decades after I-5's. But with the impending rebuild of 520, state planners have decided that the ramps will be destroyed within a short time.

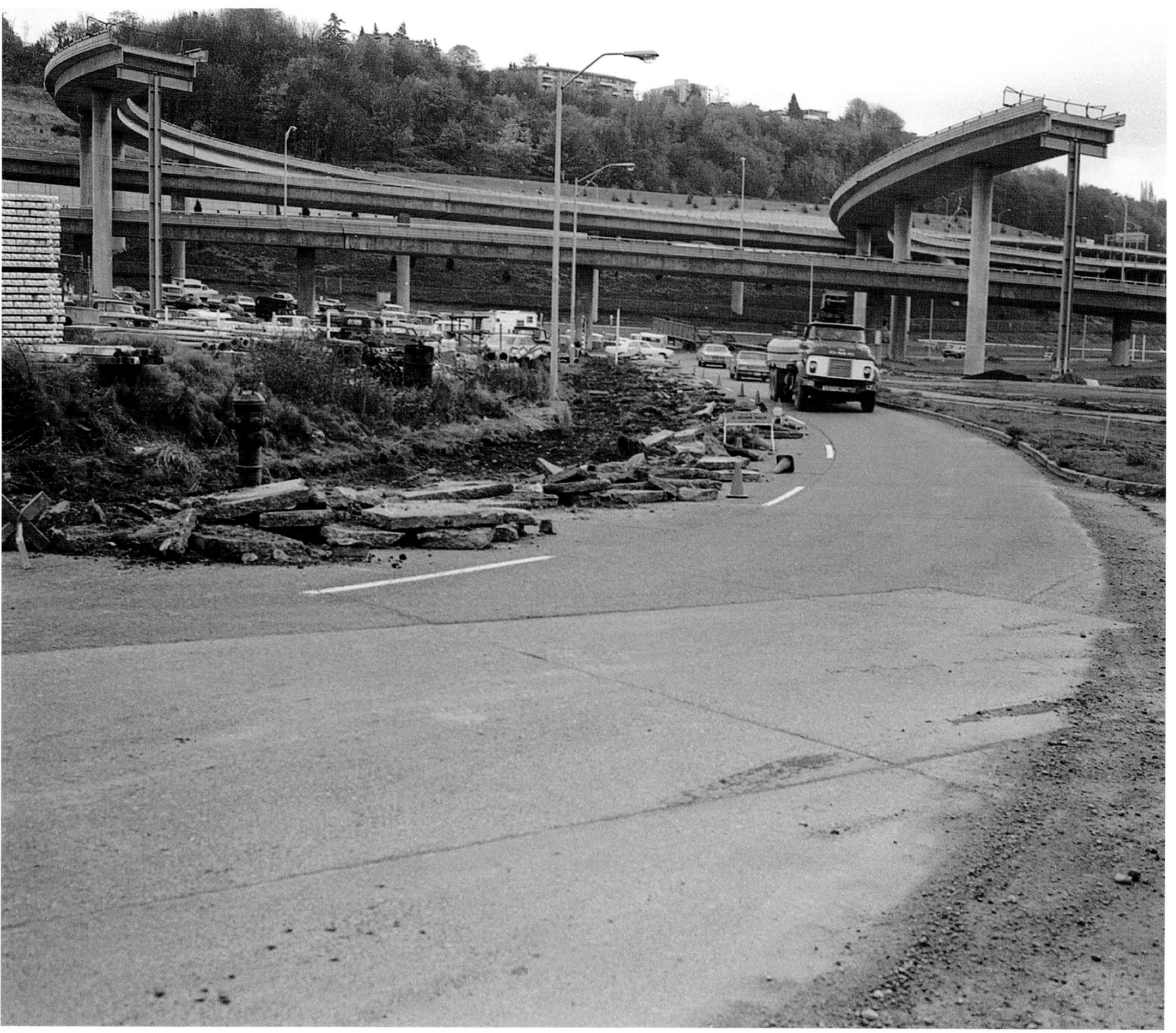

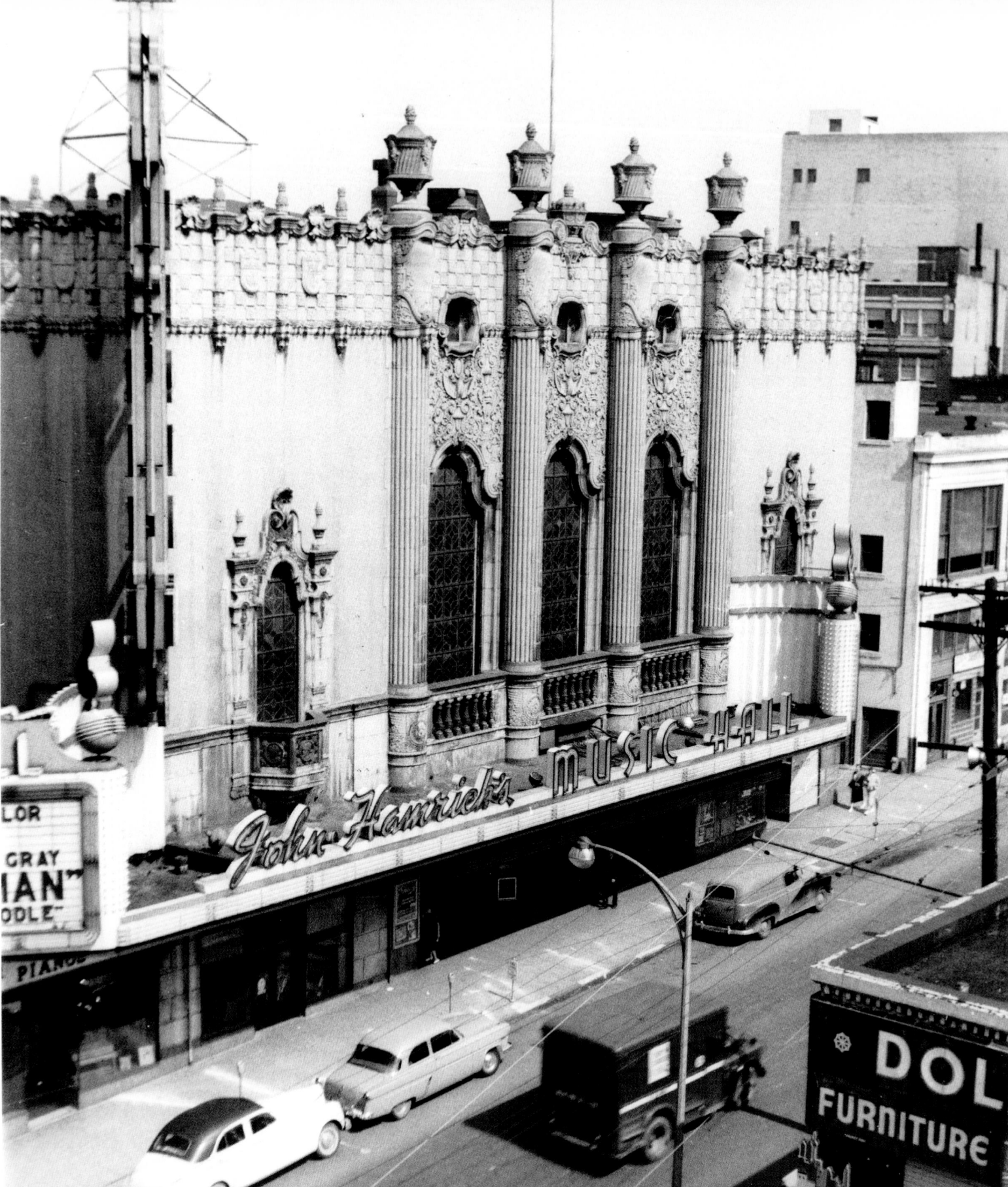

Fox Theatre DEMOLISHED 1991

William Fox's theater at Seventh Avenue and Olive Way was the last of the great theaters built in Seattle. Due to persistent financial difficulties it was reborn multiple times as a vaudeville house, movie theater, and dinner showplace.

Work on a new theater project began in early 1926 at Olive Way and Seventh, a number of blocks outside of the theater district. The Mayflower Theatre was planned as Seattle's most glamorous house for the arts. The design was described as Spanish Revival or Moorish with plaster ceilings and exterior cast stone detailing. Just as the theater was nearing completion, developer W. D. Comer was bankrupted by the failure of a previous property and sent to jail for fraud.

It took several years and a change of ownership, but in June 1929 the newly christened Fox Theatre was opened. The new owner was none other than William Fox, head of the Fox Films studio and a chain of more than 1,000 theaters across the country. Fox bought out MGM Studios in March, so opening night at the Fox Theatre was MGM's blockbuster, Oscar-winning *Broadway Melody*. Five thousand Seattleites crowded into the Fox to see one of the first musicals to use Technicolor and the first to have sound for the entire film.

For six months the Fox hosted plays, musicals and the latest movies. Then Fox Films collapsed at the start of the Great Depression. The theater struggled through the Depression, with a failed attempt by new management to rebrand it as the Roxy.

In 1934 Seattle theater manager John Hamrick reopened it yet again as the Music Hall. It would be the sophisticated complement to his Blue Mouse and Music Box theaters on Fifth Avenue. Hamrick's Music Hall staged operas, Shakespearean plays, Seattle Symphony performances, musicals, touring concerts by acts like Helen Morgan and Bob Hope, and featured first-run motion pictures.

In 1965 the Northwest's Sterling Theaters chain bought out the lease of the Music Hall along with the Orpheum and Hamrick's other two theaters. They remodeled the interior to be more appropriate for movies: the pipe organ was removed, the balcony was closed off, and a new marquee was raised. To differentiate from their Music Box, Sterling renamed the Music Hall as the Seventh Avenue Theater.

Perhaps the best remembered era of the theater began in 1977. Seattle restaurateur Jack McGovern took over after Sterling's lease expired, reopening the space as McGovern's Music Hall. McGovern grew up a short walk away and had gone to the Fox Theatre as a child. His vision was completely different, though. The garish lights and neon were removed from the facade, bringing attention back to the Spanish revival architecture. But inside it was transformed into a Las Vegas-style showroom, with showgirls, musicals and variety acts. Seats on the floor and mezzanine were removed to put in dinner tables.

Like his predecessors, McGovern struggled to make ends meet in the large space. He filed for bankruptcy in 1980, just three years after opening. By 1983 the theater had closed four times and canceled a number of shows mid-run. In 1985 his theater ended for good.

In 1987 the theater reopened briefly for dinner entertainment as the Emerald Palace. By that point, downtown Seattle finally had spread to the theater. The Washington State Convention Center and Westlake Center both opened just blocks away. The Clise family, owners of the Music Hall since the 1930s, decided to redevelop the site as a hotel. Beginning in 1985 Seattle's Landmarks Preservation Board attempted to stop demolition, but they were eventually defeated by Clise's army of lawyers.

After demolition was complete in 1991 the Clises changed their minds, leaving the property as an empty lot instead of the grand theater that had once stood. In an odd twist of fate, the organ is now the theater's last remnant. It was installed in the Bob Hope Theatre in Stockton, California in 2004 during a complete renovation of that former Fox Theatre.

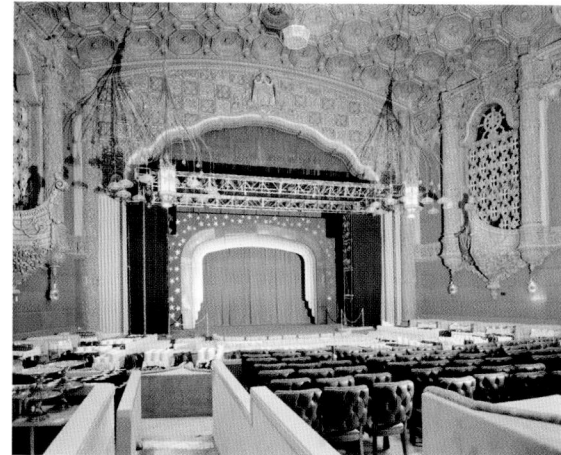

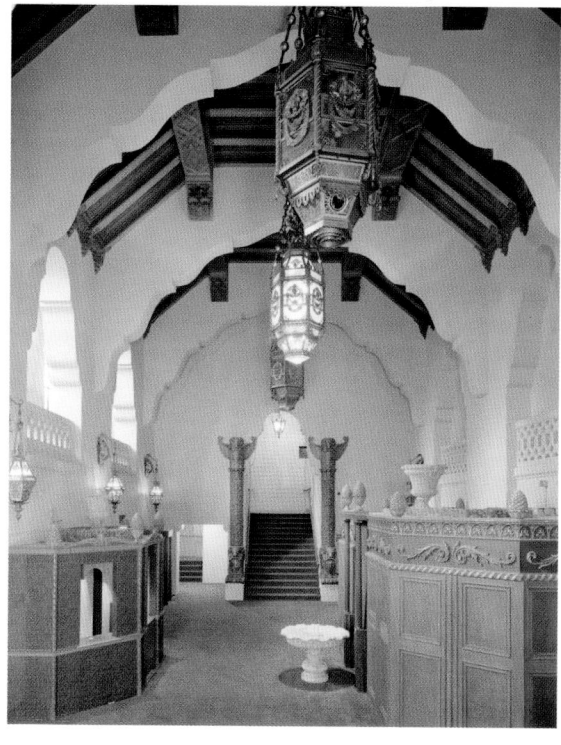

OPPOSITE PAGE *The Music Hall's Olive Way facade in the early 1950s.*

ABOVE RIGHT *The stage and auditorium in the days before demolition.*

RIGHT *Grand lights hang in the lobby foyer in its final days.*

Frederick & Nelson DOORS CLOSED 1992

Frederick & Nelson was Seattle's classiest department store, but had humble beginnings. It was formed by three miner friends who moved to Seattle in 1890 to sell plumbing and used furniture after the Great Fire. The area around them was a mix of small hotels, commercial, and light industry. A mill operated just up Pike Street. Power houses and car barns for several of the new streetcar lines hugged the side of Denny Hill and headed to northern suburbs.

In 1914 D. Edward Frederick created a stir when he announced that his store would move into a new, five-floor terracotta-clad building at Fifth and Pine. Continued investment by James Moore and the Metropolitan Building Company were changing the area quickly with large offices, high-end apartments and theaters. The day after Frederick & Nelson's land purchase was announced, the *Seattle Times* reported other transactions spiraling through the area.

The building was designed by John Graham, one of Seattle's top architects. It was clad in glazed, cream terracotta tiles. The first floor interior was lined with 30,000 feet of pink marble. Patrons could find a meal at the fifth floor grill or formal tea room or refreshment at the basement soda fountain.

The tea room featured a frozen dessert called Frangos. In 1927 the store's candy counter began selling a new mint chocolate with the Frango name. It was an instant success, and by the 1940s Frederick & Nelson was operating the largest handmade chocolate factory in America. The candies were sold individually wrapped in a hexagon-shaped box and became symbolic of Frederick & Nelson's distinctiveness and care for quality of service.

Another Frederick & Nelson classic was the Paul Bunyan Kitchen, opened in 1948 to replace the soda fountain in the basement. They sold Frango mint milkshakes, crustless sandwiches for kids,

and chicken and beef pot pies baked on site. The Paul Bunyan room became a favorite lunchtime spot for office workers, and weekend destination for kids.

The building was given a massive facelift in 1952. John Graham, Jr., son of the original architect, designed a five-story addition atop the building. The 10th floor featured a massive candy factory to produce Frangos. The loyalty of the department store's customers was reflected in one of the guests of honor, Ida Ludvigson, who had been a regular shopper since 1890.

Frederick & Nelson closed its doors in 1992 after suffering through financial difficulties and ownership turmoil. The building was occupied by one of its former rivals, Nordstrom. Another rival, the Bon Marché, took over sales of Frangos. Frangos can still be purchased at Macy's throughout the Pacific Northwest.

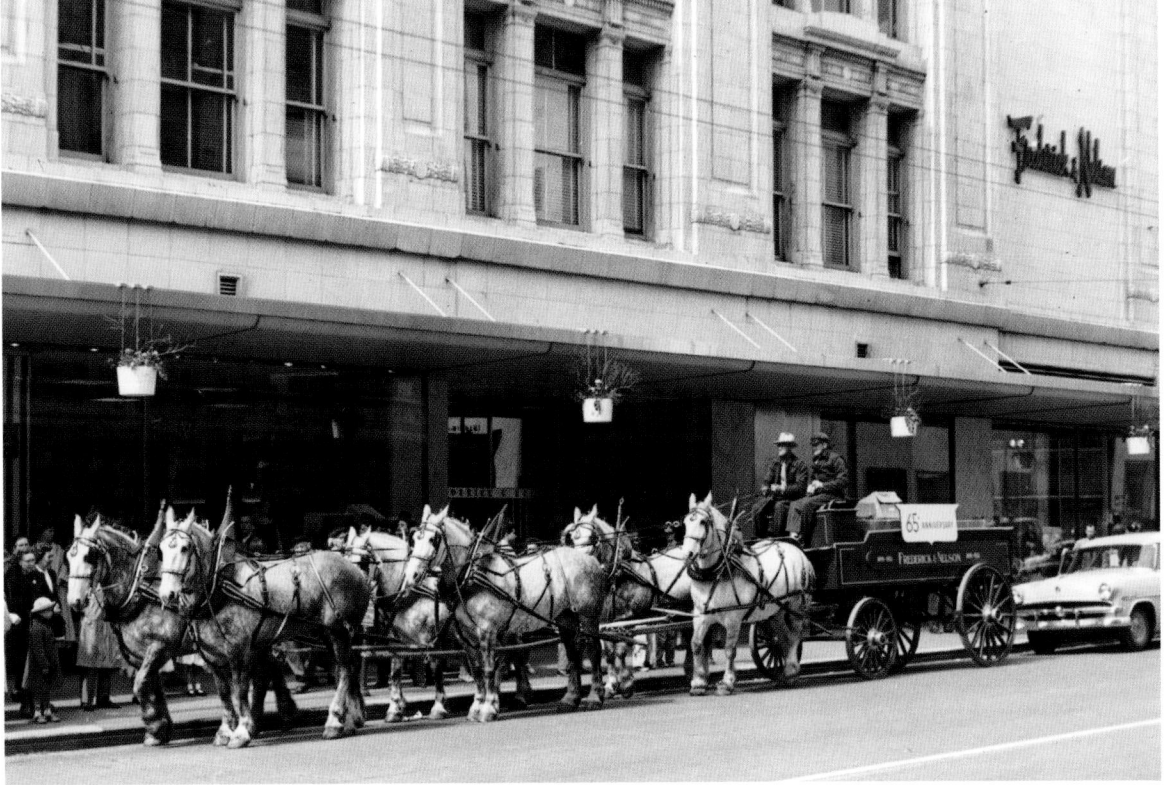

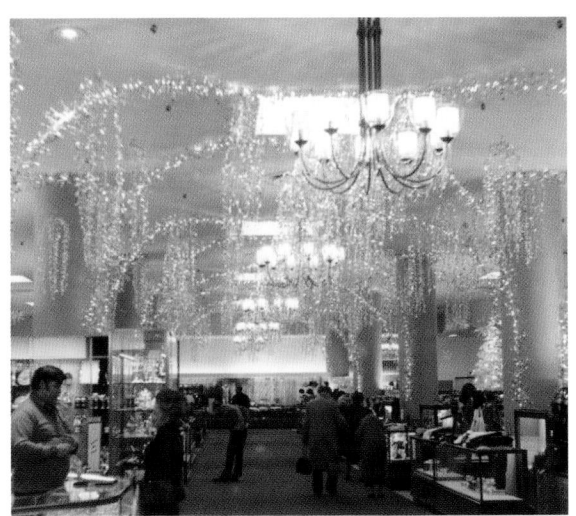

RIGHT *The Fifth and Pike store soon after opening.*

LEFT *The store's 65th anniversary events in 1955 included a horse team pulling an old delivery wagon.*

BELOW *Lights decorate the first floor displays for Christmas in 1975.*

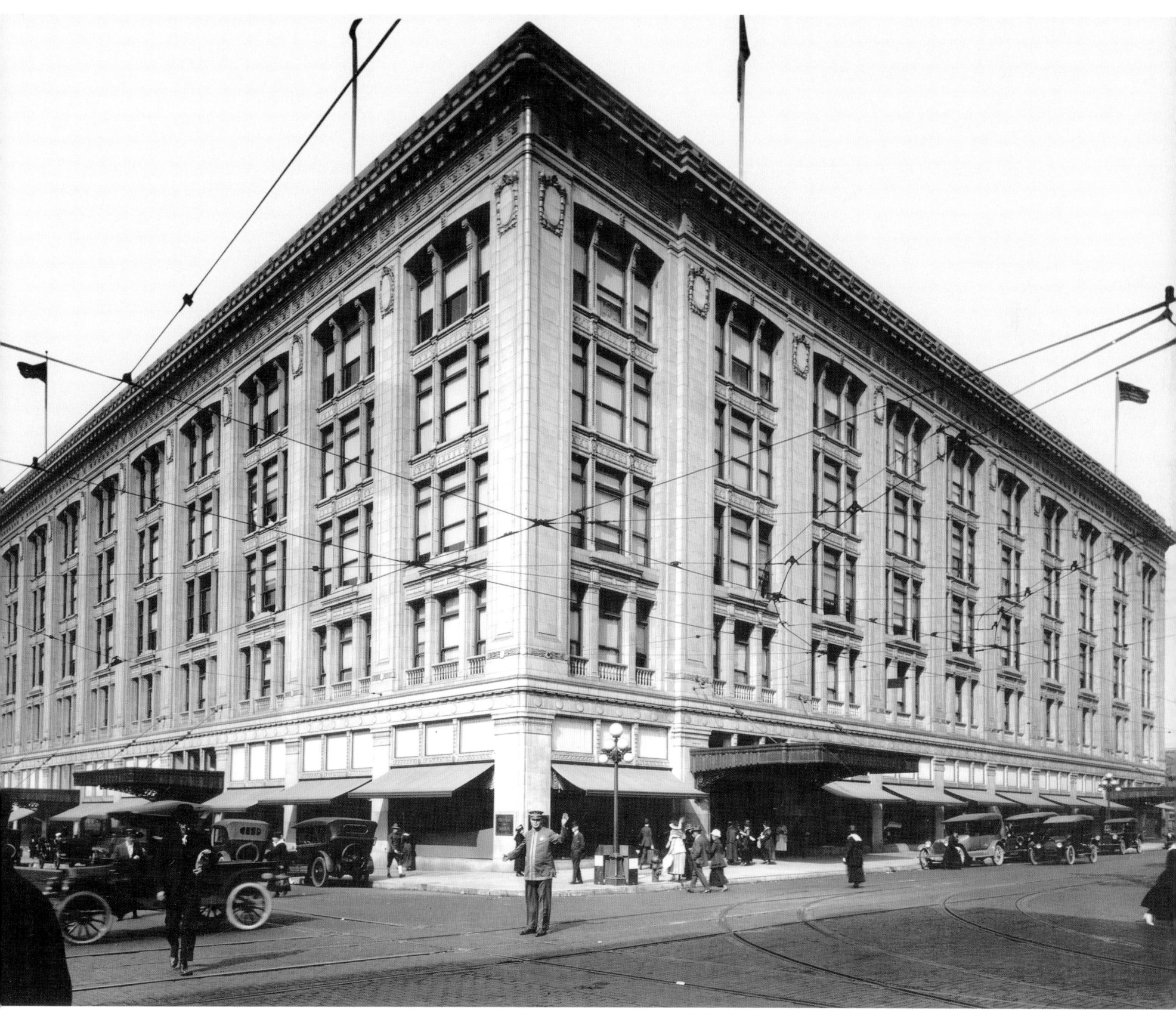

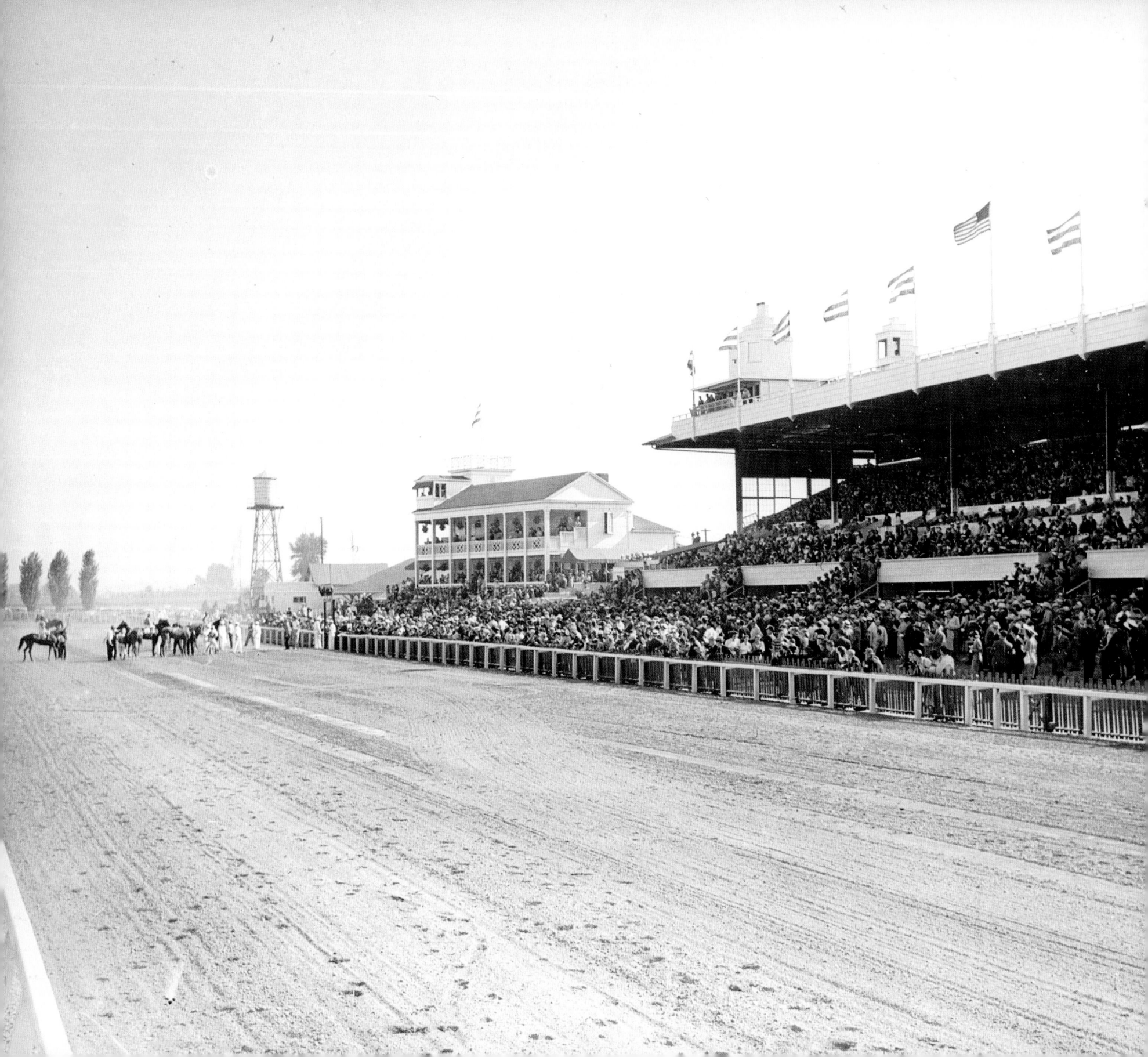

Longacres REDEVELOPED 1992

Longacres was a horse race track located just south of Seattle in Renton, Washington. An entire community developed around it during six decades of photo finishes.

In 1909 gambling was made illegal in Washington State, causing Georgetown's Meadows racetrack and its pools to shut down. One Seattleite who missed the horses more than most was real estate developer Joseph Gottstein. He grew up at the Meadows at his father's stables and worked through the 1920s to find a way to make horse racing permissible again.

After the onset of the Great Depression Gottstein's efforts found traction. In 1933 his friends in the state legislature pushed approval of pari-mutuel betting, which splits the money of the losers among the winners minus the track's charge.

Gottstein hired B. Marcus Priteca to design the facilities including judge's stand, clubhouse, barns, and grandstands with a marvelous view of Mount Rainier. It wasn't the first pairing of Priteca and Gottstein, though. Priteca was architect for Gottstein's Coliseum Theater in downtown Seattle. Amazingly, Longacres opened on August 28, 1933, just 28 days after Priteca completed designs.

Longacres became the society destination for weekend outings and the place to take out-of-town guests. Horse racing's uniqueness as something only seen on vacations or in the movies made Longacres a success in hard economic times.

Most American races are six furlongs or three quarters of a mile long. The classic horse race is 10 furlongs or one and a quarter miles. Gottstein chose to make annual Longacres invitational a difficult length right in between: one full mile. Then he added an abnormally large purse to attract attention, $10,000 in 1935's first run.

For the mile's thirtieth anniversary in August of 1965, veteran race caller Chick O'Neall shared memories of the best Longacre Miles with Seattle newspapers. He described the second Mile, won by a horse going by a pseudonym to throw everyone off. The race in 1945 was rainy and muddy. The winner, Prince Ernest, almost didn't compete for the $20,000 prize because he ran poorly in mud and his jockey fell in an earlier race and couldn't ride. The call went out and jockey Fred Milman came down from the stands to lead Prince to the stakes. His favorite race was the recent 1961 edition where Sparrow Castle and Dusky

Damion, two local horses, took 1-2 over illustrious outside competition in a thrilling race.

In 1990 Boeing purchased the land from Gottstein's descendants to build a flight training facility and more offices. When Longacres closed on September 21, 1992, it was over 59 years old and the longest operating thoroughbred track on the Pacific Coast.

In that final season Gary Baze, a popular, 35-year-old, local jockey, won his 100th race at Longacres for a total of $18 million. His father had been a trainer in Renton near the track, representative of the family relations of many involved at Longacres.

By its last run, the Longacres Mile purse had raised to $293,000. Its winner, Bolulight, was ridden by Ron Hansen who won 58 races in 37 days in Longacres' final season. The final day was a gala event of gowns and tuxes. Celebrity horses returned for a final walk around the track they had raced in their youth.

The community moved further south, opening Emerald Downs track in Auburn.

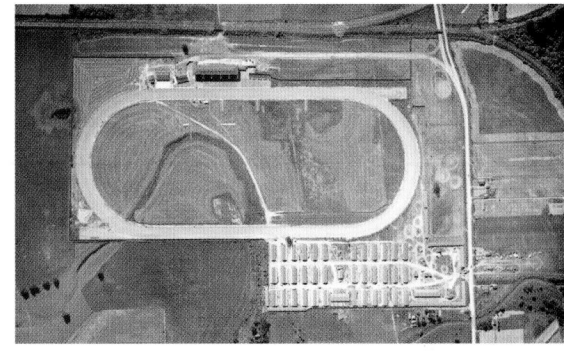

ABOVE *Aerial view of the track with stables on the bottom right and grandstand on the top.*

OPPOSITE PAGE *Horses gather at the finish line in front of a full crowd.*

BELOW *The finish line view from the judge's stands.*

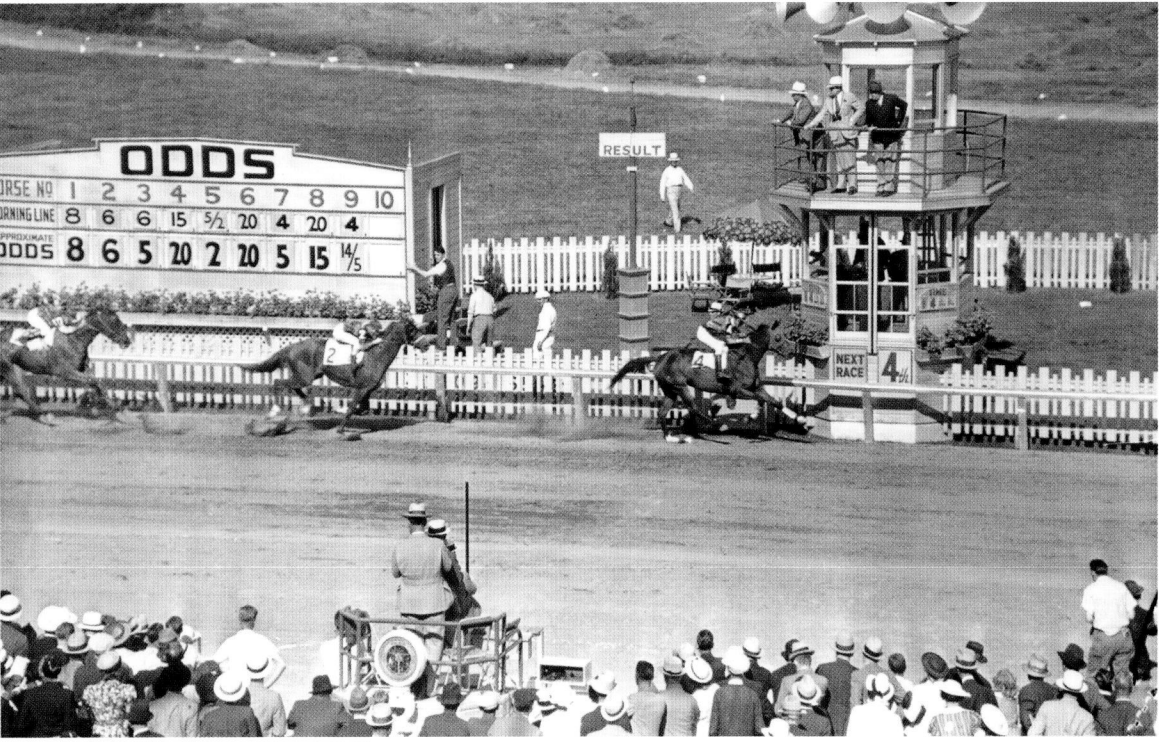

Coliseum REBUILT 1994

The Coliseum sports arena started as the Washington State Coliseum, built for the 1962 World's Fair on the former site of the Warren Avenue School. It was designed by Seattle's renowned modernist architect Paul Thiry. Thiry also was lead architect for the fair itself.

Many visitors were drawn into the Coliseum by the experimental Firebird III displayed in the General Motors exhibit. But it also featured the Library of the Future exhibit, Man Against Cancer, the French national exhibit, and was best known for the World of Tomorrow. World of Tomorrow was a multimedia show projected on aluminum cubes suspended over the main floor. It was reached by a spherical, Plexiglass, 100-person elevator known as the Bubbleator.

The building was designed by Thiry to be converted to an arena by the City of Seattle after the fair ended. So in 1963 he took charge of the remodel. Installation of seating and creation of ramps were the major tasks, but already repairs were needed to fix a leaky roof.

Water penetration was caused by the novel design of the roof. Four steel beams met at the peak and suspended panels between them by cables. In high winds the panels would shift, allowing rain to enter and fall on the crowd or court. The first major incident occurred in 1972 when SuperSonics power forward Spencer Haywood slipped on a wet spot and injured his knee.

The worst incident came in 1986: the only rainout in NBA history. Leaks were spotted in the afternoon and a tarp was placed on the roof. At game time more water was found, and a ball boy was tasked with watching for any new drips. No one was watching the tarps, though, which blew away in the wind. Water appeared in more spots on the floor and Sonic Al Wood pulled a hamstring. The game was called.

Fed up with the Coliseum, Sonics owner Barry Ackerley immediately proposed building a new arena near the Kingdome. The Seattle Center began considering conversion of the Coliseum into an open-air ice rink, perhaps with the roof fitted with Plexiglass to make it clear.

Plans for a new Sonics arena fell through after King County protested transportation impacts. Instead, in 1994 the Coliseum underwent significant changes in order to meet NBA basketball standards, payed for by $75 million of public money and $20 million by the owners of the SuperSonics. The floor was dropped, bathrooms were remodeled, seats replaced and 3,000 added, more restaurants lined the walkways, and the roof was given a new skin.

To defray costs, the naming rights were sold to the highest bidder. KeyBank chose to rename it to KeyArena. The Coliseum was recycled.

RIGHT *View of the Coliseum at the end of the fair with Elliott Bay to the left and Queen Anne Hill to the right.*

BELOW FAR LEFT *The Bubbleator carries another bemused crowd into the World of Tomorrow during the World's Fair.*

BELOW LEFT *The four raised, web steel structures meet at the center of the building. A wire mesh is strung between them to suspend the roof tiles.*

BELOW *Children slide down a concrete roof support while a police officer tells them to get down.*

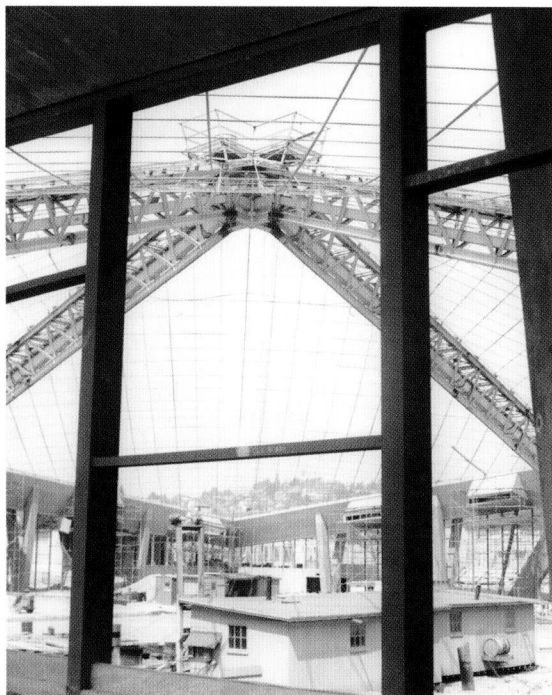

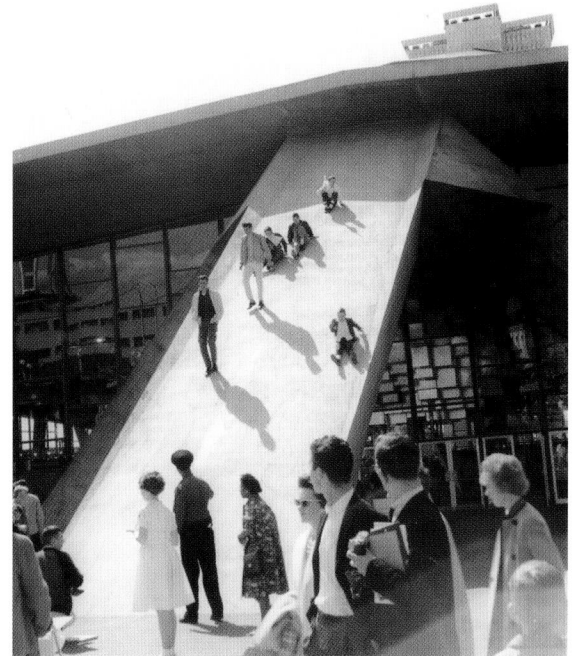

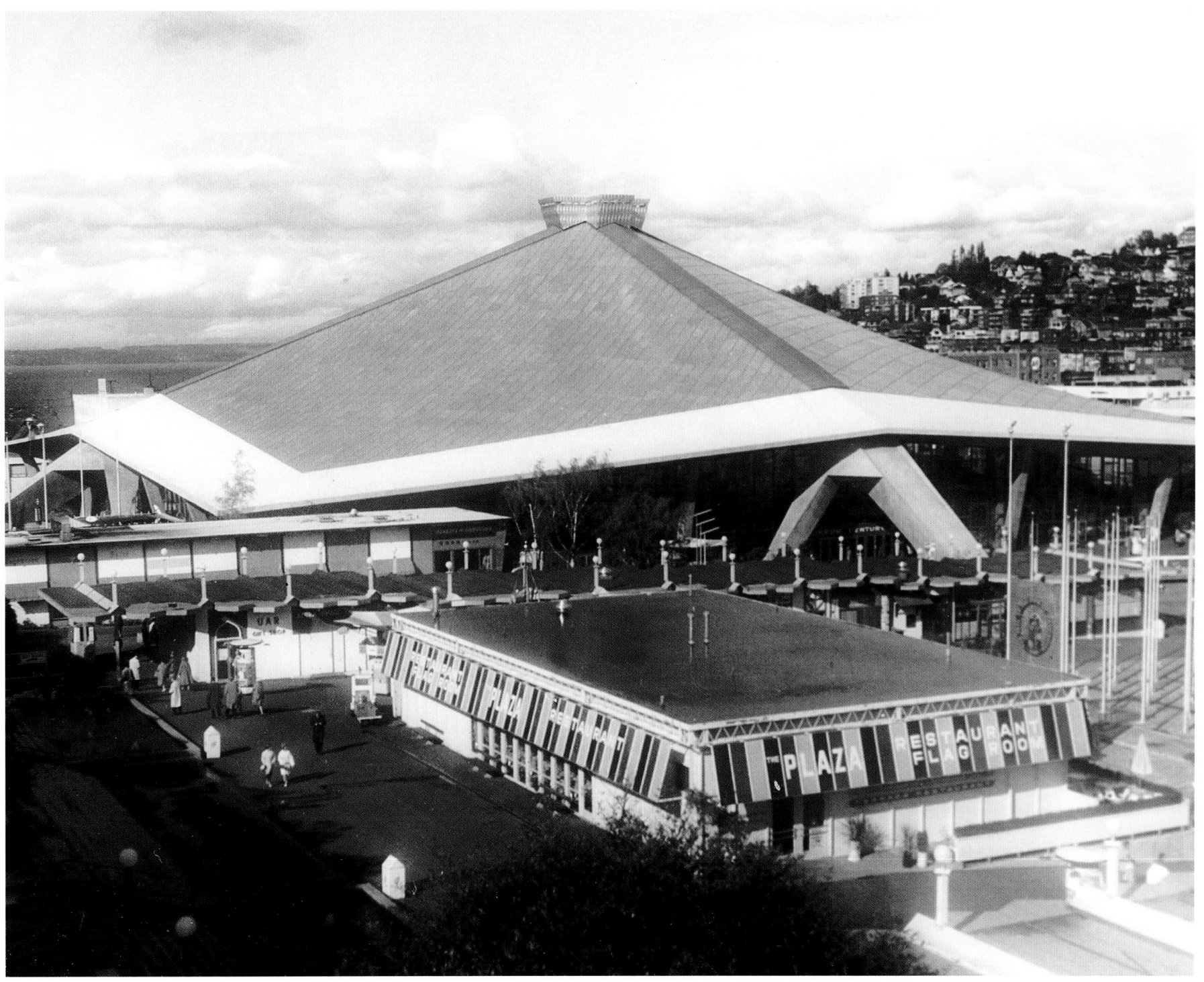

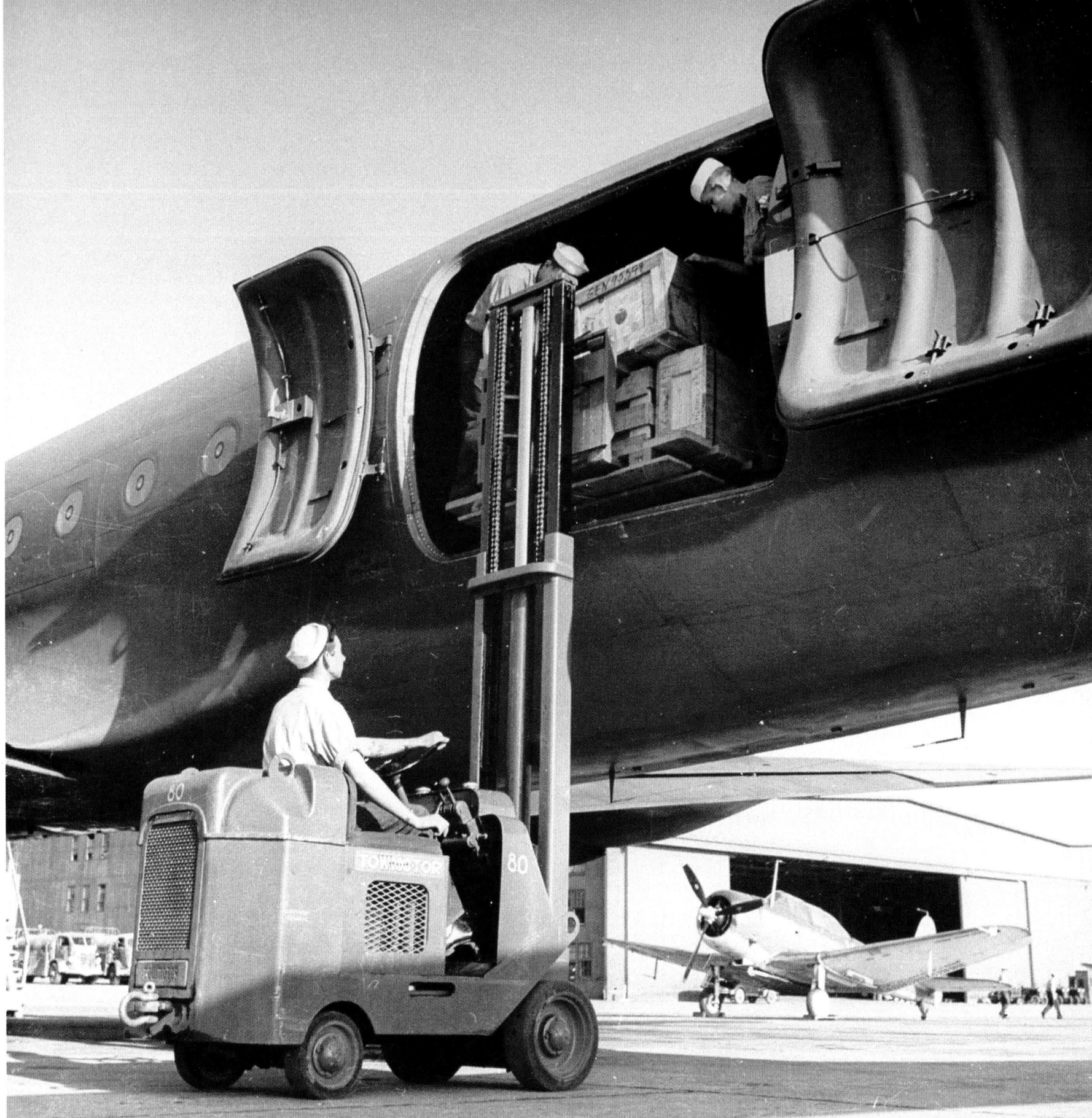

Naval Air Station Seattle DECOMMISSIONED 1995

Bill Boeing began the Northwest Aero Club in 1915 to train pilots and create a civilian air defense for the Puget Sound. The group petitioned for the Washington National Guard to take formal responsibility for air defense. In 1916 Aero Club member Terah Maroney, who gave Boeing his first ride in an airplane, was sworn in as a lieutenant and the Guard took use of his plane on loan.

The Puget Sound had no airport and the Naval Reserve needed a place to fly from near Bremerton. The Aero Club joined them to lobby for a military airfield in the Seattle area. So in 1920 King County purchased Sand Point to encourage the military to locate there. It took time for Congress to come to agreement, but they appropriated money in the waning hours of 1922 to develop the field for use by the Army and Navy reserve pilot training.

In the early years the station was literally a muddy, sod field. In addition to military training, the field was used for final assembly by the Boeing Aircraft Company and was a landing or launch point for the adventures of many aviators in the 1920s. Sand Point became focused on Naval operations after the Army began using Tacoma Field in 1927 and King County completed Boeing Field south of Seattle for civilian use in 1928.

Development of the base finally came at the end of the 1930s, with steel hangars, paved runways, a variety of administration buildings and comfortable barracks for stationed Reserve pilots. World War II brought more expansion and an enhanced mission. Defensive fortifications were put in place, barracks and officers' quarters were expanded, and the

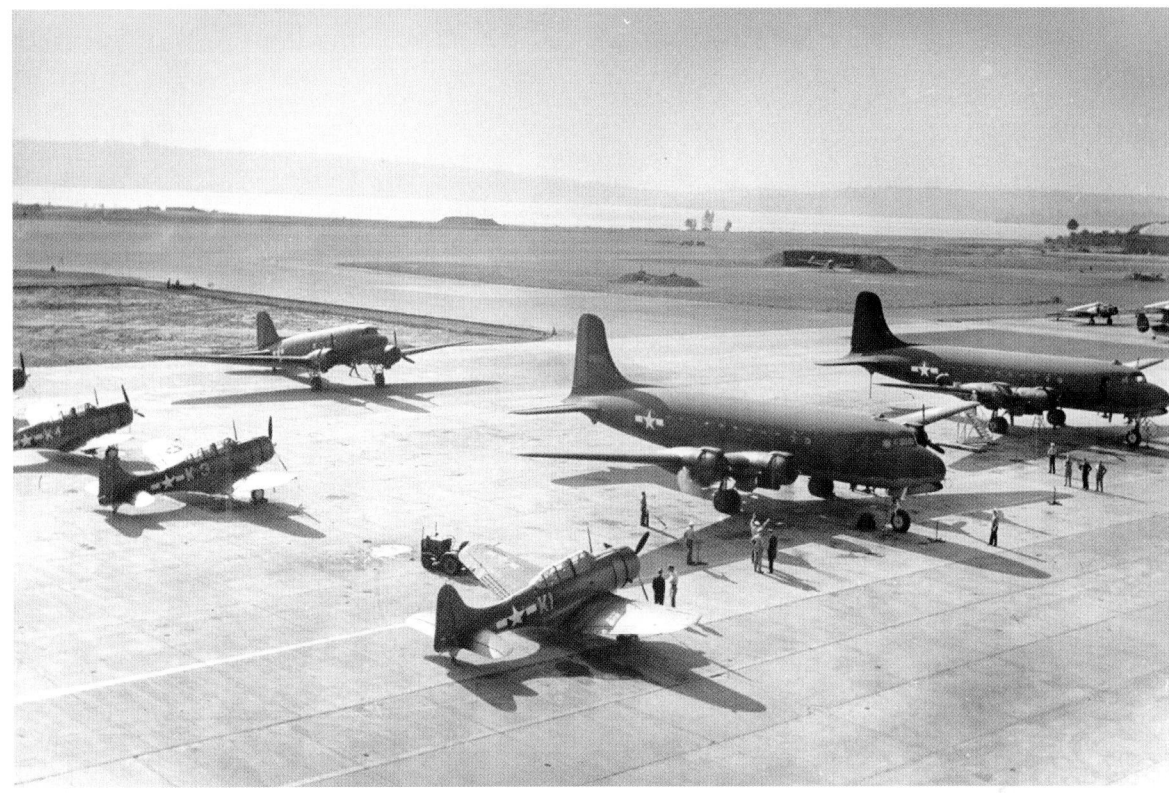

landscape was smoothed out to broaden the runways. Sand Point was turned into a repair facility for all land- and carrier-based planes in the Pacific Northwest. The base was also the logistics and storage center for outfitting the dozens of aircraft carriers built in Tacoma and Vancouver, Washington.

After World War II, portions of the base were gradually decommissioned. By 1953 NAS Seattle's runways were only used for training by the Naval Reserve. All maintenance work was moved to NAS Whidbey Island. The regional Navy headquarters were briefly moved to the grounds but in 1958 the station was dedicated to reserve activity. In 1972 roughly a third of the base was given to NOAA and a third to the City of Seattle for parkland. Navy Reserve training and support continued on the remaining third.

When Congress ordered consolidation of military bases around the country in 1990, NAS

Seattle was an obvious candidate for closure. Navy operations ceased at Sand Point in September 1995.

The City of Seattle has declared the site of Sand Point Naval Air Station to be an historic district. The buildings and grounds will be preserved for future generations to enjoy and learn from.

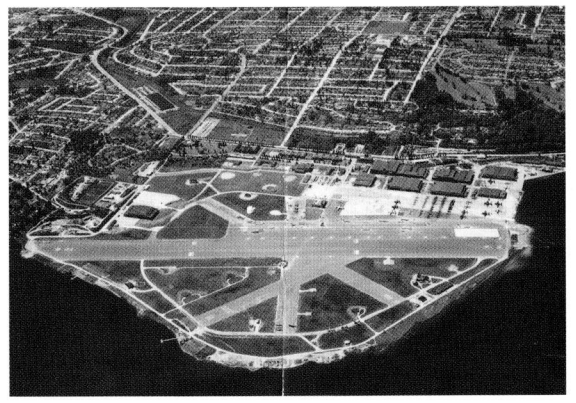

ABOVE *Fighter planes and supply planes are readied for combat in the Pacific Theater during World War II.*

LEFT *Looking west from Lake Washington over Sand Point in 1953.*

OPPOSITE PAGE *Loading supplies for Alaska to a cargo plane during World War II.*

Rainier Brewery **TAPPED OUT 1999**

Rainier Beer was first brewed in Seattle in 1893 by the Seattle Brewing & Malting Company. Seattle Brewing was formed by the consolidation of several Seattle breweries: Bay View Brewery in the tideflats along Beacon Hill; Claussen-Sweeney Brewing in Georgetown; and Albert Braun Brewing further south in the Duwamish Valley. Their timing was perfect. That year a nationwide financial collapse left them in a much better position than other breweries on the Pacific Coast.

By 1895 Rainier Beer was already on tap at taverns as far away as Honolulu, Hawaii and in 1901 Seattle Brewing opened a bottling facility in Honolulu to meet growing demand in Asia. Rainier Beer was popular in Shanghai, Nagasaki, and as the company put it "every land washed by the Pacific." The company continued to grow organically and through acquisitions.

In 1912 Seattle Brewing began advertising that expansions had made their Georgetown plant the largest brewery west of the Mississippi. That year the old Bay View facility became dedicated to bottling, transferring its brewing to Georgetown.

Washington State beat the rest of the nation to Prohibition, outlawing beer, wine and spirits in 1916. At that time, Seattle Brewing & Malting moved its factory to San Francisco, their second largest market on the West Coast. For four more years Rainier Beer continued to be made and sold, then the brewery switched to soft drinks like everyone else in 1920.

The provinces of Canada outlawed beer at about the same time as Washington State, but they were giving up by the early 1920s. Canadian breweries became wildly successful with bootlegging operations carrying their product into the United States. This was the climate which led to the Sick family's acquisition of Rainier Beer.

Emil Sick was born in Tacoma, Washington to German parents in 1894. His father Fritz was a coppersmith working in Tacoma's breweries. The family moved to Canada where Fritz started his own brewery, the Lethbridge Brewing and Malting Company in Alberta in 1901. The family weathered the Canadian Prohibition, and acquired other breweries across Canada in the 1920s.

When Prohibition was repealed in 1933, Emil and Fritz Sick were quick to return to the Puget Sound. They rented the old Bay View brewery in Seattle which had been used as a feed mill. They began making beer and buying up other brewers as they struggled to ramp up production.

In 1935 Emil Sick purchased the rights to the Rainier brand and began brewing it in the Bay View facility where it was first brewed in 1893. It was an immediate success, and Emil Sick leveraged the popularity by purchasing Seattle's struggling Pacific Coast League baseball team in 1937. He rechristened the team the Rainiers and built a new ballpark, Sick's Stadium, on Rainier Avenue along the interurban route the next year. They responded by winning the PCL pennant in 1939, 1940 and 1941.

Rainier beer returned to iconic status in Seattle. The giant R was placed above the brewery in 1954, just before Emil Sick sold majority interest to Molson and then passed away. In 1970 a series of Rainier commercials captured the Pacific Northwest's imagination with the Brews Brothers, a Rainier gear-changing motorcycle, Rainier screaming Tarzan, and Rainier singing frogs.

Rainier and its brewery changed hands several times as the international beer industry continued to consolidate. Finally in 1999 Pabst became owner, and announced that Rainier beer would no longer be brewed in Seattle under the shadow of Mount Rainier. Today it's brewed again in California.

The giant neon R is housed at the Museum of History & Industry in Seattle.

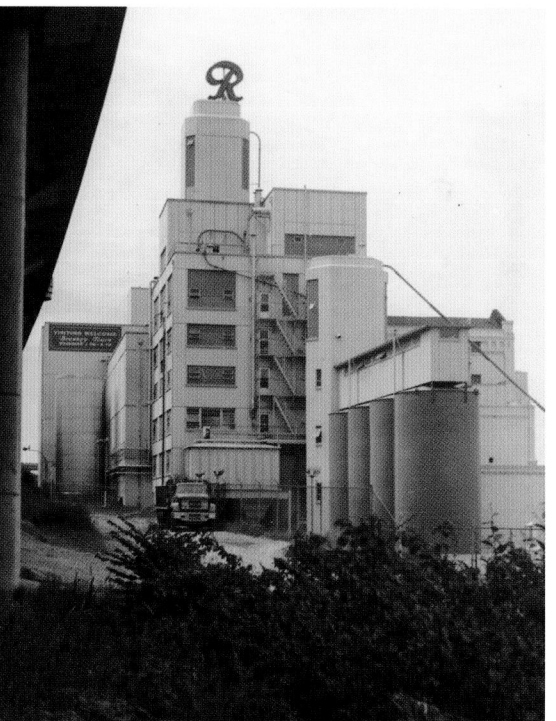

RIGHT *Rainier Beer brewery at South Forest Street and Airport Way, newly reopened in 1939.*

FAR LEFT *Sick's Stadium at Rainier Avenue South and South McClellan Street was the home of Emil Sick's Rainiers baseball team. They were Seattle's sports team for decades.*

LEFT *The big, cursive R on the top of the brewery rose high above the SoDo industrial district and was visible for miles away. After Interstate 5 was built alongside, the R became a marker on the way in and out of downtown.*

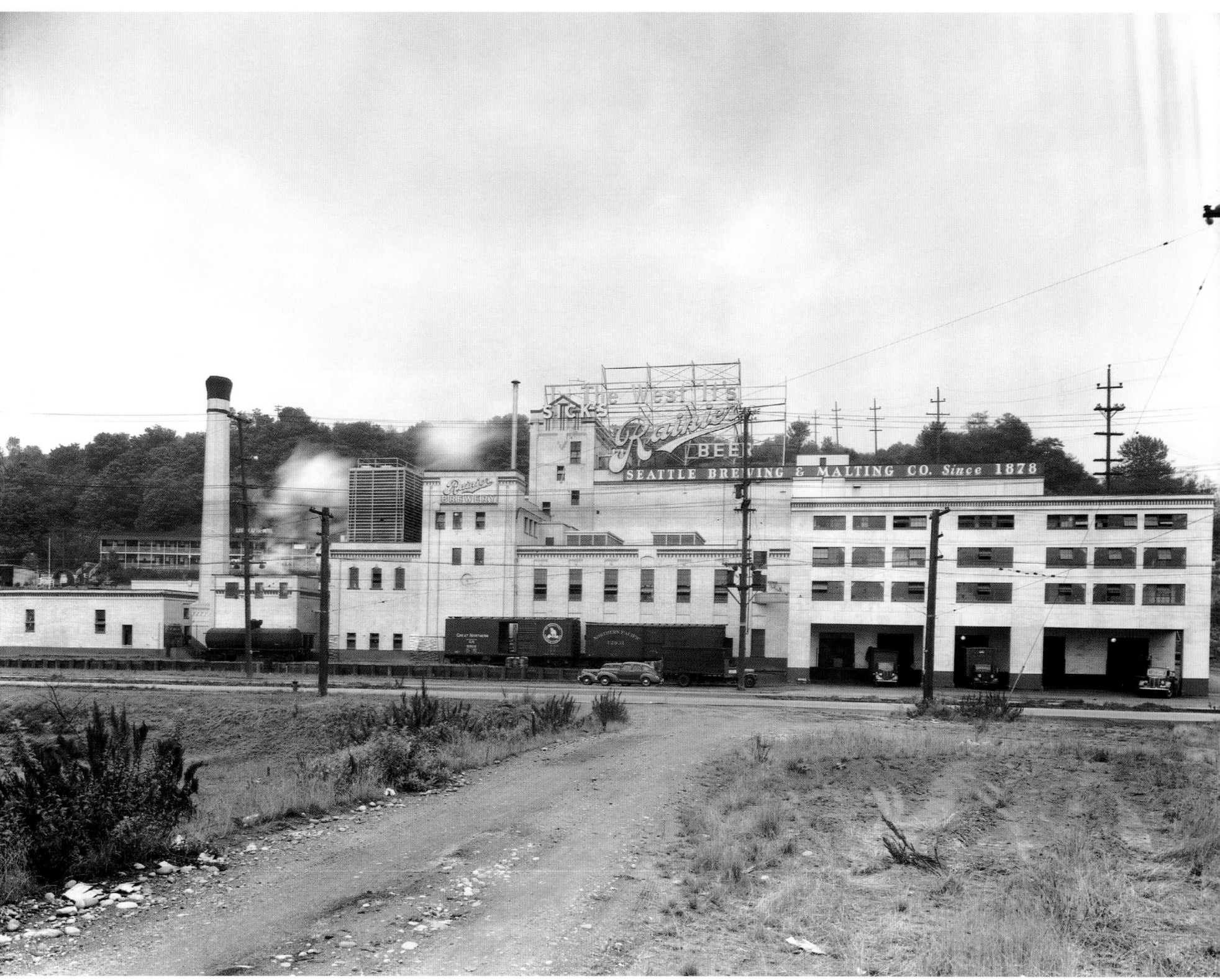

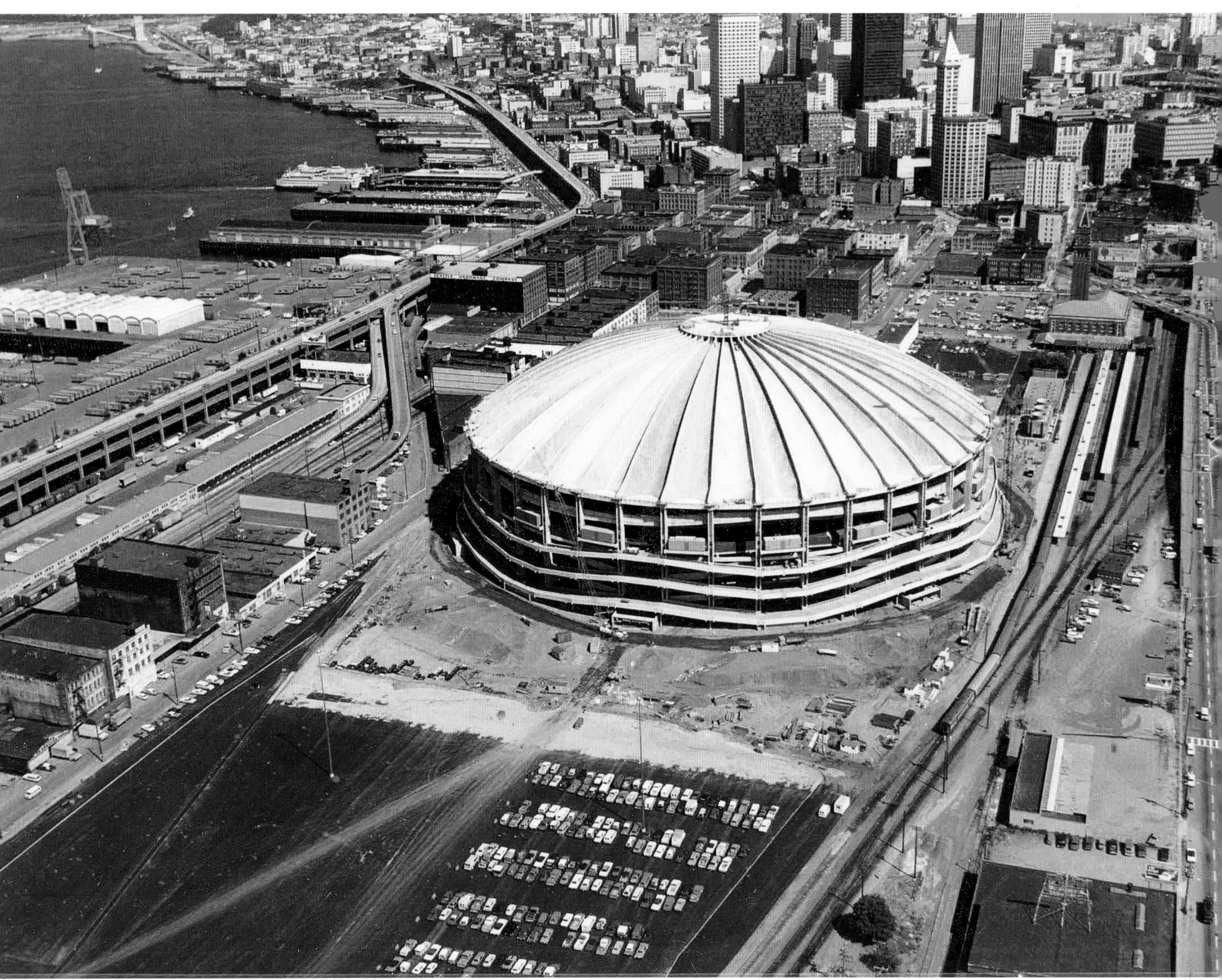

Kingdome IMPLODED 2000

Built on the former site of rail yards south of Pioneer Square and downtown, the Kingdome was Seattle's first major league sports stadium.

It took three votes before King County's citizens finally approved the $67 million expense and the location. After first proposing the Seattle Center grounds and then eliminating every other option, planners settled on the more remote area south of downtown. Still, not everyone was a fan of the idea. A group of angry Asian American youth activists from the neighboring International District interrupted the ground breaking ceremony in 1972, hurling boos, insults and mud balls at the politicians and dignitaries. They wanted help for their neighborhood. Signs read "Hum Bows, not Hot Dogs!" Construction went on.

From its completion in 1976 until implosion in 2000 the Kingdome was home to the NFL Seahawks. The MLB Mariners franchise began a year after the 'hawks, and they moved to a new home just across the street in 1999. The NBA SuperSonics also called the dome home for seven seasons, including when they won the 1979 NBA championship. The NASL Sounders played the first game ever at the stadium, and joined a full schedule of college and high school sporting events.

Despite the acoustics, a who's-who of rock bands played over the years as well. Paul McCartney's Wings, Led Zeppelin, Pink Floyd, The Rolling Stones, Metallica, Guns 'n Roses, U2 and even Madonna.

By the 1990s, the roof was in bad shape. Ceiling tiles began to fall. With both the Mariners and Seahawks threatening to leave town, the dome was done.

It took 16.8 seconds for the 250-foot high concrete shell of the dome to collapse. It still lives on though, in the name of the neighborhood it created between highways south of the city: SoDo, South of the Dome.

OPPOSITE PAGE *The Kingdome nears completion in 1975 with the south parking lot completed and the remaining train tracks on the right.*

BELOW LEFT *The Kingdome is framed by ships from Elliott Bay during Seafair in 1982.*

BELOW *Each explosive creates a puff of dust and smoke as the Kingdome implodes in 2000.*

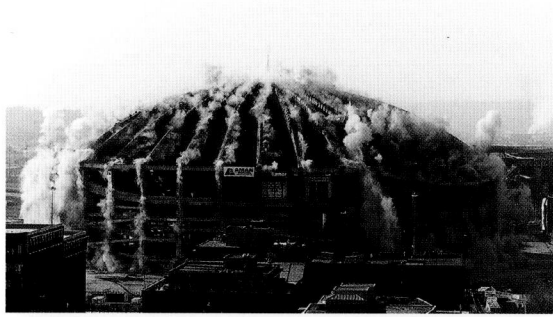

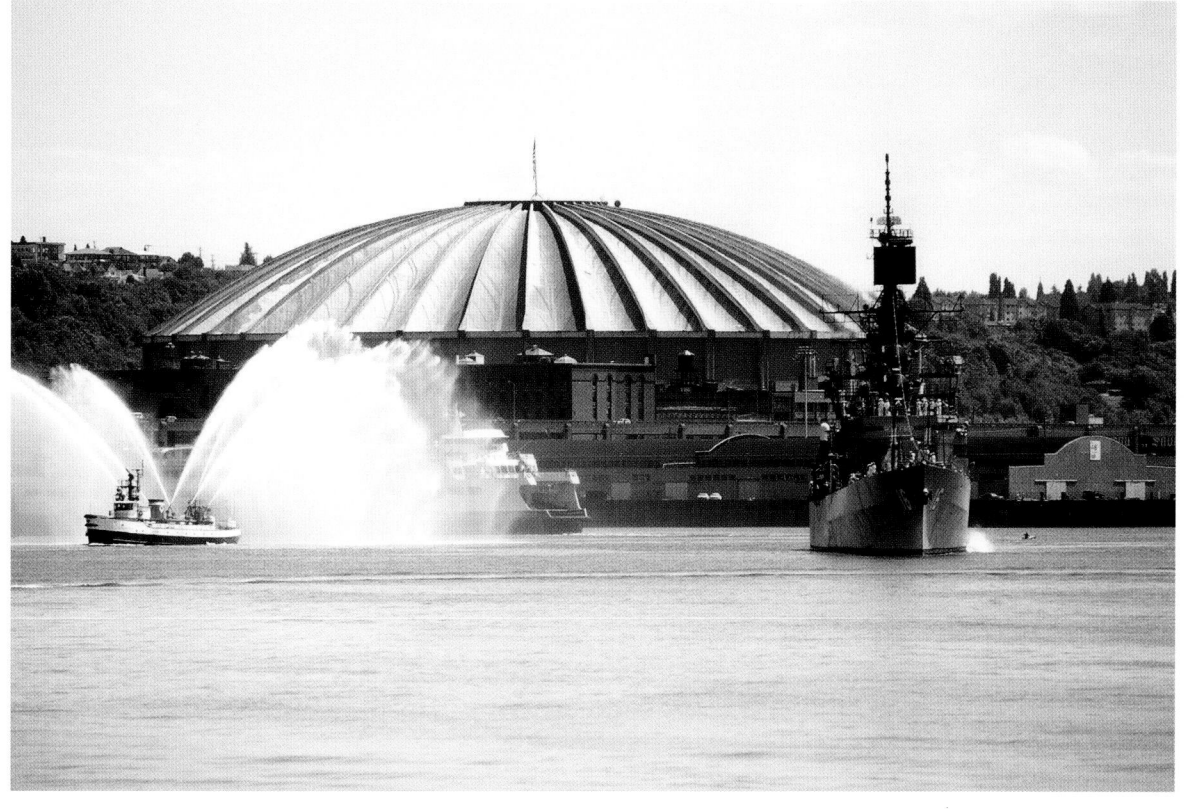

THE 12TH MAN

Seattle teams have a reputation for having loud fans, and the cavernous Kingdome served them perfectly. With 11 men on the football field, the fans became known as the 12th Man and the Kingdome as the loudest stadium in football. The jersey number 12 was retired in the fans' honor during the 1984 season, after the Seahawks' first playoff appearance. In 1989, the NFL instituted its infamous crowd noise rule in response to the 140 decibel echo chamber inside the Kingdome. Visiting teams would be given free yardage when the fans got too loud for the quarterback to make calls. Many fans have priceless memories of Denver's Hall of Fame quarterback John Elway begging officials for help. Amazingly the rule is still on the books but now never put to use.

Boeing Headquarters MOVED TO CHICAGO 2001

For decades Boeing Aircraft was the biggest employer in Seattle, the largest exporter in Washington State, and the dominant force in the Pacific Northwest.

Founder Bill Boeing's first experience with airplanes was in civil defense. He funded the Northwest Aero Club in 1915, which later became the Naval Air Reserve. No plane met his expectations so he built his own at his yacht's shipyard.

Boeing built hundreds of planes in the first decade: seaplanes for the Navy and fixed wheeled planes for the Army Air Corps and Marines. These successes set the stage for Boeing's own commercial airlines for mail in 1919 and passenger flight in 1927. The Boeing Airplane & Transport Company would go on to become United Airlines in 1934. In the years before World War II, Boeing created the world's largest landplane, the XB-15 Army Air Corps experimental bomber in 1937; and the world's largest seaplane, the 314 Clipper for Pan American World Airways in 1938.

Boeing's production increased tremendously during the war to roll out B-17 and then B-29 bombers for the Army. Employees quadrupled. Factory space quintupled. Subsidiary industries mushroomed as well with aluminum output reaching a third of national production. By the end of the war, one sixth of the population of King County worked at Boeing.

Commercial production picked up in the 1950s with the 707 jetliner. Expansion into aerospace with NASA and in particular the Apollo program continued growth in the 1960s. In 1969 the massive 747 jetliner entered production, but the economic crisis later that year and the oil crisis in 1973 hit Boeing hard. More than 60,000 of Boeing's Commercial Airplane Group employees were laid off. Unemployment in Seattle hit 17 percent.

The 1980s brought work on the B-2 bomber, the 757 and 767 and the International Space Station. The 1990s involved the F-22 Raptor fighter plane and the 777.

In 1995 the original headquarters of Boeing were demolished and management moved to an adjacent building. The real removal of the Boeing's headquarters came in 2001. Stating that they did not want to be swayed by any one of their many divisions, Boeing executives moved their offices to Chicago. Nearly $100 million dollars in tax breaks were waiting for them.

FLYING FORTRESS

Boeing's B-17 became an icon of American air superiority and synonymous with the European theater air war of World War II. After the 1935 unveiling, the *Seattle Times* called it a fighting cruiser, an aerial battle cruiser as well as simply enormous, but the headline said "Flying Fortress." B-17 production ramped quickly during the war, and the Douglas and Vega Aircraft factories began assembling them as well because of the plane's strategic importance. Almost 13,000 B-17s were built in total. More than half were built in Seattle. Twenty-five percent of planes were lost per mission in 1943 as Luftwaffe pilots learned to exploit weaknesses in the armor and gun pod defenses. P-47 Thunderbolt escorts improved B-17 effectiveness but the arrival of the P-51 Mustang signaled the end to the air war. P-51 flew just as far as B-17s, letting them hit targets all over Germany with impunity. The final B-17 was built in Seattle on April 7, 1945. All factories were switched to producing its successor, the B-29 Superfortress. One month later, Germany surrendered to the Allies in Europe.

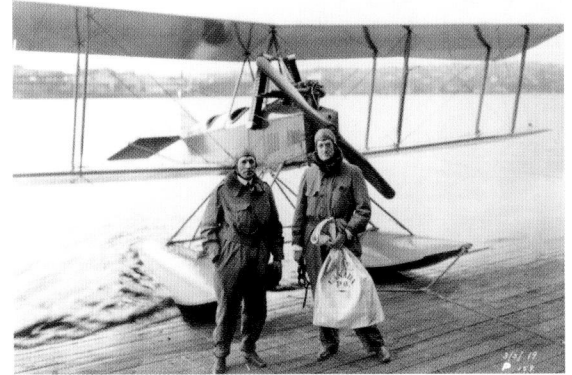

LEFT *Bill Boeing poses with a Model C and Eddie Hubbard before the first international airmail delivery in 1919.*

BELOW *Boeing Aircraft's wing room in 1922.*

RIGHT *A bomber pilot stands on stage, telling an air battle story to Boeing workers in 1942.*

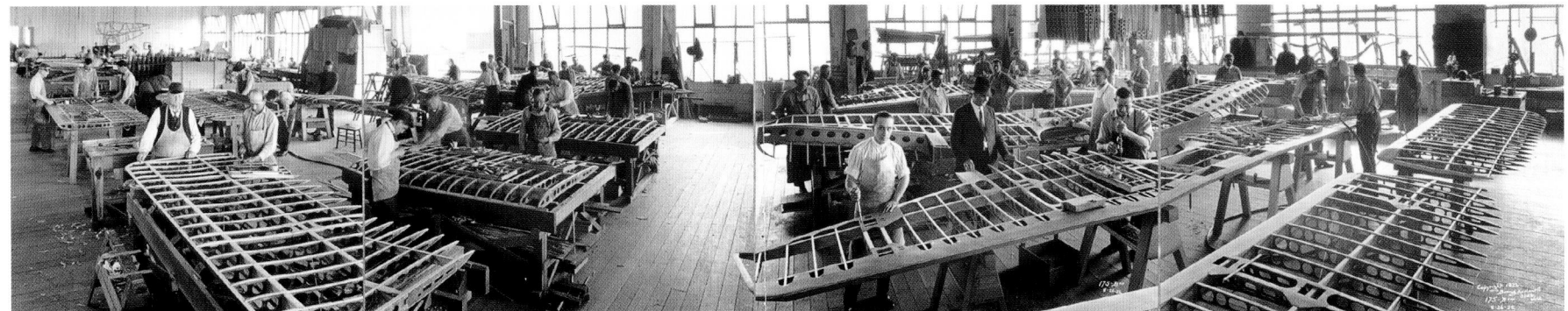

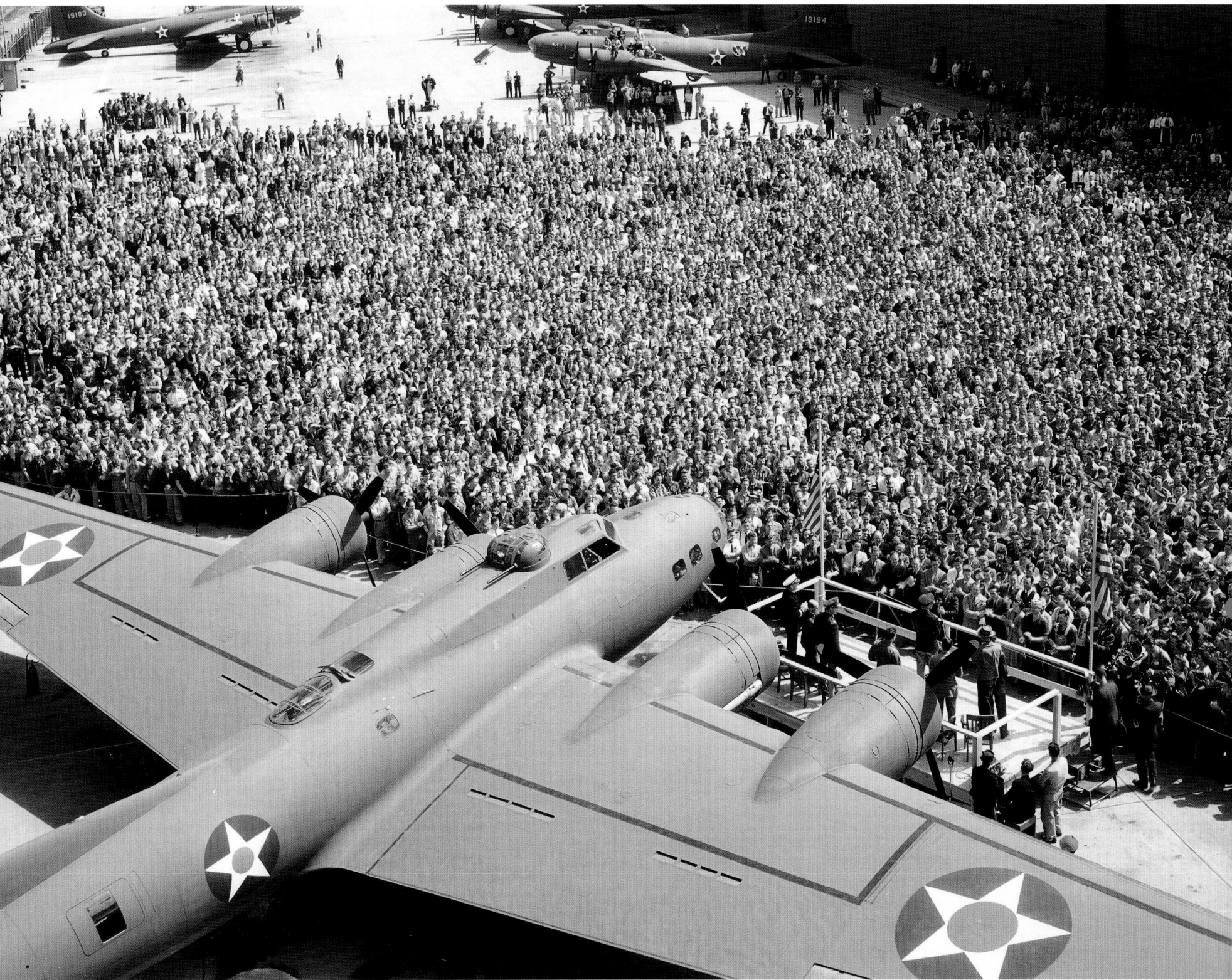

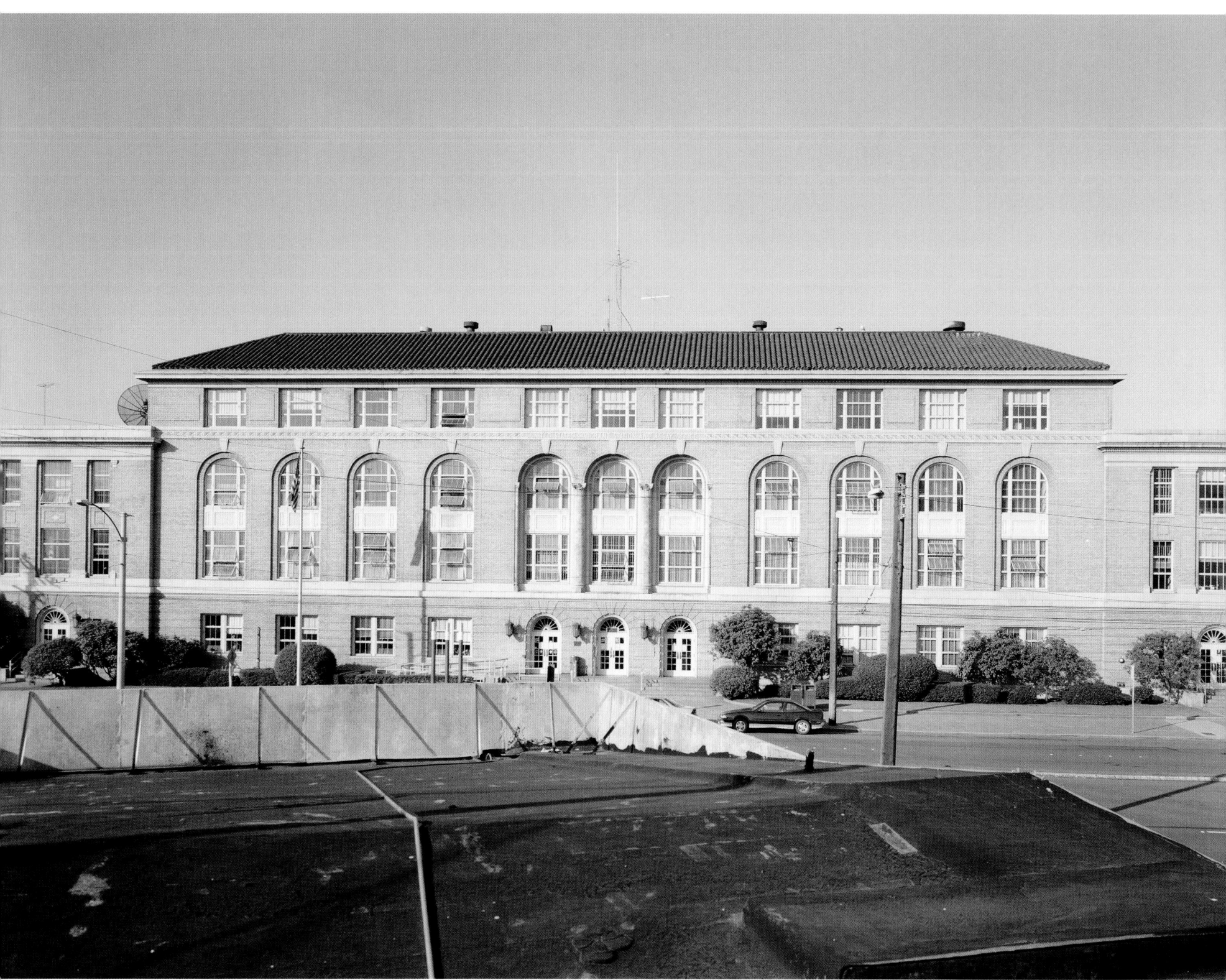

INS RELOCATED 2004

Seattle's Assay Office and Immigration Station (commonly known as the INS) was built as a public works project at the start of the Great Depression. Opened in 1931, Seattle's INS (Immigration and Naturalization Service) building was a symbol of arbitrary bureaucracy, the temporary home for imprisoned immigrants, and the weigh station for Alaska's gold.

The Assay Office purchased raw gold and other minerals from miners, smelted it, and shipped blocks to the U.S. Mint in Denver, Colorado. Seattle's office was established in 1898 after intense lobbying by the Chamber of Commerce. They saw the Klondike gold shipped raw to San Francisco's Assay Office, and were determined to have the money flow through Seattle instead. By the late 1920s the small commercial building on top of First Hill was clearly too small for the Assayer.

Seattle's Immigration Station came from Port Townsend in 1907. At that time, enforcement activity was focused on the Chinese Exclusion Act, which blocked Chinese laborers from moving into the U.S. In 1922 Japanese were stripped of their ability to become citizens, and the Seattle City Council began passing laws that only citizens could get business licenses and do other normal activities. In 1924 a long list of countries were given extremely limited immigration quotas because they were not white.

Beginning in 1926 the federal government began funding new buildings to replace rented facilities. In Seattle the Art Deco Federal Office Building at First Avenue and Marion Street was built at the same time, but it was completely different from the INS building's neoclassical Mediterranean style.

Entering the front doors in the center of the building, immigrants would line up before the massive front desk or enter a waiting room until their name was called. The first floor also included interview rooms and offices for agents. Upstairs were detention rooms that held immigrants with disputed status or who awaited deportation.

In the early years the detainees were mostly Chinese because the Exclusion Act singled them out; later, the community's decades of experience skirting the law occasionally backfired. Even as the United States became concerned about Japan's invasions of China in 1940, three-quarters of the detainees at the Seattle immigration station were Chinese.

War was already raging across Europe in early 1941, months before the United States declared war on Japan and Germany. Unable to deport European immigrants, the INS was forced to detain them indefinitely. After Pearl Harbor many Japanese-American men were brought to the INS and detained until they were proven to not be spies. Chinese detainees dwindled after the laws excluding them were repealed in 1943. INS activity returned to normal after the war, managing per-country quotas and removing immigrants with expired visas.

By 1953, 10 tons of gold passed through the Assay Office each year and it was one of the last assayers in the United States. Just before Christmas of 1954 it was announced that the office would close in two months. The people who were Scrooged out of a job included Broadway High School grads assayer-in-charge George Swarva and chemist C. L. Breland, who had both been at the office for three decades. Over the 70 years of the Seattle Assay Office, nearly 1,000 tons of gold were processed. Eighty percent of it was mined in Alaska.

The detention center was greatly reduced in 1979, and most of the INS building was converted to offices. In 2004 the INS's bureaucratic arm for managing legal immigrants moved to Tukwila. At the same time the processing and holding of illegal or under-review immigrants was moved to Tacoma, leaving the INS building empty.

The City of Seattle declared the INS building a city landmark in 2009 and the federal government surplused the building, selling it to an arts organization.

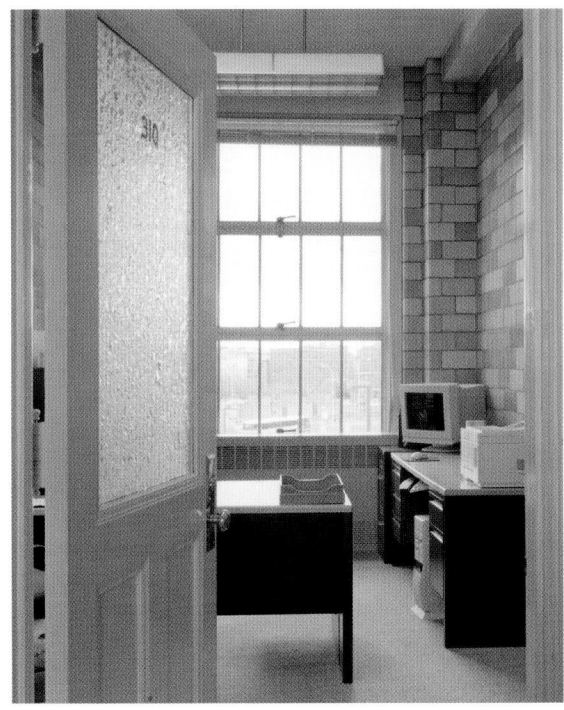

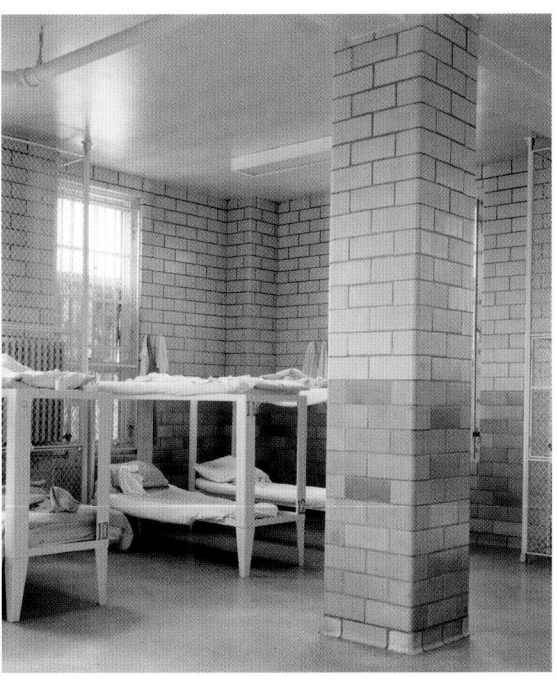

TOP RIGHT *Office in the Immigration Station.*

RIGHT *Bunk beds in the Immigration Station detention center.*

OPPOSITE PAGE *The neoclassical facade of the INS and Assay Office building along Airport Way (now Seattle Boulevard again) seen over the roof of a gas station.*

Nippon Kan DROPPED THE CURTAIN 2005

The Nippon Kan was a Japanese community theater operated in the Astor Hotel. It was built in 1909 on the slope of Yesler Hill as the Jackson Regrade cut away the ridge just a half block away. It was owned by Masajiro Furuya, Japantown's leading citizen. The building's architects, Thompson & Thompson, designed many other structures for the growing Chinese and Japanese commercial districts including the Milwaukee Hotel and Kong Yick's new headquarters.

The building had simple and unadorned facades of brick, indistinguishable from other Seattle buildings. Stepping into the Nippon Kan Theatre, though, immigrants could be transported back home for a time and their children could gain new appreciation for their culture. Kabuki was performed twice per month, and traditional dance and theatrical performances occurred regularly. Movies, variety shows, judo and kendo exhibitions, concerts, and traditional music like koto, biwa and shamisen provided entertainment. Political debates and community meetings gave intellectual stimulation.

This all came to an end in 1942 when Japanese American citizens and immigrants boarded trains for Puyallup and three years of unlawful imprisonment. Non-Japanese friends ran the hotel briefly until it was foreclosed by the lending bank. The building returned to Japanese ownership in 1946, but only the hotel apartments were put to use. The Nippon Kan remained boarded up for three decades.

In 1971, with naïve dreams of urban preservation, architect Edward Burke purchased the building for his growing practice. He and his family and friends spent the next decade restoring the theater from a derelict shell filled with pigeons and garbage into an attractive space with great acoustics. It came at high economic cost, though, requiring him to sign a stacked agreement with millionaire philanthropist Samuel Stroum during hard times.

The Burkes made special effort to reach out and connect with the remaining Japanese community. Enough time had gone by since incarceration that many were embracing this relic of their past. The revived hall once again hosted Japanese American weddings, dances, and musical performances. But it also reached a broader audience. An eclectic assortment of jazz, symphonic music, Finnish and Jewish cultural events, Northwest Asian American Theater performances, and myriad other theatrical, concert, and film events were held under the Burkes' direction.

The Burkes' ownership and management of the Nippon Kan came to a close in 1991 as Stroum took majority ownership of the facility. Unwilling to compromise, they sold their remaining share and set off for retirement. The momentum that they built up carried the theater for another decade under Stroum and his family's leadership.

After Samuel Stroum's death in 2001, new ownership was sought for the building. Several arts and community organizations considered purchase but each fell through. In 2005 a messenger company purchased the Nippon Kan. The theater seats were ripped up and replaced with desks, and the stage was converted into a dispatch office.

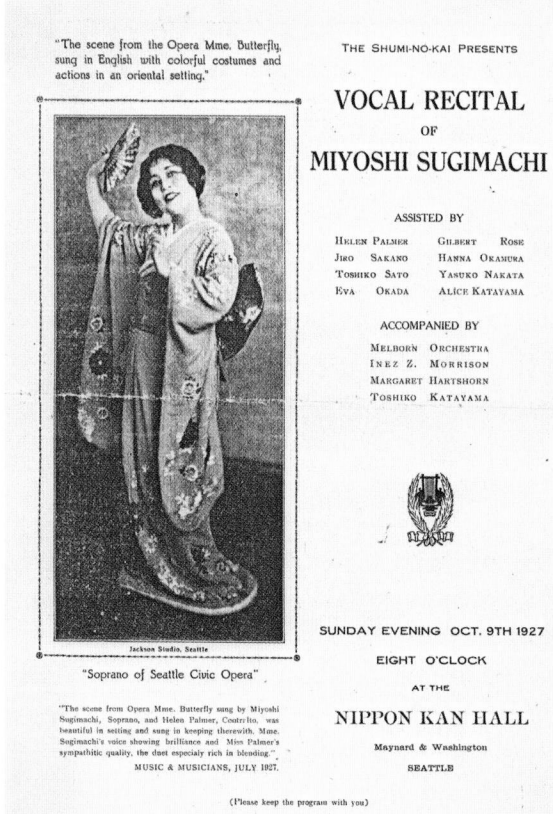

RIGHT *Asahi Club performance in 1919.*

LEFT *Advertisement for a vocal recital at the Nippon Kan in 1927.*

FAR LEFT *The Astor Hotel today, renamed Kobe Park Building.*

BELOW *The stage curtain, covered with community ads from the 1910s, now at the Wing Luke Museum.*

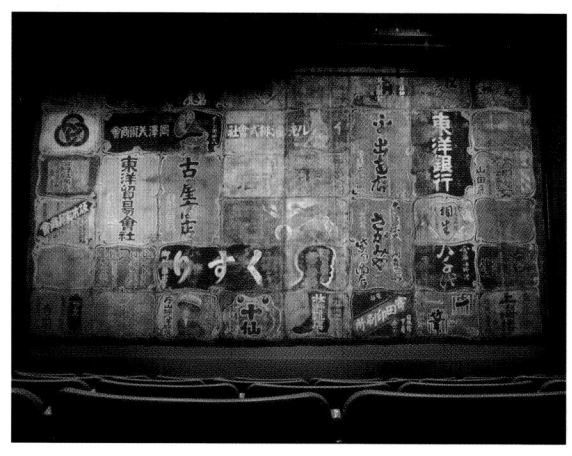

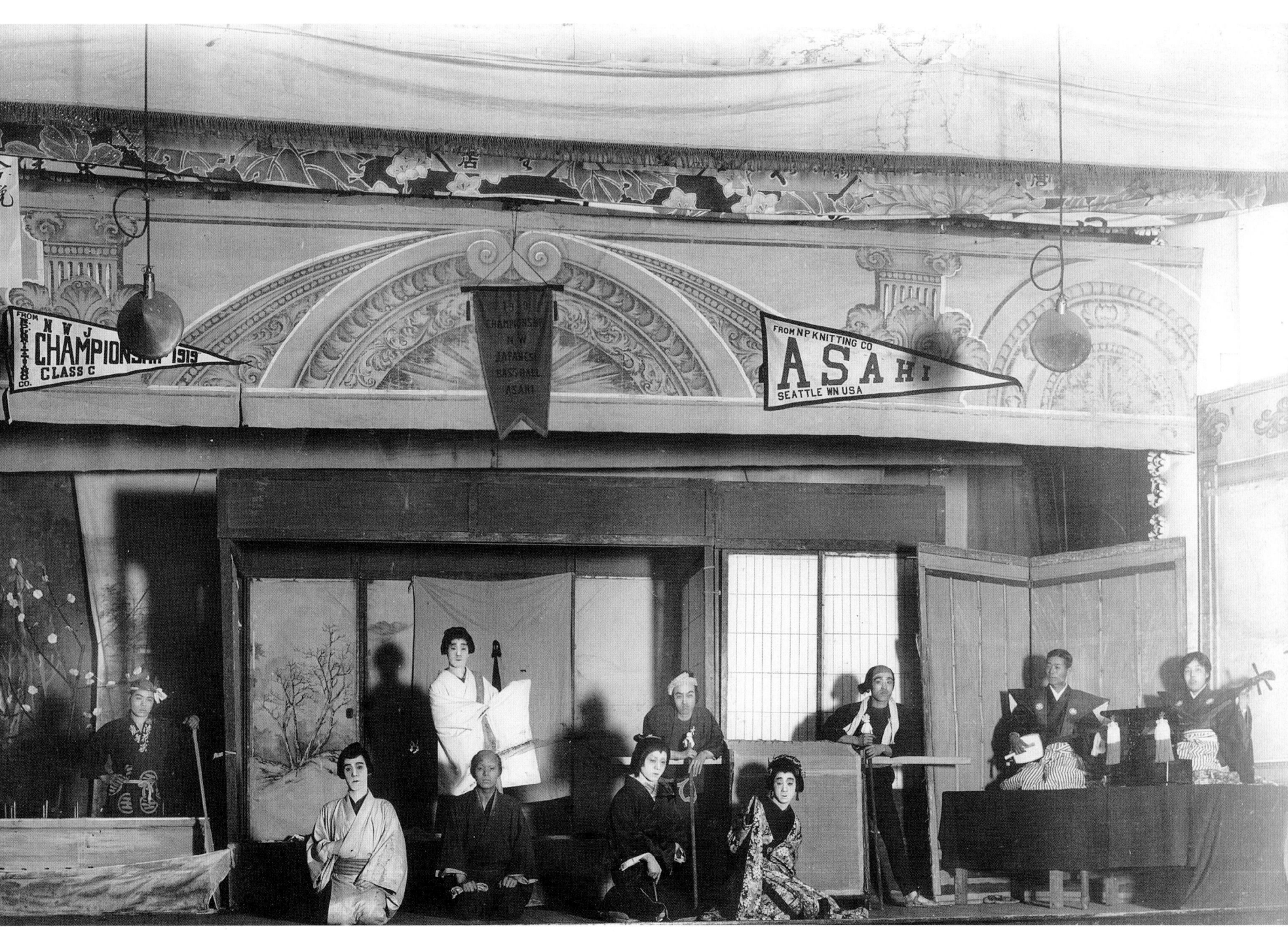

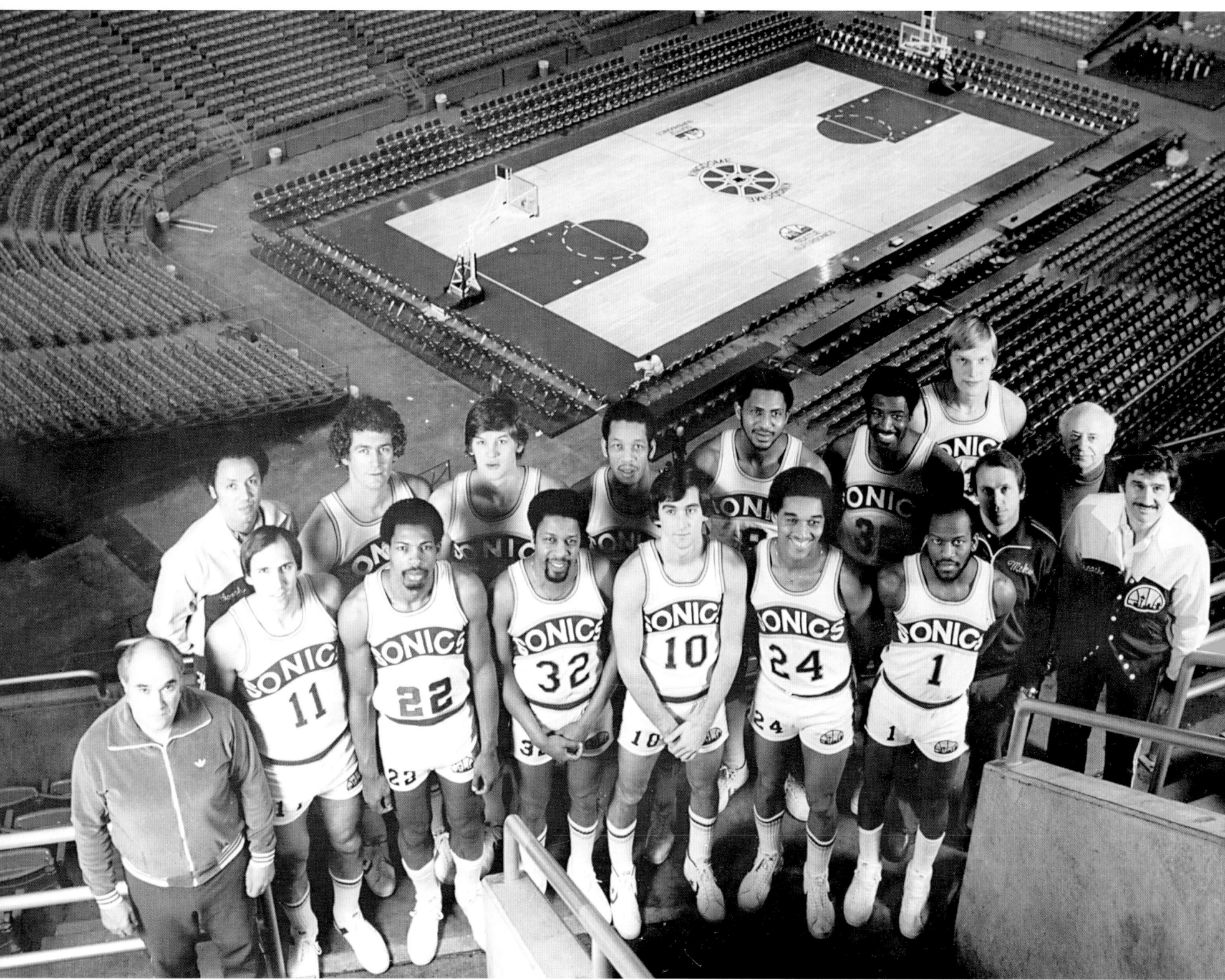

SuperSonics DUNKED 2008

Seattle was home to a variety of minor league baseball and hockey teams over the years, but in 1967 the Seattle SuperSonics became the first major league, professional sports franchise. Hot off of buying San Diego's NFL team, Sam Schulman led a group of investors to create an expansion NBA basketball team in Seattle. Fans packed the Coliseum to see games, not worried if the Sonics lost a few.

The 1973–74 season brought tremendous change for the Sonics. Legendary and newly retired center Bill Russell was hired as coach. The first three million-dollar players were hired from the ABA. And undrafted point guard Slick Watts played his way onto the team.

Slick became Seattle's first sports superstar. It was unfamiliar to him and to the city. People would see him on the street, ask him to come to their kid's birthday party, and he'd say yes. In 1976 Slick Watts won the NBA Citizenship Award after more than 300 community appearances that year. Along the way he was one of the guests of honor at the grand opening pageantry of the Kingdome.

Bill Russell was an enigmatic and unforgiving coach. He took the Sonics to their first and second playoffs but was fired in 1977 after a disappointing season. Former Sonic All-Star Larry Wilkens returned as General Manager and rebuilt the roster. A bad start to the following season brought coach Bob Hopkins' tenure to a close after 22 short games. Wilkens stepped in, and continued to make moves. Fan favorite Slick Watts became another casualty mid-season, traded to the New Orleans Jazz.

Wilkens led the Sonics all the way to the Finals that season, and they made their first two Kingdome appearances. The first was a bit odd. In May 1978, a Sonics playoff game was aired on the big screen while the Sounders played a soccer match on the field below. Just two weeks later they played for real, losing game four of the NBA Finals to the Washington Bullets in overtime in front of 39,000 fans. The Sonics would lose the series 3-4, enough to make some people superstitious.

Ignoring any bad luck in the Kingdome, the Sonics moved there for all home games the next season, and it worked. They finished the season ranked second, and faced the Bullets again in the finals. Seattle lost the first game on a last-second foul, but won the next four straight to end it at five games. The SuperSonics were the first major league team in Seattle to win a championship.

The Sonics made it to the playoffs regularly, but the team changed quickly. By 1985 ticket sales were so low that the team moved back to the Coliseum. It took another decade for the Sonics to put together the pieces for another run at the championship. Raw power forward Shawn Kemp was first in the 1989 draft, followed by point guard Gary "The Glove" Payton in 1990. Hiring coach George Karl in 1993 was the final key, and the Sonics spent the mid-90s as one of the elite teams in basketball.

Ownership had always been stable for the SuperSonics. Sam Schulman held the team for 16 years, finally selling to advertising mogul Barry Ackerley in 1983. Almost two decades later, Ackerley sold to Starbucks founder Howard Schultz in the middle of the 2000–01 season.

Schultz seemed to be Gary Payton's biggest fan at first. Things soured a bit when Schultz announced that Payton was available for trade that summer. A year later Payton was playing the best ball of his 13-year career, and continued to ask for a contract extension. Schultz felt slighted by the public demands of Payton, and at the start of the 2002 season he dealt away the Sonics' lone remaining superstar. He did it out of spite, and because he thought it was a good business decision.

In 2004 Schultz claimed he had no interest in selling the team, but was obviously hurt by public reaction to the Payton trade. Unable to convince the City of Seattle to pay for a new stadium, he sold the team just a year later. Howard Schultz expressed shock that the new owners, led by Oklahoma City's Clay Bennett and Aubrey McClendon, moved the SuperSonics to their hometown in 2008. KeyArena hosted the last SuperSonics game on April 13, 2011. The team is now known as the Thunder.

The SuperSonics' sister team Seattle Storm is still playing here. After winning WNBA Finals in 2006 and 2010, they are the only two-time champions in Seattle.

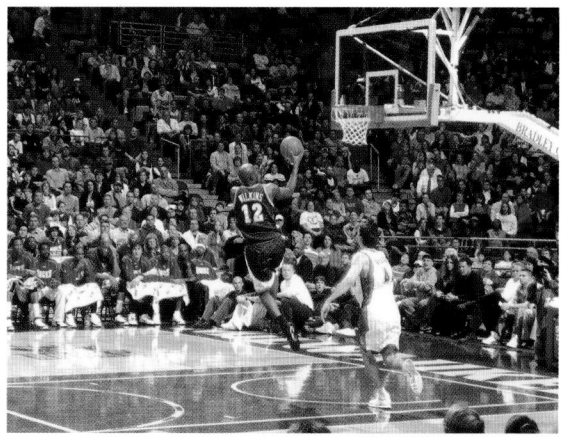

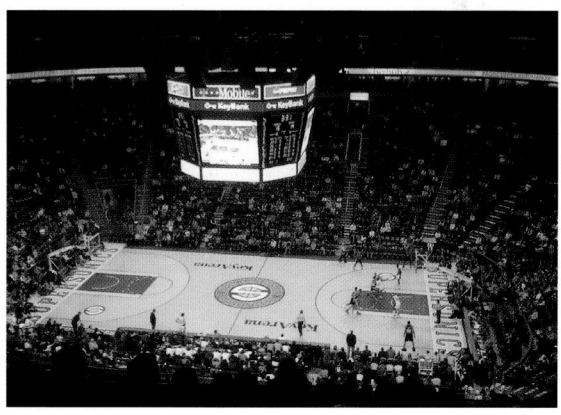

TOP *Damien Wilkins drives in for a layup.*

ABOVE *The building rebuilt as KeyArena with a Sonics game underway.*

OPPOSITE PAGE *The championship team in 1974 with the original Coliseum court behind them.*

Washington Mutual JUNKED 2008

Washington Mutual, known affectionately as WaMu, was the largest bank to fail in the 2009 mortgage crises. Bitter Seattleites continue to shun its successor, Chase Bank.

WaMu got its start in 1889 in the smouldering aftermath of the Great Fire as the Washington National Building Loan & Investment Association. Seattle had only six major banks before the fire, but Washington National was one of a dozen banks to open in the following year. It was formed by Mayor Robert Moran and several leading citizens. They were determined to found a bank that would locally reward savings and help to rebuild the city.

Just eight months after the fire, Washington National began issuing home loans. The first was to Norwegian-born Peter Nord, a seaman on a Mosquito Fleet steamer, for a new home in the new city of Ballard.

Washington National grew slowly but steadily, surviving the 1893 financial panic and growing through both gold rushes. In 1908 Raymond Frazier took over day-to-day management of the bank and also became vice-president. He brought a new philosophy to the bank based on the cooperative banks of Denmark, which he experienced as consul-general there. The bank would give secure interest income to middle-class and working families who made small-scale retail investments. Frazier lobbied the state legislature to allow true mutual savings banks, and finally the law was passed in 1915. The bank changed names as it restructured into Washington Mutual Savings Bank in 1917 with Frazier as president. Its unique position

and an aggressive advertising campaign brought in a flood of new depositors and raised the deposits more than half by the end of World War I.

Washington Mutual proved resilient again during the Great Depression, and survived with the continued leadership of Raymond Frazier. He finally retired in 1941 as the bank began making acquisitions and opened its second office in Seattle. With continued growth during the war, WaMu grew to four branches. After a 1964 acquisition the first branch in Spokane began operating, and more cities in Washington were added in the 1960s.

In 1983 Spokane's Murphey Favre was acquired. This brought Kerry Killinger to WaMu. Appointed CEO in 1990, Killinger grew WaMu to be the biggest retail thrift bank in the nation through an astounding array of mergers. In 1999, one of those mergers brought in Long Beach Mortgage, which specialized in subprime mortgages to clients without good credit. But Long Beach was really selling "liar loans," where the lender purposely falsified information about the applicant in order to approve their loan.

WaMu's mortgage portfolio rotted with the cancerous liar loans. The disease accelerated in 2005 when Killinger announced that WaMu would become the Walmart of mortgage lenders. The executive team fled the company. WaMu was overextended, lacked deep connections in Washington, D.C. and Wall Street, and was teetering.

When the 2007 economic crisis hit, WaMu was unprepared for the first time. Although Chase and the Treasury propped up WaMu in 1931, this time they worked against it. When WaMu couldn't meet the single-day customer demand for $16.7 billion in cash, federal regulators forced the bank to fail and sold its assets at a steep discount to JPMorgan Chase on September 25, 2008. After 119 years of helping thrifty Seattleites build homes, Washington Mutual was no more.

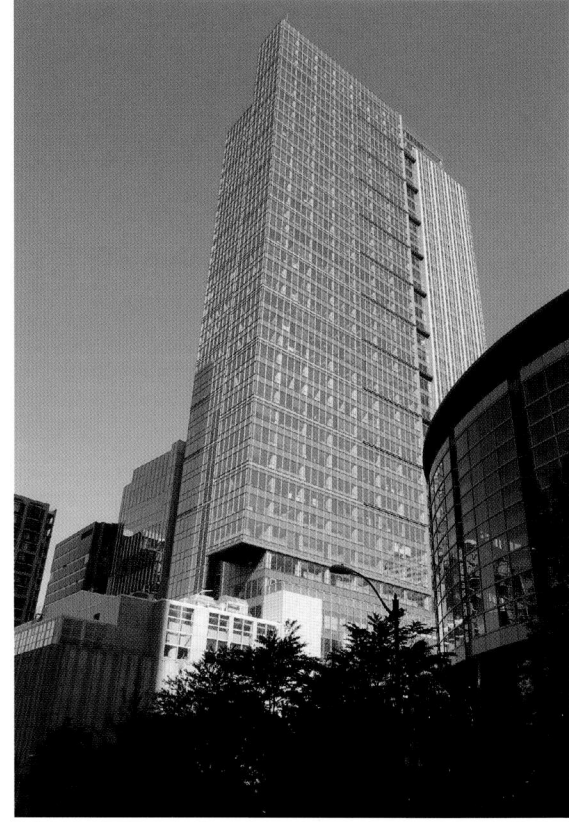

ABOVE *The WaMu Center was built atop an expanded home for the Seattle Art Museum in 2006. Benaroya Hall is on the right.*

RIGHT *Beyond Benaroya Hall is the former Washington Mutual Tower. It was completed in 1988.*

LEFT *Panoramic view of Seattle from the 48th floor of the WaMu Tower.*

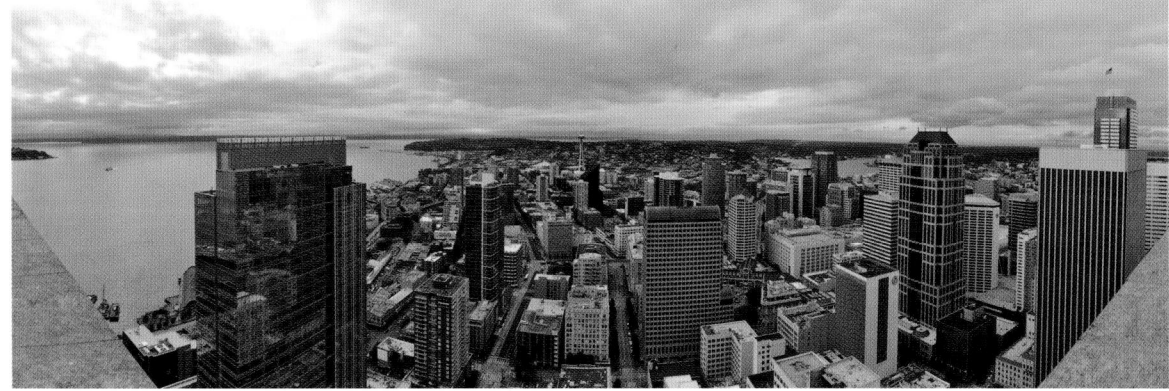

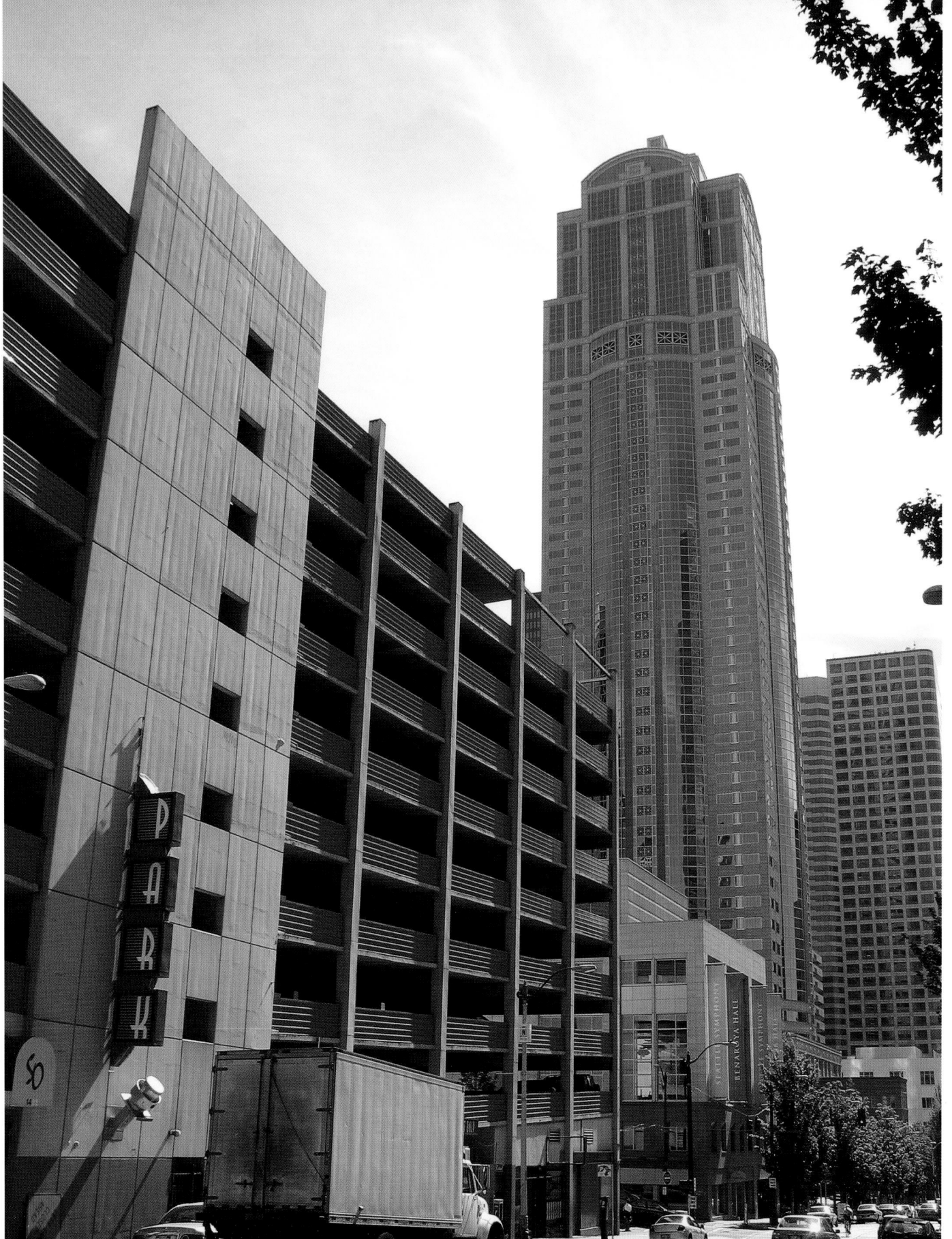

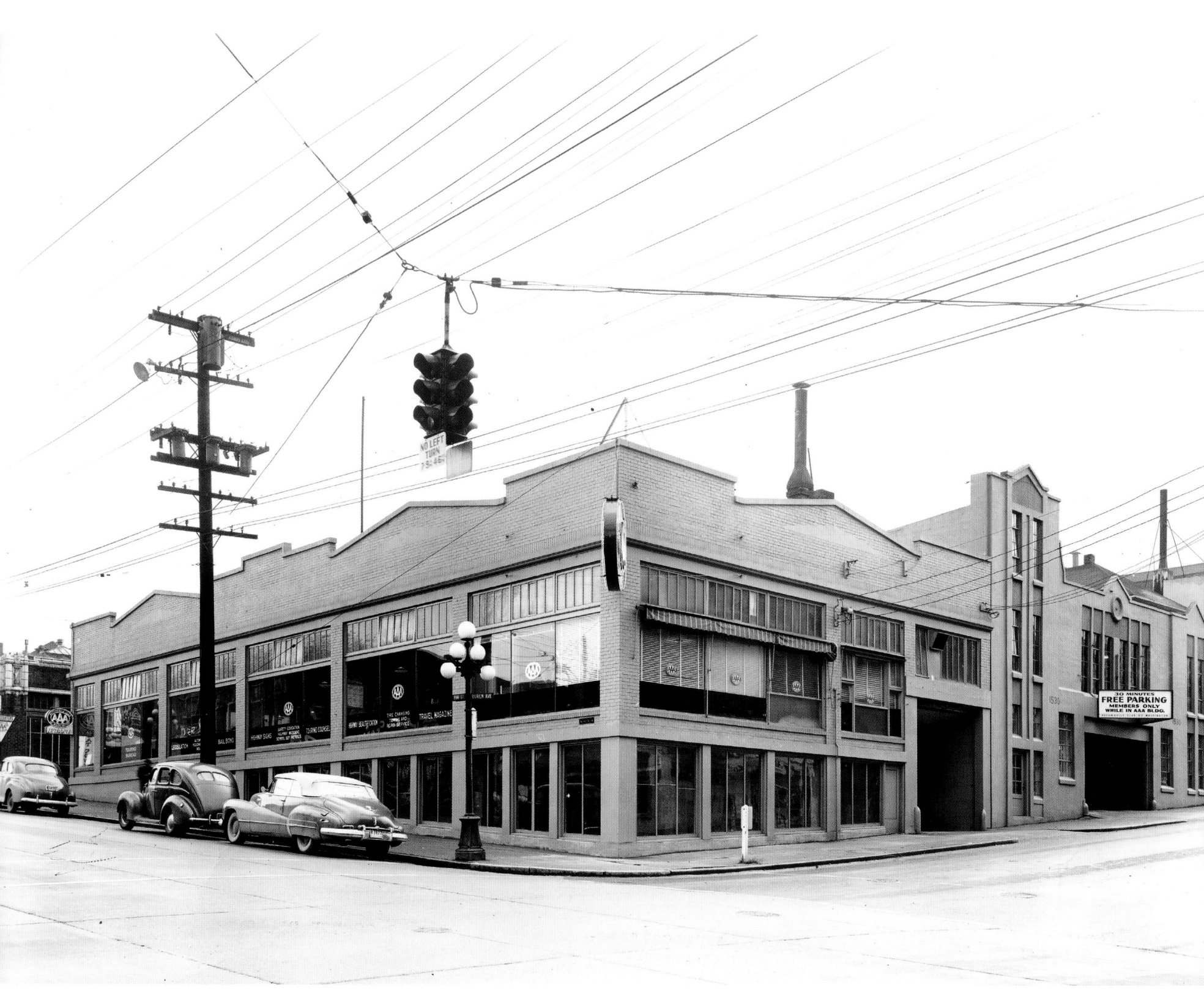

Capitol Hill's Auto Row RELOCATED 2009

There were already a handful of automobiles in Seattle in 1904 when the first auto dealership opened at Olive Street and Broadway in what would become auto row. The neighborhood is called Pike/Pine now, part of Capitol Hill. Back then it was just Broadway. The dealership started as John B. Wing Automobiles. John was the son of Frederick Wing, Assayer in Charge of the U.S. Assay Office on First Hill. After a few months Frederick and several banker friends pooled their money and backed his son's establishment, moving it to Broadway and Madison Street and changing the name to Broadway Auto along the way.

Broadway Auto's success was quickly duplicated by an assortment of auto-related businesses. They were drawn by cheap, accessible real estate close to their rich customers. Until 1903, Broadway was only easily accessed by cable cars from downtown. Then the Pike Street regrade opened access. In 1907 the Pine Street regrade made it even easier to get up the hill. And in 1909 the 12th Avenue regrade opened a route around the backside of First Hill. The regrades also flattened out the streets and turned hilly and boggy properties into blank slates. Perhaps more significantly, Pike/Pine was right in between the established mansion district on top of First Hill and James Moore's newly established high-grade community of Capitol Hill next to Volunteer Park. By

1911, 32 of Seattle's 41 automobile dealerships were on Broadway, Pike Street and Pine Street.

The 1910s and 1920s saw continued build-out of auto row. The architectural forms which still dominate the neighborhood became well-established. Dealerships had terracotta facades with high, broad windows. Some featured basement or second-floor mechanic shops accessible by the old neighborhood grade. Others used massive elevators to move cars up several floors to showrooms or service areas. Businesses dedicated to parts and repairs were less lavish, with wood or brick exteriors and smaller, subdivided commercial bays.

The array of vehicle makes sold in auto row reflected the variety caused by American innovation. Templar, Willys, Overland, Daniels, Studebaker, Pierce-Arrow, Franklin, and Winton were all popular models. Alongside them the still-familiar names of Ford, Chevrolet, Mack, Lincoln, Mercury, Dodge, and Pontiac vied for attention from passersby.

Seattle also became home to a few automobile factories, which were located south of Lake Union. In 1914 Ford cut shipping costs by sending the parts by train and assembling them in plants. In 1917 Kenworth opened their factory, and moved into larger spaces four times as their business grew. In the 1920s auto row drifted down Pike Street and

Pine Street, turned on Westlake and stretched all the way to this industrial area of Lake Union. The two mile long band had dozens and dozens of automobile businesses.

When Interstate 5 was built in the early 1960s, it removed the middle of the Pike/Pine corridor including the auto row offices of AAA of Washington. And along with other freeway construction it gave quick access to distant, undeveloped suburbs. Advertisements for Bellevue's auto row appeared in 1965, and Burien's auto row in 1968. Instead of walkable strips of showrooms, these new commercial areas had small offices set back in the lot with rows and rows of automobiles lining the street. Instead of choosing a car from a display model and waiting for it to be delivered, buyers could drive away that day.

Capitol Hill's auto row continued, though it turned to specialty, imported models that benefited from the luxurious Art Deco storefronts. Mazda, Yamaha, Citroën, Fiat, and MG were all sold from the storefronts built for American cars, but they all left as well.

In 2009 BMW Seattle announced that it was moving to a new, much larger building in another neighborhood. This left Seattle Volvo on the west end of Pike/Pine, Ferrari Maserati of Seattle on the east end, and Phil Smart Mercedes-Benz in the middle. Three small dealerships spread across a half mile could no longer be called an auto row.

As redevelopment threatened destruction of the remnants of auto row, the City Council moved quickly. Later in 2009 it enacted an Auto Row Conservation District. This would reward developers who saved historic storefronts and incorporated them into new buildings.

It was none too soon. Phil Smart sold his dealership in 2012, and the new owners announced it was moving as well.

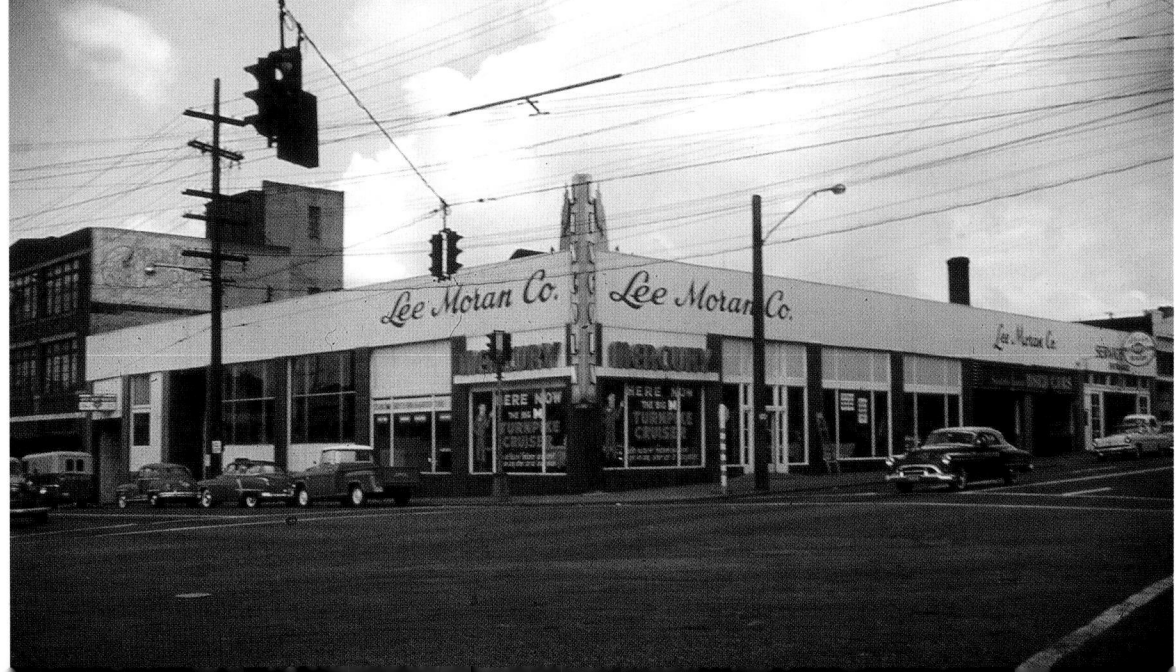

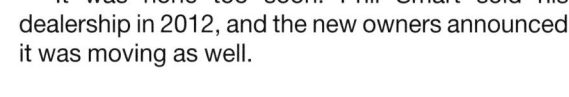

OPPOSITE PAGE *AAA of Washington's home for three decades was demolished to build I-5.*

LEFT *Currently Ferrari of Seattle, one of two dealerships left of auto row. From the late 1940s to early 1960s it was Lee Moran's Lincoln Mercury dealership.*

Schooner *Wawona* DISMANTLED 2009

Seattle's harbor can be split into four eras. Initially the central waterfront was a port focused on shipping lumber and landing the Mosquito Fleet. When gold was found in the Klondike, Seattle blossomed as an industrial and shipping center, and the waterfront transitioned to support massive ships that sailed and steamed across the Pacific. From the founding of the Port of Seattle in 1911 the downtown waterfront entered a period of decay and disinvestment, with larger vessels moving to Harbor Island and Smith Cove. Finally the area became an entertainment and tourist destination after the 1962 World's Fair.

The schooner *Wawona* first sailed in 1897, on the eve of the Gold Rush. She was from the very end of the first era, and carried lumber from Puget Sound and Grays Harbor ports to California. Around 500,000 board feet were taken each trip south, with ballast on the return. She continued this trade until 1914, when she was refitted for fishing in the Bering Sea.

By 1939 she was already described as picturesque or a "romantic old sailing schooner." News reports tracked her 1,500-mile trip back from Alaska with her 500-ton take of codfish to Seattle. Boy Scouts rode her on joyrides through the Locks.

In 1942 the Army Transport Service conscripted the *Wawona* for service in World War II, removing the masts and towing her as a barge. She was renamed the "BC-710," where BC stood in reverse for cargo barge. On the trip north she took supplies to Alaska and heading south hauled timber back, in an odd reprisal of her life as a lumber schooner.

Wawona returned to fishing in 1946, but only caught codfish for two more seasons. The economics weren't there anymore. There was a glut of cheap powerboats after the war, people weren't eating as much codfish, and it was difficult to find young men who could work a sailboat. In the fall of 1947 she entered retirement holding the world record for codfish catch by a schooner at 7.2 million fish.

In 1964 the *Wawona* was called back to duty, this time as a heritage vessel. She was purchased by Save Our Ships, which later became Northwest Seaport. S.O.S. envisioned the *Wawona* as centerpiece to the revitalization of Seattle's waterfront, and hoped to build a ship museum around her like the maritime parks in San Francisco and Connecticut. S.O.S. Chairman and Seattle City Councilman Wing Luke led the effort to raise funds to first purchase her and then restore her.

The *Wawona* was added to the National Register of Historic Places in 1970 and became a city landmark in 1977. She was moved to the south shore of Lake Union, moored outside the old Naval Armory Building in 1981, joining several other historic vessels that Northwest Seaport added to their collection. The Center for Wooden Boats provided a nice complement next door.

Wawona was beginning to finally show her age, though. Rainwater caused rot which spread year by year. An infestation of powderpost beetles honeycombed her planks. Inspection in 2005 revealed a tremendous effort and more than $15 million needed to restore her to sailing condition.

In 2006 she was closed to the public and her masts taken down before they fell. The city promptly ordered Northwest Seaport to move her to make way for the new South Lake Union Park.

Finally Northwest Seaport determined to allow *Wawona* to have death with dignity. Rather than letting her rot and sink, they hauled her to a drydock where she was disassembled and cut up. Pieces of her are now put to various uses, including the centerpiece sculpture in the Museum of History & Industry's new home in the Armory.

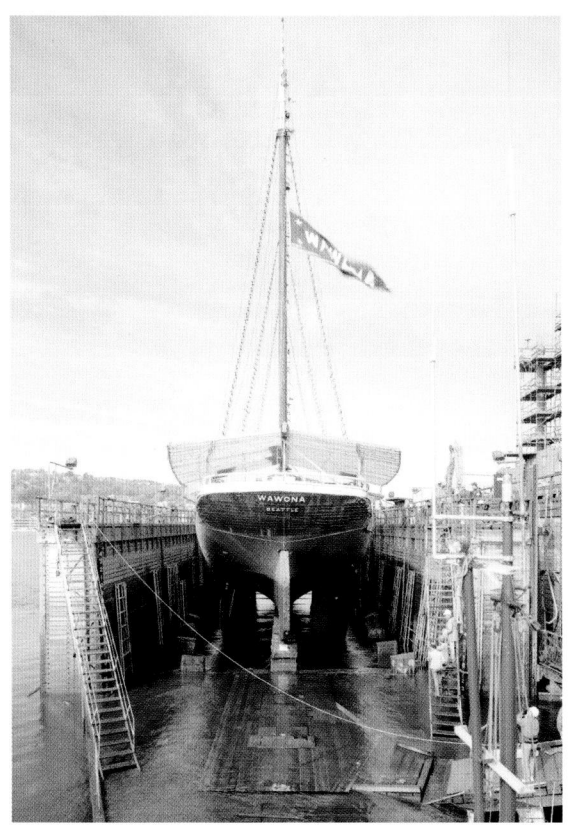

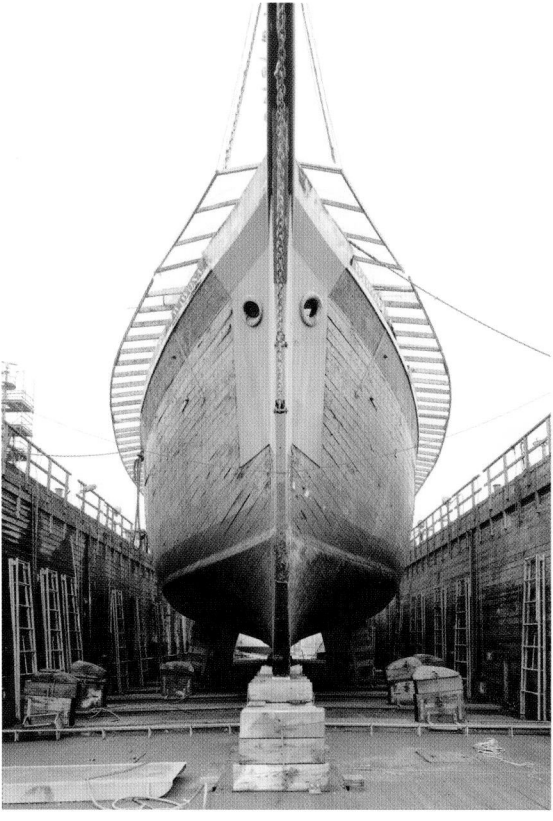

RIGHT *Docked outside the Armory with the Space Needle in the distance.*

FAR LEFT *View from the stern, in dry dock around 1970.*

LEFT *Bow view during maintenance.*

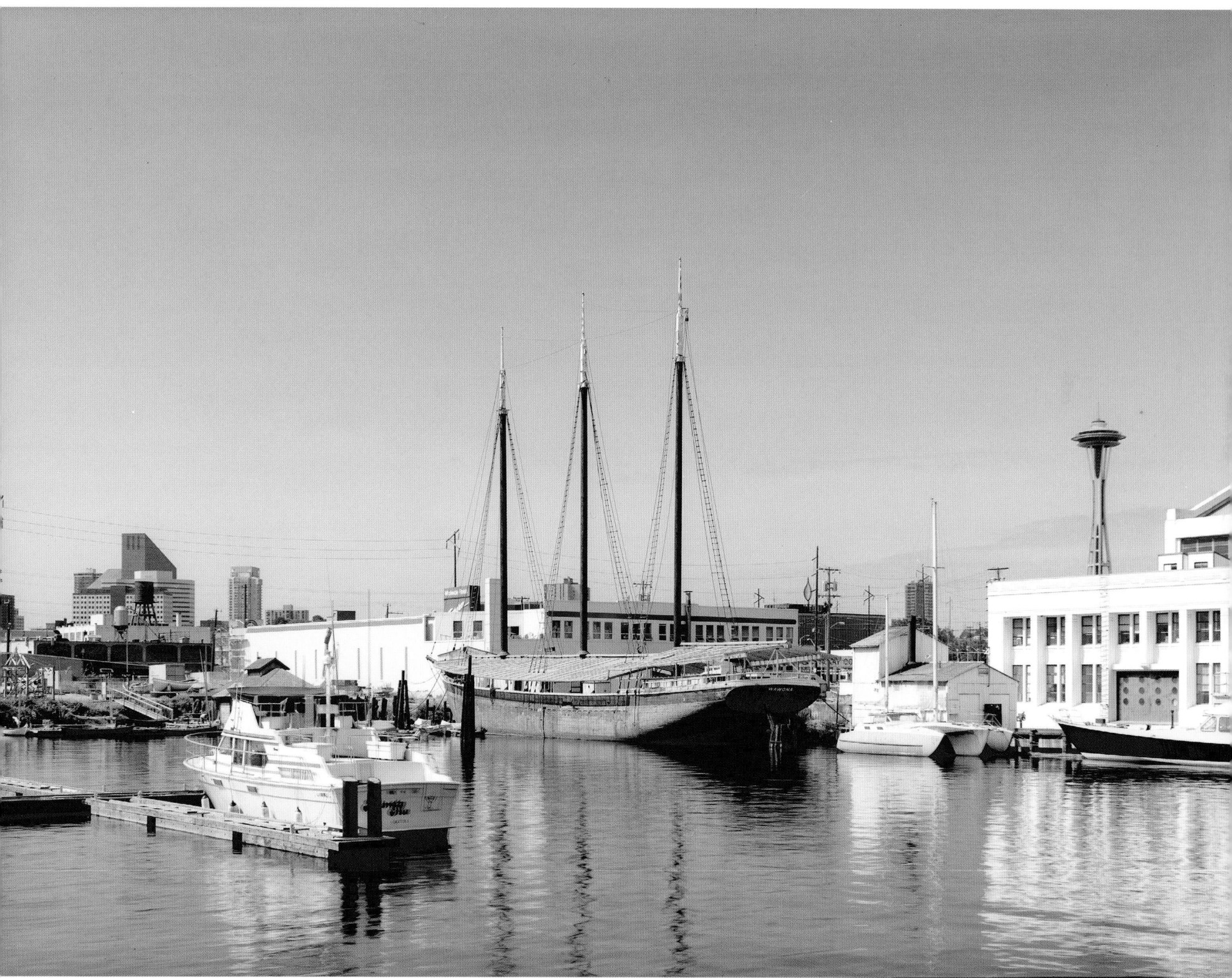

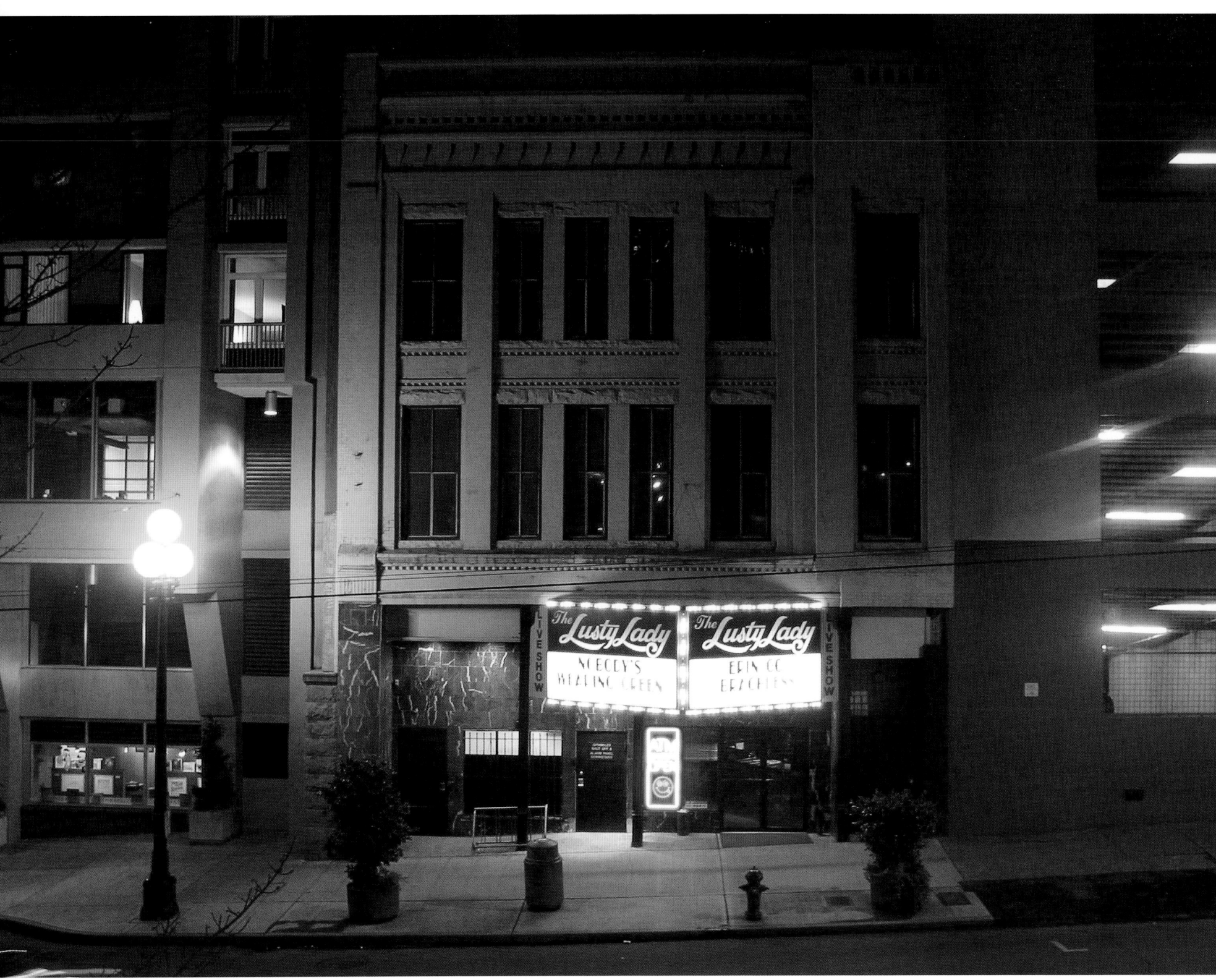

Lusty Lady CLOSED 2010

Seattle's pleasure quarters grew with the city. A gentlemen's agreement kept them south of Mill Street (Yesler Way) for a time, but after the gold rush in 1897, the brothels and opium dens blossomed.

In 1902 Mayor Thomas Humes decided that Seattle should be like Tokyo, London, Paris, and other metropolises. It was time for the houses of immorality to move into a dedicated district. Mayor Humes drew the line further south than before, at Jackson Street. The area would pick up many nicknames: Skid Road, from Mill Street's other name; the tenderloin; and the lava beds, apparently one level above a hotbed.

The backlash came in 1910, when Hiram Gill was elected mayor on an "open town" platform. Everything would be permissible everywhere. It took a full year before his chief of police faced corruption charges and Gill was forced out of office.

The expansion of the tenderloin persisted though, and it stretched up First Avenue. This area acquired its own notoriety. By the 1950s it had picked up the name Nightmare Alley from a steamy movie. Pictured in the film *Cinderella Liberty*, the name Sailor's Row came from the sailors on leave who climbed the hill for some quick fun.

Lusty Lady began showing short adult films in private rooms in the 1970s as the Sultan on First Avenue. In 1985 they switched names, added a peep show and hung a pink marquee out front. The marquee ran tongue-in-cheek puns on current events and pop culture and became a point of interest to the thousands of motorists commuting into downtown on First Avenue each day.

When the Seattle Art Museum moved in across the street in 1991, Lusty Lady's manager Darrell Davis was sure that gentrification would doom their adult entertainment. Instead, SAM and the Lusty Lady enjoyed an intimate relationship. SAM board member Mimi Gates described Lusty Lady's marquee as a city landmark.

The Recession of 2009 coupled with the growth of adult entertainment on the Internet made the Lusty Lady financially unviable. It closed on June 27, 2010 and the marquee was pulled down. With the building empty and awaiting new tenants, SAM installed a temporary marquee to carry on the tradition of punning in its absence, using "One Elles of a Show" to advertise its 2012–2013 exhibition "Elles: Women Artists from the Centre Pompidou."

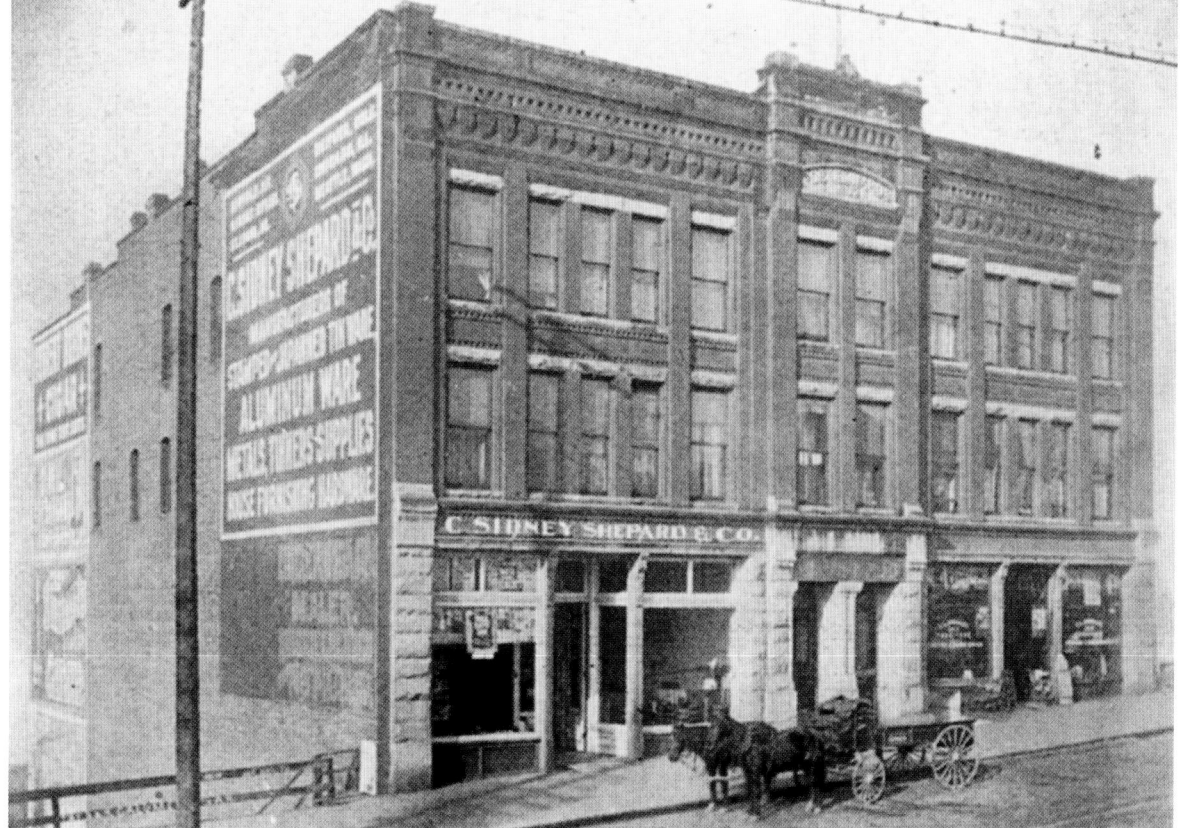

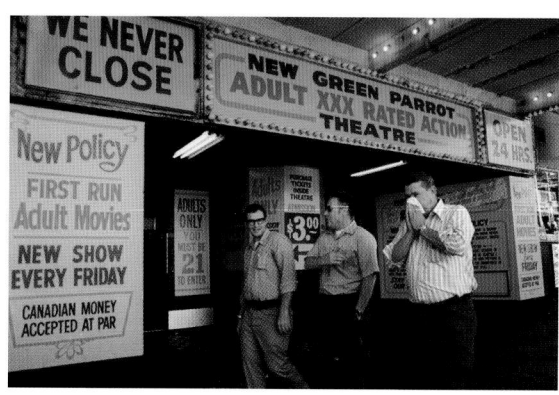

OPPOSITE PAGE *The Museum of History & Industry snatched up the marquee in 2010 and has it on display.*

LEFT *The building that later held the Lusty Lady was cut in half in 1966.*

BELOW *"Nightmare Alley" in the 1970s.*

Fun Forest CLEARCUT 2011

For almost 50 years, the Fun Forest amusement park helped parents and children have fun together and gave teens a place to sneak kisses on dates.

The Fun Forest was Seattle's first centrally located amusement park. Earlier parks were located in distant communities accessed by streetcar or bus. Luna Park was first, followed by a small amusement park at the entrance of Woodland Park from 1919 to 1934. Playland in Bitter Lake was a full amusement park, operating from 1930 to 1960 with a dance hall and race track.

Seattle Center's park started as the Gayway, the amusement area of Seattle's 1962 World's Fair. The park featured a Wild Mouse roller coaster, a Flight to Mars spook ride, the Meteor centrifugal force ride, the Space Whirl futuristic teacups, and many more.

By the mid-1980s, the Fun Forest's carnival rides were considered dilapidated and substandard but also the only part of the Seattle Center targeted at teenagers. Officials reached out to amusement park operators around the country and eventually found a receptive ear at Walt Disney Imagineering. Disney wasn't interested in just replacing the Fun Forest, though. So they were hired to deliver a plan for the entire Seattle Center.

In 1988, Seattle embraced Disney's idea to turn the Seattle Center into a family oriented place with educational, cultural, and open-space features. But Disney decided it was overstretched with other projects and declined to invest in Seattle. No other private partner emerged. Over the decades parts of the plan have been implemented, like moving the Children's Theater from the zoo.

But much of it was ignored. For example, the land across Fifth Avenue from the Center was supposed to become world-class theme park thrill rides, and instead ended up as the Bill and Melinda Gates Foundation's headquarters. Also the Fun Forest's rides and arcade were tagged for demolition, the plan to replace them with another teen-focused attraction like Disneyland's Videopolis. Instead the carousel and little Ferris wheel spun on.

The early 1990s brought new rides to the Fun Forest with the Windstorm roller coaster. But then a piece of the amusement park was cut off to build the Experience Music Project in 1996. The Flight to Mars was among the loved, lost attractions. It was moved to Texas.

In 2006 the Seattle Center began another round of planning for updates and renovations. The Fun Forest was always mentioned first as something that should be removed, although it had successfully made a profit for decades. The adult rides were first to go. Wild River floated to Coney Island in 2010. Other rides went to California, Texas, Pennsylvania and to a traveling carnival. In 2011 the kiddy rides shut down.

The kiddy rides were replaced with a Chihuly glass museum. The bigger rides became an empty lot that during the summer has an inflatable ball room, a zip-line, and other temporary entertainment. It's called the Playway.

RIGHT *A variety of rides beckoned fairgoers in the Gayway.*

LEFT *Visitors look for refreshments at the Gayway during Century 21, the 1962 World's Fair. The Fun Forest took over after the fair.*

BELOW *The garden at the Chihuly Garden and Glass museum, which replaced the remaining Fun Forest in 2011.*

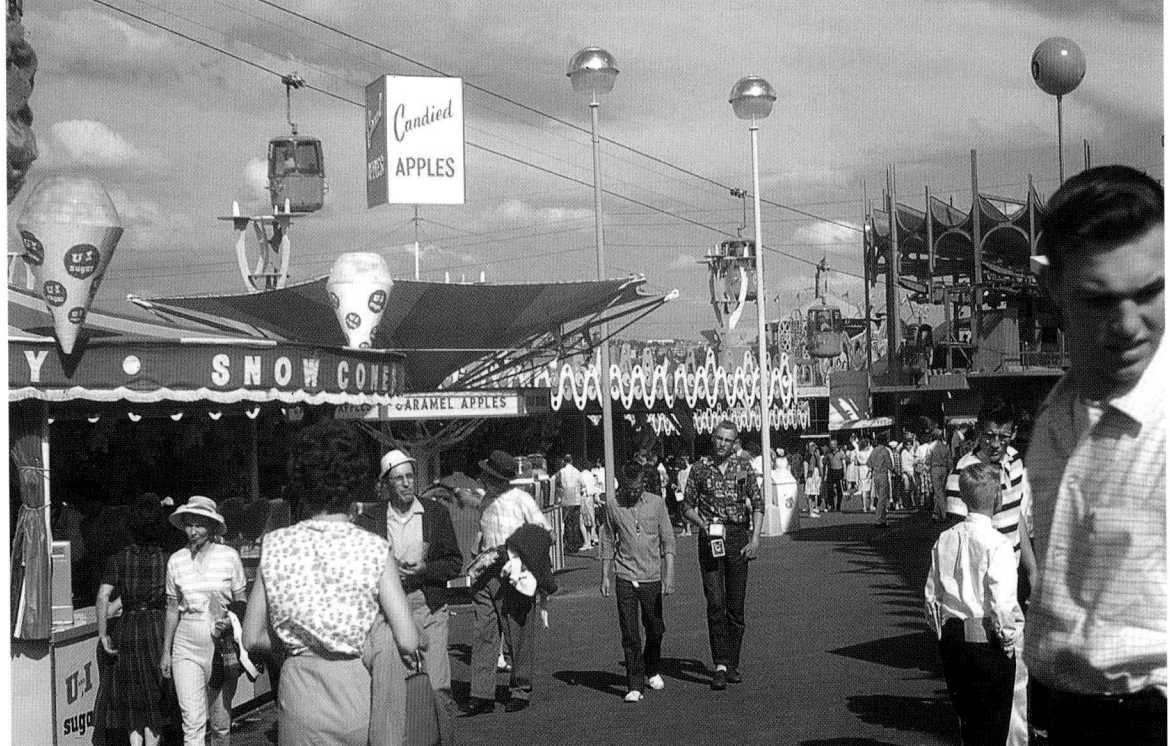

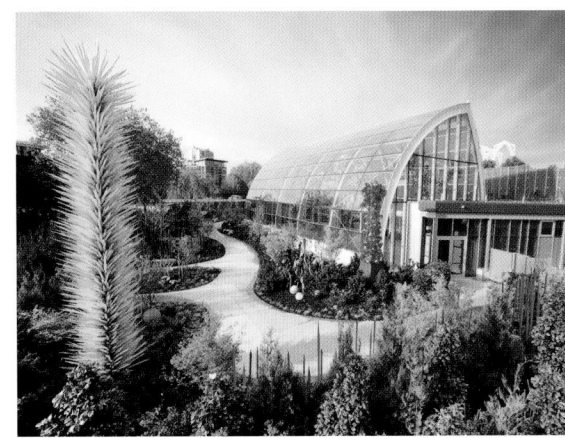

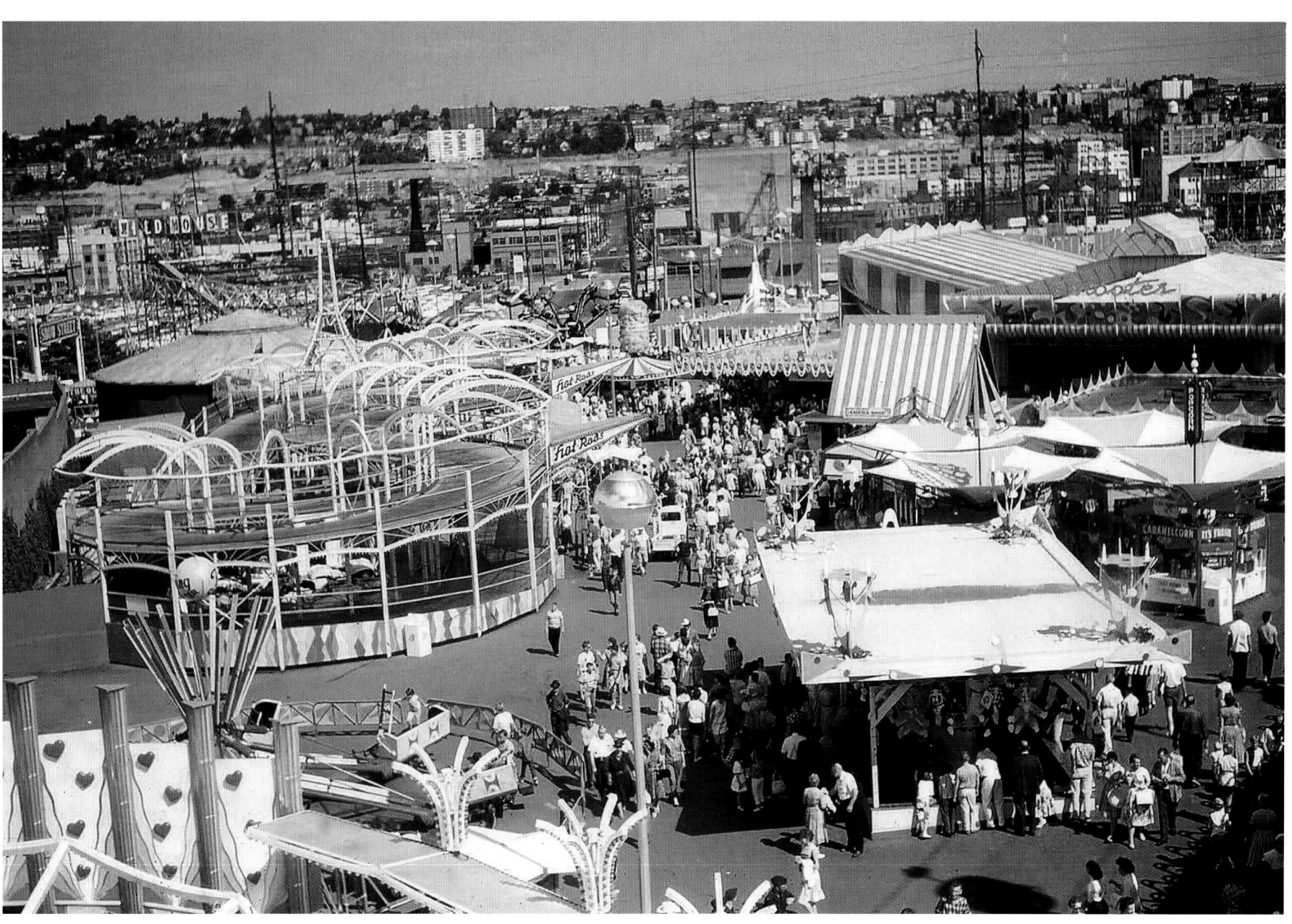

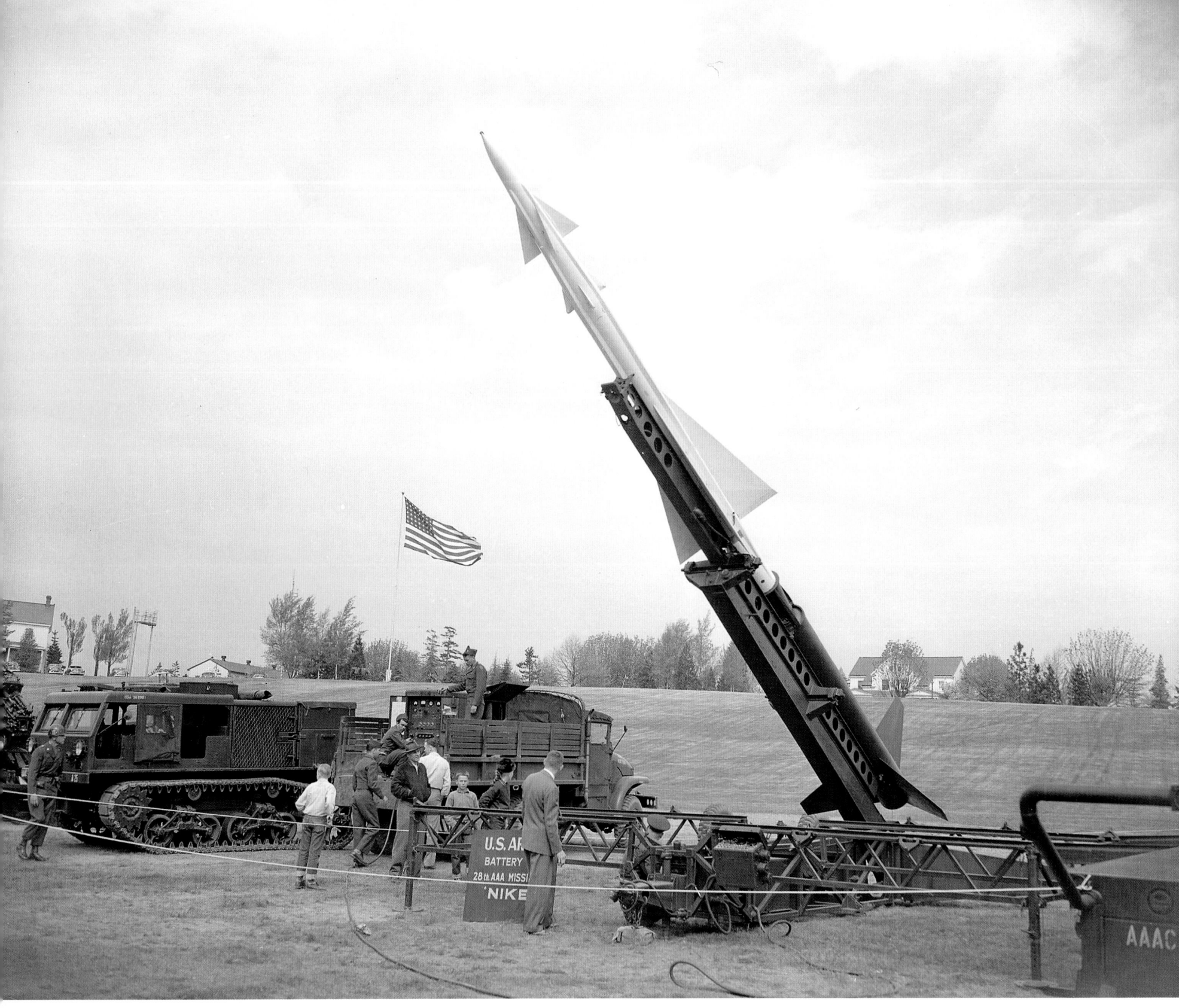

Within the image: U.S. AR... BATTERY 28th AAA MISSI... 'NIKE

Fort Lawton DECOMMISSIONED 2011

Fort Lawton was an Army garrison located northwest of downtown Seattle. It was perched on the 300-foot Magnolia Bluff, which rose out of mudflats to the north of Elliott Bay and to the south of the narrow entrance to Salmon Bay that became the Ballard Locks.

The spot was chosen in 1894 for its expansive views of Puget Sound and for the ability of artillery batteries to defend the entrance to Seattle's harbor. The establishment of the fort prepared America for a series of military actions in Asia. First came the Spanish-American War's battles in The Philippines in 1898. In 1899 the Philippine-American War began, and then China's Boxer Rebellion erupted in the same year. Both continued as Fort Lawton opened in early 1900, named after a war hero who died in The Philippines.

To support the Army's activities in the Pacific, a livestock corral and supply depot were established which sent replacement horses and mules on Army transports throughout the Pacific. Fort Lawton's corral was briefly home to the First Cavalry as they deployed to The Philippines in 1900, with 3,000 animals shipped to Manila. In 1901, 2,000 more horses, mules and other working animals were prepared for service in China. The site was particularly well suited, with the ability to train pack mules on the steep trails heading up Magnolia Bluff.

In 1902 the Army added four infantry companies to the packmasters already stationed at Fort Lawton, and moved the artillery companies to Alaska. This set the tone for the next two decades, as the troops stationed at the fort constantly shifted. Troop strength peaked as America prepared for possible involvement in World War I. The 7th Infantry Brigade took over Fort Lawton for its headquarters and stationed a battalion of infantry and a company of artillery. But they rotated out of Seattle as soon as the war was over. Despite the constantly changing personnel at Fort Lawton, Seattleites made an effort to connect with them. Newly arriving officers were invited to stately dinners and dances and camp baseball teams were invited to municipal leagues. The Army reciprocated with weekly concerts by their band, bridge parties, and put on benefit plays for the community with their children as actors.

The Army Corps of Engineers took over the facility in 1927. They were joined during the Great Depression in 1933 by new units of the Civilian Conservation Corps, a make-work program that paid jobless men to do heavy labor of civil engineering. As part of the program, the entire grounds of Fort Lawton were improved with grading, sod, tree planting, and path and road building. The engineers were moved to make way for quick-deployment troops in 1940 as tensions rose with Japan and war spread in Europe.

For almost a year Fort Lawton was nearly empty. In the months before Pearl Harbor the Army had already determined that Fort Lawton would best serve as a headquarters for an Air Corps Interceptor Command and as a training and deployment center for infantry headed to Alaska. The IC leveraged a network of civilian observers throughout the Pacific Northwest to report the approach of enemy aircraft, copying the effective program that the British used to spot incoming German bombers.

After the Pearl Harbor bombing in December 1941, anti-aircraft guns were quickly installed at Fort Lawton. The formerly empty barracks filled as Seattle shipped newly trained volunteers and draftees out to battle. More than a million men and women passed through Fort Lawton during the war, with up to 20,000 in residence at a time. The fort also passed 6,000 Italian and German prisoners of war to prisons in Hawaii.

After World War II, Fort Lawton went idle until troops began staging for deployment and recovery in 1950 for the Korean War. Then when the three-year war was over Fort Lawton never again saw use by active duty Army soldiers. The Air Force used part of the grounds for a Nike missile defense battery beginning in 1959. The Army Reserves continued to use part of the facility.

In 1961, the base was recommended to be declared surplus. The missile defense system was abandoned in 1968 and the process of surplus for the majority of the grounds began. Most was transferred to the City of Seattle, which created Discovery Park in 1973. The rest was used by the Navy, Coast Guard and Army Reserves. Along the way, the City of Seattle declared Fort Lawton to be an historic district, protected by municipal landmark preservation laws.

The Army Reserve unit moved to Marysville in September 2011. Only the old Army cemetery remains.

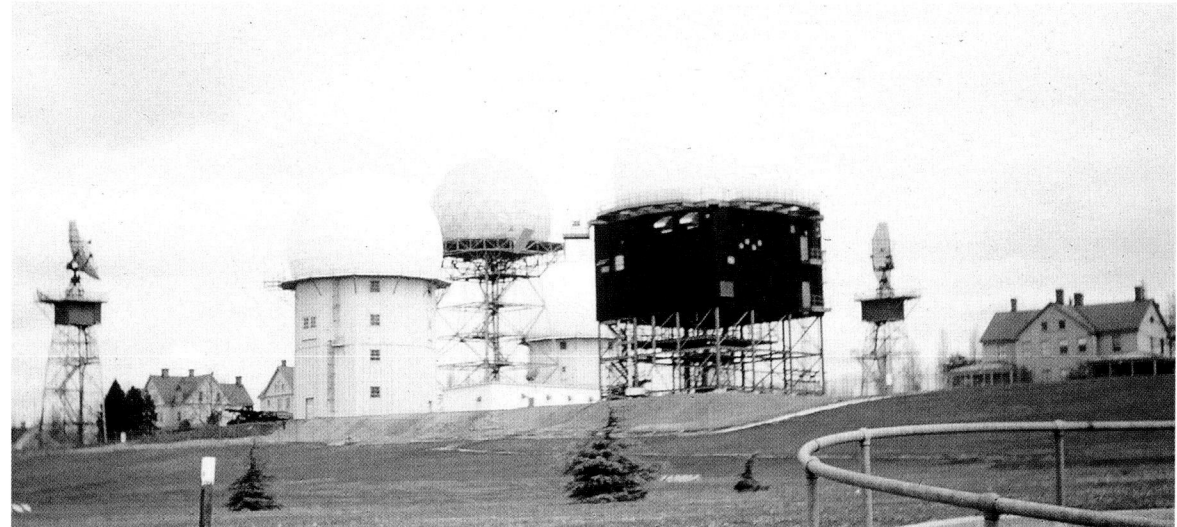

OPPOSITE PAGE *A Nike Ajax missile stands on display and ready to defend against incoming bombers.*

LEFT *Fort Lawton used several types of radar for tracking targets.*